D1474341

STUDENTS AND SOCIETY
IN EARLY MODERN SPAIN

STUDENTS AND SOCIETY IN EARLY MODERN SPAIN

RICHARD L. KAGAN

THE JOHNS HOPKINS UNIVERSITY PRESS
BALTIMORE AND LONDON

This book has been brought to publication with generous
assistance from the University Committee on Research of the
George Washington University and the Andrew W. Mellon
Foundation.

The Johns Hopkins University Press, Baltimore, Maryland 21218
The Johns Hopkins University Press Ltd., London

Library of Congress Catalog Card Number 74-6828
ISBN 0-8018-1583-5

Library of Congress Cataloging in Publication Data

Kagan, Richard L.   1943–
  Students and society in early modern Spain.

  Includes bibliographical references.
  1. Universities and colleges—Spain—History. 2. Higher education
and state—Spain—History. I. Title.
LA917.K33   378.46   74-6828
ISBN 0-8018-1583-5

FOR MOTHER AND FATHER K

CONTENTS

ILLUSTRATIONS

Maps

Figures

ABBREVIATIONS

1. ARCHIVES AND LIBRARIES

AA	Archivo del Ayuntamiento
ACM	Archivo de la Universidad Central de Madrid
ACV	Archivo de la Chancillería de Valladolid
AGNA	Archivo General del Reino de Navarra
AGS	Archivo General de Simancas
AHN	Archivo Histórico Nacional
AHP	Archivo Histórico Provincial
AM	Archivo Municipal
ARSI	Archivium Romanum Societatis Iesu
AUG	Archivo de la Universidad de Granada
AUS	Archivo de la Universidad de Salamanca
AUSA	Archivo de la Universidad de Sevilla
AUSC	Archivo de la Universidad de Santiago de Compostela
AUV	Archivo de la Universidad de Valladolid
AVM	Archivo de la Villa de Madrid
BE	Biblioteca de El Escorial
BM	British Museum
BNM	Biblioteca Nacional (Madrid)
BNP	Bibliothèque National (Paris)
BSC	Biblioteca Santa Cruz
BUS	Biblioteca de la Universidad de Salamanca
IVDJ	Instituto Valencia de Don Juan
RAH	Real Academia de Historia

2. OTHER ABBREVIATIONS

Add.	Additional manuscript
BRAE	*Boletín de la Real Academia Española*
BRAH	*Boletín de la Real Academia de Historia*
CMC	Contaduría Mayor de Cuentas
CODOIN	*Colección de Documentos Inéditos para la Historia de España*
Cons.	Consejos Suprimidos

DC	Diversos de Castilla
Eg.	Egerton manuscript
Exp. Hac.	Expedientes de Hacienda
GJ	Gracia y Justicia
Inq.	Inquisición
Jes.	Jesuitas
leg.	legajo
lib.	libro
mrs.	maravedís
NC	Nominas de Corte
pet.	petición
RABM	*Revista de Archivos, Bibliotecas, y Museos*
secc.	sección
Univs.	Universidades

PREFACE

Bureaucratic organizations, public and private, have two essential operating requirements: specialized knowledge and a steady supply of manpower equipped with this knowledge.[1] Although bureaucracies of many ages and empires have relied upon institutions of higher learning to supply them with the second of these fundamental needs,[2] far too little is known about the long-range effects of this demand upon the evolution of the educational institutions involved. Nowhere is this more true than in Europe in the sixteenth and seventeenth centuries, an age marked by the emergence of strong, monarchical government as well as growing popular interest in universities and schools.[3] One of the central themes of this book is the concept that these phenomena were closely linked, and, in essence, the book is an attempt to measure the response of Spain's universities to the growth and recruitment policies of the Habsburg state.

Of course, to suppose that "education" responds only to "bureaucracy" is a gross oversimplification of the truth. Educational institutions do far more than supply governments and other bureaucratic organizations with the manpower they require; conversely, governments are not the only ones to demand the expertise in which schools and universities specialize. Nevertheless, it is the contention of this study that the rise of bureaucratic institutions in Spain in the years between 1500 and 1700, and the changes in Spanish society that this occasioned, were the most important and far-reaching influences upon Spanish educational history during that period.

With "bureaucracy" and "education" as the starting points, this survey is not intended to be a "standard" history of education. Works of this nature are generally concerned with the history of curriculum, pedagogy, and scholarship, not to mention the history of the governance of universities and schools. Then, too, they have a special fascination with the educational planks of political parties, the lives and writings of famous teachers, and various projects for academic reform. However important, such topics are not this inquiry's primary concern. Rather, the aim here is to explore changes in the extent, utilization, and role of educational institutions within a society—in this case, Habsburg Spain—and then to assess

[1]Max Weber on bureaucracy in *From Max Weber*, ed. H. H. Gerth and C. W. Mills (London, 1948), pp. 198–244.
[2]S. W. Eisenstadt, *The Political Systems of Empires* (London, 1963), p. 66; Gerth and Mills, *From Max Weber*, p. 240.
[3]See below, Introduction.

how these changes affected the character of the educational institutions involved.

Castile, the heart of the Spanish monarchy in the sixteenth and seventeenth centuries, provides the setting for this inquiry. Following the rise and fall of the Spanish empire itself, education in Castile went from its own epoch of bouyant expansion and prosperity in the sixteenth century to one of deterioration and collapse in the era that ensued. This story is nothing new; certainly, it is common knowledge among students of Spanish history and literature that Castile in the *Siglo de Oro* possessed a number of flourishing universities, all of which declined, both in quality and prestige, in the course of the seventeenth and eighteenth centuries. Moreover, there are already numerous books and articles dealing with the internal history of Castile's schools and universities during this period. So rather than duplicate their findings, this study intends to take up where they often leave off and to set the educational institutions of the Habsburg era within their social context. In short, its aim is to consider these institutions from the perspective of an historian interested especially in the reasons for their spectacular rise and equally spectacular collapse. This approach will not be particularly pleasing to readers who are more interested in the lives of famous teachers like Luis de León or Benito Feijóo than in the matriculation records of a crowd of anonymous students; but this study, on the other hand, is directed primarily to those who are interested in the evolution of Castilian society within the early modern period, and especially in the phenomenon known as the "decline of Spain."

However, there is a paucity of material now available on the history of Castile during the Habsburg era. Studies on the nature and development of cities, population, private wealth, social classes, institutions, and other topics vital to the elaboration of this study are relatively few. And with the background evidence so flimsy, exact answers to questions associated with the history of education in early modern Spain are frequently difficult to obtain. In many instances, no more than crude hypotheses and suggestions are possible, and it is probably best to mention now, at the beginning, the tentative and exploratory nature of this study.

At this point, it is also appropriate to acknowledge those individuals and organizations who have helped me at various stages of my research. My debt, first and foremost, is to J. H. Elliott. Without his advice and encouragement, my work would never have seen the printer's ink. I should also mention H. G. Koenigsberger, Juan Linz, Francisco Marcos Rodríguez, N. G. Parker, Orest Ranum, Sheldon Rothblatt, A. J. R. Russell-Wood, Harry Sieber, and Lawrence Stone; each, in his own way, has contributed to the completion of this book. I am grateful to the *archiveros, bibliotecarios*, and *porteros* of the Spanish archives and libraries in which I have worked; and it goes without saying that their assistance, patience, and cooperation were indispensable to me. Financial aid for this project was generously provided by the Trustees of Indiana

University, the History Department of the Johns Hopkins University, and the Shelby Cullom Davis Center for Historical Studies at Princeton, New Jersey. Finally, I would like to thank John Spurbeck of Baltimore who prepared the maps, charts, and graphs and Mrs. Thomas Grover who typed the finished manuscript.

INTRODUCTION

Europe in the course of the sixteenth century experienced—in the words of Lawrence Stone—an "educational revolution."[1] The change this revolution entailed was a sudden and unprecedented increase in the number of "educated" and particularly university educated men. Previously, during the Middle Ages, higher learning was limited primarily to churchmen and members of the learned professions. But beginning more or less around 1500, new schools, colleges, and universities came into being, while private persons, municipalities, ecclesiastics, and kings endowed new masters and teaching chairs. Simultaneously, the number of students attending educational institutions increased dramatically, and in many countries the total number of university students would not be equaled again until the late nineteenth or early twentieth centuries. The reasons for this educational achievement were many. Demographic and economic trends, social and political developments, changes in job opportunities, religious beliefs, intellectual currents, and shifts in adult attitudes toward children and growing-up all played a part, although the exact contribution of each is difficult, if not impossible, to discover.

One of the aims of this study is to demonstrate that Castile experienced an "educational revolution" of its own. More importantly, Castile, with the possible exception of a few Italian states, experienced this revolution several decades before the north of Europe and to a degree which neither England nor France, let alone the German states, could match. On this particular question, therefore, the current historiographical practice which forces events and situations in under-studied Spain into a mould created by the rest of Europe should be reversed. In terms of education, sixteenth- and seventeenth-century Spain, or Castile to be more exact, should be the yardstick by which the performance of other states will have to be measured. It would be jumping the gun, however, to begin this examination of Castile's educational experience without first setting it within the broader European context.

Much of the educational advance of the sixteenth century was the result of the spread of the printing press and the mass-produced book following Johannes Guttenberg's introduction of movable type in 1453.[2]

---

[1] Lawrence Stone, "The Educational Revolution in England, 1560 to 1640," *Past & Present* 28 (1964): 41–80.

[2] See Elizabeth L. Eisenstein's two suggestive articles: "Some Conjectures about the Impact of Printing on Western Society and Thought: A Preliminary Report," *Journal of Modern History* 40 (1968): 1–56; "The Advent of Printing and the Problem of the Renais-

This new industry helped to improve the position of the literate man in European society. The person who was able to read in medieval times was for the most part a churchman, a scribe, a merchant, or a member of one of the learned professions. On the other hand, society's most important and honored class, the aristocracy, though not totally illiterate, was not expected to be endowed with bookish skills they regarded as suitable only for low-born clerks. The appearance of the printed book altered the aristocracy's stand; its widespread availability encouraged interest in reading and in less than a century rendered literacy an essential skill for all members of society's upper ranks.[3]

Additional impetus toward education came from the so-called "new monarchies" which were established in Western Europe, principally in England, France, Burgundy, and Spain, toward the end of the fifteenth century. Rulers in these states extended their powers by the appointment of thousands of officials. Lawyers and administrators, tax-gatherers and finance officials, military experts or secretaries of state all had this in common: they had to be not only literate but educated and trained for their jobs.

This was not the whole story. In a fundamentally religious age, the church remained at least as important in education as the state, and the religious controversies of the era provided a considerable stimulus for academic training. The various factions, Protestant and Catholic, eager to reform from within and to proselytize abroad, were determined to create an educated clergy. Colleges and universities were enlisted for this task and many were attached to specific doctrines and groups, particularly in Germany where each of the Protestant sects sought pulpits of their own. The churches, moreover, encouraged school and university training among the laity in the belief that early indoctrination could bolster their position against the inroads of heresy. Accordingly, teachers, both clerical and lay, were obliged to offer instruction in dogma as well as the three Rs. The "educational revolution" of the sixteenth century must therefore be set against a background of religious dissidence and hate. In large part, it was the product of particular creeds struggling to indoctrinate children in their version of spiritual truth. Continuing confessional divisions proved, however, that religious propaganda meted out to the young is not always effective; education is just as likely to spark new, sometimes dangerous ideas as it is to bolster those which society sanctions.

Books, bureaucracies, and militant religions provided the bases for the "educational revolution," but its success has also to be attributed to the populace's response to the emergence of new careers in the ruling hierarchies. Public offices, promising broad opportunities for wealth and ad-

---

sance," *Past & Present* 45 (1969): 19–89. Also useful is Lucien Febvre and Henri-Jean Martin, *L'Apparition du Livre* (Paris, 1958). For the early history of printing in Spain, see below, p. 35.
    [3]See J. H. Hexter, "The Education of the Aristocracy in the Renaissance," in *Reappraisals in History* (London, 1961).

vancement, were strong magnets for many of society's most ambitious individuals, urging them to acquire educational skills. Together, church and state served as the major employers of educated men; consequently, changes in their demands helped to determine changes in Europe's educational development, since the time had not come when agriculture, commerce, or industry required their practitioners to attend any but the primary school.

Equally important for the success of the educational revolution were the families and clans who moved regularly from school and university into official posts. Originally, the "new monarchies" attempted to man their administrations with officials trained in law and the Latin prose style popular at the time. Recruited primarily from the lower echelons of the nobility and the Third Estate, these functionaries, dependent upon their offices for honors and for wealth, formed the beginnings of an "administrative nobility" which emerged in the seventeenth and eighteenth centuries. This class, owing its titles and privileges to academic training and offices rather than chivalry and war, formed the backbone of monarchical government, and in this position, acquired immense fortunes and power. The old, warrior aristocracy, though wary of these upstarts, gradually followed suit, acquiring in turn the skills and training which could enable its members to preserve their position and influence at the royal court and to cash in on the riches which the new monarchies had amassed.

These two distinct but interrelated groups, known commonly as the nobilities "of the robe" and "of the sword," constituted, along with leading ecclesiastical officials, many of whom were their kinsmen, what might be called early modern Europe's ruling elite. And because of their wealth, culture, and patronage, the educational interests of these groups were crucial to the educational history of the era as a whole. Thus it may be said that the emergence of militant, national churches, the growth of strong monarchies, and the nobilities these governments helped to develop or transform were the most direct and sustained influences upon the history of education, particularly higher education, in Europe before the beginning of the modern age.

After 1500, higher education in Europe can be divided roughly into two general categories: the professional, specialized, largely legal training designed for civil servants and churchmen, and the humanist, Latin, largely literary training designed in the first instance for noblemen, to whom this instruction was important mainly for culture and social status rather than career. This division may be illusory, since jurists often had a background in philosophy and the classics, while the nobles who attended university commonly studied law. But it is nevertheless true that each of these categories represented an independent strain in the education of early modern Europe which, when blended together, formed a single, hybrid program.[4]

---

[4]Max Weber was among the first to distinguish the differences between the education designed to create the "humanist" or "cultivated" man and that designed to create "profes-

The humanist strain in this program dates back to the poets and pedagogues of northern Italy during the fourteenth and fifteenth centuries who
advocated instruction in the liberal arts, meaning the literature and
languages of classical Greece and Rome, as a substitute for the scholastic
education of the Middle Ages.[5] Asserting that education should not necessarily involve vocational training, they set education within the wider context of moral development and made as its goal the creation of the individual capable of and interested in public service to his prince or nation
and to God. Famous teachers like Alberti, Bruni, Palmieri, Vergario, and
Vittorino proceeded to instruct their pupils in the prose and poetry of the
ancients, shunning the logic of Aristotle which, in the hands of medieval
educators, had evolved into a professional tool for future theologians. For
them, scholastic training in logic was fruitless, leading in no apparent
direction beyond the study of the subject matter itself. Conversely, the
study of Cicero, Quintillian, and Plutarch, along with other classical
authors, would provide models of "virtuous" men and their deeds and, consequently, direct the young to emulate the examples of their ancient fore-
bearers in the "active, civic life." The goal of this liberal arts program was
a life of involvement, not of monastic or scholarly withdrawal. It was in fact
designed to create citizens rather than clerics, while aiming to improve
men's characters instead of sharpening their wits.

Speaking largely to the circles of the princely courts and to the nobility
who were their patrons, the Italian educators, along with their followers
and imitators in the rest of Europe—among others: Erasmus and Juan Luis
Vives in the Low Countries, Budé in France, Colet and More in England,
and Melancthon in Germany—urged the ruling class to shed its disdain for
learning and follow a liberal arts education, combining instruction in the
classics with its age-old training in chivalry and the martial arts.[6] Such a
background, argued the teachers, would best enable them to serve their
nations as councillors, courtiers, soldiers, and statesmen, and even as kings.

At first, the haughty aristocrats balked, preferring the life of arms to
that of letters. But opposition to the "new learning" began to wane at the
opening of the sixteenth century, since Latin studies, thanks to the influence of the humanists and early aristocratic converts to the liberal arts,
had already shed much of its old "clerkly" reputation, making it much
more attractive to noblemen and peers. Added to this were the examples of
monarchs like King Henry VIII of England and Queen Isabel of Castile,
both of whom were schooled in Latin and the classics. So it did not take
very long before courtiers took to the "new learning" themselves, if only
to preserve their influence in the courts of rulers interested in the services

sional" men, the "specialists"; see H. H. Gerth and C. W. Mills, *From Max Weber* (London,
1948), pp. 242–43.
    [5]See E. Garin, *L'Educazione in Europa, 1400–1600* (Bari, 1957), esp. pp. 124–57.
    [6]See ibid.; W. H. Woodward, *Studies in Education during the Age of the Renaissance,
1400–1600* (Cambridge, 1906).

of "educated" men.[7] Soon Latin became all the rage. Private tutors, hired especially to teach Latin and Greek, proliferated in wealthy households, and many a young nobleman, tutor in tow, attended a court academy organized specifically to instruct the court aristocracy in the liberal arts. Private libraries also came into vogue as humanist authors, making the best of the printing press, promoted their educational program on an international scale. Among Europe's early "best sellers" were classical works and educational tracts, notably those by Castiglione and Erasmus, along with Ascham, Elyot, and More.

In addition, instruction in the liberal arts was institutionalized. Beginning early in the sixteenth century, various colleges and universities accommodated the new curriculum, some more quickly than others, and new chairs in Greek and Latin literature were added to supplement if not to replace those in the traditional areas of scholastic study. And when existing universities did not readily accept the humanists' program, new educational foundations were formed wholly dedicated to the "new learning." Paris thus gained the College of France with the help of Francis I; Oxford, the Colleges of Corpus Christi and the Cardinal (later Christchurch); Cambridge, St. John's College followed by Trinity; and Spain acquired the University of Alcalá de Henares, famed for its Trilingual College.

Despite this new popularity, the liberal arts never managed to dominate the university curriculum. It is a common misconception that the Renaissance emphasized the liberal arts to the exclusion of other disciplines. It is true that pedagogical thinkers of the epoch lauded Greek and Latin literature above all other subjects, and it is also true that most institutions of higher learning in Europe sooner or later heeded the call by adding the "humanist" program to their curriculum. But neither did these institutions neglect the scholastic education characteristic of the Middle Ages which aimed at the production of professional specialists trained in jurisprudence, medicine, and theology. In fact, the sixteenth century marked a heyday for such subjects, particularly law, a favorite among university students on the continent. Of course, the study of jurisprudence in the sixteenth century had acquired a new historical and philological dimension, thanks to the work of legal scholars such as Cujas, Forcadel, Alciato, and Vasco de Quiroga.[8] But "humanist" law was slow to shed its

[7]A good example of a monarch interested in improving the education of the aristocracy was the Emperor Charles V. His courtiers in the Franche-Comté had complained to him about the role given to the low-born Cardinal Granvelle in the important affairs of state, whereas they found themselves neglected and ignored. Charles supposedly said in reply: "What do you want me to tell you—that you are ignorant, without learning and education? Give your children an education, and I will have them serve me; otherwise, do not expect me to make them public servants but only soldiers, cavalrymen, or domestic servants in my household." Cited in Lucien Febvre, *Philippe II et le Franche-Comté* (Paris, 1911), p. 429.

[8]The best introduction to the jurisprudence of the Renaissance is Domenico Maffei, *Gli Inizi dell'Umanésimo Giuridico* (Milano, 1956).

"clerkly" reputation at a time when the administrative requirements of both church and state required more and more trained lawyers and other officials schooled in the law. Consequently, the universities remained rooted in the past: homes for professionally oriented students and others interested in the law for practical, utilitarian reasons. For these students a liberal arts education served mainly as background for the more specialized disciplines from which a living could be earned. As a result, the universities of continental Europe (England's experience was somewhat different, since the study of law was centered wholly at the Inns of Court after Henry VIII ended instruction in canon law at Oxford and Cambridge) paid more attention to the "certification" than to the "education" of the young, allowing professional training to take precedence over innovative scholarship and thought.[9] In the long run, it was this vocational emphasis which cost many of Europe's leading universities their place in the mainstream of intellectual life, since by neglecting studies in philosophy, natural history, and other speculative subjects, they had little opportunity to join in the emergent, rational-scientific culture of the seventeenth and eighteenth centuries.

In order to find the causes for the exaggerated juridical character of Europe's universities, one must look to the demands of the "new monarchies" and the militant churches of the sixteenth century for educated men. Generally, those with a background in law were preferred, and, indeed, this subject led to opportunities for employment that none of the other university disciplines could match. Across Europe, royal councils, regional tribunals, popular assemblies, and cathedrals fell increasingly under the sway of legally trained and educated men.[10] In the Middle Ages legal education had also offered easy access to lucrative administrative careers, but in the sixteenth century—an age marked by the rapid expansion of government, spiritual as well as secular—it began to do so on a vast and unprecedented scale, both in competence and scope. For commoners, the lower nobility, and even for the landless sons of the aristocracy, law was *the* road to wealth, influence, and social prestige. Perhaps their model of success was England's Thomas Cromwell (1485?–1540): a lawyer who rose to occupy a powerful position on the king's council and at the royal

---

[9] Legal education in England during the sixteenth century has recently been examined in Wilfrid R. Prest, *The Inns of Court under Elizabeth I and the Early Stuarts, 1590–1640* (London, 1972). I owe the terms "education" and "certification" to David Reisman and Christopher Jencks, *The Academic Revolution* (Englewood Cliffs, N.J., 1969), p. 44. Karl Mannheim's essay, "On The Nature of Economic Ambition and Its Significance for The Social Education of Man," deals briefly with the relationship between "education" and "career." See his *Essays on the Sociology of Knowledge*, ed. Paul Kecskemeti (London, 1952), pp. 247–49.

[10] On the backgrounds of the deputies to popular assemblies in England and in France, see J. E. Neale, *The Elizabethan House of Commons* (London, 1949), pp. 290–91, and J. Russel Major, *The Deputies of the Estates General in Renaissance France* (Madison, 1960), pp. 138–42.

court of Henry VIII before establishing a household which, as the Earls of Essex, later ranked among England's peers.

It would, of course, be exaggerating to suggest that law's popularity in the universities of the sixteenth and seventeenth centuries had only to do with such "careerism." Europe then consisted of societies dominated increasingly by a "rule of law" imposed by absolute monarchs interested in internal order and domestic peace. Under this restraint, litigation became a regular feature of daily life. Though dueling remained fashionable among the aristocracy, and blood-feuds still disturbed the countryside, the bulk of western Europe's citizenry after the late sixteenth century settled more and more of their differences in court.[11] Thus even among families who scorned "professional" education for their sons, training in jurisprudence was something of value, and, together with those who viewed the subject along more vocational lines, they guaranteed that the universities retained their clerkly, professional image.

A change occurred in the course of the seventeenth century when, after generations of office-holding and the gradual acquisition of lands, titles, and wealth, many of the families who had been in the habit of sending their sons to university ceased to do so. Responsive to aristocratic principles, many sons of the office-holding class, long a major contributor of university students, eschewed judicial posts for honorific charges at the royal court and for commissions in the military, while the careers of others were made secure through the purchase of public office. Gradually, a tradition of legal education was lost; judicial robes were discarded and replaced by the luxurious appurtenances of gentlemen. During this changeover, the custom of attending university was largely forgotten.

Meanwhile, the universities attempted to keep in step with the changing interests of the ruling caste. Having formerly served as a means to power, the universities evolved into institutions designed to temper that power with elegance and grace. Gowns of scholarly black gave way to bright silks as the universities became playgrounds for the rich. The old, professional curriculum, unsuited to the new, genteel spirit, languished as teaching passed from the lecture halls to colleges and tutors whose interests were more in harmony with students' "cultivated" tastes. Concomitantly, the university's age-old tradition for advanced learning and thought suffered from decay. Scholars deserted the universities for newly established private and royal academies, leaving the former saddled with instructors more interested in cultivating gentlemanly habits among their students than in writing and research. More and more, the university came to be a center for those who looked upon education as a social asset rather than an exercise in learning or preparation for a career.

It would be wrong to suggest that this transformation was complete. Sons of the ruling elite, particularly at the large universities of continental

[11]See Lawrence Stone, *Crisis of the Aristocracy, 1558-1641* (Oxford, 1965), pp. 234-70.

Europe, represented only a fraction of the students. Whereas gentlemen in England managed to dominate the universities of Oxford and Cambridge by means of the college system, on the continent they only succeeded in gaining control of a few colleges within the larger institution. The remainder of the students resembled those youths who had enrolled at universities since their inception—the future professionals: lawyers, physicians, theologians, and teachers. For these students, certainly the majority, higher education still represented a preparation for a livelihood, and their relationship to the university was linked to its survival.

By the end of the seventeenth century, Europe's educational revolution had run its course. Attendance at the universities had slipped; even secondary education was depressed. Apparently, Europe had lost faith in organized education. This change was linked in part to the difficult economic conditions of the century, and contemporaries were quick to blame an excess of education for economic stagnation and decay.[12] Authors in France and Spain further noted that education beyond the level of literacy served only to encourage youths to enter careers in government and the church, turning them away from more useful and productive pursuits in commerce, farming, and the crafts. Furthermore, it was clear that the educational revolution had done little to solve Europe's continuing religious problems, nor had it stemmed the threat of revolt, both political and spiritual, from within. Indeed, in the face of new ideas which challenged established churches and monarchies in the seventeenth century, intensive education for the laity, once touted as the harbinger of orthodoxy and order, was suspect and viewed with increasing misgivings. Kings and royal ministers even lost faith in the liberal arts education of the aristocracy which they had once so forcefully espoused, and it was no accident that in the first half of the seventeenth century independent, but almost simultaneous and analogous, schemes were presented in England, France, and Spain to alter and improve the training of this powerful class.[13] In short, by the middle of the seventeenth century it was patently clear that the educational revolution had not born the fruits its "humanist" heralds had promised.

In the meantime, university matriculations continued to decline, while a few wealthy students managed to entrench themselves behind college walls. Many ordinary students, hurt by the economic difficulties of the era, simply stayed away. Others, aware that the positions to which a law

[12]See below, pp. 20, 43–44. For French criticism of "excess" education, see BNP (see Abbreviations): Ms. Fr. 17307, "Memoire pour diminuer le nombre des etudiants," folios 230–31.
[13]See below, pp. 38–39, for the Count-Duke of Olivares's suggestions. For a similar plan submitted by Richelieu, see his *Lettres Instructions et Papiers d'Etat*, ed. M. Avenel (Paris, 1863), 5: 721–23; *Recueil General des Anciene Lois Françaises*, ed. Isambert and Taillander (Paris, 1829), 16: 466–70, and BNP: Ms. Fr. 18828, folios 679–92. *The Journals of the House of Lords* III: 36–37, mentions a proposed academy for the English nobility.

degree once led were distributed on the bases of money and family ties, sought other instruction, generally outside the university. Many chose to finish their formal education at the secondary level, perhaps to enter one of the many venal offices which proliferated during the seventeenth century or to follow a career in the behemoth armies which were characteristic of the times. Religion, the New World, and openings in trade and commerce—partly the result of continuing European expansion overseas—offered other careers to talented and ambitious youths, and they too were in a position to push university aside. On the whole, the seventeenth and eighteenth centuries appear to have been an era of shrinking job opportunities for university graduates, while new positions which did not require a prolonged academic education came to the fore. And since the former had served as a major catalyst for university study, many would-be students failed to enroll, leaving the centers of higher education to the rich, the clergy, and those hard-core professionals which society could still absorb.

The outcome was the end of the universities' Golden Age. In 1600 the university was a populous, flourishing institution, respected for its learning and called upon for its advice. One hundred years later, the university was in decline. Its students were few and its curriculum, grounded in the medieval past, was under attack. Meanwhile, much of learned opinion was moving to institutions closer to the royal court, since the university's continuing overemphasis on the study and teaching of law had caused it to lose much of its intellectual preeminence and scholarly prestige. Though criticism of the university's decadence mounted and plans to update them appeared repeatedly in manuscript and in print, these institutions, controlled by groups who had little interest in innovation or reform, fought hard to remain unchanged.

This dynamic shift in the importance of the university between 1600 and 1700 was a European phenomenon, but it is not the purpose of this study to explore this question in continental terms. The reasons for this turnabout will only be examined within one country, the kingdom of Castile, but these may then be able to serve as guidelines for a study of the educational experience of Europe as a whole.

STUDENTS AND SOCIETY
IN EARLY MODERN SPAIN

part I
THE EDUCATIONAL SYSTEM
OF HABSBURG SPAIN

The requirements for entrance to university have varied from place to place, century to century, but in the western world since the Middle Ages, two have been exceptionally long-lived. One, still operative, is literacy in the vernacular. The other, lingering in some countries but rapidly passing out of fashion, is proficiency in the Latin language. To enter the universities of early modern Europe, both were essential, and together linguistic instruction in Latin and the vernacular constituted the bulk of primary and secondary education. Training in literacy, the main purpose of the elementary school, involved then a small but significant minority of the population and nowhere did it begin to become universal before the nineteenth century.[1] Latin, on the other hand, taught primarily at the secondary school, was fundamentally the privilege of an elite destined for careers in the liberal professions, the church, and the upper echelons of secular government. Furthermore, Latin, at least after the beginning of the sixteenth century, was the mark of an educated, cultured man and essential for membership in the ruling elite.

Unlike European societies of today, schooling in the sixteenth and seventeenth centuries was organized primarily on a local or independent basis and only began to be centrally administered and directed toward the end of the eighteenth century. Previously, central governments served only as loose licensing agencies and an occasional source of funds, allowing private individuals, municipalities, and ecclesiastical officials to provide for nearly all of the institutions of learning below the university level. Schools, consequently, developed haphazardly, and this created a confused educational patchwork, uneven in quality, character, and geographical distribution. The best schools were clustered in prosperous regions and those pockets of wealth and privilege—the cities and towns. Conversely, small villages and impoverished regions were undereducated and backward, often without regular, organized instruction. And since so many schools depended upon the charity of the rich, they tended to reflect the interests of this class. In practice, this meant that Latin schools were better

---

[1]The best introduction to the subject of literacy in history is Lawrence Stone, "Literacy and Society in England, 1640-1900," *Past & Present* 42 (1969): 69-139. Also useful is Carlo Cipolla, *Literacy and Development in the West* (London, 1969).

organized and financed than those which taught only literacy. And though it is true that most schools, primary as well as secondary, offered a number of scholarships to poor children while a few, notably those operated by religious orders, were free to all comers, the vast majority were semi-private institutions, charging tuition fees which were beyond most families' means. As a result, the bulk of Europe's population was left ignorant and illiterate.

In this regard, Habsburg Spain was no exception. Here early education was performed by four distinct but overlapping and often complementary agencies: the family, the private tutor, the "school of primary letters," and the grammar or Latin school. A wealthy male child might benefit from all four, a pauper or a girl only from the first, but the exact usage of these institutions for particular social groups is not known. Schools have left behind few records concerning their history, let alone their students, while family records which provide insights into educational practices exist only for a few important families. Furthermore, surprisingly few Spaniards of the sixteenth and seventeenth centuries wrote diaries or journals recalling their early lives and education, one consequence, perhaps, of a strongly confessional society in which personal details are confided to priests rather than paper and ink. In spite of such problems, a brief sketch of early education in early modern Spain is still possible, and this can serve as an introduction to the universities of the same period.

chapter 1
EARLY EDUCATION

THE FAMILY AND THE HOME

Among the educational institutions that existed before the modern era, the family is the one about which the least is known. The intimacy of home life rarely produces written documents and when these do exist they come from the exceptional family which kept an archive of its own, whose activities led to a notary, or whose problems wound up in the courts. In some cases, a correspondence revealing the details of home life survives when a parent happened to be away from his family, but this too is the exception. Recent works by French, English, and American historians have begun to explore domestic life in the past, but nothing comparable exists for Spain.[1] For these reasons the following discussion of the educational activities of the Spanish family in the early modern period is meant only to be a suggestive interpretation based upon very scanty information, largely literary in character, and upon findings for families in countries other than Spain. A second qualification is that the family to be discussed can only be considered representative of the elite: the noble and the rich. The family life of the popular classes, urban and rural, remains unexplored.[2]

In the first place it appears that families in sixteenth- and seventeenth-century Spain were decidedly patriarchal, the father making all important decisions about the organization of the home, the upbringing and schooling of the children, and their eventual marriages and careers.[3] The mother, whose influence was perhaps more strongly felt with regard to her daugh-

---

[1]The best introduction to the topic of children in history is Philippe Ariès, *Centuries of Childhood, A Social History of Family Life*, trans. Robert Baldick (New York, 1962). See also John Demos, *A Little Commonwealth, Family Life in Plymouth Colony* (New York, 1970); David Hunt, *Parents and Children in History* (New York, 1970); A. Macfarlane, *The Family Life of Ralph Josselin: An Essay in Historical Anthropology* (Cambridge, 1970); Ivy Pinchbeck and Margaret Hewett, *Children in English Society* (London, 1969), vol. 1; and Lawrence Stone, *Crisis of the Aristocracy, 1558-1641* (Oxford, 1965), chap. 11. An interesting collection of studies on the subject of children in history can also be found in the *Annales de Démographie Historique*, "Enfants et Sociétés," 1973.

[2]Insights into some of the problems faced by peasant families in sixteenth-century Spain are available in Michael Weisser, "Crime and Subsistence: The Peasants of the "Tierra" of Toledo, 1550-1700" (Ph.D. dissertation, Northwestern University, 1972).

[3]Literary evidence for patriarchalism in Spanish family life of the sixteenth and seventeenth centuries can be found in Ricardo del Arco y Garay, *La Sociedad Española en las Obras de Lope de Vega* (Madrid, 1941), p. 628. By the same author see "La Vida Privada En La Obra De Cervantes," *RABM* 56 (1950): 500. Also useful are P. W. Bomli, *La Femme dans L'Espagne*

ters, was clearly out of the picture so far as her sons were concerned. In the event of the father's death, paternal authority and responsibility would usually go to the closest male relative on the father's side, although in exceptional circumstances the mother would take command. And if the mother remarried, the step-father would still look to the original father's family for advice when making important decisions about his newly adopted children.[4]

Second, paternal authority was exerted most forcefully in the case of the eldest son—symbol of the family's lineage, the object of family hopes and aspirations, and the one to whom the bulk of the family's wealth would go through Spain's strong laws of primogeniture and entail—the *mayorazgo* system. He was carefully watched over, disciplined, and controlled until a successful marriage could be arranged; the family's fortune, prestige, and good name were too valuable to allow him to run free. The eldest son was therefore often a homebody, allowed outside the father's watchful eye only in special circumstances, usually educated in or near the home, and rarely allowed on his own to attend university—proverbial hotbeds of sin and corruption.[5]

For the first-born and even for the younger offspring, submission to the family lasted well beyond childhood. Although Spanish youths were often endowed early with independent rents and clerical benefices, granting them a measure of financial independence which may have clashed with paternal claims to absolute authority, fathers continued to assert their control over their sons long after puberty.[6] Younger sons were undoubtedly the most successful at achieving early independence, and they were often free to determine their own careers, select the university of their choice, and follow the subject matter they wished. Eventual preferment, however, rested in large part upon family prestige and the good services and influence of the father. Few sons would willingly break from the family and place their future careers in jeopardy. Independence of action, therefore, was carefully circumscribed even as the sons matured.

---

du Siècle d'Or (The Hague, 1950); and Caroline B. Bourland, "Aspectos de la Vida de Hogar en el Siglo XVII según las novelas de Doña Mariana Carvajal y Saavedra," *Homenaje a Menéndez Pidal* (1925), 2: 332.

[4] A good example of this is the relationship between Mateo Vázquez and the son of his sister, Maria, widow of Andrea Barrasi. Vázquez, secretary to Philip II, directed the upbringing of his two nephews, Mateico and Agustinillo, even after the remarriage of their mother to Jerónimo Gasol. See J. Hazañas y La Rua, *Vázquez de Leca, 1573-1649* (Seville, 1918), chaps. 2, 3.

[5] There were exceptions, however. The Count of Lemos, nephew to the Duke of Lerma, was a student at the University of Salamanca; see Marquis de Rafael, *El Conde de Lemos* (Madrid, 1911), pp. 13-14.

[6] Mateo Vázquez de Leca, nephew to Philip II's secretary, received income from various offices which had been entrusted to him at an early age by his father and uncle. Subsequently, his stepfather attempted with partial success to deprive him of this revenue. See Hazañas, *Vázquez de Leca*, chaps. 3, 4.

In contrast, the years up to the age of five or six were ones of relative freedom and indulgence for children of either sex, first-born or otherwise.[7] Tended first by a wet-nurse, later pampered by the servants, and treated with special care in order to guard against disease, the child's early years were, especially in comparison with the years after seven or eight, characterized by a rather lax discipline. Harsh punishments were not unknown, but they do not appear to have been used methodically to break the child's will or to dampen his independence. On the contrary, there are indications that some families purposely allowed young children to cultivate their own interests, although not without some encouragement and guidance by the father. An example of such casual control was the suggestion made by the royal secretary of Philip II, Mateo Vázquez, that in the home of his nephew, Agustinillo, aged five, there be a room of "arms" and another of "letters" to see to which the boy was most inclined. Agustinillo's step-father, Jerónimo Gasol, another royal secretary to Philip II, soon noted that the child "would be more inclined to the profession of arms than to study."[8] Such early educational encouragement on the part of parents may only have been indicative of highly ambitious, "careerist" families, but it appears likely that children of the upper classes were allowed to develop independently though not impudently. Subject to a relatively carefree routine implemented primarily by household servants, the young child's major obligations involved toilet-training, respect for parent authority, and adherence to the rituals of the Catholic faith.

Childhood independence and freedom, however, halted abruptly after the age of six when a new stage in life began and the child had reached what French ecclesiastical law termed the "age of discretion."[9] This change was heralded symbolically by the exchange of childhood robes for clothes modeled upon those of adults and by the taking of first communion which brought the child into the adult congregation of the church. Formal, rigorous instruction in literacy and religion now began, and apprenticeship contracts were arranged.[10] Meanwhile, strict obedience and dis-

---

[7]Ariès, *Centuries of Childhood*, part I describes the routine of childhood during the *Ancien Régime*, while Arco, "La Vida Privada En La Obra De Cervantes," pp. 600–04, offers brief comments about the life and dress of Spanish children. Angel Valbuena Prat, *La Vida Española en la Edad de Oro Según sus Fuentes Literarias* (Barcelona, 1943), gives references to this subject as well. Also interesting is A. Rodríguez Marin, "Varios juegos infantiles del Siglo XVI," *BRAE* (1931). Juan Luis Morales, *El Niño en la Cultura Española* (4 vols., Madrid, 1960), provides a useful historical bibliography of pediatrics in Spain.

[8]Hazañas, *Vázquez de Leca*, pp. 15–16.

[9]Louis de Hericault, *Les Loix Ecclesiastiques de la France . . .* (Paris, 1730), chap. I, art. xxx, p. 14. In the Middle Ages, the "age of discretion" appears to have come somewhat later. The Council of Beziers in 1246, for example, fixed it at seven, while the synodial statutes of Tournai in 1346 placed it around ten, "*cirecter dicennium*"; cf. J. Toussaert, *Le Sentiment Religieux en Flandre a la Fin du Moyen Âge* (Paris, 1963), p. 160.

[10]Cristóbal Pérez de Herrera in his *Amparo de los Legítimos Pobres* (Madrid, 1608), recommended that at the age of eight poor boys be given jobs and girls be sent to find work as servants. This work is cited in Morales, *El Niño*, 1: 129.

cipline became a fundamental rule of thumb. Contemporaries warned that "the worst pestilence that can befall a town is the liberty and disorder of youth," and to forestall this eventuality, children of seven and eight were subject to stern controls.[11] The whip was no longer an instrument of intermittent discipline, but a tool used regularly to force the child to submit to the family's as well as the schoolmaster's will.[12]

The years between six and eight therefore represented a turning point for the child, one that in the modern family is at least partially delayed until adolescence. At that juncture the father made decisions that determined much of his child's adult life. Tutors and schools were selected and the type of education chosen often dictated to the child his later vocation and career. A decision regarding holy orders was frequently determined before the age of nine as well, this being the youngest age at which a youth could take religious vows and become eligible for ecclesiastical rents.[13] In other words, the child, prodded by the whip, entered a training period—the latency period in the parlance of modern psycho-analytic theory—in which he would be equipped to enter the adult world in terms of education, religion, vocation, and dress.[14] It is clear that sixteenth-century Spaniards, particularly those connected with schools, foundling homes, orphanages, and the like, regarded the years after six as a stage in life during which children had to be moulded in order to prepare them for adult responsibilities.[15] This transitional stage ended only with the coming of puberty, which contemporaries officially pegged at twelve for girls and fourteen for boys.[16]

[11]Pedro López de Montoya, "Libro de la Buena Educación y Enseñanza de Nobles," in Las Ideas Pedagógicas del Doctor Pedro López de Montoya, ed. E. Hernández Rodríguez (Madrid, 1947), p. 257.

[12]BE: Ms. L.I.13, "Advertencias sobre el remedio que se podria poner para que los maestros de escuelas saquen con brevedad los muchachos en ellos buenos lectores y escribanos y contadores," folio 264, cites the complaints of schoolmasters during the 1580s "who say that one of the reasons they cannot teach the boys well is that some of the fathers order them not to whip [their sons], and if they do it, the fathers immediately remove their boys from the schools." For other arguments on leniency toward children in the sixteenth century, see Felix G. Olmedo, Diego Ramírez Villaescusa 1459–1537 (Madrid, 1944), p. xxiii.

[13]See Hazañas, Vázquez de Leca, chap. 2, for decisions made by Mateo Vázquez regarding the schooling and future careers of his nephews. Curiously, young Agustinillo, aged six, who only a year earlier had demonstrated a preference for a room of "arms" and his distaste for "letters" by the tears he shed in school, was ordered into the household of the Archbishop of Zaragoza and launched onto an ecclesiastical career.

[14]On the general question of children's passage to adulthood in the Ancien Régime, see Ariès, Centuries of Childhood, pp. 25–26. For a critique of Ariès' views, see Natalie Zemon Davis, "The Reasons of Misrule: Youth Groups and Charivaris in Sixteenth-Century France," Past & Present 50 (February 1971): 61, note 63.

[15]See p. 12.

[16]See Hericault, Loix Ecclesiastiques, chap. V, art. ii, p. 78. In Spain, Hernando de Salazar, "Tratado que se dio el Rey el año 1643 sobre materias de gobierno y hacienda," BNM: Ms. 2375, folio 234v, claimed the age of fourteen for boys was "that of puberty." Antonio Xavier Pérez y López, Theatro de la Legislación Universal de España y las Indias (Madrid, 1791) 20: 71, notes that in traditional Spanish law boys under fourteen and girls under twelve could not be accused of incest. Presumably, the law rested upon the premise that children below these ages were sexually immature.

It was during these years that the child might also be removed from the parental home and placed under the care and authority of others. In the eighteenth century there is some evidence that boys and girls as young as three or four years of age were placed in the care of women known as *amigas*, who directed the equivalent of a modern nursery school, but it is not known whether this was a widespread practice or even when it first began.[17] In general, children remained at home until the "age of discretion." At that point sons of the aristocracy, in accordance with the medieval tradition of wardship, might be sent to become pages at the royal court, while others were placed in the residence of a friend or relation to be trained in the arts of chivalry and war. Other children were boarded at a variety of monasteries and schools, and youths who were destined for the church might enter the household of a prelate. Children of humble origin were commonly sent out of the house to find work as servants and domestics, and other families, seeking a particular craft for their offspring, would apprentice them to a master artisan, allowing the latter to educate and train the children as he saw fit.[18] The extent of these "putting-out" practices is difficult to discover, but they were certainly practiced on a regular basis, varying from family to family and class to class, even though such customs had their liabilities, as bans upon carnal relations between masters and servants suggest.[19]

PRIMARY EDUCATION: THE TEACHING OF LITERACY

The art of learning how to read and to write in the vernacular, to perform simple arithmetic calculations, and to recite parts of the Catechism and a few simple prayers were the first responsibilities which many new six- and seven-year-olds had to face. For this task ABC-primers, Spanish grammars, and reading notebooks were available by the opening of the sixteenth century, to be published thereafter in growing numbers.[20] Thus anyone wishing to undertake the instruction of the young had the necessary tools if not the

[17]AA Granada: leg. 894, "Visita a las escuelas de Granada, 1774-75."

[18]For examples of these contracts, see Agustin G. Amezúa y Mayo, *La Vida Privada Española en el Protocolo Notorial* (Madrid, 1950), pp. 203-09. Not all of these arrangements were successful. Young Alonso de Contreras, apprenticed, so he later said, without his consent by his mother to a silversmith, refused to carry water for his new master's wife. "I said to her that I had not come to be a servant but to learn a craft." He then ran away to home where neighbors defended his action, believing that a boy should not be compelled to do something against his will. See *The Life of Captain Alonso de Contreras, Written by Himself*, trans. C. A. Phillips (New York, n.d.), p. 15.

[19]AA Granada: leg. 1864, royal pragmatic of 25.XI.1565.

[20]Examples of these texts are Juan de Iciar, *Recopilación Subtillissima Intitulada Orthographia Practica* (Zaragoza, 1548); Pedro de Madariaga, *Libro Subtilissimo Intitulado Honra de Escribanos* (Valencia, 1565); and Juan de la Cuesta, *Libro y Tratado para Enseñar Leer y Escrivir* (Alcalá de Henares, 1589). Henry Thomas, "An Unrecorded Sixteenth-Century Spanish Writing Book, and More About Gothic Letters," *Estudios Ofrecidos a Menéndez Pidal* 3 (1952): 412-20, mentions a similar work by Alonso Martin de Canto which dates from the 1530s.

necessary skills, wisdom, and patience. Pedagogical techniques were those common to centuries of school teaching: memorization, endless repetition and review, constant practice and copying, always aided by the free use of the cane upon the bored, inattentive, lazy, and mischievous.

The least common medium of instruction but that with the greatest prestige was the private tutor, living in the home, serving as teacher, companion, and social director for the child. Comfort and privacy, direct, personal communication, constant attention and supervision, a routine especially suited to fit the child's particular interests, and the ability of parents to keep a close tab on both tutor and pupil alike were strong arguments in favor of such instruction, and by the middle of the sixteenth century Spain's aristocracy were already well-accustomed to the presence of these teachers in their homes. Class bias and prejudice, as well as the reputation of schoolmasters for brutishness and cruelty, also prompted the use of the tutor among this class; the young grandee who was taught at home would not have to mingle with children of lesser rank nor suffer the public indignity of the whip.

Whatever the potential merits of private tutors, drawbacks existed as well. Incompetent, poorly trained, corrupt, and immoral tutors were as common as good ones, making careful selection by the parents essential. But according to Ambrosio de Morales, chronicler to Philip II, "parents selected tutors as if they were buying a velvet chair,"[21] a comparison which suggests that Spain's aristocracy gave little thought to something so commonplace. And if the selection of tutors was indeed so casual, one can imagine that mistakes were many and the tenure of many tutors relatively short, thus prolonging the child's education or leaving it to household servants or to the parents themselves.

Competent or incompetent, private tutors were rarely found outside the households of the aristocracy. Though other families may have sought their services, private tuition at home was expensive. In addition to a regular stipend, tutors required a room and frequently a servant of their own, and the number of Spaniards who could afford their services was always at a minimum. Even then, private tutors were not always in demand. Mateo Vázquez, Philip II's secretary, elected to have his nephews learn their lessons in small, private schools.[22] And for men of similar circumstances—high government officials, leading lawyers, wealthy merchants—tuition at home was probably an exception, perhaps a privilege accorded only to the oldest son. These ambitious, forward-looking families paid considerable attention to the proper education of their sons; rather than shield their children from

---

[21]Cited by E. J. Zarco-Bacas y Cuevas, *Relaciones de Pueblos del Obispado de Cuenca* (Cuenca, 1927) 1: cviii. A similar complaint was made by Juan Gutierrez Tello, an army officer in Seville, who in 1650 attributed part of what he called the "ignorance" of the times to the fact that noblemen put great care in looking for a good *picador* for their horses, "little or none in looking for a good master for the education of their sons"; cited in Felipe Picatoste, *Estudios Sobre la Grandeza y Decadencia de España* (Madrid, 1887) 3: 144.

[22]See Hazañas, *Vázquez de Leca*, pp. 16–17.

the realities of the wider world, they placed them into the competitive and disciplined atmosphere of the school which rewarded drive, obedience, and hard work. Not surprisingly, these same families provided most of the financial support for primary and secondary schools during the Habsburg era. But it is important to recognize that wealthy mercantile and office-holding families in the course of the seventeenth and eighteenth centuries were continuously acquiring titles of nobility, landed estates, and larger, more spacious homes, adopting for themselves, in short, the external trappings of aristocratic life. Simultaneously, their educational habits turned inward, aping the private, hearth-centered instruction typical of the old grandee class.

One alternative to the private tutor was private tuition outside of the home. "Masters of primary letters," embodying the continuation of medieval craft traditions in which scribes and notaries taught writing to their sons and a few apprentices, could be found in most Spanish towns. As early as 1370 these instructors were sufficiently numerous and their services sufficiently popular to warrant Henry II (1369–79) of Castile to establish licensing procedures to guard against unskilled and incompetent masters.[23] The monarchy's weakness at this time ensured that this decree would have little effect, although it did set an important precedent by subjecting the writing masters to royal as opposed to ecclesiastical control.

In practice, Spain's masters of primary letters remained free of most external regulation and control until the early sixteenth century, when new interest in learning the art of literacy and new religious concerns prompted intervention into their affairs. At issue was the fear that the cheap editions and translations of the sacred texts which followed the introduction of printing into Spain in 1473 would encourage the populace to interpret scripture on their own. There was also concern that the masses might be tempted by heresies imported from abroad in the form of pamphlets and printed books. Accordingly, the Spanish church took steps to place the instruction of primary letters under its thumb. One of these was a 1512 ruling by the diocese of Seville ordering all parish priests and sacristans to teach the three Rs.[24] Other dioceses appointed "visitors" to examine the "masters of the children's schools" for their religious orthodoxy.[25] Such measures met only with limited success, but similar concerns led to a royal decree in 1573 that excluded from the teaching profession *conversos* as well as individuals whose forefathers had been brought before the Inquisition. Furthermore, municipally appointed inspectors were asked to see "what books they [the writing masters] are using, if they are [doctrinally] correct or not, if the books are apt for the said Art, and if they have been [previously] examined by the Royal Council."[26]

[23]See Lorenzo Luzuriaga, *Documentos para la Historia Escolar de España* (Madrid, 1916) 1: 5–9.

[24]See E. García y Barbarín, *Historia de la Pedagogia Española* (Madrid, 1909), p. 65.

[25]Olmedo, *Ramírez de Villaescusa*, pp. xxiii–iv.

[26]Luzuriaga, *Documentos* 1: 12–13.

Implicit in such rulings was the notion that children were particularly susceptible to religious propaganda, and as a corollary to this, the belief that ideas implanted early in life were indelible. Contemporaries believed that if instruction in morals and religion was initiated after a certain age, it would be nothing but a waste of time, since by then the child would have already formulated the ideas and principles he would keep for life. The statutes of the Colegio de los Niños de la Doctrina, an orphanage in Toledo, stated expressly that its incoming wards "have to be between the ages of seven and ten since the latter is the latest at which good doctrines and customs can be imprinted."[27] It follows that sixteenth-century rulers placed great stock in the value and efficacy of early education; it moulded the Christian and the citizen for life. Diego de Simancas, a noted jurist of the era, put it this way: ". . . one of the most important functions of the State must be that children and youths are correctly educated and perfectly taught since subjects who are poorly trained as children grow up to be the worst enemies of the homeland."[28] And for a society as preoccupied with the maintenance of orthodoxy as sixteenth-century Castile, the proper regulation of elementary education was indispensable. Subsequently, a continuous stream of rules and regulations handed down by municipal authorities, churchmen, and kings chipped away at the independence of the "masters of primary letters."[29] Religious orthodoxy was of the highest priority, and this meant that the masters had to be proven Catholics. Otherwise, these instructors managed to preserve much of their freedom. Fathers interested in their services would seek out a local master, agree to pay him a certain sum, and seal the contract before a notary. Only rarely did ecclesiastical, royal, or even municipal officials intervene in the negotiations.

Operating therefore as private instructors, the cost of the lessons provided by the "masters of primary letters" was rather steep. In 1532, for example, Gomez Mosquera, resident in Santiago de Compostela, hired two masters at the cost of six gold ducats to teach his son Alonso to read and to write "in a script that scribes are able to sign."[30] Other contracts reveal similar arrangements, although by the end of the century the services of a writing master for one year in Santiago and other nearby cities cost eight ducats and more, not to mention quantities of livestock and grain.[31] This was a sum few ordinary Spaniards could afford.[32] According to contracts

[27] AM Toledo: registro Ms., "Colegio de los Niños de la Doctrina."

[28] Cited in Zarco-Bacas, *Cuenca*, p. cxv.

[29] For documents concerning the crown's policy toward primary schools in the sixteenth century, see BE: Ms. L.I.13.

[30] Cited in Pablo Pérez Constantí, *Notas Viejas Galicianas* (Vigo, 1925), 1: 350. This volume lists a number of similar contracts.

[31] Ibid., 1: 383.

[32] A day laborer in Old Castile in the 1530s earned no more than five ducats a year, and no more than seven or eight in the 1550s; private tuition was clearly out of reach. Even a master builder earning about 60 ducats a year would have been hard-pressed to spend 10 per-

from Galicia, private lessons were arranged only by a limited number of families, and then by wealthy landlords, lawyers, or master artisans in a luxury trade. Families of more moderate means sent their offspring to organized private and semiprivate schools, and it was there, in classrooms, that the majority of Spanish children who learned to read and write were taught.

Documentation for these "little schools" is almost nil, since few attained a level of organization that surpassed a lone master and one or two assistants; record-keeping, consequently, was at a minimum. Yet it is clear that such schools existed in numerous localities by the opening of the seventeenth century. The size of each depended on the popularity and price of the individual schoolmaster. Those who were eager for cash or exceedingly ambitious took on as many students as they could attract. So Alonso Martin de Canto, resident in Salamanca during the 1530s and author of *The Art of Writing All Forms and Types of Letters*, noted that he taught 150 pupils daily,[33] while fragments of a 1642 inquiry in Madrid reveal schools ranging in size from 38 to 140 pupils.[34]

These relatively large classes suggest that individual attention was at a minimum, while keeping order must have occupied much of the school day. Presumably, teaching, most of which was done through the use of printed *cartillas* that demonstrated the rules of orthography and different writing styles, was rather difficult, and the pace at which students learned very slow. Such problems were compounded by an eight-hour day with a break only at lunchtime. Students were often bored, tired, and restless, and the recommendation of one sixteenth-century writer that special officers be hired to round up truants suggests that the schools could have been made more attractive.[35] Other difficulties stemmed from the harsh physical punishments inflicted by masters intent on maintaining discipline and order. Such rigor earned for them the description of "barbaric idiots" from Cristóbal de Villalón and a reputation for "bestiality" from Sebastian de Covarrubias.[36] Municipal and ecclesiastical authorities also complained of their cruelty:

they [the schoolmasters] should not treat the children or the adolescents cruelly, because this does nothing more than to make them hate to study. Treat them with kindness, applauding them loudly when they deserve it, praising them with due discretion in order that they are encouraged to go ahead with their studies. Further-

cent of his income on a private education for his son. These salary figures are approximations of actual wages; cf. Earl J. Hamilton, *American Treasure and the Price Revolution in Spain, 1501-1650* (Cambridge, Mass., 1934), app. vii; Bartolomé Bennassar, *Valladolid au Siècle d'Or* (Paris, 1967), pp. 293-302.

[33]See Thomas, "Spanish Writing Book," p. 416.

[34]AVM: 2/376/19.

[35]See BE: Ms. L.1.13, folio 264v.

[36]Cristóbal de Villalón, *El Scholástico*, ed. M. Menéndez y Pelayo (Madrid, 1911), p. 106; A. González Palencia, *Datos Biográficos del Lic. Sebastian de Covarrubias y Horozco* (Madrid, 1925), p. 217.

more, the masters should have for their students the hearts of fathers, and they should look at them in this light, not as cruel witches who only enjoy themselves when they are making others suffer.[37]

Fees in these schools varied according to what each pupil was taught. The cheapest—two *reales* a month—were for pupils learning only to read; those learning to read and write paid four; and those learning all of the three Rs paid six. Presuming that the academic year lasted eleven months, it is possible to estimate that the cost of learning the three Rs in a private school was nearly six ducats a year, an expense that remained beyond the reach of Castile's working population, except for those few boys lucky enough to be accepted "*de limosna*," that is, according to whatever they could afford to pay, or for free. The abridged program, costing only two ducats a year, was more accessible, and the fact that approximately one-third of the students in Madrid's schools in 1642 paid only this sum may be an indication that reading was a skill common among portions of the city's popular classes.[38]

But the system of sliding fees utilized in Madrid's schools may have also fostered within each classroom a separation of students which worked against those of humble origin and background. One can imagine the poorest students, the "readers" paying only two reales apiece, clustered in the back of the classroom and the sons of more prosperous families who were each paying six reales seated in front. Since teaching was grounded upon the premise that the master would collect a sum of money in accordance with the time he spent with each student, those paying the highest fees must have been favored to the detriment of others paying less, and this is exactly the situation which one petitioner late in the sixteenth century described.[39] If such practices were widespread, it is easy to understand why contemporaries complained that too much time was required to teach children the rudiments of literacy. And in this perspective, it is also possible to see that the introduction of free primary education in the nineteenth century involved not only a widening of educational opportunities for the poor but also the end of a situation in which the poor, even though they might be in school, were permanently disadvantaged vis-à-vis children of wealthy backgrounds.

[37]Olmedo, *Ramírez de Villaescusa*, p. xxiii.

[38]Owing to the nature of the school program, reading was always much more prevalent than writing. For this reason, studies which purport to measure "literacy" by the incidence of signatures in a given population should be examined with care. For a brief discussion of some of the problems involved in measuring rates of literacy in the past, see Stone, "Literacy and Society in England, 1640–1900," *Past & Present* 42 (1969): 98.

[39]See BE: Ms. L.I.13, folio 213. That there were problems of division by social class in these schools is suggested in a story told by Alonso de Contreras. After playing hooky with the son of a constable, Contreras remembered that on the following day the schoolmaster, to punish him, "laid on with a parchment rod 'til he drew blood. This was done at the instance of the boy's father who was richer than mine." In revenge, Alonso, after school, stabbed the constable's son with a knife. See the *Life of Alonso de Contreras*, pp. 12–13.

In light of the discriminatory practices of many schoolmasters, the uneven quality of their instruction, and their eagerness to charge exorbitant fees, many towns, beginning in the middle of the sixteenth century, were prompted to bring private schools under some form of municipal control. This movement began in Spain's largest cities and aimed especially at rooting out incompetent masters and those charging excessive fees. A 1610 petition to the municipal council in Jérez de la Frontera, for instance, complained that the city's fourteen schoolmasters included individuals so ill-trained as to be unable to teach, among them several part-time teachers who were cobblers, barbers, and one who was only a student himself.[40] Similarly, the city of Seville took steps to shut down schools of unlicensed masters, while attempting to fix the fees which masters could collect.[41] In Madrid, the situation was worse. Here as elsewhere, royal edicts on the licensing of schoolmasters had proven ineffective, and in 1600, with the consent of the Royal Council of Castile, the *corregidor* of Madrid was instructed to appoint examiners who were to inspect the credentials of "masters teaching in houses as well as those in private houses."[42] Anyone not examined would be barred from teaching the three Rs, but in a city of 100,000 people, that was growing rapidly, many masters continued to teach on the sly. Twenty years later the corregidor ordered another inquiry into Madrid's schools, and on this occasion 44 masters were discovered, although the corregidor added that "there are others, unskilled and ignorant, who give lessons in houses and in the streets."[43]

Eager to impose strict licensing procedures were Madrid's established schoolmasters who, in the guise of maintaining educational standards, sought to limit their competition. This campaign was headed by Juan Diaz Morante, author of a book on how to teach the three Rs, who was later named to be a "master examiner" with the task of inspecting the credentials of all schoolmasters in Madrid. Writing in 1625, he complained "that there are more than 60 public masters, not including the many secret ones, and among these there are no more than three or four who know anything. For this city, fifteen *good* masters are enough."[44] Morante added that unqualified masters, by charging low prices, jeopardized the careers of the reputable ones, since the "multitude prefer the cheapest schools." To bring an end to this state of affairs, he proposed a series of examinations to eliminate all but the most qualified teachers as well as a halt in the licensing of new masters, so that the total number of schools and schoolmasters would gradually decrease.

---

[40]See H. Sancho de Sopranís y Juan de la Lastra y Terry, *Historia de Jérez de la Frontera* (Jérez, 1965), 2: 317.

[41]See AA Sevilla: lib. 22, nos. 1, 6, 7; J. Guichot y Parody, *Historia del Excmo. Ayuntamiento de la . . . Ciudad de Sevilla* (Sevilla, 1903), 2: 313; and Salvador Montoto, *Sevilla en el Imperio* (Sevilla, n.d.), p. 111.

[42]AVM: 2/376/1, *decretos* of 3, 26. VI.1600.

[43]AVM: 2/376/10.

[44]AVM: 2/376/12, letter of 20.III.1625.

In subsequent years Morante continued his campaign, arguing that if Madrid was to have good teachers, stiff examinations in the capital would not be enough, since ill-trained masters from other towns where licensing procedures were lax constantly drifted into the court city. Emphasizing this point, Morante claimed that the certification of schoolmasters should only be allowed in Madrid, because "there are not six masters in all of Old and New Castile, let alone all of Spain, who know the art [of the three Rs] well enough to be good examiners."[45]

In many respects Morante's complaints were justified. The capital was populated by the rich, the noble, the educated, the people most likely to seek an education for their children and pay well for it. As Madrid attracted beggars and thieves who hoped to live as parasites off the royal court, it also attracted teachers from other towns. This influx reached a peak during the second quarter of the seventeenth century, flooding the capital with schoolmasters, many of whom were no more than charlatans.[46] Teaching in doorways and in stairwells, these unlicensed preceptors, or *leccionistas* as they were known, invariably charged lower fees than the established masters who ran organized schools. In danger of losing part of their clientele to this cut-rate competition, the licensed masters protested that ". . . among the leccionistas are some illiterates who have pretended to be masters with their own schools and with this title they loiter about the Court. From their classes completely ignorant persons who do not know how to read, write, or count have graduated. These unknown, 'foreign' leccionistas have given rise to other, more serious problems as well."[47] Among these problems, so the regular masters alleged, was a reduction in their own ranks from 50 to 31.[48]

Viewed from another perspective, there was good reason for the leccionistas to exist. The established masters, however qualified for their work, had been charging excessive fees. In 1642, for example, Madrid's corregidor stated the fees demanded by the masters forced "many poor people to stop instructing their sons."[49] Thus the leccionistas, though endangering the position and prosperity of the licensed schoolmasters, may have been able to teach literacy to segments of Madrid's population who would have otherwise remained ignorant.

In the end, the regular schoolmasters emerged victorious. In order to bring to a halt the unwanted competition and to protect their own interests, they organized in 1666, with the help of the crown, into a confraternity or guild, the Hermandad de San Casiano, that was empowered to set licensing procedures and to regulate student fees.[50] By 1695 the schoolmasters ex-

[45]AVM: 2/376/13, letter of 5.V.1626.
[46]See AVM: 2/376/2–9, 11, 26. These contain teaching licenses issued by the city of Madrid.
[47]Cited in Luzuriaga, *Documentos* 1: 25.
[48]Ibid., p. 25.
[49]AVM: 2/376/19, letter of 9.XI.1642.
[50]See Luzuriaga, *Documentos* 1: 41 ff.

cluded from their newly self-proclaimed "noble" profession individuals who had previously exercised "vile and indecent" offices and prohibited "preceptors of grammar" from teaching primary letters, asserting that "the teaching of the one is incompatible with the other."[51] The guild subsequently limited the number of schools in Madrid, attempted to raise the standards required of new masters, and set the texts to be used, presumably with the aim of improving elementary education within the court city.

Abuses, however, remained, and this situation led the Bourbon monarchy in the second half of the eighteenth century to intervene in the guild's activities and to assume the supervision of elementary education in Madrid and elsewhere on an unprecedented scale. Charles III (1759–88) and his son, Charles IV (1788–1808), acting on the premise that a literate society was vital to economic growth and religious orthodoxy, created the beginnings of a national program for elementary education in Spain. Examinations of new masters were given over to the Royal Council, elaborate licensing procedures were established, and in Madrid a normal school to train teachers, Spain's first, was created in 1780. By the close of the century the capital had twenty-four officially recognized schools of which eight, created by Charles IV in 1791, were designated as Royal Schools.[52] So after centuries of sporadic and uneven regulation, primary education had at last become an instrument of national policy, designed to aid the kingdom rather than line the pockets of the schoolmasters.

Attempts by the Spanish Bourbons to organize public primary education can be traced not only to their interest in the ideas of the French Enlightenment but also to precedents within Spain itself. For centuries town councils and private individuals had been setting aside rents and revenues in order to organize rudimentary forms of public elementary schools, and, to a lesser extent, their work was matched by that of the Catholic church. Cathedral and collegiate churches commonly offered lessons in literacy to boys preparing for the priesthood, and secular students, paying fees, were frequently allowed to attend. The religious orders did much the same, particularly the Jesuits and Franciscans, both of whom provided free instruction. Officially, parish priests were also expected to teach the three Rs, although the extent and the quality of their contribution remains unknown. In most instances public instruction in literacy was the work of the towns. Schoolmasters were hired out of public funds and the fees, if any, charged to students were subject to municipal regulation. In addition, many town councils required local schools to admit a number of paupers free.[53]

---

[51]Ibid., p. 135.

[52]Ibid., p. 240.

[53]These contracts were often very precise; that of Betanzos, a town near La Coruña, might serve as a typical example. The Master Juan Domínguez de Busto received from the town in 1582 a six-year contract which stipulated that "he had to teach the students the 3 Rs, Christian doctrine, and all that a good master ought, and this for the salary he will arrange with the persons whom he teaches; moreover, he is obliged to teach without any remuneration three sons of poor residents that the city will send to him, and that when these are

Arrangements of this nature were hammered out by hundreds of municipalities in the sixteenth century, although it is significant that large cities like Madrid, Seville, and Toledo, for example, did not follow suit. Despite pressure on officials in these cities to provide some form of subsidized instruction, they left instruction in literacy to private and religious schools, doing little more than supervise the work of these institutions and make sure that a number of poor children were admitted gratis.[54] It would appear, therefore, that the tradition of public support of education in Castile was strongest in the small, provincial towns where the population was neither sufficiently large nor wealthy to support private schoolmasters of note.

So, with the exception of a handful of large metropolitan centers, the sixteenth century in Castile was marked by an extraordinary willingness on the part of municipal authorities to invest in public primary education. Teachers were paid and schools built out of the municipal budget, while subsidies offered to cathedrals and convents opened hitherto private classes to the public. At the same time, private schoolmasters were brought under some form of municipal control. The reasons for this early primary school movement are unclear. The appearance of the printed book in the late fifteenth century had certainly placed a premium upon literacy, spurring interest in learning how to read and write. But apart from families who sought to train their sons as notaries and scribes, there was never any pressure from below, no widespread, manifested desire on the part of the masses to obtain the necessary skills. Indeed, for most people living in the sixteenth and seventeenth centuries, literacy was no more than a luxury. Economically, its value was limited, and though it might offer some protection against forged documents, literacy was not worth the time, trouble, and expense it took to acquire.

Nevertheless, literacy was on the rise in sixteenth-century Castile, and this was a phenomenon directed and supported by people near the top of society, namely, the wealthy bourgeois and noblemen occupying positions on the local *concejos*, the town councils. Underlying their support was the conception that reading and writing were skills vital to the community at large and not simply a professional elite. Here one finds the influence of Renaissance humanists who stressed the importance of "learning" and "culture" for the citizenry, but, and perhaps more importantly, town fathers realized that literacy would allow the young, particularly the offspring of the poor, to enter into the Christian commonwealth. Spaniards in the six-

---

'taught,' the city can send three more in their place." His maximum fees were set at one *real* a month for each pupil taught to read, one and one-half reales for those learning to read and write, and two reales for those busy with the 3 Rs. In addition to his fees, Busto was to receive an annual salary, paid by the town, of 6,000 mrs. This contract is cited in Pérez Constantí, *Notas Viejas Galicianas*, p. 385.

[54]Zarco-Bacas, *Cuenca*, pp. cxviii–ix cites a petition to the city of Toledo which advised the establishment of municipally sponsored schools.

teenth century admitted the innocence of baptized infants, but they also believed that children who were left uneducated and unattended would follow their supposedly natural, "evil" instincts, become worrisome brats, and then lead depraved, criminal, and even heretical lives.[55] Such reasoning was evident, for example, when the city of Seville in 1548 stated that neglected orphans would eventually become sinful and criminal in their habits "because having been brought up free and without a 'boss,' they divert themselves; and that having been raised in liberty, when adults, they necessarily become destructive of the public good, corruptive of good customs, and disquieting to people and towns."[56] To overcome such tendencies, it was understood that children should be placed in schools or at least in the care of conscientious adults to make sure that they were taught how to become loyal, obedient, pious, and industrious subjects. Such aims for childhood education were nothing new, but in the sixteenth century the program was emended to include the three Rs so that the means of indoctrination might be improved.

To achieve such goals Castile's cities began to establish schools and foundling homes for the care and instruction of abandoned infants, orphans, and the children of the large number of paupers (*pobres*) who constituted much of the urban population. The city of Seville maintained at the Cortes of 1548 that in the two years since it had built a House for the Instruction of Christian Doctrine in 1546 there were "fewer thieves than before, less disease and contagious illness, and more doctrine and better example among the poor."[57] Hoping for similar results, other towns followed suit, supporting free or low-cost education for the poor and providing instruction in literacy, religion, and a number of "useful" trades.

Such subsidies, however, were unthinkable without a religious rationale. Fear of heresy was rife in the sixteenth century, and literacy was regarded as an excellent means by which the young could be taught the fundamental tenets of the faith. Religious orthodoxy could then be achieved, but only so long as subversive literature could be kept out of reach. The town councils and the Spanish Inquisition shared this crucial task; the former would provide for, or at least look after, teachers and schools; the latter, through censorship, would keep the "poison" out. And together these agencies managed to preserve religious uniformity in Spain, a feat that no other European nation, with the exception of Portugal and the states of Italy, was able to achieve.

Simple Christian charity was also vital to the primary school movement of the sixteenth century. During this era of prosperity pious burghers, infused with Renaissance conceptions of learning, contributed freely to the spread of elementary education. The rationale they employed may have

---

[55]See AA Sevilla: Secc. 3, tomo 11, no. 52. This is a petition of 2.IX.1545 which lists some reasons for establishing an orphanage in Seville.

[56]Cortes de Valladolid, 1548, pet. 206. See also AA Sevilla: Secc. 3, tomo 12, no. 3.

[57]Ibid.

been similar to that of Baltasar de los Reis, a Sevillian bookseller, who submitted the following petition to the aldermen of his city: ". . . I admit that for the love of God I want to give the poor children an ABC-primer that I have made because such a primer costs ten *maravedís* and poor widows do not have that sum to spend on such a book."[58] Similarly, a petition in the Cortes of 1594 requested that the price of ABC-primers be held at four mrs.; it was alleged that these notebooks were selling at three and four times this price, "with harm to poor people whose sons, because they are children, ruin them."[59] On another scale, such reasoning led to municipal subsidies to primary schools.

Thus for a mixture of social, religious, charitable, and personal ends, local authorities in the sixteenth century regarded public support of educational institutions to be an essential task, an effort which enabled the spread of lay literacy to make substantial if still limited gains. However, problems of finance and administration hampered this effort from the start, threatening not only the existence of the municipal schools but the continuing extension of literacy itself. Jérez de la Frontera's difficulties may have been typical.[60] Master Firmiano de Marquina, the city schoolmaster, was also retained by the city council to write special letters to important dignitaries. In spite of his two posts, Marquina complained that he could not support himself, and in 1587 he quit. A new master was obtained, only to leave a few years later, and in 1600 the city complained that as a result of a local epidemic all of its writing masters, public and private, had either fled the city or were taken ill.

During the seventeenth century mounting inflation, monetary chaos, and administrative mismanagement continued to exact a heavy toll from the municipal schools. Short of money, many towns defaulted on their contracts with schoolmasters. They in turn raised their fees, but this often did little more than cause the number of students in attendance to fall. So, with uncertain and shrinking incomes, many schoolmasters abandoned the smaller towns for the larger cities, an exodus which left many communities without trained teachers, while triggering Madrid's complaints about "foreign" leccionistas.

The root cause of the difficulties faced by the municipal schools in the seventeenth century was not necessarily financial. Underlying this lack of support was a change in the attitudes of the rich toward education for the poor. Authors writing during this period of economic stagnation and decline were quick to point out the average Spaniard's supposed revulsion to manual labor, asserting that "excessive" education was its source.[61] They

---

[58]Guichot, *Ayuntamiento* 2: 314.

[59]Cited in Zarco-Bacas, *Cuenca*, p. cxvi, and Pérez y López, *Theatro*, vol. xiii, p. 20. See also the *Leyes de Recopilación* (Madrid, 1775), Lib. I, tit. vii, ley 30.

[60]The following is taken from Sancho de Sopranís, *Jérez de la Frontera*, 2: 316–17.

[61]See below, p. 43.

argued that schooling served only to encourage youths to abandon the fields and workshops for other less economically productive pursuits, particularly those in the church. Saavedra Fajardo, a political writer during the reign of Philip IV, even maintained that education weakened the nation's defenses, since it weakened men's wills and corrupted their spirits. The more ignorant the populace, he wrote, the stronger the ruler.[62] And while it is true that Saavedra Fajardo, along with other writers who were critical of education, aimed most of his fire at Latin schools and universities,[63] the opinions of these writers seem to have helped to shape a reluctance on the part of Spain's urban patriciate to spend public monies for schools which had apparently brought only negative returns. As Castile's economic and political problems continued unabated, this skepticism was reinforced, compounding still further the difficulties of the municipal schools.

One other manifestation of this probable shift in opinion was a decline in the contributions of private individuals to public primary schools. Of course, there were those like Antonio de Varreda who left 100 ducats in his will to the "best" schoolmaster in Talavera de la Reina, with the proviso that twenty boys be taught for free.[64] But in general it appears that the pace of such giving slacked off, particularly in the years following the decade of the 1620s.

To some extent, the increasing charitable role of the religious orders in public primary education compensated for the decline in private giving. Noted for their contributions to Latin and university education, as well as for their efforts to teach Indians in the New World, the religious orders did not take an especially active role in elementary education in Castile until the new Society of Jesus began to establish colleges of its own in 1547.[65] In most of their colleges, the Jesuits offered free instruction in literacy as well as Latin, and in towns such as Huete, Logroño, and Plasencia they alone offered free instruction in the subject. Other municipalities, unable to secure qualified teachers on their own, looked to the Jesuits for aid, offering an annual subsidy if the Society guaranteed regular instruction. Guadalajara, for example, agreed in 1631 to finance one chair in Latin grammar and one "master of primary letters" if the Society supplied the necessary

---

[62]*Idea De Un Príncipe Político Christiano* (Munich, 1630), Empresa 66. This point of view is also expressed in P. Fernández de Navarrete, *Conservación de Monarchías* (Madrid, 1621), Discursos XLVI–XLVII and Abad Joseph Arnorfini de Illescas, "Discurso Hispano político sobre el estado presente de la Monarchía, 31.III.1622" (BM: Add. 28, 455, folios 136 ff.).

[63]See pp. 43–44.

[64]AHP Toledo: lib. 422, f. 52 v. The testament is dated 27.IV.1651.

[65]In the Americas the religious orders had been active in bringing literacy to the conquered Indian population, ostensibly to aid in their missionary effort, right from the very start. In 1512, for example, the Franciscans had printed in Seville 2000 "cartyllas de ensenar a leer" for an expedition to the Americas. See F. J. Norton, *Printing in Spain, 1501–1520* (New York, 1965), p. 13.

teachers,[66] this being an arrangement that was subsequently adopted by the cities of La Coruña and Pontevedra.[67]

Unfortunately, the Jesuits' efforts to improve elementary education in Castile were too little and too late. Their colleges, along with those of the other religious orders, were relatively few in number and only a handful were situated in rural areas where the teaching of literacy was at its worst. Furthermore, the state of Castile's economy in the seventeenth century was such that opportunities for free instruction were not sufficient to convince many families that they ought to send their sons to school instead of to work, the income from which could bolster the family purse.[68]

At the opening of the eighteenth century, Castile was saddled with a decaying system of municipal schools. Owing to the uncertain economy and a lack of private support, many had already closed. In others teaching was entrusted to unskilled instructors who themselves could barely read and write. In all probability, the incidence of literacy had ceased to advance and it may even have been on the decline. The end of the War of the Spanish Succession (1701–14) and the coming of the new Bourbon dynasty brought the promise of progress and reform, but recovery was slow and initiated only piecemeal. And even when Charles III made it his policy to reorganize the existing hodge-podge of schools and to create more free places for the children of the poor, improvements were limited to the larger, more prosperous towns. Rural communities, like Alcalá de las Gazules in Andalucia, could write: "Because of the lack of competent instruction in [Latin] grammar and even in that of primary letters, the youth of this town are generally very 'rustic'."[69]

The expulsion of the Society of Jesus from Spain and its dominions in 1767 seriously hampered efforts to improve the teaching of literacy. Naturally, the problems were at their worst in towns where the Jesuits had taught. Though private teachers and other religious orders moved in to fill the gap created by the expulsion of the Jesuits, costs were so high and money so short that many towns suffered more than a temporary lapse in instruction. In 1769, for example, an official in the town of Huete complained that the new masters appointed by the municipality were too young and inexperienced to teach properly, and he feared that unless something was done to improve the local school, Huete would in a few years become a totally illiterate community.[70]

[66]See F. Layna Serrano, *Historia de Guadalajara y Sus Mendozas en los Siglos XV y XVI* (Madrid, 1942), 4: 24.

[67]See AHN: Cons. leg. 13183, report of Galicia, 1764.

[68]In 1764 the town of Arcos de la Frontera reported: "the population of this city is in general composed of poor people. For this reason fathers commonly direct their sons into exercises that enable them to help support their families." As a result the city claimed that local schools were short of students. See AHN: Cons. leg. 13183, report of Arcos.

[69]AHN: Cons. leg. 13183, report of Alcalá de las Gazules, 1764.

[70]AHN: Cons. leg. 13183, report of Huete, 29.II.1769. The city of Caceres also mentioned a shortage of teachers at this time; see, in this same *legajo*, the report of Caceres, 5.IV.1768.

At this moment of crisis, however, the crown began to take seriously its commitment to bolster Castile's backward network of primary schools. Thanks to the influence of reformers like Pedro Rodríguez of Campomanes (1723–1803), *fiscal* (royal attorney) of the Royal Council of Castile under Charles III, and Gaspar Melchor de Jovellanos (1744–1811), Minister of Grace and Justice to Charles IV, both of whom lobbied for the establishment of free primary education in Spain, some progress was made. Royal subsidies helped towns to reopen schools and hire teachers, while a flood of edicts devised new categories of urban and rural schools, new teacher-training procedures to fit each category, tax grants to support the establishment of new schools, and more scholarships for the poor. It is unfortunate that existing studies on these reforms are few, making it difficult to know their effectiveness or if parents responded by sending their children to school. Certainly, there was progress in some of the larger cities, but in small towns and country villages little in the way of more and better schools was achieved. And despite subsequent school reforms during the first half of the nineteenth century, Spain's population in 1860, according to official statistics, was 75 percent illiterate, one of Europe's worst scholastic records.[71] This figure suggests that in previous centuries no more than 10 to 15 percent of the population could read and write.[72] Regardless of the Bourbons' good intentions, Spain in the *antiguo régimen* remained a kingdom overwhelmingly composed of illiterates.

THE ILLITERATE

Those who were unable to read and write were most numerous by far in rural areas, the educational backwaters of early modern Spain. Organized schools in the hamlets and villages which dotted much of the Castilian countryside were few, and even in those localities where instruction was offered, either by a private master or the parish priest, its quality was notoriously low. Literacy, consequently, particularly in the smaller settlements, was much more the exception than the rule, a fact which is graphically illustrated in a series of tax lists (*padrónes*) prepared for Castile during the reign of Philip II (1556–98).[73] For example, in Serranillo, a community of 30 *vecinos* (or about 150 inhabitants) in the province of Ciudad Real, the scribe preparing the *padrón* noted: "I testify that since there is nobody in the said village who knows how to sign for the *alcaldes* (mayors), nor do they [the alcaldes] know how to do it either, it is not signed."[74] Countless other hamlets with fewer than 100 vecinos were in similar

[71]See Lorenzo Luzuriaga, *El Analfabetismo en España* (Madrid, 1919), p. 44.
[72]My estimate is slightly above that of Manuel Fernández Alvarez, *La Sociedad Española Del Renacimiento* (Salamanca, 1970), who claims that only 10 percent of Spain's population in the sixteenth century was literate (p. 193).
[73]These can be found in AGS: Exp. Hac., serie I.
[74]AGS: Exp. Hac., serie I, leg. 82, Serranillo.

straits; local officials, unable to sign their names to the padrón, made only their marks.[75]

The reason for this is obvious. Literacy *a priori* requires instruction, but small villages in the sixteenth century rarely possessed a resident who was able, let alone willing, to teach. It follows that nearly the entire village, with the possible exception of the priest, a few town officials, and a handful of rich peasants, was unable to read and write. On the other hand, only in village communities of substantial size, that is with 500 vecinos and more, did primary schooling begin to be organized and literacy become something less of a rarity.[76] Orgaz, a wool-producing village of 550 vecinos even had a *bachiller de gramática* who was supposed to teach Latin, although in 1576 he was listed as a pauper.[77] Yet this serves to illustrate that even those communities large enough to have a schoolmaster were not always more literate than those that did not, since these teachers, in the absence of subsidies, were obliged to charge fees which only a small minority of the local population was willing and able to afford. Looking for students, the schoolmasters of rural Spain were constantly on the go, moving from village to village in an attempt to gain a meager living from a countryside in which both the interest in and the incidence of literacy was uniformly low.

There were exceptions, of course. Villages which possessed an exceptionally pious or charitable señor might benefit from an endowed school, while others which happened to be near a monastery had an opportunity to educate their children free. Furthermore, there were village scribes who taught the three Rs to an apprentice or two, and conscientious priests would often do the same. There are references, for instance, "to parish priests and clerics" in villages in the north of Spain who taught "in their own houses for those who wish to attend."[78] But not all village *curas* were so diligent. Uneducated themselves, many had neither the inclination nor the ability to teach their young parishioners anything more than to recite the Catechism and to understand parts of the Christian ritual. Such training, moreover, was often wholly by memory drill, since books, paper, and ink were luxuries in Spain's impoverished countryside. To be sure, a

[75]For example, see AGS: Exp. Hac., serie 1, leg. 82, El Arguidalin; leg. 91–96, Daymalos; leg. 91–97, Vaños.

[76]The distribution of Castile's rural population in the sixteenth century is known only for a few areas; cf. Noel Salomon, *La Campagne de Nouvelle Castille a la Fin du XVIe Siècle* (Paris, 1964), p. 42; and Michael Terrasse, "La Region de Madrid D'Apres Les 'Relaciones Topográficas," *Melanges de la Casa de Velázquez* 4 (1968): 153. It should be noted, however, that over one-half of the population of Old Castile in the middle of the eighteenth century lived in villages of less than 100 vecinos (cf. *La España del Antiguo Régimen*, ed. Miguel Artola, Fasc. III, *Castilla la Vieja* [Salamanca, 1957], p. 41). And in the province of Salamanca, at the same time, only 15 percent of the population lived in settlements larger than 500 vecinos. 40 percent lived in communities with 100–500 vecinos, and the remainder were scattered in villages smaller than that (cf. ibid., Fasc. 0., *Salamanca* [Salamanca, 1966], pp. 27–36). Such a dispersed pattern of settlement made it difficult to organize rural schools.

[77]AGS: Exp. Hac., Serie 1, leg. 180; leg. 39.

[78]AHN: Cons. 5495, no. 2, letter of the Bishop of Mondoñedo, 28.IV.1785.

number of village boys, thanks to the good graces of an interested lord or bishop, were able to attend choir schools in nearby towns, and a few of these were sent on to grammar schools, seminaries, and universities. But the vast majority of rural children remained unsponsored. Consequently, Spain's peasantry, too poor to support a schoolmaster, too hardworking to take time out for classes, remained overwhelmingly illiterate until the opening years of the twentieth century.[79]

But before one attributes the ignorance of the peasantry to a shortage of cheap village schools, it is also necessary to consider the peasantry's attitude toward booklearning itself. Spain's rural population never exhibited a strong, concerted demand for literacy, if only because this skill was long considered a luxury, wasteful and time-consuming, which provided few tangible benefits for those who acquired it. Hours spent in school meant hours lost in the fields, while whatever paperwork a peasant might ordinarily encounter could be handled by the village priest or a local scribe. And even if a peasant did manage to learn how to read and write, given the social and economic realities of rural life, his chances to improve his lot depended less upon these skills than upon ambition and hard work. Moreover, the high rates of infant and child mortality which prevailed among the peasantry until the late eighteenth century may have also created attitudes toward children which placed little premium upon education. If children were so delicate, poor peasants may not have stressed the importance of investing in the future of something so impermanent and vulnerable as that of a child.

The consequence of the shortage of rural schools and whatever attitudes the peasants attached to education was that the bulk of the rural population in Spain remained illiterate generation after generation. In an epoch which attached increasing importance and prestige to the ability to read and write, the peasantry stood apart. Lacking those skills, the road to further education, to the clergy, to offices, to wealth, and political power was blocked, except for a few children sponsored by the rich. The peasant remained an isolated figure, cut off from the urban, literate world by poverty and ignorance. Alone, he could maintain superstitions, magical beliefs, myths, and an oral tradition which had long passed out of fashion in

---

[79]Luzuriaga, *Analfabetismo*, p. 14. The school legislation initiated by the Bourbons in the second half of the eighteenth century did little to establish rural schools or raise levels of rural literacy. The province of Navarre in the north of Spain, having been well-served by the Jesuits before their expulsion, was a well-educated region by Spanish standards. Yet twenty years after the Cortes of Navarre passed a measure in 1787 requiring all towns and villages to provide free and obligatory primary schooling, a regional survey indicated that only the cities and larger towns of the province had anything resembling formal schools and paid masters. Nearly one-half of the villages replying had no schoolmaster whatsoever, and in those that did, he was supported by student fees. One village, Goñi, responded pessimistically that its children benefited little from the local schoolmaster, since fathers were unwilling to pay the necessary fees, and, consequently, the children rarely attended classes. In 1910, illiterates in Navarre, the third best-educated province in Spain, still represented 43 percent of the population. See AGNA: Instrucción Pública, leg. 3.

more literate circles.[80] And this figure no doubt represented a strange, mysterious, and potentially dangerous fellow to the educated and the rich.

The peasantry was not the only undereducated group in Spanish society. Comparatively, the urban workers—the daily wage-earners in the shipyards, the watercarriers, the attendants in the wool trade, the journeymen—were little better off than their country cousins. Urban priests were normally far better educated than the rural curas, and in the larger towns most held university degrees.[81] Consequently, they may have taken greater initiative and been more successful in educating the poor of their parishes. Moreover, city schools, public and private, offered either reduced fees or free places for paupers, while the convents of those religious orders which offered free instruction to laymen were usually located near or within the towns. But the question remains: did the city's poor ever take regular advantage of these opportunities? One way to answer this is to determine the proportion of persons who signed parish registers at the time of their marriage or the baptism of their children, and this is indeed the way the incidence of literacy in historical societies is frequently (though somewhat mistakenly) calculated.[82] Unfortunately, in most of Castile these registers are signed only by the priest and not by the interested parties. One exception is a register that was kept by the parish of Nuestra Señora la Vieja in the city of Burgos between 1587 and 1589.[83] In the first year twenty-six baptisms were entered, and in nine of the cases the godfather or *padrino* "did not know how to write." In the next two years there were respectively thirty-five and thirty-seven baptisms; eight padrinos signed in the first instance, four in the second. The figures for not signing would have probably been higher except that one literate person in the parish regularly served as padrino, and on other occasions clerics, students, scribes, and notaries were used to witness the event. More important is the fact that those padrinos who were unable to sign included a dyer, a gardener, two shoemakers, and a butcher, that is, skilled and semiskilled workers. Similarly, a certain Diego Martínez, a tailor resident in Madrid, claimed in a dowry contract of 1599 that he "did not know how to read" nor did a carpenter in Madrid in 1561.[84]

This information is nothing more than a handful of isolated cases from which no conclusions should be drawn, but it would be surprising to learn that literacy was common among unskilled and semiskilled workers in sixteenth-century Spain. Even late in the eighteenth century, an educational survey in Granada, a city with an abundance of private school-

[80]See Robert Mandrou, *De la Culture Populaire aux 17e et 18e Siècles* (Paris, 1964).

[81]The university degrees of these *curas* can be verified in the *vecindarios* of Philip II's reign. See, especially, those for Granada, Madrid, Seville, and Toledo in the AGS: Exp. Hac., serie I.

[82]See note 38 in this chapter.

[83]AM Burgos: Ms. register "Bautizados en la parroquia de Nuestra Señora la Vieja (= Rua), 1586–1592."

[84]Amezúa y Mayo, *Vida Privada Española*, pp. 22–24, 147–49.

masters, indicated that large numbers of children, particularly those of beggars and poor workers, arrived at puberty illiterate.[85] Analphabetism remained the rule in most Spanish cities and towns until well into the nineteenth century, and so it was that the city, like the countryside, harbored its own isolated class, defined as much by culture as by income. Moreover, in the city where the contacts between rich and poor, cultured and uncultured, literate and illiterate were far more immediate and more striking than in the village, tensions between the two groups were perhaps more tense, more excitable than in the placid countryside. It may be no accident that with few exceptions the city was the stage for social strife in Spain between the sixteenth and eighteenth centuries.[86]

The poor were joined by another uneducated, semiliterate class of persons: women from all social classes. As recently as the middle of the nineteenth century, an incredible 86 percent of Spanish women were recorded as illiterate.[87] Thereafter the establishment of free girls' schools raised female levels of literacy quickly, but before this epoch, Spanish girls were taught only by their parents and occasionally by a private tutor or a teacher in an orphanage or convent school. Furthermore, their training was customarily limited to the rudiments of literacy, religion, and the so-called "labors of their sex": sewing, embroidery, lace-making, etc.

Naturally, there were exceptions. Santa Teresa de Ávila, able to read the letters of St. Jerome (but only in Spanish) before she was out of her teens, was only one among a small group of female authors during the sixteenth century.[88] And, surprisingly enough, around 1500 a number of women—one was the daughter of Spain's famous classicist, Antonio Nebrija—taught at the University of Salamanca, although it is not known whether their appointment was the result of Queen Isabel's influence—the presence of a female monarch may have raised the overall position of women in Spanish society—or whether, in the first wave of Renaissance studies in Spain, Latinists were treated with respect regardless of their sex.[89] Spanish girls in the sixteenth century were also allowed to sit in the same classroom as boys, but this practice met with increasing criticism and gradually disappeared. By the end of the seventeenth century the schoolmasters' guild of San Casiano emphasized the moral and spiritual dangers of teaching both sexes at once; it was then judged evil to have a *maestro* teach girls,

[85]AA Granada: Leg. 894, letter of 9.I.1777.

[86]Urban centers certainly appear to be the stage of most of the rioting in the strife-torn year of 1766; cf. Laura Rodríguez, "The Spanish Riots of 1766," *Past & Present*, 59 (May 1973): 131.

[87]Luzuriaga, *Analfabetismo*, p. 44.

[88]Saint Teresa's education is described briefly in her autobiography, *La Vida de la Santa María Teresa de Jesús*, ed. *Biblioteca de Autores Españoles*, vol. 53 (Madrid, 1861), chaps. 1–3. For reference to other educated Spanish women in the sixteenth century, see Guillermo Furlong, *La Cultura Femenina en la Epoca Colonial* (Buenos Aires, 1951).

[89]See T. Oettel, "Una Catedrática en el Siglo de Isabel la Cathólica," *BRAH* 107 (1935): 289 ff., and Vicente Beltrán de Heredia, *Cartulario de la Universidad de Salamanca* (Salamanca, 1971), 3: 303–15.

and even worst for a maestra to instruct boys, since under her influence it was thought that boys were in danger of becoming effeminate.[90]

Across Spain, the seventeenth and eighteenth centuries coincided with the gradual separation of girls' and boys' schools in large cities and towns, although in smaller communities, too poor to support separate establishments, the sexes continued to mingle.[91] Private schoolmasters also violated the rules on sexual segregation, and in the late eighteenth century an official inspection of the nursery schools in Granada revealed young boys in the care of women and vice versa.[92]

With these exceptions, Spain in the seventeenth century created two worlds, one for men, one for women, separated symbolically by the iron grills on the windows of the townhouses of the rich.[93] Indeed, this century, apparently marking the first great age of the *dueña* in Spain, also brought a new emphasis on the cloistering and protection of women; hard times may have placed a premium on advantageous marriages, with the result that the surveillance of girls became all the more important. In addition, counter-Reformation moralists and preachers dwelt vividly on the dangers of sin, and their warnings suggested the need to protect women by isolating them from the opposite sex until the age of marriage and beyond. Such attitudes and practices continued into the eighteenth century, when foreign travelers wrote of the ignorance of Spanish girls and the close parental supervision to which they were subjected until a beneficial match could be arranged. Thus by the end of the Habsburg era women in Spain seem to have lost much of what appears to have been an earlier epoch of independence and freedom. The result was a cultural pattern of feminine isolation and submission that was not to be broken until well into the twentieth century. This isolation no doubt encouraged a lingering fascination with amorous tales about rich, young, and handsome lovers, such as Don Juan, just as it encouraged the extreme piety and religious devotions made famous by mystics such as Santa Teresa.

Barred from boys' schools, girls in the seventeenth century had few of their own. Most of the larger cities supported orphanages and foundling homes for parentless girls, where they would be cared for and taught religion, literacy, and skills considered appropriate to their sex, but places were limited and many poor and abandoned girls, left on their own, roamed the streets as beggars, prostitutes, and thieves.[94] Rich girls on the other hand had their own tutors, some of whom, even in the seventeenth century,

[90]See Luzuriaga, *Documentos* 1: 37, 94.

[91]In 1768, for example, schools of "mixed" sexes were banned in Cuenca; see AA Cuenca: leg. 1248, *expediente* 2.

[92]AA Granada: leg. 894, visita of 1774–75.

[93]On the question of feminine isolation in the seventeenth century, see Charles V. Aubrun, "L'Espagnole du XVe au XVIIIe Siècles," *Histoire Mondiale de la Femme*, ed. Pierre Grimal (Paris, n.d.), 2: 477–78.

[94]Lic. Alonso Ruiz, head of the Home and Hospital for Orphan Girls in Seville, complained in 1639 about the abundance of young girls begging in the streets "who do not wish to work but to take alms from the 'legitimate' poor, the sick who cannot work, and the old."

might be men.[95] Convents also took in a number of girls, and instruction offered by nuns was undoubtedly the most widespread means of organized education for women before the eighteenth century. Only then did the crown call for the establishment and regulation of girls' schools.[96] Meanwhile, the Society of Jesus, using contracted female instructors, offered lessons in literacy to girls as well as boys.[97] By the end of the century new girls' schools had been established in Madrid, and, significantly, their program included instruction in Latin and mathematics.[98]

In spite of similar improvements in other large cities, female education in the early nineteenth century remained woefully inadequate in comparison with that of boys.[99] Still accepted was the old motif, so common to Lope de Vega's plays: "When a woman knows how to sew, stitch, and mend, what need has she to know grammar or to compose verse?"[100] Such opinions changed only at the end of the nineteenth century, when numerous girls' schools were founded, and by the opening of the present century the proportion of illiterates among females in Spain was 65 percent, a decrease of nearly 20 percent since 1860, and a figure which meant that Spanish women were only 13 percent less literate than Spanish men.[101]

Sixteenth-century Spain harbored one other group, isolated and illiterate: the *Moriscos*, remnants of the old Moorish population living mainly in the south and east of the peninsula. Efforts to catechize this alien group were many, but efforts to educate them were few, another indication that Spain never wished to assimilate her Moorish population completely. Isolated attempts at education did take place and references to colleges specifically created for the Moriscos exist, but the effectiveness or regularity of this instruction is not known.[102] Most Moriscos in the cities lived apart from the Christian population in their own *barrios* or districts; there the

He wanted also a solution to the problem of *cantoneras* (prostitutes). See AA Sevilla: Secc. 4, lib. 24, no. 1.

[95]Jerónimo de Barrionueva makes reference to a "licentiate-preceptor who gave lessons to women" in Madrid during the middle of the seventeenth century. See his *Avisos*, ed. A. Paz y Melia (Madrid, 1892), 3: 317.

[96]See AHN: leg. 7294 which contains the findings of a 1714 inquiry into the state of girls' schools in Castile.

[97]See J. Malaxechevarria, *La Compañía de Jesús por la Instrucción del Pueblo Vasco en los Siglos XVII y XVIII . . .* (San Sebastian, 1926).

[98]Although girls' schools had existed previously in Madrid, they did not receive official recognition until 1783 when thirty-two such institutions were established by the crown; see Luzuriaga, *Documentos* 1: 221–32. On new girls' schools in Córdoba, see AM Córdoba: Secc. 6, leg. 1, no. 12.

[99]According to an inquiry conducted in Navarre in 1807, boys' schools outnumbered those for girls nearly two to one; see AGNA: Instrucción Pública, leg. 3.

[100]See Aubrun, "Le Espagnole . . .," p. 477. One play of Lope de Vega in which this motif is particularly evident is *La Doncella Teodor*.

[101]Luzuriaga, *Analfabetismo*, p. 13.

[102]The College of San Miguel in Granada, created in 1526 to teach *moriscos*, was converted in less than two decades into a college for Old Christians; see F. Montells y Nadal, *Historia de la Universidad de Granada* (Granada, 1870), 1: 552. BM: Add. 28,353, folio 114, a 1588 *consulta* of the Council of Aragón, refers to a "College of the Newly Converted" in Valencia.

activities of Christian schoolmasters and priests penetrated but little. And once the Moriscos were dispersed across Castile, following the revolts in Granada and the Wars of the Alpujarras in the 1570s, they lived on the margin of the Christian cities, away from masters and from schools. Rather than educate the Moriscos, the crown in 1609 decided upon the expulsion of the minority from Spain.

For reasons of wealth, location, sex, and racial origin, the bulk of the population in Habsburg Spain found the skills of literacy either difficult or impossible or not worth their effort to obtain. This training, although not exclusive to, was nevertheless designed for and organized by an elite: urban, prosperous, near or at the top of the social hierarchy. After an initial extension of the school and probably of literacy in the sixteenth century, economic problems and a reluctance on the part of the rich to invest in charitable education for the poor fostered expensive private education to the detriment of the public schoolmaster. Simultaneously, many existing schools fell under the control of the regular clergy. During this epoch, progress toward mass literacy in Spain seems to have slowed, initiating a period of educational stagnation which continued well into the eighteenth century. Improvements then followed, especially when the crown began to take a direct interest in primary education and to create a nation-wide system of public schools. Gradually, the number of Spaniards who knew how to read and write increased, but little progress was made in this direction until the last quarter of the nineteenth century. In the earlier epoch, literacy was found in small pockets, outlined by social rank, geography, and sex, and this gulf between city and country, rich and poor, men and women, Christian and non-Christian, had its repercussions in the secondary schools and universities of Habsburg Spain.

chapter 2
LATIN AND THE
LIBERAL ARTS

Secondary education in Habsburg Spain was represented by the grammar school or *colegio* or *escuela de gramática*. Here Latin grammar was the key subject and the use of the textbook written by Antonio de Nebrija in the late fifteenth century almost universal, particularly after 1598 when the Royal Council of Castile ordered that no other be used.[1] Reading was largely confined to Latin literature, and the authors who were read are common to generations of schoolboys: Caesar, Cicero, Horace, Livy, Virgil, et al. Instruction also included Christian doctrine as well as geography, history, mathematics, philosophy, and rhetoric, although here too, classical sources were preferred. Pedagogical techniques differed little from those employed in primary schools, except that discipline was much more severe. Sixteenth-century writers urged that physical punishment by the schoolmaster should not be applied to pupils under the age of eight. Thereafter, restraint was advocated, but the cane seems to have been liberally applied nevertheless.

Normally, Latin education did not begin much before the age of eight or nine, or at least not until the child had mastered the basic skills of literacy in the vernacular, and would last from four to six years. Thus Martin Pérez de Ayala and Antonio de Covarrubias, both noted sixteenth-century scholars, and Juan de Palafox y Mendoza, a famous seventeenth-century bishop, each began to learn the "rudiments of grammar" at the age of ten and completed their study of Latin at about the age of fifteen.[2] Latin training, however, did not always follow on the heels of primary education, particularly during the sixteenth century. Judging from boys well into their teens and young adults about the age of twenty who were just beginning to learn the language, clerical, military, or vocational training interrupted their school careers. Only in the eighteenth century, when adolescence began to be identified with school, did Latin education come to represent a stage of growing up, with pupils of more or less

---

[1]See E. Esperabé Artega, *Historia Pragmática é Interna de la Universidad de Salamanca* (Salamanca, 1914), 1: 631.

[2]See A. F. G. Bell, *Francisco Sánchez, El Brocense 1523-1600* (Oxford, 1925), p. 212; D. Genaro García, *Don Juan Palafox y Mendoza, Obispo de Puebla y Osma* (Mexico City, 1918), p. 20; and Rafael Gilbert, "Para el antiguo régimen universitario," *Homenaje a Johannes Vincke* 2 (Madrid, 1962-63): 456.

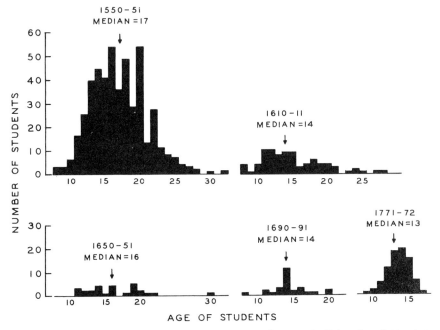

Fig. 1. Age of students: first year of grammar (class of menores), University of Alcalá de Henares. The median age drops while the age-spread narrows. Across time, therefore, the students are increasingly younger and of the same age.

the same age advancing in orderly fashion from class to class, year by year (Fig. 1).

This long, difficult, and rigorous education was mandatory for students seeking to enter the church or to pursue studies in one of the higher disciplines of law, medicine, philosophy, or theology at the universities. In this sense Latin belonged to a vocational tradition that dated from medieval times, but it was not until the late fifteenth century that Latin also became an end in itself, the mark of an educated, cultured man, and of popular interest to the ruling classes in Spain. Why Latin became so important is a story in itself.

"ARMS VERSUS LETTERS"

A common generalization frequently applied to Europe in the Middle Ages is that the landed, military aristocracy was hostile to learning of any sort and regarded these "bookish" skills as suitable only for monks and low-born clerks. While it is uncertain whether this scornful attitude applied to literacy in the vernacular, Latin, the technical language of the church and jurisprudence, acquired this stigma if only because the nobility had little need to learn it. When the occasion arose to write or interpret some Latin clause or contract, there was always a clerk in the magnate's household or a nearby ecclesiastic to do the necessary work. In Spain, the nobility's aversion to the language was also deepened by the association of Latin learning outside the church, that is, among physicians, university professors, and translators of Arabic texts, with scholars of Moorish or Jewish extraction, an alliance which undoubtedly placed Latinists in an uncomfortable social position. However, the opening of the fifteenth century brought the beginnings of change to this tradition, and the barriers between the men of letters and those of the sword began to fall, opening an extended debate over the question of "arms versus letters" which lasted nearly a century.[3]

Outside of a native tradition in Latin located within the church and the famous translation schools of Toledo, interest in the classical literature and the pure Latin of antiquity was brought to Spain, as it was to northern Europe, from Italy in the course of the fourteenth and fifteenth centuries. Following the reconquest of nearly all of Iberia by the Christians in the twelfth and thirteenth centuries, economic, cultural, and religious ties between the two Mediterranean peninsulas drew close. These were further strengthened by the rise of the Aragonese-Catalan trading empire in the fourteenth century, and once the Aragonese gained a foothold in southern Italy, Alphonso V's (1416–58) humanist court at Naples provided Iberia with a window open to the ideas and customs of the early Italian Renaissance.[4] Furthermore, the famous *studios* of Italy, largely as a result of difficulties faced by Spain's own universities in the fourteenth and fifteenth centuries, attracted significant numbers of Spanish students. The Spanish College of San Clemente at Bologna, founded by the Cardinal Gil de Albornoz in 1369, served both as a response and a stimulus to this tradition.[5] Many of Spain's leading scholars, including Antonio de Nebrija, Juan Ginés de Sepúlveda, and Antonio Agustín, were graduates of this institution.

By the opening of the fifteenth century a steady stream of Spanish ambassadors, merchants, prelates, scholars, and statesmen were in a position to carry the teachings of Renaissance Italy back to their homeland. This was a society steeped in a military, crusading tradition where, as one contemporary humanist critic wrote: "The courtiers of the time praise blasphemy and despise grammar; the latter a crown of glory, and the former, an abuse. None of them know any Latin let alone good Cas-

---

[3]On this question see Peter Rusell, "Arms versus Letters: Towards a Definition of Spanish Fifteenth-Century Humanism," in *Aspects of the Renaissance: A Symposium*, ed. A. R. Lewis (Austin, 1967), and Nicolas B. Round, "Renaissance Culture and Its Opponents in 15th Century Castile," *Modern Language Review* 57 (1962).

[4]See Andrés Soria, *Los Humanistas de la Corte de Alonso el Magnánimo* (Granada, 1956).

[5]See Berthe M. Marti, *The Spanish College at Bologna in the 14th Century* (Philadelphia, 1966); J. Beneyto Pérez, "La Tradición Espanola en Bolonia," *RABM* 50 (1929): 174 ff. One of the most famous Spaniards to study abroad was Fernando de Córdoba (1425–86?); see A. Bonilla y San Martín and M. Menéndez y Pelayo, *Fernando de Córdoba y los Orígenes del Renacimiento en España* (Madrid, 1911).

tilian."[6] Slowly, hesitantly, a "Latinizing" movement gained momen-
tum, and by the early sixteenth century the Italian tutor at the Spanish
court, Peter Martyr d'Anghiera, could boast that "Castile follows me with
honor and with love; almost all of the Castilian princes drew their love of
letters from my store."[7]

Spain's supposed transition from "medieval barbarism and ignorance," a characterization exaggerated by contemporary Latin scholars, to
"Renaissance learning and culture" occurred in much the same way as in
England, France, and the Low Countries. Drawing mainly upon the ideas
of the Italian humanists, who preached the virtuous, noble qualities of
Latin learning put to public, civic use, a campaign was begun by a handful
of noblemen and prelates who, surrounded by a following of paid scholars,
demonstrated and propagandized the joys of learning to their peers. Spain
in the fifteenth century saw a succession of these poet-patrons: the Marquis of Santillana, Juan de Lucena, Alfonso de Cartagena, Enrique de
Villena, and others who complained vehemently in their writings about
the "ignorance" of Spanish noblemen, exhorting them to complement
the life of arms with the study of letters. To emphasize their point of view,
the Marquis of Santillana in 1437 wrote Prince Henry, the future Henry IV
of Castile, that "knowledge does not blunt the iron of the lance nor
weaken the sword in a knight's hand."[8] Of course, "knowledge" to this enlightened group signified only a familiarity with Latin grammar and classical literature, and a man could be called ignorant even though he was
literate in the vernacular and versed in the classics, through the numerous
translations then being produced. But in spite of the propaganda of the
poets and the patronage of classical scholars by Juan II (1406–54) of Castile
at his supposed "proto-Renaissance" court, the small, isolated body of Latin
scholars did not, in one author's opinion, "succeed in creating a class of
nobles either literate in Latin nor favorably disposed to learning."[9] Based
upon the stigma of tainted lineage, chivalric prejudice, and a hierarchical
conception of society which placed the scholar and the knight in separate
social categories, opposition to the "new learning" of Italy apparently remained strong.[10] The turbulent reign of Henry IV (1454–74) probably did
little to erase old attitudes or alter the existing tradition of military education among the aristocracy; that era of chronic civil war offered little inducement for the grandees to eschew arms for the pleasures of the
classics.

Under Ferdinand and Isabel, the Catholic kings (1474–1504) Castile
gradually returned to peace and a climate more favorable to the develop-

[6]Enrique de Villena quoted in Round, "Renaissance Culture," p. 210.
[7]Epistle no. 622 translated in Caro Lynn, *A College Professor of the Renaissance* (Chicago,
1937), p. 111.
[8]Quoted in Rusell, "Arms versus Letters," p. 49.
[9]See Round, "Renaissance Culture," p. 205.
[10]See Rusell, "Arms versus Letters," pp. 51–52.

ment of literary tastes was created. The royal court itself served as a source of scholarly patronage, rewarding men of learning with offices and jobs. Internal order, economic growth, administrative reorganization offering new positions for the learned, and renewed cultural and diplomatic contacts with the Italy of the mature Renaissance, all contributed to heighten interest in the study of Latin. Moreover, the introduction of the printing press into Spain in 1473 and, after 1480, the free importation of books printed abroad for "the improvement and glory of the nation" gave a new immediacy to the art of learning how to read and write.[11] Spain's own presses, active in twenty-five towns by 1500 produced over 500 titles by that date, and in the following two decades another 1,307 items were printed, of which 18 percent represented texts of classical authors.[12] The coming of the book, coinciding with an era of peace, prosperity, patronage, no doubt served to popularize interest in literacy, both in Latin and the vernacular.

So in comparison with earlier decades, the Spain of the Catholic kings was alive with interest in Greek, Latin, and Hebrew, even Arabic, and classical scholars and tutors, many imported from Italy, abounded. New chairs devoted to Latin grammar and literature were added to the universities, while lectures on humanist topics drew great crowds of students.[13] "*Armas y letras*" in the course of this reign became fashionable ornaments for a grandee to display, and the rather lackadaisical crusades in Granada and North Africa afforded ample opportunities to cultivate both.

As in much of Europe, individual patronage, by monarch, nobleman, or prelate, was the focal point for initial interest in the study of Latin and the writings of the ancients among the nobility. Queen Isabel, a Latinist herself, wished to instruct not only her own children but those of her leading courtiers in the humane letters. Through the influence of Cardinal Pedro González de Mendoza, a great patron of learning and a member of the noted literary family to which the Marquis of Santillana had belonged, the Queen in 1492 invited the Italian Peter Martyr, himself a living embodiment of the "arms and letters" ideal, to begin a Latin academy at the royal court.[14] Several years later Martyr's academy was joined by a second palace school under the tutelage of another Italian, Lucio Marineo Siculo, a well-known scholar who had previously taught at the University of Salamanca.[15] The message of these two famous teachers to their aristo-

---

[11]Cortes de Toledo, 1480, ley 98.

[12]See Conrad Häebler, *The Early Printers of Spain and Portugal* (London, 1894), p. 85; F. J. Norton, *Printing in Spain, 1501–1520* (New York, 1965), pp. 125–28.

[13]See Anghiera's account of his reception at the University of Salamanca in 1488; *Opus Epistolarum Petri Martyris Anglerri Mediolanensis* (Parisiis, 1520), i. 57.

[14]For Martyr's reactions to this proposal, see Lynn, *A College Professor*, p. 110. J. H. Mariejol, *Pierre Martyr d'Anghiera: sa Vie et Ses Oeuvres* (Paris, 1887), is the best biography of this noted scholar.

[15]See Lynn, *A College Professor*, pp. 112–13.

cratic audiences was common to that of other European humanists: chivalry when combined with Latin eloquence and the study of the liberal arts and then placed in the service of one's prince would bestow upon an individual the highest attainable fame, merit, and virtue. Queen Isabel, according to the chroniclers, rewarded only such men, and the aristocracy, anxious to remain in their inherited positions of leadership, began to adapt to the new learning.

What this did, however, was help to overturn the character of Latin schooling in less than a century. Previously, the church, as the primary guardian of the knowledge of antiquity, had monopolized the field, teaching Latin to cleric and laymen alike in monasteries and cathedral schools. Though this tradition survived and was strengthened by the subsequent establishment of seminaries specifically designed for the training of priests,[16] church schools in the course of the sixteenth and seventeenth centuries were obliged to compete with a growing number of educational institutions, each of which aimed at bringing Latin to an important and growing segment of Spain's population. The church, fearful that children might be entrusted to irresponsible teachers, reacted with an attempt to bring all of Latin education under its direction and control. This effort began in earnest when the Council of Trent ordered that masters of grammar, laymen included, be licensed by ecclesiastical officials. In Spain, the church continued its fight as the dioceses, one after another, ordered that schools could only be opened with the bishop's consent.[17] But these rulings met with no more than partial success. The church had failed to recognize the changing place of classical studies within Spanish society. During the Middle Ages, Latin had predominantly been a specialized idiom, the language of scholarship, diplomacy, and religion. And while Latin's usefulness in this respect was not to be diminished for hundreds of years, in the course of the sixteenth century it was rapidly becoming an established part of lay culture as well. Accordingly, its instruction passed frequently to secular masters who stood beyond the jurisdiction of the church.

THE EDUCATION OF THE ARISTOCRACY

For the privileged classes, Latin education followed the custom established by instruction in literacy and remained within the home. Again, the private tutor, first popularized during the reign of the Catholic kings,

---

[16]On seminaries, see Vicente de la Fuente, *Historia de las Universidades* (Madrid, 1884–89), 3: 176, and Domínguez Ortiz, *La Sociedad Española en el Siglo XVII* (Madrid, 1963, 1970), 2: 10–11. The history of one pre-Tridentine seminary is presented in Francisco Martín Hernández, *El Colegio de San Cecilio, de Granada* (Valladolid, 1960). And on the general state of clerical education in the early eighteenth century, see the reports of Spain's bishops assembled in the AHN: Cons. leg. 7294.

[17]See Domínguez Ortiz, *Sociedad Española*, 2: 182–83.

was the preferred medium of instruction. Generally a young university graduate, the tutor's duties went well beyond the teaching of Latin grammar, or, as one author suggested, his major purpose was "to teach virtue and good habits, using for this the doctrine and precepts of Moral and Natural Philosophy."[18] In addition, the tutor was supposed to teach modern languages, mathematics, history, and astrology, along with the chivalric and martial arts: horsemanship, the use of arms, courtesy, eloquence, poetry, dance, etc. The overall aim of the program was to create the cultured "gentleman," skilled in Latin and literature as well as war, the archetype immortalized in Castiglione's *The Courtier*.

Whatever advantage instruction before the hearth may have offered, the use of a Latin tutor did not win universal approval. Pedro López de Montoya, recognizing that only a very few tutors were equipped for their tasks, advocated that young nobles leave home and attend organized schools: "It is very important for nobles to study and to learn in communal schools in the company of other students . . . because the masters who ordinarily teach in such places are much more advanced in erudition and in virtue since they have risen to the positions they hold as a result of their talents. They have also gained public approval for exercising their office of master with dignity."[19] He also suggested "that it would be advisable for sons of nobles to go to universities and take advantage there of the wisdom of the great masters which they cannot have in their own homes."[20]

The degree to which Spain's aristocracy preferred private tutors to organized Latin schools is a matter for debate. Literary evidence and travelers' reports indicate that tutors remained the most popular and certainly the most fashionable means of instruction for young grandees from the sixteenth to the eighteenth century. Even the renowned colleges of the Jesuits failed to attract them.[21] These schools, competitive and austere, where the sons of the rich mingled with those of the poor, were more successful with children of lesser ranks than with those of the grandees. Similarly, only a handful of the titled nobility attended university, and those who did went not to study Latin but the law.[22]

If Spain's aristocracy never rushed headlong into formal institutions of learning, there is ample evidence to suggest that the grandees gradually overcame much of their earlier disdain for literature and culture. During the sixteenth century nobles and other wealthy Spaniards began to amass large private libraries, although it remains uncertain whether these col-

[18]López de Montoya, "Libro de la Buena Educación, in *Las Ideas Pedagógicas del Doctor Pedro López de Montoya*, ed. E. Hernández Rodríguez (Madrid, 1947), p. 310.
[19]Ibid., p. 382.
[20]Ibid., p. 385.
[21]The Colegio Imperial, a school run by the Jesuits and expressly designed to educate the sons of the aristocracy, never proved popular among this class. For a (partial?) listing of students who attended this college, see José Simón-Diaz, *Historia del Colegio Imperial* (Madrid, 1952), 1: app. ix.
[22]See below, pp. 183–84.

lections were used for didactic purposes or mere display.[23] The grandees' active participation in the literary academies and informal *tertulias* which flourished in the seventeenth century also points to their growing taste for culture.[24] Indeed, learning as such became so ubiquitous among the aristocracy that it stirred complaints about their growing distaste for a military way of life. One critic wrote: "that which is most noble is now reputed as the most vile and low . . .; . . . those who would have once led armies, now are content with a place on one of the [royal] councils."[25] These remarks, exaggerated to be sure, nevertheless describe the evolution of Spain's warrior aristocracy into a genteel class whose life revolved around the royal court.

This evolution, moreover, attracted the attention of the rulers of Habsburg Spain. Ironically, the crown, though initially an advocate of the education of the aristocracy along humanist lines, began to lament the new program's eventual results. The Spanish grandee was a courtier, soldier, statesman, and royal councillor, often a financial official, provincial governor, viceroy, admiral or a trade official in Seville. Moreover, despite his largely urban existence, he was a landowner involved in countless legal suits and financial dealings. In many respects, the informal, Latin, typically "Renaissance" education obtained from his tutor and from his books failed to fit his many roles, a problem of which the crown was soon well aware. Philip II worried especially about the failure of the aristocracy to take an active part in Spain's local militia,[26] considered the importance of educating this class for its presumed "natural" tasks on the battlefield when he organized a court academy in 1583 under the direction of Juan de Herrera.[27] The curriculum, in addition to Latin studies, included practical, technical subjects: architecture, artillery, fortifications, hydraulics, cosmography, and navigation; a program, in other words, designed to train the technicians Philip needed for war.

Forty years later, Philip IV and his energetic minister, the Count-Duke of Olivares, with the aid of Jesuit instructors, established a similar academy, the Colegio Imperial or Reales Estudios de San Isidro.[28] Their stated aim was to educate the sons of the nobility, particularly the eldest sons who rarely attended university, in order to prepare them for the important roles they would have to play as the "natural" leaders of the nation. The college offered a diverse course of study which included politics, economics, geography, history, mathematics, navigation, and military sci-

[23]See Bartolomé Bennassar, *Valladolid au Siècle d'Or* (Paris, 1967), p. 509, and José Antonio Maravall, *La Oposición Política Bajo Los Austrias* (Madrid, 1972), p. 29.

[24]See José Sánchez, *Academias Literarias del Siglo de Oro Español* (Madrid, 1961), pp. 194–302.

[25]Cited in Domínguez Ortiz, *Sociedad Española*, 1: 177.

[26]AGS: DC, leg. 25, f.l., *cedula* of 6.IX.1572.

[27]See Simón-Diaz, *Colegio Imperial*, 1: 47; Rafael Altamira, *Historia de España* (Barcelona, 1906), 3: 545.

[28]Simón-Diaz, *Colegio Imperial*, 1: 64–66.

ence.[29] Opened in 1629 amidst elaborate pomp and ceremony, the Colegio Imperial was a near fiasco. Five years later the Cámara de Castilla, noting that only sixty students were enrolled in the upper division of the college, went so far as to suggest that the crown end its annual subsidy of 10,000 ducats to this "useless" institution.[30]

One of the reasons why the nobles had failed to appear was a bitter campaign launched against the Colegio Imperial by Spain's leading universities, all of which regarded this institution as a threat to their own existence.[31] Another was that the Jesuit instructors were asked to teach subjects in which they had little or no competence. This objection was raised by a Jesuit resident in Rome who claimed that the material covered in one year by the friar who taught in the Chair of Fortifications "would be read amply by a soldier from Flanders in three months."[32] This critic also inferred that the building in which the college was housed was not of a suitable standard. Court politics was yet another reason why the nobles stayed away; many grandees, in protest against Olivares and his policies, left the royal court for their country estates.

Olivares, himself a former student at the University of Salamanca, was haunted by the necessity of training the aristocracy in a proper fashion. So even as the Colegio Imperial floundered, he put forward another educational scheme in 1636 that was designed to train nobles for military and political careers.[33] Based upon a network of special academies, in Madrid as well as the provinces, the plan allowed for a number of free places and hoped to attract noblemen from foreign countries. But again these plans came to naught, and until his death Olivares was plagued by his belief in the "lack of military leaders" (falta de cabezas) in Spain, scapegoat for his disastrous military and political ventures.[34]

With the accession of the Bourbon monarchy, the crown renewed its effort to reorient the education of the aristocracy. This began in 1714 with a plan to establish schools expressly designed for this privileged class. In a letter to Spain's universities asking them to comment on the merits of this scheme, the fiscal of the Royal Council of Castile had noted that "One of the most serious problems which the Monarchy faces is that the nobility of the first and second ranks who do not follow the road of civil or canon law or theology have neither colleges nor equestrian schools in which they are able to learn rhetoric, mathematics, and the other arts. The situation is so prejudicial that if any caballero wishes to educate his sons, it is neces-

[29]The purpose of the Colegio Imperial was in many respects similar to a "Faculty of Political Science" proposed in 1619 by Sancho de Moncada, Restauración Política de España (Madrid, 1746), discurso VIII. Also see Maravall, Oposición Política, p. 208.

[30]Cited in Domínguez Ortiz, Sociedad Española, 2: app. xxviii.

[31]AGS: GJ, leg. 972, letter of 17.XII.1623.

[32]For details of this controversy, see AGS: GJ, leg. 972; Simón Díaz, Colegio Imperial, 1: 66–67.

[33]BUS: Ms. 2064, folio 8, Memorandum of the Junta de Educación, 12.I.1636.

[34]G. Marañon, El Conde-Duque de Olivares (Madrid, 1936), app. xx.

sary to send them to colleges in Bologna, Rome, Florence, and other regions."[35] In the proposed schools the fiscal envisaged a program which encompassed music, dance, lawn games, and the use of arms, in addition to more academic subjects. Nothing came of this project until Philip V revived the old Colegio Imperial as the Seminario Real de Nobles in 1725, but even this privileged institution, in and out of existence for nearly fifty years, failed to alter the educational habits of Spain's aristocracy. An English traveler, Major William Dalrymple, explained in 1774 that "The nobility educate their sons at home, under the tuition of some pedantic or artful priest, who, wishing rather to please than instruct, employs his pupil's time in agreeable trifles."[36] Other visitors to eighteenth-century Spain criticized the aristocracy for their backwardness and lack of education, and one, striking an ironic note, hinted that titles and rank were more important to this class than intelligence and culture.[37]

Such opinions are exaggerating the truth, but it is certain that Spain's aristocracy, secure in lands and titles, given over to lives of luxury and ostentation, and still at the top of the social hierarchy, did not seriously alter their educational habits in the course of three centuries. Their instruction, evolving in such a way as to include not only the traditional studies in the classics but also history, natural sciences, political philosophy, and practical tracts of various kinds, began and usually remained within the home. School attendance and foreign travel remained at a minimum. This reluctance to leave their palaces should in part be attributed to a desire for social exclusiveness, but it must also be recognized that the curricula of Spanish schools and universities failed to appeal to the special interests of this class. These institutions were censored by an intellectually conservative church and administered either by a schoolmaster's guild neither exceptionally innovative nor competent or by clergymen whose aims often differed from those of the nobles. In the classroom books on estate management, military affairs, modern history—an euphemism for the deeds of great men, i.e., nobles—and other subjects of special interest to the aristocracy were never taught. In the end, the crown's attempts to reorient the education of the aristocracy served only to aid the interests of new noble families of administrative backgrounds who associated the special academies with social status and prestige; the older aristocracy, able to educate themselves as they saw fit, simply stayed away.

GRAMMAR SCHOOLS

For less privileged families, the grammar school was the most popular means of Latin education. Though a number of these dated from medie-

---

[35] AHN: Cons. leg. 7294, no. 4, letter of 29.XI.1713.
    [36] Major William Dalrymple, *Travels through Spain and Portugal in 1774; with a Short Account of the Spanish Expedition against Algiers in 1775* (London, 1777), p. 72.
    [37] J. García Mercadal, *Viajes de Extranjeros por España y Portugal* (Madrid, 1962), 3: 676.

val timcs, most were created out of private and municipal funds in the years following the reign of the Catholic kings in response to growing demands for Latin-trained clergymen and officials and to the new prestige accorded to gentlemen skilled in the classics. One of the first towns to subsidize such a school was Madrid. There are references to an institution of this kind as early as 1346, although it is doubtful whether this school was offering regular instruction in Latin much before the middle years of the fifteenth century.[38] By 1480, however, Madrid was paying a regular salary to a *bachiller de gramática* and a year later ordered that "no person be allowed to open a school of grammar except for the *bachiller* paid for by the city without the express license of the town council upon pain of 10,000 mrs. fine and exile for two months from this city and its district."[39] A decade later the town council referred to its school as the place "where all of the sons of *caballeros* and the leading residents of the city learn,"[40] but competition was growing and by the early sixteenth century the town council was having to order local residents to send their boys to the municipal school; apparently, a number had been learning grammar at the not too distant and newly founded university at Alcalá de Henares.[41]

Alcalá de Henares, Burgos, Cuenca, Guadalajara, Jérez de la Frontera, Murcia, Soria, and other towns too numerous to list, were other municipalities which established grammar schools of their own.[42] The task of selecting teachers was generally given to the town councillors or to the royal *corregidor*, and this was often done after a public competition known as an *oposición*. The masters were then given contracts which lasted anywhere from three or four years to life. Monthly fees paid by students supplemented their regular salaries, but qualified, capable instructors were always in short supply, and this tended to drive salaries and stipends up. Taking advantage of the situation, many instructors, including the noted grammarian Baltasar de Cespedes, moved regularly from town to town,

---

[38]A. Millares Carlos y J. Artiles Rodríguez, *Libros de Acuerdos del Concejo Madrileño* (Madrid, 1932), 1: 156. See also AVM: 2/482/29. Murcia was another town which had supported a Latin school in the Middle Ages. In 1374 its *concejo* was paying 300 mrs. annually to a "maestro de gramatica" who taught the "hijos de hombres buenos"; cf. Julio Valdeón Barngue, "Una Ciudad Castellana en la Segunda Mitad del Siglo XIV: El ejemplo de Murica," *Cuadernos de Historia* 3 (1969): 230.

[39]Millares Carlos, *Concejo Madrileño*, 1: 49, 120.

[40]Ibid., 1: 120.

[41]Ibid., 1: 227.

[42]See A. de la Torre, "Los Estudios de Alcalá de Henares Anteriores de Cisneros," *Estudios Ofrecidos a Menéndez Pidal* (Madrid, 1952), 2: 627–54; for Burgos, see AGS: Exp. Hac., serie 1, leg. 62; AA Cuenca: leg. 1495, *expediente* 28; Layna Serrano, *Historia de Guadalajara y Sus Mendozas en los Siglos XV y XVI* (Madrid, 1942), 3: 384; 4: 21–24; Sancho de Sopranis, *Historia de Jérez de la Frontera*, (Jérez, 1965), 2: 193, 307–12; J. Torres Fuentes, *Estampas de la Vida Murciana en los Reinados de los Reyes Católicos* (Madrid, 1958); pp. 10–13; for Soria, see F. Lucas Zamora y V. Hijes Cueva, *El Bachiller Pedro de Rua: Humanista y Critíco* (Madrid, 1957), and M. García y García, "La Enseñanza en la Provincia de Soria en la Primera Mitad del Siglo XVI," *Celtiberia* 17 (1959): 133–38.

searching for more profitable contracts, more students, and higher fees.[43] Naturally, this situation created havoc for the towns, although a number of them, including both Logroño and Oviedo, attempted to minimize the problem by offering subsidies to a religious convent or a local cathedral chapter in order to have classes formerly reserved for members of the clergy opened to the general public and thus guarantee instruction on a regular, orderly basis.[44] Private charity also helped towns to establish schools of their own, and in many instances these gifts determined which localities would have Latin schools and which would not. Thus Juan Pérez de Cabrera, archdeacon of Toledo, established Cuenca's College of Santa Catalina early in the sixteenth century; Haro, a town in the province of Burgos, acquired a school in 1608 thanks to a former native then resident in Peru; a local widow gave Vivero, a town in Galicia, a Latin school in 1583; and a physician, Juan Martínez de Población, endowed a school in his native Frómista, near Palencia.[45] Benefactions such as these were crucial to the establishment and support of Latin schools, but it also meant that the distribution of these schools often had little to do with the size, prosperity, or educational concerns of a particular region or town.

In sum, municipal and popular willingness to contribute to secondary education in the sixteenth century led to a sharp rise in the number of Latin schools, a record not repeated in Spain until the nineteenth century. By 1600 these existed in hundreds of communities, large and small; Fernández de Navarrete estimated their number at 4,000.[46] Although the accuracy of this particular figure may be in doubt, it is certain that almost every town of substantial size, that is, those with 500 *vecinos* or more, possessed a Latin school of its own. In smaller communities organized schools were less common, but independent preceptors, supported by student fees, and, occasionally, parish priests, took up the slack.

Open to question is the number of students studying Latin grammar in any one year. Existing documents make occasional reference to a school with 200 pupils or a preceptor with 25, but the only continuous series of matriculation registers for the sixteenth century are those for the faculties of grammar attached to Castile's universities. Benefiting from the general

---

[43]Despite a contract worth 102,000 mrs. a year, Baltasar de Céspedes left his teaching post in the town of Medina de Rioseco for a more lucrative position in the faculty of grammar in Valladolid, only to switch a few years later to the University of Salamanca. Such wanderings were commonplace among teachers in the sixteenth century. See Gregorio de Andrés, *El Maestro Baltasar de Céspedes y su Discurso de las Letras Humanas* (El Escorial, 1965), pp. 58–59.

[44]For Logroño, see F. Bujanda, *Historia del Seminario de Logroño* (Logroño, 1948), pp. 18–19; for Oviedo, see G. Miguel Virgil, *Colección Histórica-Diplomática del Ayuntamiento de Oviedo* (Oviedo, 1889), p. 458. Less successful in providing regular instruction was the town of La Guardia; cf. E. Enciso, *La Guardia en el Siglo XVI* (Victoria, 1959), p. 110.

[45]These schools are listed in the AHN: Cons. leg. 13183. See the reports of the provinces concerned.

[46]See Navarrete, *Conservación de Monarchías* (Madrid, 1621), discurso XLVI.

enthusiasm for Latin studies, these faculties in the middle decades of the
century taught as many as 5,000 to 6,000 students a year, nearly half of
whom were enrolled at the famous universities of Salamanca and Alcalá
de Henares (Figs. 9 and 10, pp. 213–14). But this was their apogee; thereafter, the proliferation of municipal schools and local colleges deprived the
universities of their clientele, since most parents, for reasons of economy
and convenience, preferred to have their children study close to home.[47]
This also helps to explain why so many towns in the sixteenth century
established grammar schools. Like Medina de Rioseco, they did so in order
that "fathers would not have the obligation to spend their money sending
their sons to study outside of the town."[48]

Outside the universities, it is impossible to arrive at any accurate estimate for the total number of boys studying Latin, although it appears certain that a peak may have been reached around the year 1600. A figure of
70,000 schoolboys has even been suggested for this date.[49] This estimate is
way out of line, but it can serve as an indication that Latin education at the
opening of the seventeenth century was by no means uncommon. In fact,
its popularity was such that it engendered the criticism of contemporaries
who were looking for solutions to the economic and political problems
which Castile then faced. Latin, as widespread as it was, quickly became a
scapegoat for the monarchy's many ills. Would-be reformers, known commonly as *arbitristas* (literally, "economic projectors"), began to question the
purpose of educating so many boys in Latin, asserting that its study served
only to encourage youths to abandon economically productive careers for
those in the parasitic cadres of government and the church. Furthermore,
the arbitristas, anxious to return Spain to prosperity and to restore her
former glory, advocated a reduction in the number of Latin schools and a
reorientation of education in favor of craft skills, mechanical trades, farming, and other "useful" occupations which they believed had fallen into
neglect.[50] Typical of their criticism is a remark written by Pedro de Valencia
in 1608:

"Nowadays every farmer, trader, cobbler, blacksmith and plasterer, each of whom
love their sons with indiscreet affection, wish to remove them from work and seek

[47] A certain Doctor Gallego told the University of Salamanca in 1584 that one reason for
the decline of its faculty of grammar was that "many of the students who used to attend no
longer do so because all of the towns are teaching grammar with more harmony and order
than the University"; cited in Andrés, *Baltasar de Céspedes*, p. 58.

[48] Ibid., pp. 58–59.

[49] J. Zarco Cuevas, "El Lic. Miguel Caja de Leruela y las Causas de la Decadencia de
España," in the volume *Estudios Sobre la Ciencia Española en el Siglo XVII* (Madrid, 1935),
p. 527.

[50] Much of this literature has been summarized in Zarco Cuevas, "Miguel de Leruela";
this article was also published separately. Other references may be found in Navarrete,
Conservación de Monarchias, discurso XLVI; Saavedra Fajardo, *Príncipe Político*,
empresa LXVI; and M. Alvarez de Ossorio y Redin, *Apéndice de la Educación Popular*, ed.
P. Rodríguez de Campomanes (Madrid, 1775–77).

for them a more glamorous career. Toward this end, they put them to study. And being students, they learn little but they become delicate and presumptuous. Consequently, they remain without a trade or are made into sacristans or scribes.[51]

On the surface, this unprecedented campaign against Latin schooling was a straight-forward effort to redirect the aims of early education. But it also entailed what could be called an "aristocratic reaction," an attempt on the part of the nobility and those who aped noble status to protect the interests, jobs, and even the unique culture of the social elite.[52] During the fifteenth and sixteenth centuries the spread of Latin education had allowed many commoners access to important positions in government and the church; in other words, Latin had served, directly and indirectly, as an agency for upward social mobility. However, in the seventeenth century, when Castile's faltering economy endangered the financial security of the elite, unlimited instruction in Latin appeared as a threat, since it was thought to allow more and more commoners to qualify for positions customarily reserved for the upper-class. Implied in the arbitristas' criticisms, therefore, was an attempt to fix a status quo in society and, especially, to seal off access into the elite. Such attitudes were consistent with the conception of a fixed social hierarchy in which every person from birth was destined for a certain task, presumably, the occupation of his father. Ideally, education would serve only to make each person a Christian, obedient to his king and social superiors, and equipped to handle his inherited tasks, but nothing more. Latin was to be taught to the wealthy, noble, "naturally superior" members of society and consequently beneficial to the nation as a whole, since its leaders would be instilled with the high moral qualities that a classical education was thought to bestow. But, if extended to the masses, it would only encourage aspiration to jobs above their natural station and thus weaken the nation and threaten the place of the ruling elite.

Furthermore, it was no accident that this criticism was contemporaneous with large-scale sales of office by the crown and the award of hundreds of new patents and scores of new titles of nobility—Castile's version of the "inflation of honors"—which made noble families, particularly those of recent vintage, all the more insecure. Latin, though connected with these developments only in a marginal fashion, conveniently served as a target upon which part of the blame could be affixed.

The campaign against Latin, recurrent throughout the seventeenth and eighteenth centuries, was first translated into direct action early in the reign of Philip IV. The *Junta de Reformación*, charged to recommend solutions for the manifold problems of the Castilian government and society, made the following proposal in 1621 to the young king:

[51]Cited in Zarco-Cuevas, "Caja de Leruela," p. 526.

[52]To prove this assertion, more detailed biographical information about the social origins, careers, and aspirations of the *arbitristas* is necessary. Unfortunately, little is currently known about these writers although one awaits in this regard the publication of Jean Vilar's thesis, *Les Espagnols du Siècle d'Or devant la Crise: l'Arbitrisme*.

. . . it would also help to reform some grammar schools newly founded in villages and small places, because with the opportunity of having them so near, the peasants (*labradores*) divert their sons from the jobs and occupations in which they were born and raised, and put them to study from which they benefit little and leave for the most part ignorant because the preceptors are not much better. It would be sufficient to have such schools in large and well-known towns, where they have been located for a long time, and also in the capital of each district.[53]

Philip responded in 1623 by deciding that only towns with a royal *corregidor* would be allowed to have grammar schools, and then, only one apiece. Since Castile had approximately seventy such towns, this decree was obviously intended to bring about a drastic cut in the number of Latin schools. Outside of these municipalities, only those schools which had an endowed income of 300 ducats a year would be allowed to continue, but this was something which very few possessed. Philip also stipulated that classes in Latin in foundling homes and orphanages were to stop and that the wards be taught more "useful" skills.[54]

This decree, promulgated anew by ecclesiastical officials, had uncertain results.[55] If effective, it would have brought an early end to the study of Latin in all but a few selected towns. But like most royal orders of the *antiguo régimen*, the proclamation and the enforcement of a law were two different things. Though a number of schools may have been forced to close, countless private preceptors continued to teach on the sly. The most this decree probably achieved was to slow the century-long spread of Latin education, though it could not even have managed this without increasing upper-class suspicion toward popular education. The outcome was that the years following the promulgation of Philip IV's edict coincided with a sharp drop in the foundation of new grammar schools.[56] Simultaneously, financial difficulties obliged many municipalities to reduce and sometimes to end their subsidies to local schools. Uncertain finances caused teaching at many schools to be interrupted, sometimes for years. Disruptions of this nature occurred in Sanlúcar de Barrameda when the town council ended its payments in 1663 to the local Jesuit college,[57] and schools in Guadalajara and Logroño were suffering from problems of a similar kind.[58]

Such difficulties would seem to have been widespread, and this makes it easy to believe that the later seventeenth century marked a period of

[53]A. González Palencia, *La Junta de Reformación (1618–25)* (Valladolid, 1932), p. 28.

[54]*Leyes de Recopilación*, Lib. I, tit. vii, ley 34.

[55]The Bishop of Cuenca issued orders in 1626 akin to those of the royal *cédula* of 1623; see Zarco-Bacas, *Relaciones de Pueblos del Obispado de Cuenca* (Cuenca, 1927), p. ciii.

[56]A notable exception was the Real Colegio de Estudios Mayores de la Purísima Concepción, founded in the town of Cabra (Córdoba) in 1679. Subsequently, this college was annexed by the University of Granada. See M. S. Rubio González, *Historia del Real Colegio de Estudios Mayores de la Purísima Concepción 1679–1847* (Sevilla, 1970).

[57]See Pedro Barbadillo, *Historia de la Ciudad de San Lúcar de Barrameda* (Cadiz, 1947), p. 151.

[58]See Bujanda, *Seminario de Logroño*, pp. 9–10, 16–17; Layna Serrano, *Guadalajara*, 4: 23–24.

regression and decay not only for the teaching of literacy but for Latin as well, a situation which Spain's first Bourbon king, Philip V (1701–46), endeavored to correct. An inquiry into the state of the kingdom's Latin schools in 1714 revealed a common set of woes: a shortage of school revenues, a lack of schoolteachers, and a scarcity of pupils.[59] In the decades that followed, conditions improved slowly as many schools, benefiting from the general improvement in the Spanish economy, began to receive new or increased subsidies from municipal governments. Private benefactions were also on the rise, and a number of towns, thanks to this largesse, acquired Latin schools for the very first time. By mid-century, Latin schooling was well on the road to recovery, but this prosperity served only to revive the monarchy's old fears about the efficacy of such training. Consequently, on June 26, 1747, Ferdinand VI (1746–1759) reaffirmed Philip IV's decree limiting the number and distribution of Latin schools in Spain, although on this occasion, no new schools of any kind would be permitted in communities with less than 300 vecinos.

The following year the royal corregidores were asked to report on schools in their districts, presumably to determine which ones ought to be suppressed. Their responses, available for thirty cities, illustrate the mixed and somewhat chaotic nature of secondary education in eighteenth-century Spain.[60] The amalgam of tradition, charity, municipal subsidies, and time had left behind a confusing patchwork of schools, teachers, and preceptors with the costs and the quality of education varying widely from city to city, region to region. But in spite of this apparent confusion, the crown continued its stand against the unlimited instruction of Latin. A century before, increases in the number of schoolboys were held partly responsible for the decline of Spain, since educated youths were accused of abandoning fields and workshops to the detriment of the national economy. Now, for much the same reasons, Latin was regarded as a check upon Spain's recovery. Primary education was permissible since it was believed to encourage better discipline, religious orthodoxy, and social order among the population and, perhaps, even to be of some practical utility to the poor. But when the reformer Pablo de Olavide designed his new colonies in the Sierra Morena in southern Spain, the program expressly stated that "schools of grammar and other higher faculties will be prohibited in these towns since their inhabitants are to dedicate themselves to agricultural labor, stock-raising, and mechanical trades."[61]

The Intendant of León said much the same in 1764 when he remarked that if

[59]See AHN: Cons., leg. 7294.
[60]See AHN: Cons., leg. 13119.
[61]Cited in J. Rubio Gonzáles, *Historia de una Ciudad: La Carolina, 1767–1967* (Madrid, 1967), p. 146.

Agriculture, Skills, Industry, and Commerce are to flourish in proportion to the fecundity and fertility of the land and the excellence of its fruits and products, it would be wise to reduce significantly the number of schools in the district of [León] . . . since having them near at hand encourages many fathers to devote their sons to study and to direct them into ecclesiastical careers, secular or regular, without examination or proofs of vocation, separating them from the offices and exercises that they [the fathers] have professed and that are of such importance to the population, to the strength, and to the wealth of the State, and with very grave harm to Society, and to the general public good and utility.[62]

Implied in these statements and others like them is the idea that Latin is suitable only for society's middle and upper ranks, while the laboring classes should be educated only so far as to encourage work, obedience, and religion. Spain's "enlightened" leaders, in other words, sought to limit instruction in Latin in the hope of checking upward social mobility among the lower orders of society and thereby assure the monarchy of an abundant and docile supply of labor which would restore the nation's ailing economy.

In 1764 the crown, at the initiative of the Count of Campomanes, ordered an educational census of Castile that was presumably designed to be used in future royal policy toward Latin schools. This inquiry, undertaken by royal corregidores and intendants, took several years to complete. Unfortunately, only part of the materials collected for this census are extant,[63] but enough survives that it is possible to estimate that approximately 25,000 boys were enrolled in Latin schools in 1767,[64] a figure that is roughly equal to 4 to 4.5 percent of boys between the ages of seven and sixteen.[65] Castile, obviously, was training only a small minority of her young in Latin, yet in the crown's opinion, they were still far too many.

The census indicated that a relatively high percentage of boys from rural towns were studying Latin, and this undoubtedly reinforced the

---

[62]AHN: Cons., leg. 13183, report of León, 1764.

[63]Materials for fourteen provinces have been assembled in the AHN: Cons., leg. 13183.

[64]I have dealt with this census at length in my article, "Latin in Seventeenth- and Eighteenth-Century Castile," *Revista Storica Italiana* 85 (Giugno, 1973): 297–320. The estimate is no more than a crude doubling of the 12,180 listed as studying Latin in the provinces which the census surveyed. The justification for this maneuver is a simple one; the fourteen provinces accounted for approximately one-half of the land area of the kingdom of Castile, and together they had a population of 3.1 million, approximately one-half of Castile's total population as listed in the Count of Aranda's census of 1768. Therefore, if one can assume that the scattered fourteen provinces (they embrace nearly all of Lower Andalucia, Extremadura, and Galicia as well as large parts of León, Old Castile, and La Mancha) are fairly representative of the kingdom as a whole, it might not be unreasonable to expect that the total Latin school population of Castile was roughly double that of the census provinces, perhaps even more since major cities like Córdoba, Granada, and Madrid would have added a substantial number of schoolboys.

[65]A rough estimate of the total number of boys aged seven to sixteen is provided in Aranda's census of 1768. This is summarized in Antonio Domínguez Ortiz, *La Sociedad Española en el Siglo XVIII* (Madrid, 1955), p. 60.

crown's position. Though small villages (100 vecinos or less), which in parts of the kingdom housed more than one-half of the total population, contributed less than 10 percent of Castile's schoolboys, nearly half came from large villages and rural towns (100–1,000 vecinos).[66] The remainder (about 44 percent) hailed from cities with 1,000 vecinos or more, although this does not mean that boys in the city had more of an opportunity to learn Latin than their counterparts in the small, rural towns.[67] Actually, it was just the other way around. Seville, for example, had only 620 boys enrolled in Latin schools in 1764, a figure equal to approximately 6 percent of boys of school age. In comparison, La Bañeza, a town of 2,000 inhabitants near León, had two masters, paid by the municipality, who together taught Latin to over 150 pupils, 60 of whom were local boys. This means that approximately one third (37.5 percent) of La Bañeza's boys were in school. Similarly, Villadiego, a village of about 1,000 inhabitants in the province of Burgos, had an endowed preceptor with 100 students. This figure suggests that boys came from elsewhere to study in Villadiego, but it also indicates that a large proportion of its own children were in school. Large numbers of schoolboys in other towns this size means that contemporaries were probably correct when they said that Latin schools worked to the detriment of farming and the crafts. The city may have led to a concentration of preceptors and schools, but its large population, its reluctance to invest heavily in public education, and its strong demand for unskilled workmen, apprentices, and domestics actually inhibited the spread of secondary education. Indeed, it would appear that urbanization, at least in the eighteenth century, worked against rather than for the rise of the popular secondary school. On the other hand, the small, agricultural, less stratified, and possibly more paternalistic community appears to have encouraged the study of Latin, since this skill, much more than those in the crafts, provided a means of equipping those surplus youths the town's restricted economy could not absorb to strike out on their own, even if this only meant to enter the church.

One other fact of importance underscored by the census was the disproportionate distribution of Latin schooling about the kingdom. Regionally, Old Castile was the best educated part of the kingdom, and parts of New Castile and Extremadura among the worst (Table 1). And in general the kingdom was less educated in the south than in the north, with the exception of the provinces of Cadiz and Seville. However, too much should

[66]The figure for the percentage of the population living in villages with less than 100 vecinos refers to areas in Old Castile and León; cf. *La España del Antiguo Régimen*, ed. Miguel Artola (Salamanca, 1967). Presumably, this figure would be lower in Andalucia.

[67]Communities this size accounted for a small minority of Castile's population except in Andalucia, a region noted for a plethora of large- and medium-sized cities. On the other hand, only 10.28 percent of Old Castile's population lived in units larger than 500 vecinos and in the province of Salamanca cities with over 1,000 vecinos accounted for no more than 11.9 percent of the population. These figures have been drawn from *La España del Antiguo Régimen*.

Table 1. Educational Census of 1764-67: Schoolboys by Province

Province	% Boys in school
Valladolid	12.6
Burgos	7.3
Zamora	7.2
Seville and Cadiz	4.7
León	4.5
Palencia	3.9
Badajoz	3.6
Ciudad Rodrigo and Salamanca	2.9
Soria	2.9
Avila	2.6
Cuenca	1.8
Plasencia	.1

Source: AHN, Cons. leg. 13183.

not be read into this distribution, since the availability of schools, and, consequently, of the number of boys studying Latin, had much more to do with the charitable bequests of the sixteenth century than with patterns of wealth and population in the reign of Charles III.[68] Nevertheless, the prevalence of Latin learning among the small, rural towns typical of Old Castile served only to stiffen the crown's resistance to the spontaneous and unchecked development of Latin schools. Without controls, it was believed Latin would serve only to undermine the recovery of Castile's economy which, by the 1760s, was already well underway.

Latin throughout the seventeenth and eighteenth centuries played many roles. It was a practical tool for the learned professions and the church, a distinct but ancillary part of high culture, and a filter through which a small minority of the young destined for universities, careers in the liberal professions, and important religious and secular posts were allowed to pass. Of course, this filter was imperfect. At all times, it allowed through a small number of the poor, many of whom were sponsored by charity and

[68]Curiously, in regional terms, the educational patterns of secondary schooling in the 1760s correspond well with those of a century later (cf. *Informe sociólogico Sobre la Situación Actual en España.* Fundacion Foessa [Madrid, 1970], maps 14.2, 14.3, 14.7). Despite the continuing economic decay of Castile in relation to the prosperity of the "periphery" of the peninsula and regardless of the educational policies of different regimes, each with programs designed to equalize educational opportunities by region if not by class, Valladolid in particular and Old Castile in general remained the best educated regions of Spain throughout the nineteenth century. Even in 1932 this situation holds true, a phenomenon which might lead to the conclusion that the utilization of various public services, such as schools, by different regional populations operates independently of politicians, governments, and their reforms. The cultural baggage of the past, local customs and traditions, and the parental attitudes toward children that they foster would thus seem every bit as important as wealth and population patterns in determining the causes for one region's "knowledge" and another's "ignorance." But for the historian, working without the benefit of modern survey information, it is almost impossible to measure the influence of such cultural factors upon the social phenomena of the past.

the church, but most of the popular classes were excluded. The reasons for this were partly cost, partly the investment in time which Latin education required, and possibly because most people regarded Latin as foreign to their interests and irrelevant to their daily material needs. Thus Latin, though never the exclusive preserve of the rich, the well-born, and the ecclesiastics, was designed for and moulded to suit their particular vocations and careers. In the long run, classical education in early modern Spain may have served only to set further apart the elite from the rest of society, and consequently lessen possibilities of mutual understanding between the literate and the nonliterate, the rich and the poor, the rulers and the ruled, divisions which parliamentary governments in nineteenth- and twentieth-century Spain found so difficult to bridge.

THE SOCIETY OF JESUS

With the rise of municipal schools in the sixteenth century, the role of the church in secondary education was seemingly on the wane. But even before the crown launched its attack upon the teaching of Latin, many of these local institutions were encountering difficulties on their own. Runaway inflation, sustained in part by the massive importation of bullion into Castile from the New World, was cutting into fixed school revenues and precipitated in countless cities the interrelated problem of insufficient funds and unqualified teachers. In Guadalajara, for example, the College of Santa Catalina, a school financed jointly by the town council and a legacy left by a local citizen, faced chronic disorders. Troubles began in 1553 when "Master Cueva, reader of grammar," complained that his salary of 8,000 mrs. was too low and threatened to leave town. Matters were settled temporarily when his pay was raised to 11,500 mrs., but in the following decades, the city, heavily in debt, skimped on its obligation to contribute both firewood and funds to the college. Consequently, difficulties in securing competent teachers arose. One rector, Licentiate Antonio Millán, was dismissed because he went home at night to his wife, leaving the students who boarded in the college alone and undisciplined. His replacement, a priest, proved no better. Problems of this nature continued, and in 1619 the city was considering a recommendation from one of its aldermen that the college be turned over to the Society of Jesus "inasmuch as students benefit the most in cities and districts where the fathers of the Society govern and teach instead of preceptors, 'foreign' to the city, who do not care about anything but their own comfort and salary." After years of sporadic negotiation, the Jesuits were invited in 1631 to assume control of Guadalajara's troubled college. Under this arrangement, the college prospered, and Latin grammar was taught regularly in the city until the expulsion of the Jesuits from Spain in 1767.[69]

[69]The above is adapted from Layna Serrano, *Guadalajara*, 4: 21–24.

Guadalajara's troubles and their eventual solution were far from unique. Oviedo and Pontevedra came to similar arrangements with the Jesuits, while other towns, among them, Huete and Logroño, unable to organize schools of their own, also looked to them for aid.[70] Spain's universities did the same, since the shortage of qualified masters to teach in their faculties of Latin grammar was particularly acute. The University of Valladolid was the first to do so, and its 1581 contract with the Society of Jesus stated that "because of the great shortage of readers and masters of grammar that exists in the university and because of the serious problems this situation causes among the students, the Fathers of the Society of Jesus . . . have been comissioned for four years to read grammar and to teach good customs to the students."[71] This agreement, approved by the Royal Council of Castile, stipulated that the Society would receive 300 ducats a year to teach grammar, rhetoric, and Greek and that this instruction would be gratis. Apparently, the Jesuits turned out to be a great success, and the number of students studying grammar at the university was said to have risen from less than 200 to over 700 in the space of a few years.[72] With this example before them, five other universities—Granada, Lérida, Santiago de Compostela, Toledo, and Valencia—followed Valladolid's lead and turned to the Jesuits.[73]

On the other hand, those universities which attempted to teach Latin on their own ran into serious trouble. With skilled masters wanting, the faculties of grammar at the universities of Alcalá de Henares and Salamanca, both of whom were staunch enemies of the Jesuits, lost students at a spectacular rate (Figs. 9 and 10, pp. 213–14). In part, this decline was the result of competition from the municipal schools,[74] but the colleges of the Jesuits, expanding rapidly in the late sixteenth century, dealt the decisive blow. The faculties of Latin grammar managed to survive at these universities by attracting students from the local population, but this was not enough to halt a progressive decay. One had to await university reforms

[70]See Miguel Virgil, *Ayuntamiento de Oviedo*, pp. 458, 495; Enrique Fernández Villamil, "La Preceptoria y Estudios de Pontevedra a Través de Cuatro Siglos," *Cuadernos de Estudios Gallegos* 1 (1944): 266; AHN: Cons. leg. 13183, report of Galicia, 1764; J. J. Amor Calzos, *Curiosidades Históricas de la Ciudad de Huete (Cuenca)* (Madrid, 1904), p. 69; and Bujanda, *Seminario de Logroño*, pp. 9–10, 16–17.

[71]AUV: Lib. 517, folio 8.

[72]AUV: Lib. 517, folio 11. In spite of this success, the university broke its contract with the Jesuits in 1588 on the grounds that the Society had refused to let anyone but its own members teach grammar at the university. Instruction was subsequently suspended for a number of years before other instructors were named, but by 1597 the university turned once again to the Jesuits for help, "since one has seen the improvement they bring to the habits of students as well as to the teaching of grammar." See Andrés, *Baltasar de Céspedes*, pp. 63–79.

[73]The Royal Council of Castile approved the turnover of Granada's faculty of grammar to the Jesuits in 1583 after it heard of "the great shortage of grammar preceptors and that the sons of Granada's residents are going outside of the city to learn this subject at great cost to their patrimony"; cited in Montells y Nadal, *Historia de la Universidad de Granada* (Granada, 1870), 1: 116.

[74]See below, p. 43.

in the nineteenth century, however, before these faculties were suppressed.

With Castile's major universities out of the picture, the Society of Jesus quickly became the leading organizer of secondary education in Habsburg Spain. Interested in awakening religious fervor among the populace through teaching and eager to take up where other schools had failed, the Jesuits developed an extensive network of colleges and schools. And in sharp contrast with municipal schools, independent preceptors, and the universities, all of which charged their pupils monthly fees, the Jesuits offered free instruction except for those few students who were housed and fed within the college in the *internat*. The Jesuits, moreover, had a pedagogical program superior to that of many other schools.[75] Municipal and university classes of grammar had often been irregular and uneven owing to the shortage of qualified teachers, while many preceptors and tutors were ill-trained and incompetent. The Jesuits, in contrast, offered a well-organized four- to six-year course of graduated study in grammar and philosophy, with additional training in theology, mathematics, geography, history, and astronomy, not to mention instruction in morality, self-discipline, and religion. Furthermore, in many of their colleges the Jesuits taught primary letters as well as Latin, affording families the opportunity to educate their children cheaply but thoroughly at a single school: a service no other scholarly institution in Spain could offer. Jesuit teachers, though often young and inexperienced, were dedicated, well-educated clerics interested as much in the moral development of their pupils as in their formal education. Such attention, institutionalized in the *Ratio Studiorum*, the credo by which all Jesuit schools taught, won for the Society broad and long-lasting popular support.

The hallmark of the Jesuits' teaching was the *internat*, the program administered for those few wealthy students who boarded within the college. These pupils, a minority of the students in any one college, lived under a strict pedagogical routine which lasted twenty-four hours a day nearly eleven months a year. In this cloister, cut off from the evils and temptations of the outside world, the isolation was almost complete. Latin was the only language allowed to be spoken; only classical authors (in the original) were read; and even a subject such as geography, smacking too much of the contemporary world, held a diminishing place in a curriculum devoted to creating a mythical world of classical heroes and great deeds which the students were admonished to emulate. To make this pedagogical environment more secure, vacations were short and parental visits were curtailed. Meanwhile, constant surveillance regulated behavior and ensured proper discipline day and night. The students were even

---

[75]An excellent discussion of Jesuit education can be found in Georges Snyders, *La Pedagogie en France aux XVIIe et XVIIIe siècles* (Paris, 1965). Much of the following two paragraphs is drawn from this valuable work. The best history of the Jesuits in Spain is Antonio Astraín, *Historia de la Compañía de Jesús* (7 vols., Madrid, 1912–26).

asked to spy on one another in order to make sure the rules were enforced when the masters were temporarily absent. Learning consisted of long hours of classes and study, although this routine was interrupted regularly by periods of supervised play and occasionally by dramatic performances on classical themes acted before invited relatives and guests. Excellence and hard-work were promoted through competition, with prizes being awarded to those students who excelled in their work. This rigorous program, implemented in all of their large colleges, gave the Society a reputation for excellence which few private tutors and municipal schools could match; and this too contributed to their lasting popularity and success.

Unfortunately, the almost complete lack of matriculation registers for these colleges does not allow us to know the kinds of students the Jesuits educated. It has been asserted that in Madrid they catered for the sons of the nobility, while the municipal school taught those of the "middle class,"[76] but this is probably inexact. Presumably, the origins of the Jesuits' students in Spain matched those of their college in Bordeaux, France, where it has been demonstrated that the sons of government officials and merchants dominated the college, but not to the exclusion of children of lesser ranks.[77] In Spain, it can be assumed that only the high aristocracy, wary of all forms of organized education, and the illiterate poor stayed away.

Two measures of the Jesuits' success in secondary education are the number of colleges they established and the number of students they taught. The first of their colleges in Spain opened in 1547 at Gandía, a Levant town near Valencia, and later grew into the Jesuits' first university. Other colleges followed quickly, and by 1600 the Society, with the help of local patrons, had established colleges in most of the kingdom's major cities and towns. Thereafter, Spain's troubles dampened the pace of their expansion and by the opening of the eighteenth century the establishment of new colleges had come to a halt. By then, however, the Jesuits maintained no less than 118 colleges in Spain, 92 of which were located with the Crown of Castile, in addition to 20 seminaries for the training of priests (Map 1).[78] The largest cities, as might be expected, had the largest complement of these colleges; Madrid and Seville, for example, boasted 4 apiece. Regionally, the Society was best represented in the north of the peninsula, particularly the Basque provinces and Old Castile, where they possessed a total of twenty-one colleges, along with Andalucia, where they had colleges in no less than twenty-eight towns. Other areas had

[76]See Domínguez Ortiz, *Sociedad Española*, 2: 192.

[77]See F. de Dainville, "Colleges et Frequentation Scholaire au XVIIIe Siècle," *Population* 3 (1957): 468.

[78]There are differences regarding the exact number of Jesuit colleges in Spain. Included here are only their teaching institutions—colleges and seminaries—as found in Lud. Carrez, *Atlas Geographicus Societatis Jesu* (Paris, 1900), *Assistentia Hispaniae*, and in A. Guglieri Navarro, *Documentos de la Compañía de Jesús en el Archivo Histórico Nacional* (Madrid, 1967).

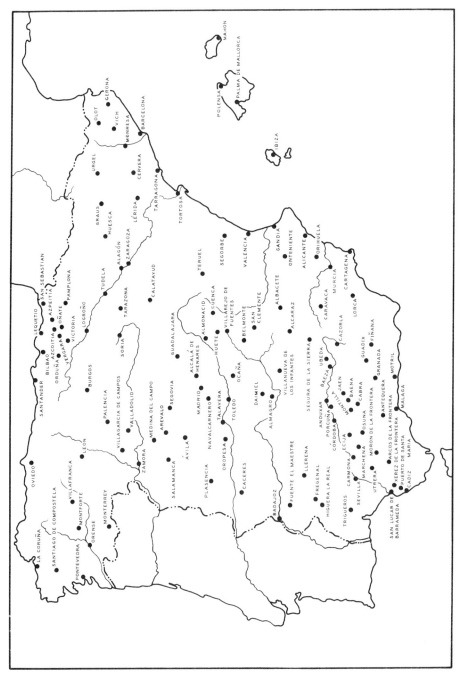

Map 1. Schools and colleges of the Society of Jesus in Spain. (*Sources:* Carrez, *Atlas Societatis Jesu;* Guglieri Navarro, *Documeños de la Compania de Jesús.*)

proportionately fewer colleges, but, as Map 1 clearly shows, by the middle of the eighteenth century the Jesuits had at least one establishment in every province of Spain.

Matriculations are perhaps a more accurate test of the popularity and influence of the Jesuits, since they represent the willingness of families to send their offspring to the Society's schools. Most of these records have been lost,[79] but it remains clear that wherever the Jesuits opened a college, students were never in short supply. In Seville, for example, the Jesuits were teaching 500 students in 1563, about 800 a decade later, and over 1,000 by 1590.[80] Moreover, with the help of the city, a new college, that of San Hermenegildo, had been built to accommodate this crowd. Matriculations at Córdoba grew at a similar pace, reaching the 1,000 mark by 1588.[81] Even in smaller towns, the Jesuits' record was outstanding. Their college in Monterrey in Galicia, for instance, enrolled 400 students annually during the 1560s, nearly 1,000 by 1582, and approximately 1,200 by 1588.[82] Other colleges enjoyed similar prosperity, and though it is only a rough estimate, the total number of students taught by the Jesuits in the kingdom of Castile toward the end of the sixteenth century was something on the order of 10,000 to 15,000 a year, the vast majority of whom were studying Latin grammar.[83]

The progress of matriculations at Jesuit colleges in the seventeenth century is more obscure. Most colleges recovered quickly following the severe plague which opened the century, and by the 1620s the University of Salamanca complained that the Jesuits in Madrid enrolled "2,000 students in their schools, many of whom have been brought from the University of Alcalá de Henares, as a result of which that university has become so deserted that scarcely anyone attends class."[84] In subsequent decades, war, mounting taxation, and inflation accompanied by demographic decline may have caused matriculations to fall, but, owing to the lack of accurate figures, this is only an assumption which remains to be proved. In Pamplona students in the Jesuit college at the end of the seventeenth century numbered 300 to 400 a year.[85] This figure, equal to the number of students enrolled in this college one hundred years earlier, suggests that matriculations were on the rise following the difficult, middle decades of the

[79]Only those for the college of Pamplona between 1670 and 1720 survive; cf. AHN: *Jesuitas*, lib. 192.

[80]Astraín, *Compañía de Jesús*, 1: 589; 4: 172.

[81]Ibid.

[82]Ibid.

[83]This figure is no more than an educated guess. The eleven colleges which existed in the Jesuit province of Castile in 1593 taught Latin to approximately 3,500 students. If one includes those who were studying the 3 Rs, the liberal arts, and theology, the total is well over 5,000 (cf. ARSI: *Provintia Castilla*, lib. 14 II, folios 228v-297). Other colleges in Andalucia, Galicia, Asturias, and Navarre would have raised the grand total to 10,000 or more.

[84]AGS: GJ, leg. 972, "Memorial de la Universidad de Salamanca," 1627.

[85]AHN: *Jesuitas*, lib. 192.

century. However, the history of Pamplona's college may not correspond
to what was happening elsewhere, and it is possible that the Society's
other colleges resembled that in León which was said to have lost students because of declining economic circumstances.[86]

Whatever the precise experience of individual colleges, it appears
certain that the total number of students taught by the Jesuits at the opening of the eighteenth century was no greater than and possibly below that
of a century before. The War of the Spanish Succession took an additional
toll, and, in spite of a brief recovery during the 1720s and 1730s, the Jesuits
lost ground once again in the years immediately preceding their expulsion in 1767. In 1764, for example, commentators in Palencia, Soria, and
Zamora remarked that the Jesuit colleges located in those cities had had
more students "in the past."[87]

If the Jesuits' position was weakening at a time when secondary
school education in Castile was on the rise, the causes may be found in
the revival of municipal schools, increases in the number of independent
preceptors, and the belated entry of the other religious orders into public
education. By mid-century the Augustinians, Dominicans, and Franciscans
had begun to challenge if not supplant the hegemony of Jesuit schools,
managing to siphon off part of what would have previously been the Society's exclusive clientele.[88] More serious for the Jesuits was the threat
posed by the independent preceptors who, despite monthly fees of five to
ten reales, were increasing both in number and popularity. In 1728, for
instance, the rector of Córdoba's Jesuit college complained of a serious
shortage of students at his institution and placed the blame on "an inunda-
tion of preceptors . . . so copious that one stumbles upon a preceptor at
nearly every street corner."[89] And in Antequera, where free instruction
was offered by the Jesuits as well as the Franciscans, two private preceptors enrolled twenty students between them, each of whom paid fees
of six reales a month.[90] It was the same elsewhere; if a preceptor—known
commonly as a *pedante, domine,* or *dio-sero*—was present, a number of
students preferred to pay for their instruction and perhaps benefit from
classes that were smaller and less disciplined than those in the religious
colleges.

Thanks to the educational census of 1764–67, it is possible to see the
extent to which the Jesuits controlled the teaching of Latin in Castile.
While municipal schools accounted for nearly half of the pupils (45 percent)

[86]AHN: Cons. leg. 7294, no. 3, letter of 6.I.1714.
[87]AHN: Cons. leg. 13183, reports of the provinces of Palencia, Soria, and Zamora.
[88]In Antequera, for example, the Jesuits enrolled sixty students in 1764, while a school
opened by the Franciscans only ten years before managed to attract thirty; cf. AHN: Cons.
leg. 13183, report of Seville.
[89]AM Córdoba: Secc. 6, leg. 1, no. 4. A municipal investigation subsequently indicated that Córdoba had only nine such preceptors, but as a result of the rector's complaints,
nearly all of them were forced to stop teaching.
[90]AHN: Cons. leg. 13183, report of Seville, 1764.

Table 2. Educational Census of 1764–67: Schoolboys by Religious Order

Religious order	No. of pupils	No. of houses (mid-18th)
Augustinians	116	128
Benedictines	39	63
Dominicans	480	213
Franciscans	219	425
Minimos of St. Francis de Paul	66	79
Fathers of the Pious Schools	20	17
Calced Religious (Carmelites)	18	78
Calced Trinitarians	15	73
Society of Jesus	3,572	132
Total	4,545	

Source: AHN. Cons., leg. 13183; La Fuente, *Historia Ecclesiástica*, 3: App. 13.

and the independent preceptors another fifth (about 20 percent), approximately one-third of the students attended religious schools. Of these, the Jesuits claimed the lion's share; their 3,500 pupils represented nearly 80 percent of those who were taught in religious schools and about 30 percent of the total number of schoolboys listed in the census (Table 2).[91] In the 1760s, therefore, the Jesuits, in spite of losses which they had incurred in the previous half century, still represented a major force in Castilian education. Their strongholds were Galicia and the province of Seville; in the former they taught close to 60 percent of all students, in the latter, 40 percent. The Basque provinces and Madrid were also Jesuit fiefs,[92] but census materials for these areas do not exist.

Against this background it is easy to understand why the expulsion of the Society of Jesus in 1767 precipitated an educational crisis. Although the crown intervened, allowing towns to hire instructors with revenues confiscated from the Society and to open schools in the buildings the Jesuits had deserted, many problems remained. Trained masters were expensive and in short-supply, and many communities were obliged to hire incompetents.[93] Difficulties continued and a new series of educational censuses, beginning in 1772, underscored the gravity of the situation.

The first of these inquiries covered the province of Seville, a region especially hard-hit by the expulsion.[94] Of the thirty organized schools that had existed in 1767, only nineteen remained. A subsequent inquiry in

[91]In the fourteen provinces of the census, the Franciscans maintained only five schools; the Augustinians and the Dominicans each had only four.

[92]For a history of the Jesuits in the Basque provinces, see Malaxechevarria, *Compañia de Jesús por la Instrucción del Pueblo Vasco en los Siglos XVII y XVIII . . .* (San Sebastian, 1926).

[93]AHN: Cons., leg. 13183, report of Cuenca includes complaints of this nature from officials in the town of Huete.

[94]AHN: Cons., leg. 13183, report of Seville, 1772.

1775 showed little improvement, yet the regent of the royal *audiencia* in Seville, who had been in charge of this census, recommended that no new grammar schools be established, particularly in smaller communities, since they would only encourage the masses to abandon their work in industry and the fields. Another survey, conducted in 1778 by the *chancilería* in Valladolid for Castile north of the Tagus River, indicated that there were fewer organized schools but more independent preceptors than in previous years.[95] Though many towns requested the crown's help to revive their schools, the president of the chancillería called for the suppression of most of the smaller schools still in existence and an end to all but a few of the independent preceptors. He also advocated the amalgamation of small schools into larger institutions, the standardization of teaching methods and texts, and the creation of a special board of examiners to select new teachers and to keep in touch with the "*sabios*" (or scholars) of Europe in order to learn of new ideas and techniques relevant to the teaching of grammar and the liberal arts. But few, if any of his suggestions were put into practice; meanwhile, Latin education in Castile continued to decay. Complaints from Galicia in 1785 about shortages of schools, skilled teachers, and pupils point to the lasting effects of the expulsion of the Jesuits in 1767.[96]

One of the major reasons for the failure of Latin schooling to recover quickly after 1767 was the crown's failure to come effectively to their aid. Suspicious of the results that widespread, popular instruction in Latin might bring, the monarchy under Charles III left the bulk of the organization and financial support of Latin schools to private individuals, municipalities, and the church. The most that it did for secondary education was to revive the old Seminario de Nobles in Madrid and to establish similar schools in Valencia and Vergara. And even though the crown was willing to provide some temporary financial assistance to the towns most affected by the expulsion of the Jesuits, in the main it acted only as a loose regulatory agency and an arbiter of educational disputes. Active intervention had to await the coming of the nineteenth century, beginning with Charles IV's involvement in the establishment of a number of specialized technical schools.[97]

Before this belated attempt at centralization and control, the only agency in Spain which had attempted to establish order amidst the chaos and confusion of the teaching of Latin was the Society of Jesus. To assess

[95]AHN: Cons., leg. 13183, report of the Chancillería de Valladolid, 1778.

[96]AHN: Cons., leg. 5495. The town of Mondoñedo complained about the "lack of endowed masters in most of the villages" (folio 38), while the Bishop of Mondoñedo said about the same thing in a letter dated 28.IV.1785. La Coruña claimed that its children learned the three Rs too late, that is, when they were "already adult and then passed into the study of grammar at an age better suited for instruction in crafts."

[97]There was a plan offered in 1792 for a college designed for nobles from the New World that was to be established in Granada, but the institution never got off the ground. See AA Granada: leg. 894, 1792.

the results of its contribution is difficult. At the outset, it is important to recognize that only a minority of the students who went through the Jesuits' schools entered the church; the greatest number by far entered secular careers, many in government. And one can probably assume that with the exception of leading court families, many of whom educated their children at home, a large proportion of crown officials in the years between 1600 and 1770 had been brought up under the Jesuits' care. One can only guess, of course, as to the outcome of such shared experiences among this elite. The fact that their education, at least in content, had changed marginally over the years, locking them into a program which emphasized the study of Latin, antiquity, and the image of order and stability presented in the world of Imperial Rome, perhaps helps to explain the dull, methodical nature of Spanish imperial politics, where the hackneyed ideas of "one monarch, one religion, one sword" prevailed. Like the schools' curriculum, the politics of the age consistently looked backward, toward a mythical Golden Age, that of Rome incarnate in the person of the Emperor Charles V, rather than seeking inspiration from the realities of the present or looking to the future.

Indeed, the *internat*, by bringing together sons of wealthy families destined to be Castile's future leaders and encouraging them from an early age to pursue their own interests and ambitions, but always within a fixed, immutable framework, may have itself contributed to class-exclusive policies, the protection of privilege, and the status quo in Castilian society to the detriment of social reforms aimed at improving the lot of the laboring poor. Here one is tempted to point out that the major reformers of the late eighteenth century—the Count of Aranda, Campomanes, and Jovellanos—had all been raised outside of Jesuit auspices, although the unsuccessful reformer, Pablo de Olavide, had been taught by the Society in Peru. But too much should not be read into this, because the program of other Latin schools closely resembled that of the Jesuits in content if not in form and in method. Thus Castile's long-standing resistance to innovation and to reform may be linked to a system of Latin education which at its heart taught the elite unquestioning obedience to authority and tradition. In Castile these ideas apparently helped the monarchy to maintain a relatively peaceful society, controlled and disciplined from within, and resigned to imperial defeat, financial disorders, and the arbitrary nature of absolute government. Internal tensions, rather than assuming a violent nature, as in seventeenth-century England or eighteenth-century France, found their outlets in religious fanaticism, persecution of racial and religious minorities, exploitation of empire, migration to the New World, and hostility to foreigners and their ideas.

But this is undoubtedly exaggerating the importance of Latin education in Castile. More certain is that Latin served as an important agency for upward social mobility, particularly in the years between the reign of the Catholic kings and the opening of the seventeenth century. It did this in two ways. A knowledge of Latin, however rudimentary, conferred a measure of status and prestige; those who knew something of the language acquired a reputation for learning and wisdom, and this in turn helped them to obtain key positions in the public and the private domain. Furthermore, Latin schooling provided access to the universities, whose degrees helped to boost talented commoners and members of the lower nobility into positions of wealth and importance. By the middle of the seventeenth century, however, Castile's depressed economy and the efforts of new noble families to protect their political prerogatives and social position made sure that Latin was stripped of this particular role. After the 1620s, Latin in fact served increasingly as a wedge against upward social mobility. Though the church demanded it, the elite feared the consequences of its spread, and, consequently, the crown moved to restrict its instruction to society's upper ranks. Under these circumstances, one can begin to understand why Latin education remained a local, private, and largely uncoordinated and spontaneous effort, except in the hands of the trusted Jesuits, where it helped to buttress the existing social and political order.

In any event, it might be argued that Latin was beneficial to Spanish society, since it provided the church with a link to its earliest years, gave the upper classes a distinct education they could call their own, and allowed the nation's rulers access to the Golden Age of Imperial Rome, which they could aspire to restore under the banner of Catholic Spain. In addition, as noted above, the ancient language conferred social status and in some cases offices and jobs, helping in this regard families at the middle rather than those at the bottom of the social scale. On the other hand, a pedagogical preoccupation with the Latin language and ancient culture in general helped to block curricular change at universities and schools, or, as Jovellanos put it: "The Latin language, for reasons which are hidden to my poor reason, has raised itself up to the dignity of the one and only legal idiom of our universities, and what is more, it is conserved in them, despite past experience and disappointment."[98] Meanwhile, Latin schools, by the expense and difficulty of their program, helped to thwart the advance of the intelligent, more ambitious and talented poor or at least direct them into nonproductive and nonreproductive ecclesiastical careers, thus canceling long-range prospects for families of lowly origin to rise on the social scale.

But this too is exaggerating the influence of the Roman tongue and that of early education in general. Perhaps the most that should be said is that Latin went hand-in-hand with "robe" culture in Castile. In the sixteenth century Latin abetted the rise of a new social and political elite—

---

[98]Gaspar Melchor de Jovellanos, "Memoria Sobre la Educación Popular," ed. *Biblioteca de Autores Españoles* (Madrid, 1858), 46: 236. The translation is that of John H. R. Polt, "Jovellanos y la Educación," in *El P. Feijóo y su Siglo* (Oviedo, 1961), p. 328.

the nobility of the robe—which owed its position to advanced education and the offices of the crown. But in the seventeenth century Latin education became increasingly restrictive as this elite, gradually assimilating itself into the established aristocracy, while seeking to protect its position from below, sought to make Latin the exclusive privilege of the noble and rich. In short, Latin, the instrument by which many of Castile's ruling families had originally come to power, was then used by this same elite to protect the stability and the fixed social order of the *ancien régime*.

chapter 3
THE UNIVERSITIES

Upon completing his course in Latin grammar, the student with the opportunity and the interest to continue his studies looked to the university. Commonly known as *estudios generales* before the seventeenth century, later as *universidades*, these institutions were distinguished from the grammar schools by their teaching chairs in the advanced faculties of law, medicine, and theology and the right to grant licenses or degrees of scholastic attainment—the baccalaureate, master's license, and doctorate. *Estudios particulares*, or simply *estudios*, often rivaled the universities in size but lacked either the full complement of faculties or the right to grant academic degrees. These simple estudios included many of Spain's grammar schools which taught theology and the liberal arts in addition to Latin grammar but had no power to grant degrees, only certificates of study. In the same category were various institutions which taught all of the prescribed university subjects but could grant degrees only to certain groups, the members of one religious order, for example.[2]

Universities in Spain, as in other European nations, began during the Middle Ages. By 1450 the kingdoms of Castile and Aragón had six estudios generales, four of which were fully operational and rather well-known. The oldest was at Salamanca, a city in the old kingdom of León in western Spain, not far from the Portuguese border. It had originated early in the thirteenth century, received the official recognition of King Alfonso X in 1248 and the sanction of the papacy in 1255, which enabled it to be known as *studium generale* and to grant academic degrees, the right of *jus ubique docendi*.[3] Salamanca was soon rivaled by another estudio general at the not far distant town of Valladolid, the first in the kingdom of Castile,[4] and then by others at Huesca in the kingdom of Aragón and at Lérida in the principality of Catalonia.

[1] The best introduction to the history of Spanish universities is La Fuente, *Historia de las Universidades* (Madrid, 1884–89). More recent is G. Ajo y Sainz de Zúñiga, *Historia de las Universidades Hispánicas* (8 vols., Madrid, 1957–72). G. Reynier, *La Vie Universitaire dans l'Ancienne Espagne* (Paris, 1902), provides a more impressionistic account as does Alberto Jimenez, *Historia de la Universidad Española* (Madrid, 1971).

[2] The *estudio general* in the Dominican convent at Jérez de la Frontera was reserved for members of this order, and after 1564 all outsiders were banned from its classes. See Sancho de Sopranis, *Historia de Jérez de la Frontera* (Jérez, 1965), 2: 309.

[3] See V. Beltrán de Heredia, "Los Orígenes de la Universidad de Salamanca," *Acta Salmanticensia* 1 (1953): 16, 17, 23, 30. He claims that the university opened its doors in the year 1218–19.

[4] See M. Alcocer Martínez, *Historia de la Universidad de Valladolid* (6 vols., Madrid, 1918–31).

Beyond a few basic facts, little is known about the early history of these institutions. The work of kings rather than popes, they led an uncertain existence, especially during the wars of the fourteenth and early fifteenth centuries. The major subjects were the laws, canon and civil, if only because theology was not an official part of the university curriculum. Salamanca, for example, relying upon classes offered by nearby religious convents, did not acquire a faculty of theology until 1394, more than a century after its official foundation. Pope Martin V (1417–31) expanded the number of Salamanca's theology chairs and sanctioned the theology faculty which had begun in 1411 at Valladolid with the help of King John I; nevertheless, the holy science continued to take second place to studies in law. In this respect Spain's medieval universities bore a close resemblance to their Italian counterparts, notably Bologna, upon whose government and organization they were modeled. The universities of northern Europe, Oxford, Cambridge, and Paris in particular, famous for their studies in arts and theology, were markedly different. Moreover, the latter were the *universitas* or corporation of masters rather than students, while the collegiate tradition, so strong in the north by the late fourteenth century, came slowly to the universities of Spain, never to assume the importance it would achieve in Paris or in England.

After the middle of the fifteenth century the fortunes of higher education in Spain improved decisively. At that point Spain's universities, now numbering six, were institutions at the periphery of society, far removed from the mainstream of religious and secular life. Poor in rents, low in reputation, many Spanish youths avoided them, preferring instead to study abroad: physicians at Montpellier, lawyers at Bologna, some of whom were supported by the Spanish college in that city, and theologians at Paris.[5] But in the century following the opening of the reign of Ferdinand and Isabel, the universities of Spain grew in number, size, and prestige. Between 1474 and the early seventeenth century, twenty-seven new universities were established, giving Spain a grand total of thirty-three. In addition, Spaniards organized universities in their new American territories at an astonishing rate. The first, under Dominican auspices, arose at Santo Domingo on the island of Hispaniola in 1538, to be followed by others in Mexico City (1551), Lima (1551), Las Charcas (1552) in what is now modern Bolivia, Bogotá (1580), and Quito (1586). Universities in Argentina, Chile, and Guatemala came in the seventeenth century. In total, Spaniards of the Golden Age established or reorganized no less than forty universities, including those in Spanish-controlled territories in Europe, a record no other Europeans could match.

---

[5]A recent study has demonstrated that Spanish students, especially those from Aragón and Catalonia, were fairly numerous at the universities of southern France during the fifteenth century. See Jacques Verger, "Le recrutement géographique des universités francaises au début du XVe siècle d'apres les suppliques de 1403," *Mélanges d'Archéologie et d'Histoire de l'école francaise de Rome* 82 (1970).

Map 2. Universities in Habsburg Spain.

In Spain itself the universities, new and old, were situated almost without exception in major towns and clustered in two regions: Catalonia and Old Castile. The former, a small but populous and relatively pros- perous region around Barcelona, maintained six universities by 1620. In comparison, the much larger but sparsely populated and impoverished kingdom of Aragón, lying just to the west, had only three, while the king- dom of Valencia and the Balearic Islands boasted five. The nineteen re- maining universities lay within the borders of the Crown of Castile: the administrative, economic, and political heart of the Spanish empire (Map 2).

Of the nineteen only six were to be found south of the Tagus River, which runs across the middle of the peninsula, separating Andalucia, Extremadura, and much of New Castile from the northern half of the king- dom. In general, the south was a poor, backward, illiterate region. Its sparse population consisted mainly of landless peasants working for wealthy landowners who lived in the towns; industry was light, limited mainly to pottery-making and silk, while mercantile activity centered in and around Seville, gateway to the New World. Moreover, outside of Córdoba, Granada, and Seville, the south had no major administrative or ecclesiastical seat. Castile north of the Tagus, on the other hand, was a prosperous, densely populated region. Towns like Burgos and Medina de Campo thrived on the international trade in merino wool; cathedral chap- ters were plentiful and rich; and in the years before Philip II settled his capital in Madrid, it was here that Spain's peripatetic court spent most of its time. Home for a major part of Castile's nobility and boasting a tradition of municipal support for primary and secondary schools, little wonder that the north of Castile acquired eleven new universities, more than any other region in Spain.

Accompanying the proliferation of universities in the sixteenth century was the rise of colleges within them. These institutions had existed in Spain since the creation of the College of Pan y Carbón at Salamanca in 1386,[6] but in the fifteenth century the universities had acquired only a handful of new colleges. Thereafter, they multiplied. Salamanca had only two colleges for lay students before 1500, but acquired twenty-eight in the course of the century which followed, not including those colleges the religious orders built for themselves.[7] Similarly, the University of Valladolid received six such communities in the century following the reign of the Catholic kings, while the new University at Alcalá de Henares added eight colleges to the seven created at the time of its foundation in 1508.

Modeled after the Spanish college in Bologna, the colleges were small, semiautonomous communities. Members elected their own officers and administered the rents set aside by their founders for their support. Elections to scholarships were generally handled by the scholars themselves, although in some colleges selected patrons had the right of nomination. All of Spain's colleges were semimonastic in character and strict rules regarding dress and discipline, the tenure of each scholarship, and the subjects to be studied were minutely set forth in constitutions and statutes. But other than repetition exercises and mock examinations, no organized teaching took place within the colleges. In this regard university colleges in Spain contrasted sharply with their counterparts in England and France, the reason being that while many of the colleges in the north of Europe had been designed for graduate students who later took on undergraduates as boarders, pupils, and wards, all but six of Spain's colleges were for undergraduates who were expected to attend university lectures.

Initially, the goal common to the university college in Spain was to provide poor or orphaned students with an opportunity to attend university, and toward this end most of these communities had special statutes barring students whose private income exceeded a certain level. This charitable aim was complemented by that of regional improvement; each college was generally restricted to students from specific provinces and towns. A few imposed further limitations: four were reserved for students

[6]See Santiago Nogaledo Alvarez, *El Colegio Menor de 'Pan y Carbón,' primero de los Antiguos Colegios Seculares de Salamanca, 1386-1780* (Salamanca, 1958).
[7]See L. Sala Balust, *Constituciones, Estatutos, y Ceremonias de los Antiguos Colegios Seculares de la Universidad de Salamanca* (4 vols., Madrid, 1962-66), and, by the same author, "Los Antiguos Colegios de Salamanca en la Matrícula Universitaria," *Hispania Sacra* 12 (1959): 131-64.

who belonged to one of Spain's military orders; two, notably San Lázaro and Santa Catalina at Salamanca, were restricted to members of the founder's family; while the College of the Conception, established in 1608 at Salamanca, required its scholars to defend the doctrine of the Immaculate Conception. College founders also stipulated whether the scholars were to be laymen, tonsured or full-fledged priests, noble or plebeian; thus, Spaniards from every estate were represented in the colleges' scholarships.

Noteworthy among the host of new colleges and about which more will be said later were the six colegios mayores.[8] Four of these were at Salamanca, one was at Valladolid, and another at Alcalá de Henares. The oldest, the college of San Bartolomé, was established at Salamanca in 1401 by Diego de Anaya, Archbishop of Seville, and subsequently served as the archetype for the later foundations.[9] These included Santa Cruz (1484) at Valladolid; San Ildefonso (1508), the core of the new university at Alcalá; and the remaining three at Salamanca: Cuenca (1510); San Salvador, known as Oviedo (1517); and Santiago el Zebedeo, called del Arzobispo (1521). As in the case of San Bartolomé, the later foundations were the work of wealthy prelates.

These six colleges were distinguished from the others by their wealth, special graduation privileges which reduced examination fees for their members by as much as one-half, and the regulation that a baccalaureate was necessary for admission. Students entering these communities were therefore not young beginners but mature scholars who had already spent considerable time at university. Selected on a competitive basis, they were required to be "poor." In return they received full financial support from the college for a stipulated number of years, enabling them to remain at university and to prepare for advancd degrees. In other words, from their inception, these colleges were expected to provide their universities with an academic elite.

As in the case of the colegios mayores, prelates were the major patrons of Spain's new institutions of higher learning. The lay aristocracy hardly participated at all. Aside from the small college of Santa Catalina at Alcalá, gift of the daughter of the Counts of La Coruña, the universities at Osuna and Gandía were the only important contributions of this class. A possible explanation for this is that Spain's aristocracy had little liking for the professional character of university education. As in the case of early education, the charity of Spain's titled families failed to reach those institutions in which they had little direct interest or concern.

Royal sponsorship was also infrequent, even though the crown contributed indirectly to all new foundations by means of special tax privi-

[8]See below, Part III, Chap. 7.
[9]See J. Roxas y Contreras, *Historia del Colegio Viejo de San Bartolomé* (3 vols., Madrid, 1766).

leges. The University of Granada, founded by Charles V in 1526 to help train clerics to work in the recently conquered but as yet unconverted kingdom of Granada, was the most lavish contribution of the Habsburg kings. The colleges of the military orders at Salamanca, King's College at Alcalá for the sons of servants in the royal palace, the colleges for English and Irish Catholic refugees, and Philip II's small university within his palace-monastery at El Escorial were the only other pure royal foundations of note. In the main, the Habsburg kings, isolated from their people, often abroad and with interests leaning toward dynastic questions and the great affairs of state, left the work of university-building to groups more in touch with local and regional educational needs.

Thus it was up to the clergy to do the necessary work, and together Spain's wealthy prelates provided at least nine of the twenty-seven universities created after 1474.[10] Churchmen of lesser rank added another three.[11] Armed with papal bulls, special royal confirmations and privileges, and church rents set aside for the purposes of construction, salaries, and endowment, these ecclesiastics sought to foster the development of higher education in Spain. In their founding statements the need for "science" was continually stressed, while "ignorance" was decried, but frequently little else was said. Ostensibly, their primary goal was religious; in the sixteenth century a cultured clergy and an educated laity were considered essential for the maintenance of the faith. Threatened by heresy from abroad, universities could help protect Spanish orthodoxy from within. Universities could also provide church and state with skilled, educated officials—a goal popular in Spain, thanks to the strong influence of Erasmus.[12] Such considerations, however, fused with those of regional improvement and pride. For instance, when the town of Burgos petitioned Philip II in 1589 to expand a local college into a university, it referred to the reasons why that community had first been built: ". . . the cardinal Iñigo Lopez de Mendoza, former Archbishop of Burgos [1527–39], realizing the lack of "lettered" persons in his diocese and that for reasons of poverty and necessity the inhabitants could not leave for other universities and support themselves during their studies, ordered the establishment of a college in Burgos and left some rents so that chairs and faculties could be read."[13] In a similar vein the Dominican order, attempting in 1580 to ex-

---

[10]In the Crown of Castile prelates established the universities at Alcalá de Henares, Burgo de Osma, Oñate, Santo Tomás (Seville), and Santiago.

[11]The University of Baeza was largely the work of Rodrigo López, *clérigo*, and his brother Pedro, a canon in Palencia. Juan López de Medina, archdeacon of Almazán, founded the University of Sigüenza with the help of Cardinal Pedro González de Mendoza, and Rodrigo Fernández Santaella, an archdeacon in Seville, was responsible for the University of Santa María de Jesús (Seville).

[12]See Marcel Bataillon, *Erasme et Espagne* (Paris, 1937).

[13]AGS: Patronato Royal, Cortes de Castilla, leg. 71, folio 169. The efforts of Burgos to make its Colegio de San Nicolás into a university had begun as early as 1581; cf. Beltrán de Heredia, *Cartulario de la Universidad de Salamanca* (Salamanca, 1971), 3: 574. This bid was subsequently denied by the Royal Council of Castile.

pand their estudio particular Jérez de la Frontera into a university, claimed "that the city could profit from a small university and avoid the travels, troubles, and expenses that its sons now suffer to graduate and which sometimes dissuade many worthwhile students who could otherwise benefit from such studies."[14] Local feeling was sufficiently strong in sixteenth-century Spain for prelates and other would-be founders to have little need to justify their projects on additional grounds.[15] And once one or two prelates built their universities, the others, in a competitive spirit, followed suit. During an age in which education and learning, no matter how vaguely defined, were considered beneficial to the society at large, the honor attached to university-building was an attribute few of Spain's prelates could ignore. The large number of hastily planned and inadequately financed colleges and universities that never succeeded suggests that sheer emulation and concern over one's reputation in generations to come had as much to do with the proliferation of academic institutions as other more exalted intentions and goals.[16]

In organization and design, the universities created by the ecclesiastics differed widely from those of medieval origin. Salamanca, Valladolid, and Lérida, in line with the Italian tradition, were open, "democratic," universities in the sense that the students through their "nations" elected university officials from among their own ranks and through open competitions elected their instructors. Though colleges developed, they were never constitutionally granted control of university government and teaching. Moreover, since a majority of the students lived outside college walls, life in the older universities remained relatively undisciplined and free; continuous complaints about student riots, violations of scholarly dress, and the indiscriminate use of arms give an indication of the atmosphere that prevailed.[17]

The laxity as well as the democratic aspects of the medieval universities contrasted with the more confined, disciplined character of the sixteenth-century institutions. Shaped more in the tradition of Paris than Bologna and founded in an age of religious upheaval and discontent, the founders sought to infuse their universities with the discipline and routine of a monastery. Their contribution was uniquely Spanish: the college-university. In this arrangement a small, endowed college reserved for selected scholarship students served as the administrative, financial, and academic core of a larger university. Officers elected by the college were

[14]Sancho de Sopranis, *Jérez de la Frontera*, 2: 310.
[15]In some instances, local feeling worked against the rise of new universities. The University of Salamanca in 1513 requested the Bishop of Malaga to help stop the establishment of an university in Seville "because it would be very harmful to the quality of the University of Salamanca, which is generally regarded as the best in the world . . ."; cited in Beltrán de Heredia, *Cartulario*, 3: 427.
[16]A notable failure was the *estudio* at Ejea de los Caballeros in Aragón which had even managed to secure a papal bull authorizing its transformation into an *estudio general*.
[17]See below, p. 203.

university officers and teaching took place within the college by instructors appointed by the college scholars. The remaining students, the majority by far, played no part in university government nor in the selection of their instructors.

The small university founded at Sigüenza in 1477 by Juan López de Medina, archdeacon of Almazán with the aid of el Gran Cardenal, Pedro González de Mendoza, was Spain's first college-university,[18] but the largest and most famous of these institutions was that at Alcalá de Henares.[19] Established by the Cardinal Cisneros, Archbishop of Toledo and later Regent of Spain, the center of this university was the Colegio Mayor de San Ildefonso. Its twenty-four scholars elected among themselves a rector and governing council which automatically became that of the university. Furthermore, college students generally managed to dominate the university's teaching posts. With the exception of the universities at Granada, Oviedo, Valencia, and Zaragoza, all of the universities founded in the sixteenth century were organized along similar lines, although in certain cases a religious convent replaced the college; hence the name: "convent-university."[20]

The latter aside, Spain's universities in the sixteenth century, the largest and most famous ones above all, were fundamentaly secular institutions. University instructors in England had to be clergymen, but in Spain anyone who met the qualifications of age, education, purity of blood, and who was an orthodox Catholic was allowed to teach. Monks, though never barred from university chairs, nevertheless confined their activities to their own convents and monasteries, except for the few who lectured publicly in theology and the arts.

In spite of these arrangements, it would be difficult to argue that the universities of sixteenth century Spain were wholly secular institutions. Religion and religious ceremony were integral to university life. Catholic orthodoxy was mandatory for every student and teacher, and the ideas put forth in the classrooms were scrutinized by the Inquisition's censors and spies. Students remained subject to the jurisdiction of religious authorities, specifically, the *maestrescuela* of the local cathedral and his subordinates. But it is also true that with the erosion of papal power in Spain after the late fifteenth century, more and more university disputes went to crown officials. Though the maestrescuela continued to rule upon student misdemeanors and crimes, the university rector, the corregidor—the local representative of the crown—and the Royal Council of Castile became the universities' major courts of appeal. Disputes once directed to a bishop or the Pope went directly to the Royal Council, and this body,

[18]See I. Montiel, *Historia de la Universidad de Sigüenza* (2 vols., Maracaibo, 1963).

[19]See Martín Esperanza, "Estado de la Universidad de Alcalá Desde Su Fundación Hasta El Año 1805," ed. A. Melgares y Marín, *RABM*, (1903), 8: 58 ff.; 228 ff.; 300 ff.

[20]These included the universities at Almagro, Avila, El Escorial, Sahagún-Irache, Toledo, Santo Tomás in Seville, and Toledo.

acting as a primitive ministry of education, guarded over university statutes, initiated constitutional, curricular and disciplinary reforms, while
playing an ever increasing role in the selection of university teachers and
the regulation of student life.

The interest which the crown displayed in such matters was a phase in
the consolidation of political and jurisdictional power in the hands of the
monarchy after the reign of Catholic kings. But at the same time it was
indicative of the new and growing importance which universities had
acquired for the rulers of Spain. Royal interest in these institutions centered upon their role as training schools for the officials staffing Castile's
militant church and the newly reorganized royal administration. These
university-trained officials, commonly known as *letrados*, a term which
applied broadly to any lettered individual and specifically to jurists, had
been integral to the legal profession, the universities, and the high clergy
since the Middle Ages.

Letrados had also served as royal advisors since the reign of Alfonso X
(1252-84), but they did not become regular crown officials until the end of
the fourteenth century. Thereafter, monarchical weakness and civil war
helped to increase the number of letrados in the crown's employ; their
knowledge of Roman law served as a useful weapon against local and
feudal jurisdictions which challenged the royal prerogative. The Catholic
kings, bent on increasing the power of the throne over and above the head
of Castile's independent, rebellious aristocracy, dramatically extended the
letrado's role in royal government. This policy began at the Cortes of
Toledo in 1480 when the rulers initiated a series of administrative reforms which were gradually to create a new hierarchy of political power
in Castile that was independent of the aristocracy, directly controlled by
the monarchy, and staffed overwhelmingly by university-trained letrados.[21]

What developed was a collegiate system of government, fully independent of the old government of the royal household. A number of
councils with competence over matters ranging from faith to finance
formed the core of this new administration. At the provincial level new
legal tribunals were erected and the existing one, the chancillería at
Valladolid, was expanded and given new powers. And in the towns the
use of an official known as a corregidor whose job was to represent and
protect royal interests at the local level was extended.

The primacy of the letrado in this new administrative hierarchy reflected the dual function of its offices; every post from the *corregimiento*

---

[21] I have described these reforms in greater detail in chapter II of my Ph.D. dissertation, "Education and the State in Habsburg Spain" (Cambridge University, 1968) (cited
hereafter as "Education and the State"). See also El Conde de Torrenaz, *Los Consejos del
Rey Durante La Edad Media* (2 vols., Madrid, 1884), and José Antonio Maravall, "Los
hombres de saber o letrados y la formación de su conciencia estamental," *Estudios de
historia del pensamiento español* (Madrid, 1967), pp. 347-80.

to seats on the royal councils combined judicial with administrative duties, a combination which can be traced back to the origins of monarchical government itself. Inherent in the letrado's new position in the royal government was a medieval conception of kingship in which law-giving and justice were regarded as the primary function of the monarchy.[22] Moreover, it was in the financial and political interests of rulers to deploy a centralized system of justice based upon the imperial code of Justinian, which could work to supplant the existing jumble of local and feudal laws.

In order to restrict access to the new positions, the Catholic kings enacted on July 6, 1493 at Barcelona the following law:

"We order that no letrado can have any office or post of justice, investigator, or *relator* in our council, tribunals, or chancellories nor in any city, town, or village in our kingdom unless he has a notarized document certifying that he has studied canon or civil law for a minimum of ten years at a university in our kingdom or in foreign lands."[23]

For the universities of Castile this regulation, apparently unique in Renaissance Europe, with the exception of neighboring Portugal, had far-reaching consequences even though the requirement for ten full years of study was never enforced. The kingdom's highest educational institutions now had a formal, permanent link with the royal administration, since they were to be the sole source of its vital functionary, the letrado. And now that the monarchy had placed its confidence and its trust in the hands of the letrados, it began to look beyond them to the institutions in which they were trained, seeking to ensure high educational standards.

In the late fifteenth century royal supervision of university life was a thing of the past. Though Alfonso X and other thirteenth-century monarchs had been active in the creation and support of the estudios generales, the chaotic and war-torn years of the fourteenth and fifteenth centuries weakened royal power, enabling the papacy to gain virtual control over Spain's universities.[24] Rome's influence reached its apogee in 1420 when Martin V issued new statutes for Salamanca, a university previously subject to royal government and control.[25] The papacy continued to hold the upper hand until the reign of the Catholic kings, then the monarchy's newly acquired powers of clerical patronage and the need to train skilled officials of its own prompted royal intervention into university life. Much more than in the past, it was in the interests of the mon-

---

[22]On law and the medieval monarchy, see J. A. Strayer, *The Medieval Origins of the Modern State* (Princeton, 1970).

[23]*Nueva Recopilación de las Leyes de España (1566)* (Alcalá de Henares, 1569), Lib. III, tit. ix, ley 2.

[24]See V. Beltrán de Heredia, *Bulario de la Universidad de Salamanca* (3 vols., Salamanca, 1966–67), esp. the Introduction.

[25]These have been published in Esperabé Artega, *Historia Pragmática é Interna de la Universidad de Salamanca* (Salamanca, 1914), vol. 1.

archy to take a larger share in the regulation and support of higher education, a policy consistent with Queen Isabel's own interest in Renaissance learning and which apparently induced the rulers to offer financial aid to sons of noblemen and royal officials who were at university.[26]

The beginnings of this new era of monarchical control over Castile's universities can be traced to the Cortes of Toledo in 1480 when Ferdinand and Isabel ordered all letrados who had graduated after 1464 to certify the legitimacy of their academic titles before the Royal Council of Castile; increases in the student population and new positions for letrados had apparently led to false certificates of study and degrees.[27] This order was followed by a series of decrees designed to fix matriculation and graduation fees, ensure legitimate examinations and degrees, and to end corruption in the system through which students elected their instructors.[28] The purpose of these laws is evident: a desire by the monarchy to secure quality education in order to ensure quality churchmen and letrados. Subsequently, the royal decree replaced the papal bull as the supreme arbiter of university life,[29] and these institutions, as in the case of universities in the north of Europe, became the servants of kings, national churches, and national culture, as popes, the Church Universal, and the international culture of the humanists were ousted from academic life.

Accordingly, Castile's rulers, no longer faced by papal opposition, were free to intervene directly into university affairs, both to regulate and to recruit. Goaded by a Cortes eager to maintain the order of university life,[30] the crown judged academic disputes, ordered new statutes, appointed university officials, and with its own concerns in mind, demanded contributions for the royal war-chest and broke university regulations whenever it saw fit.[31] The universities, dependent upon the monarchy for judicial protection, tax exemptions, and permission to alter founding statutes, were obliged to conform to standards and rulings set independently by the crown. By mid-century royal intervention in collegiate and university affairs was routine; thus when Philip II in 1559 forbade Spanish students to study abroad except in certain "safe," Catholic areas in order to prevent the spread of heresy to his Iberian kingdoms,[32] he completed a process that had been under way since the time of the Catholic kings—the "nationalization" of education so that it could serve the interests of the state no matter what they might be. In this regard, the subsequent history

[26]See p. 183.
[27]Cortes de Toledo, 1480, ley. 108.
[28]*Nueva Recopilación*, Libro I, tit. vi, leyes 5, 16, 17.
[29]Beltrán de Heredia, *Bulario*, I: 180.
[30]See, for example, the Cortes de Madrid, 1528, pet. 49; Cortes de Madrid, 1534, pet. 126; Cortes de Valladolid, 1555, pets. cix, cxiii; Cortes de Madrid, 1563, pet. xxvi.
[31]Esperabé Artega, *Universidad de Salamanca*, vol. 1, publishes much of this university's official correspondence, including royal orders and pragmatics of university administration and government.
[32]These were the universities in Bologna, Rome, Naples, and Coimbra.

of the universities of Castile was to a large degree determined by the history of the monarchy itself.

part II
OFFICE AND HONOR

chapter 4
INCENTIVES TO STUDY

Castile before the nineteenth century had a wide variety of students, each with different reasons for matriculating at Salamanca or Seville. Alongside grandees, few of whom bothered to acquire university titles and degrees, were the preprofessionals, grinding through the long course toward a doctorate. These two types represented opposite poles; the majority of students were somewhere in between, but it is impossible to know exactly why they went to university. Their diaries are virtually nonexistent and their notebooks are yet to be found; thus what is known about the reasons why these youths chose to study comes mainly from what others said about them. Such sources, however, are commonly distorted and exaggerated; the old, the adult, in any age, have a tendency to put forward gross generalizations, even total misconceptions about the goals and motivations of the young. But it is curious that contemporaries in sixteenth-century Castile, many of whom were university graduates themselves, shared one opinion as to why students went to university. They were unanimous in their appraisal that students were interested primarily in the jobs to which academic titles could lead. The term they used was *premio* or reward, meaning an office in the civil service or the church or merely a pension or income of some sort. If this strong sense of "careerism" existed in Habsburg Spain, it was not peculiar to the university; one historian a few years ago used the term "empleomania" in order to describe the strong perference seventeenth-century Spaniards displayed for careers in public office.[1] In part empleomania is symptomatic of a society in which the dominant upper- and middle-class values are "aristocratic" in the sense that manual labor and commercial enterprise are demeaned while that of the *rentier* is applauded, even if the rentier's income is derived from office rather than land. Furthermore, it is symptomatic of a preindustrial, overwhelmingly agricultural economy in which the major employer of the small minority of males not engaged in food production, crafts, and other manual jobs is government, spiritual and secular. In Habsburg Spain neither industry nor trade was sufficiently developed to support more than a fraction of the nonlaboring population. Investment was limited largely to government finances, overseas trade, and, above all, land and a variety of public offices. It was toward these charges that university education led, since

---

[1] K. W. Swart, *The Sale of Offices in the Seventeenth Century* (The Hague, 1949), p. 32.

real estate, finance, and trade, at least in the sixteenth and seventeenth centuries, were never thought to require any formal education beyond that of literacy, numeracy, apprenticeship, and on-the-job experience.

Documentation for this "careerist" interpretation of university students in Castile is not overabundant, but a few quotations from contemporaries should prove the point. For example, in reference to students belonging to the colegios mayores, members of the Royal Council who were in charge of appointments to royal office advised Philip III that "they [the colegiales] see as the goal of their studies service to Your Royal Majesty and with this in mind, they spend their time and money in preparation, seeking only to be rewarded by Your Royal Hand and not by the practice of law."[2] These councillors, university graduates in their own right, consistently saw royal offices as the goal of the colegiales, and this view was shared by others less directly involved in the business of appointment. The Licentiate Mantilla, writing to Philip II in 1587 on the necessity of maintaining orderly self-government in the colleges, made the following suggestion: "The best means to achieve this end is for Your Majesty to dangle government posts in front of their eyes and then let them know that whatever news comes to Your Attention, the good will be rewarded, and the evil punished."[3] An anonymous statement in 1636, commenting upon whether the colegios mayores were under ecclesiastical or royal jurisdiction, put it this way: ". . . it appears that the principal aim of the colleges is more political than spiritual because most of the colegiales are training for Your Royal Service in secular posts."[4] Finally, Doctor Juan Queipo de Llano, president of the chancillería in Valladolid and a graduate of the Colegio Mayor de San Bartolomé, could be said to have summed up current opinions of the colegiales when he wrote: "the love of letters brings only a few to the colleges."[5]

Though members of the colegios mayores constituted only a small segment of the universities, countless ordinary students shared in their aspirations. This is at least the conclusion that could be drawn from the following statement written by the *Junta de Educación* in 1636. "Because they [the students] direct their studies towards the 'rewards,' both ecclesiastical and secular, that they hope to gain afterwards, the principle that must stimulate those within the university to work and to take advantage of their surroundings must be the just distribution of the 'rewards'."[6] Unfortunately, students' views on this question are difficult to obtain, but a brief reference as to why they sought academic titles may be found in a passage written in 1631 by a graduate of the College-University of Sancti

[2]*AHN: Cons. leg. 13529, consulta* of 6.IX.1608.
[3]IVDJ: Envío 90, folio 706.
[4]BUS: Ms. 1925, folio 21, "Discurso sobre si los Colegios Mayores son de la Jurisdicción Real o Pontífica . . . ," p. 24.
[5]AHN: Cons. leg. 7138, letter of 17.XI.1638.
[6]BUS: Ms. 2064, folio 8, Memorandum of the *Junta de Educación*, 12.I.1636.

Spiritus in Oñate: "Necessarily, I had to do some work in this noted college; but one day I knew that I had to leave it, and if I hoped to reach greater honors, I would have to imitate other great men who reached these prizes through their virtue and continuous work in their studies. In truth, I was not lacking in these motives in 1625 when I began to read a lesson from ten to eleven in addition to the obligation to read philosophy every morning and afternoon."[7]

Another glimpse into the student world lies in the famous 1617 work of Cristóbal Suárez de Figueroa, *El Passagero*.[8] In the advice which a physician gives his son about which university career to follow, "laws and canons," "a noble and illustrious profession, the heart and soul of the cities," receives the highest recommendation because of its "security of promotions." The father then comments on the ease with which the necessary degrees are earned and on the possibility of obtaining a "perpetual seat," meaning an office with life tenure, either in the "West," the Indies, or in one of the tribunals in Spain. These positions, the father claims, will supply anyone with all of his needs. And then hinting at the honors and riches that await law graduates who obtain the valued posts, he queries: "Is there anyone who does not want *Mayorazgos*, *Comendadores*, *Consejeros*, *Títulos*, if it is possible?" The wise father, however, soon died, and the son, a rather independent fellow, opts for theology "because of the secure rewards it customarily brings to its bearer in the competitions for professorships and high offices."

It seems reasonable, therefore, to consider the prospect of civil or ecclesiastical office or at least a career in one of the liberal professions as a strong inducement to higher education in Habsburg Spain. Naturally, not all students, particularly the offspring of leading noble families, shared in this careerism. Yet it would be difficult to dispute that the Castilian universities of the sixteenth and seventeenth centuries were filled with students lacking in professional aspirations. The remainder of this chapter is intended to outline the availability of such professional offices and careers, since the fluctuating prospects of employment were crucial to the changing fortunes of the universities in Castile.

The majority of government positions open to letrados were in a complex of offices that for want of a better description can be called the letrado hierarchy, that is, those positions which were subject to the ten-year rule on legal study set by Ferdinand and Isabel.[9] Its roots consisted of hundreds of lesser magisterial offices distributed among the towns of

---

[7]BUS: Ms. 1925, folio 172, letter of 27.VI.1631.

[8]Ed., Sociedad de Bibliofilos Españoles (Madrid, 1914), pp. 174–73.

[9]A more detailed description of the offices comprising the letrado hierarchy can be found in Kagan, "Education and The State," chap. III. Published works on the nature of government in Habsburg Spain include the short introduction by Dr. J. M. Batista i Roca to H. Koenigsberger, *The Government of Sicily under Philip II of Spain* (London, 1951) and M. J. Gounon-Loubens, *Essai sur l'Administration de la Castille au XVIe Siècle* (Paris, 1860). Also useful is M. Dánvila y Collado, *El Poder Civil en España* (6 vols. Madrid, 1885).

Castile, a variety of lesser judicial posts in the councils and tribunals of the crown, and what were called "temporal offices" of justice, positions in which the officers were appointed on a short-term, revolving basis. Among these temporal posts the only ones which did not belong exclusively to letrados were the *corregimientos*. In frontier and rebellious regions and in some of the larger cities, corregidores were men of a military background. Known as *capa y espada* officers, corregidores of this genre were obliged to have with them one or more letrado deputies to preside over matters of law and justice. Common in the early years of the sixteenth century when the monarchy was still insecure, these "unlettered" corregidores gradually disappeared.[10] By the seventeenth century, jurists, both as corregidores and deputies, dominated this class of offices.[11]

More senior positions in the letrado hierarchy comprised those offices known as the *plazas de asiento*, that is, offices with life tenure that provided the office-holder with retirement at half-pay after twenty years of service. They included the well-paid, influential magisterial positions of *oidor*, *fiscal*, and *alcalde* on all royal tribunals in Castile and the New World and were monopolized by letrados. Higher up were the positions on the letrado councils situated at the Royal Court, among them, the councils of Castile, *Cruzada*, Supreme Inquisition, Military Orders, and the *Contaduría Mayor de Hacienda* or Auditor's Office of the Exchequer. The Council of the Indies and the magistrates of its subordinate body, the *Casa de Contratación* (House of Trade) in Seville, were also part of Castile's letrado hierarchy, although this council, in response to demands for military expertise among its members, admitted a number of capa y espada (literally, cape and sword, i.e., noble) members in the seventeenth century. Acting much like a council were the supreme criminal magistracies of Castile, the *Alcaldes de Casa y Corte*, all of whom were letrados. The Council of Italy was also a letrado council but outside the sphere of Castilian government, as was another letrado preserve, the Council of Aragón.

The Castilian church and the inquisition also reserved numerous positions for letrados. After the early sixteenth century most of the cathedral clergy were university graduates, and parish churches in the larger cities went also to priests holding university degrees. Judgeships on the local tribunals of the inquisition located in Spain, Spanish possessions in Europe, and the New World were for letrados as well, while the

---

[10]In 1512 less than one-half of Castile's corregidores were letrados (Tarsicio de Azcona, *Isabel la Católica* [Madrid, 1964], p. 343), but by the middle of the sixteenth century their share of this class of offices had risen to over 60 percent (BM: Add. 28352, ff. 95–95v; Add. 28353, folio 104).

[11]By the eighteenth century *capa y espada corregidores* numbered only seventeen, that is, less than 25 percent of the officers occupying these posts. See Domínguez Ortiz, *La Sociedad Española en el Siglo XVIII* (Madrid, 1955), p. 35. For a survey of the history of the corregidor in Castile, see B. González Alonso, *El Corregidor Castellano (1348–1808)* (Madrid, 1970).

important office of Inquisitor General alternated between graduates in theology and in canon law.[12]

Letrado positions in government, the inquisition, and the church were not the only public charges open to university graduates in law. These offices were unique in that they were exclusively reserved for letrados, but countless other royal and municipal offices, most of which entailed few judicial duties, might employ law graduates, although they were never obliged to do so on a regular basis. Credentials for these charges rested primarily on an individual's money and family ties as well as his "prudence, virtue, skills, and experience." University never became a formal requirement for these posts, although literacy and, increasingly, Latin were essential.[13]

These "non-letrado" offices numbered in the thousands and comprised the bulk of the civil service at every level of Castilian government. Collectively they can be known as the "capa y espada" hierarchy.[14] The duties of this hierarchy were so diverse as to defy easy description: diplomacy, war, taxation, municipal government and police, and the regulation of virtually everything that could be regulated. At the top stood the Council of State presided over by the king and where leading letrado officials mingled with grandees, cardinals, and military men; at bottom was the lowly castle warden, the inspector of weights and measures in a market town, the porter in a town hall.

Few of this hierarchy's recruits were letrados. Many may have attended university, perhaps even taken a first degree, but only a handful remained for the post-graduate studies and advanced academic titles that placed letrados into a world of their own. One must keep in mind that letrados were able to acquire capa y espada offices through purchase or from the crown in return for services rendered, but for the most part the capa y espada hierarchy was not interested in university graduates, particularly those in law. Consequently, it remained open to men of diverse educational backgrounds and qualifications. The letrado hierarchy, on the other hand, set apart from the bulk of administrative offices through its special educational requirements, developed in the course of Habsburg rule a close relationship with Castile's universities, the institutions which alone supplied its personnel.

---

[12]Julio Caro Baroja, *El señor inquisidor y otras por oficio* (Madrid, 1968), pp. 18–23, sketches the education and career of an "ideal" inquisitor, emphasizing his legal background.

[13]Latin was certainly required for the important post of secretary of state; cf. José Antonio Escudero, *Los Secretarios de Estado y del Despacho* (Madrid, 1969), 2: 388–94.

[14]See Kagan, "Education and the State," chap. III.

chapter 5
THE LETRADO HIERARCHY

On the eve of the Habsburg accession to the Spanish monarchy the structure of the letrado hierarchy was nearly complete and the path to future administrative development in the Indies had been laid. Loyal to the collegiate principle of government set by the Catholic kings, Charles V and his successors kept their basic administrative inheritance intact, expanding old councils and tribunals when necessary, adding new ones in response to changing administrative and territorial demands.[1] The elaboration and refinement of the letrado hierarchy was matched by an expansion in the total number of letrados in the crown's employ (Table 3).[2] These increases abated only at the end of the sixteenth century, when advances in the Castilian economy and population had also come to a halt.

Similarly, the expansion of letrado places in the New World, the inquisition, and the church was largely a phenomenon of the sixteenth century. The legal tribunals of the Indies, implemented in the course of the sixteenth century, rarely expanded above their original complement of men,[3] and the history of the local tribunals of the inquisition was much the same.[4] There is also evidence to suggest that Castile's cathedral clergy, sharing in the general prosperity of the era, expanded in the course of the sixteenth century, while in the following century, an epoch marked by economic difficulties and decline, it suffered from stagnation or, at best, marginal growth.[5]

[1] Ibid.

[2] Ibid.

[3] Among the nine American *audiencias* which had been created in the sixteenth century, only those at Lima and Mexico City, both of which had increased from their original complement of four places to eight, had grown significantly since the time of their foundation. See BNM: ms. 1447, "Memorial y Resumen Breve De Noticias De Las Indias . . . ," (Madrid, 1654) and E. Schäefer, *El Real y Supremo Consejo de las Indias* (Seville, 1947), vol. II.

[4] Most of these tribunals were established in the late fifteenth and early sixteenth centuries and were originally staffed by three senior letrado officials—two *oidores* and a *fiscal*—along with a letrado assessor. Added to these officials were theological and other legal advisors, a physician, a *juez de bienes* to determine the value of confiscated goods, and an *abogado de fisco* to settle financial problems. By the middle of the seventeenth century these tribunals had each added no more than one or two letrado places, although the subaltern, largely *capa y espada* staff had expanded significantly. See Henry Kamen, *The Spanish Inquisition* (London, 1965), pp. 143–44, and AHN: Inq., lib. 323, "Relacion de la Personal . . . 1666–67."

[5] At least this is what happened to the cathedral chapters of Ávila, Granada, and Salamanca. The number of canonries in each expanded during the early sixteenth century and then leveled off (see Archivo de la Cathedral de Granada: Libros Capitulares; Archivo de la Cathedral de Salamanca: Calandario; and J. P. López-Arévalo, *Un Cabildo Catedral de la Vieja Castilla: Ávila, Su Estructura Jurídica, siglos XIII–XIX* [Madrid, 1966], p. 78).

Table 3. Plazas de Asiento in Castile, 1500-1700

Council or Tribunal	1500	1566	1601	1691
Royal Council of Castile	13	16	18	21
Indies	—	9	13	14
Military Orders	4	5	5	8
Supreme Inquisition	3	5	7	9
Finance	—	6	6	6
Alcaldes of the Court	4	4	9	8
Valladolid	12	26	26	28
Granada	8	25	25	27
Seville	—	11	12	14
Navarre	—	11	12	12
Galicia	4	6	6	9
Canaries	—	4	4	4
House of Trade	—	2	3	4
Misc. Fiscales at Court	—	2	2	2
	48	132	148	166

[a]Council presidencies are not included in these figures, since nonletrado officials often occupied them.

[b]Capa y espada councillors of the Indies are not included in these figures.

Source: ACV: Libros de Acuerdo, libs. 2, 6; AGS: Comiseria de Cruzada, leg. 516; CMC, 1ª época, leg. 1587, 1697; CMC, 2ª época, leg. 461, 467; NC, leg. 1–4; AHN: Cons., lib. 724, 731; Inquisición, lib. 246, 284, 577, 1246; BM: Sloan Ms. 3610, f. 8v, "Relación de los Consejeros de las Ordenes Militares." AHN: Ordenes Militares: MS. Consejo, Sign. 1286 C. J. J. Salcedo Izu, *El Consejo Real de Navarra en el Siglo XVI* (Pamplona, 1962), App. V. E. Schäefer, *El Consejo Real y Supremo de Indias* (Seville, 1935), 1:240, 246, 263.

The absence of accurate figures and accounts does not allow for a precise estimate of the total number of letrado places available at any one time in Castile. Far too little is known about local government and the rank-and-file of the church to make any estimate more than a roughly calculated guess. In terms of the letrado hierarchy alone the crown in the early seventeenth century offered about 150 *plazas de asiento* on the tribunals and councils of Castile, and if these same places on the *audiencias* of the Indies are included, the total rises to about 225. But these high offices represented only a fraction of the total number of letrado offices in the crown's gift. The subordinate letrado personnel of the councils and tribunals, the corregidores and their deputies, and miscellaneous judicial officers probably accounted for another 200 places. In total, the King was

In the seventeenth-century diocesan rents in many areas of Castile were in decline. Presumably, this did not allow for the expansion of the cathedral clergy (see Marquis de Saltillo, "Prelados de Osma en el Siglo XVII, 1613–82," *Celtiberia* 6 (1953): 177–90, and "Prelados de Badajoz en el Siglo XVII," *Revista de Estudios Extremeños* 8 (1952): 157–82). Fr. Manuel Risco, *Iglesia de León, y Monasterios Antiguous y Modernos de la Misma Ciudad* (Madrid, 1792), p. 35, notes that by the mid-eighteenth century the number of prebends in the cathedral of León had declined from 55 to 40. If such a pattern holds true for Castile's other dioceses, then the seventeenth century was almost certainly an epoch of decline or stagnation for the cathedral clergy.

responsible for the appointment of approximately 400 to 500 letrado officials, and if one includes subordinate letrado positions in the New World,
then this figure should be raised substantially. Such an estimate, however,
does not include municipal offices such as *alcadías*, many of which were
reserved for letrados. These may have amounted to several hundred places
for the Crown of Castile alone.[6]

To letrado positions in the government must be added those in the
inquisition and the church. Inquisitors did not have to be clerics, and the
Holy Office offered between seventy and eighty senior magisterial positions to qualified letrados, and perhaps twice that figure if lesser legal
officials in the inquisition's employ are considered. The task of estimating
the number of letrado positions in the church is more troublesome. According to Antonio Domínguez Ortiz, the cathedral clergy in Castile
around 1630 included 343 dignitaries and 928 canons, in addition to thirty-
five offices of archbishop and bishop, most of whom were letrados.[7] To
this group—the "intellectual elite of the clergy"—must be added priests in
the larger towns, royal chaplains, important priors, and similar high-
ranking ecclesiastical officers who were always university-trained men.
Moreover, if positions in Castile were filled, a cleric could always migrate
to the New World.

Employment opportunities for letrados, however, were not limited to
offices in the ruling hierarchies alone. Hundreds of places existed for law
graduates as *abogados*—Spain's equivalent of the barrister—in the royal
councils, tribunals, and municipal courts, even though there seems to have
been a sharp drop in their number after the opening years of the seventeenth century.[8] Abogados had considerable opportunities for wealth and
the legal profession was itself considered "noble,"[9] a fact not unconnected
with its popularity and prestige. Qualified abogados, particularly in the

[6]J. M. Batista i Roca in Koenigsberger, *Government of Sicily*, p. 31, estimated that
Castile in the early seventeenth century had 530 judicial offices. Though firm evidence is
still lacking, it would appear that his estimate is far too low.

[7]Domínguez Ortiz, *Sociedad Española*, 2: 39.

[8]The number of registered *abogados* at the *chancillerías* of Granada and Valladolid
increased sharply in the course of the sixteenth century, reaching a peak in the 1580s and
1590s when there were no less than forty-nine abogados inscribed in the Libros de Acuerdos
of the latter, nearly twice as many as a half century before (ACV: Libros de Acuerdos).
Then, after criticism about parasitic abogados and the high costs of justice, Philip III
ordered a cut in the number of barristers who would be allowed to plead before the tribunals
and councils of the crown (BNM: Ms. 12179, folios 76–79). By the end of the seventeenth century, as few as twelve abogados were registered at the chancillería of Valladolid. The number of abogados licensed to practice in the royal councils in Madrid fell in the twenty years
following Philip III's edict, but recruitment into that city's Colegio de Abogados rose thereafter, although never to a point equal to that of the century's opening decade. Between 1600
and 1609, for example, 104 abogados were admitted into this "college"; cf. Pedro Barbadillo
Delgado, *Historia del Ilustre Colegio de Abogados de Madrid* (Madrid, 1956), 1: 177–223.

[9]For the rules and regulations of the legal profession in Spain, see Pérez y Lopez,
Theatro de la Legislación Universal de España y las Indias, vol. 1, "Abogado." Bennassar,
Valladolid au Siècle d'Or (Paris, 1967), p. 368 gives an indication of the substantial salaries
successful lawyers could earn.

sixteenth century, were able to assume regular offices, making the profession a promising stopover for ambitious men on the way up. In addition, jurists could hope to teach at a university. Teaching posts at large universities such as Salamanca and Valladolid were well-paid, prestigious, and much in demand.[10] Alternatively, Castile's litigious city councils, cathedrals, guild corporations, and other public institutions, along with wealthy private individuals were accustomed to retain legal advisers on a permanent basis, and positions such as these were always available in Castile and the New World.

In sum, opportunities for letrados were substantial. The majority of these positions, however, were either created or set aside for letrados in the era between the reign of the Catholic kings and the opening of the seventeenth century. Previously, the letrado was a marginal figure in Castilian society, a learned specialist, represented in a few small universities and a handful of places in the cathedral chapters, monasteries, and courts of law. But thanks to Ferdinand and Isabel and the Habsburgs, he acquired a central position in Castile, and as his numbers increased, so did his political influence and social prestige. Once regarded as a mere clerk, base and low-born, scorned by the prevailing aristocratic standards of the day, the letrado, through his offices, gradually assumed an important place on Castile's social ladder. In Valladolid, for example, the letrados of the chancillería ranked, through their salaries, investments, and loans, among that city's wealthiest inhabitants.[11] And at a time when money more and more helped to determine (or at least buy or marry into) social status, much of the increasing prestige of letrados rested upon their wealth.

In the first instance their fortunes were based upon their salaries. An *oidor* on a royal audiencia in the middle of the sixteenth century earned 150,000 mrs. a year, and this sum was augmented by as much as one-half by an annual *ayuda de costa*. Salaries, moreover, kept pace with, perhaps ahead of, the price rise. By 1600 oidores in Valladolid earned over 300,000 mrs. a year, while inquisitors in 1679 collected as much as 500,000 mrs. apiece.[12] Already substantial salaries were then boosted by the incalculable sums letrados clandestinely received in the form of bribes, gifts, kickbacks, embezzlement, and the like. And inasmuch as letrados were exempt from royal levies and taxes, the riches they earned they kept or spent or invested in land, government bonds and annuities, trade and finance. "Letters were a path to wealth,"[13] and there is no doubt that in Habsburg Spain, an epoch when, as Quevedo admitted, "*Poderoso caballero es Don Dinero* [A Powerful Knight Is Sir Money]," no other occupation or career offered such possibilities for economic and social advancement.

[10]See below, pp. 164–65.
[11]Bennassar, *Valladolid*, pp. 247–50, 357, 365–66.
[12]AHN: Inq. lib. 271, folio 646.
[13]Bennassar, *Valladolid*, p. 357.

It was the latter which gave the letrado's career its maximum value. In Habsburg government, a life-time of office-holding led to periodic promotions but no annual increments in pay. Instead kings rewarded their loyal officials with *mercedes*, a catchall rubric for a cash grant; the right to establish a *mayorazgo*, a fee-paying office; permission to make a certain office part of a family's inheritance; pensions; membership and *encomiendas* in one of Spain's military orders; or, most cherished of all, patents and titles of nobility. Such honors were never reserved for letrados, but letrados received their share. The expansion in the number of aristocratic titles in Castile after 1600, for example, was to a significant but unknown extent the result of letrados turned *títulos*. Among them was the first Count of Villaoquina who was previously a professor of law at Salamanca and had later held letrado offices on the audiencia of Seville, the chancillería at Vallodolid, the Council of the Cruzada, and, finally, the Royal Council of Castile.[14] The advancement of Diego de Riano y Gamboa was also typical of this new class of titled nobles; first a doctor in canon law from the University of Salamanca, he was named *fiscal* of Valladolid in 1619, then oidor in Granada, fiscal and oidor on the Royal Council of Castile, president of Valladolid's chancillería, General Commissioner of the Cruzada, and, at the end of his life, president of the Royal Council of Castile, the kingdom's first office. In reward for his lifetime of letrado service, he was named Viscount of Villagonzalo de Pedernales in 1658.[15] The Counts of Ayanz, Boadilla, Castroponce, Ervias, Francos, Fuente el Salce, Gomarra, Grasnedo, and Guaro, along with the Marquises of Almodovar, Chiluebes, Palacios, Rosa, Vega del Pozo, and Villagarcía were others who earned their titles in much the same way.[16] But as no systematic study of Castile's new nobility exists, it is impossible to determine the extent to which titled families in seventeenth-century Castile were also letrado families, or how long it took for those families to secure their rewards. Nevertheless, it is indisputable that a sizable percentage of Castile's new titled families were of letrado backgrounds. Like her neighbor to the north, Castile in the seventeenth century acquired a "nobility of the robe." In Castile's case, however, the term "aristocracy of the robe" might be more apt, since so many of the new títulos were *hidalgos* (i.e., lesser nobles) at the start.

The established aristocracy, jealous of their prerogatives and afraid of losing influence at court, resented these letrado upstarts, although this did not prevent them from marrying into letrado families for reasons of political power and wealth. In the course of time the older aristocracy also

---

[14]See L. Ferrer Ezquerra and H. Misol García, *Catálogo de Colegiales del Colegio Mayor de Santiago del Cebedeo, del Arzobispo de Salamanca* (Salamanca, 1956), no. 328.

[15]He subsequently became Count of Villariezo; see Domínguez Ortiz, *Sociedad Española*, 1: 40.

[16]These promotions are cited in the student registers of the colegios mayores; see p. 125, note 24.

directed some of their sons, the younger ones in particular, onto the path of letters and offices. Pedro Núñez de Guzmán, son of the Marquis of Montealegre, brother of the Marquis of Camarasa, became a councillor of Castile after a long letrado career beginning at the University of Salamanca. Pedro de Cortés, grandson of the conqueror of Mexico, son of the second Marquis del Valle, rose through a variety of letrado offices to become fiscal on the Council of the Military Orders. The Dukes of Albuquerque, Cardona, Feria, and Gandía, the Counts of Medellín and Salvatierra, along with many other título and grandee families launched one or more of their sons on similar office-holding careers. Rare before the later sixteenth century, the increase in the number of sons of títulos turned letrados was linked to the possibilities of wealth and power that letrados could achieve.

Not all letrados, however, were alike. The royal councillor with powerful court connections was far removed—geographically, culturally, socially, and financially—from the *abogado* in Almería or the *alcalde* in Andúxar. In this group, the gradations of office, influence, and wealth were many and far apart. The elite represented those who held the valuable *plazas de asiento*, and these were the positions to which most letrados, from the lowly investigator (*pesquisidor*) in Galicia to the oidores in Lima and Mexico City aspired. Such plums were the goal, the acme of the letrado's career, but they were scarce, the competition was intense, and as the decades went by, the standards upon which this letrado elite was selected gradually restricted these places to a privileged circle of families. This contraction in turn affected the whole of the letrado's world, from the university to the Royal Council of Castile.

chapter 6
RECRUITMENT TO OFFICE

When the letrado hierarchy was still in its infancy, that is, during the reign of the Catholic kings, chroniclers tell us that the rulers were able to make letrado appointments themselves. According to one account, Ferdinand and Isabel carried with them a little book in which they jotted down the names of persons qualified for office whom they happened to meet in their travels. When a vacancy occurred, they had only to consult this book to find the right man.[1] However romanticized, this picture of Ferdinand and Isabel making their appointments directly, without the formal help of intermediaries, suggests that the rulers themselves were able to set the standards through which letrados would gain access to royal office. These were relatively straightforward. Office-holders were required to be at least twenty-six years of age (twenty-five was the legal age of majority), to have studied jurisprudence for the requisite number of years at a recognized university, and, after 1505, to be versed in the laws of the realm.[2] Before assuming their posts, officials were to be examined by the Royal Council, but it is questionable whether these examinations were always carried out.

In many instances these educational criteria took precedence over those of geography, racial background, and social rank. Despite protests from Castilians, "foreigners" from the Crown of Aragón were known to have assumed important places in Castilian government, and even qualified *conversos*—notably Doctors Micer Alfonso de la Caballería and Cabrero, both members of the Royal Council—gained access to letrado posts.[3] Furthermore, it was possible for a letrado of lowly origin to assume important posts in the royal government. The councillors Pedro de Oropesa, Palacios-Rubios, and Toribio Gómez de Santiago came from "peasant stock," although most of the royal councillors belonged to Castile's large noble but often poor and landless *hidalgo* class.[4] Doctor

---

[1]See Galíndez de Carvajal, "Anales Breves del Reinado de los Reyes Cathólicos," *CODOIN*, 18: 229, 235. I have outlined the procedures through which letrado officials were appointed in greater detail in Kagan, "Education and the State," chap. IV.

[2]*Neuva Recopilación*, Lib. III, tit. ix, ley 2; Cortes de Toro, 1505, ley 2.

[3]See Kamen, *Spanish Inquisition*, pp. 19–20. Galíndez de Carvajal, "Informe que . . . dío al Emperador Carlos V . . . ," *CODOIN*, 1: 124.

[4]See ibid., pp. 122–27; Torrenaz, *Los Consejos del Rey Durante La Edad Media* (Madrid, 1884), 1: 199ff; and AGS: NC, leg. 1.

Galíndez de Carvajal, a royal councillor himself, wrote that the Catholic kings appointed "skilled, prudent persons even though they were of the middle classes,"[5] while Diego Hurtado de Mendoza, writing in the mid-sixteenth century, said: "The Catholic Kings placed the administration of justice and public affairs into the hands of letrados, people mid-way between the great and the small . . . whose profession was the law."[6] Apparently, technical skills and individual merit in the era of the Catholic kings determined nomination to letrado posts more than family tradition or distinguished birth.

With employment therefore resting largely upon a university education in jurisprudence, the burden of training the crown's letrados fell directly upon Castile's leading universities: Salamanca and Valladolid. Graduates from these institutions dominated the magistracy, and from time to time professors left their university chairs for the more lucrative and honored places offered by the crown. Lorenzo Galíndez de Carvajal, who left his professorship at Salamanca in 1504 for a place on the Royal Council of Castile, is a case in point.[7]

Among the new graduates employed by the crown, those from the Colegio Mayor de San Bartolomé at Salamanca attracted special attention. Noted for its high academic standards, rigid discipline, and a tradition of training civil and ecclesiastical officials, this small college provided Ferdinand and Isabel with no fewer than eight royal councillors, six bishops, and numerous lesser officials.[8] With this outstanding record, it is little wonder that a contemporary proverb stated: "all the world is filled with the sons of San Bartolomé."[9]

After the deaths of the Catholic kings and their immediate successor, the Cardinal-Regent Cisneros, Castile's direct, personal methods of appointment gradually disappeared. The rapid expansion of the Spanish dominions and the size of royal government rendered the old procedures obsolete. Charles V was always on the move, frequently far away from Castile, and the business of letrado appointments fell to the president of the Royal Council of Castile and the royal secretary, Francisco de los Cobos. Together they gathered the necessary information and prepared short memoranda or *consultas* which outlined the merits of prospective candidates for offices. From these consultas the monarch made the final choice. After the death of Cobos in 1547, the presidents of the Royal

[5]Galíndez de Carvajal, "Anales Breves . . . ," p. 229.

[6]Diego Hurtado de Mendoza, *Guerra de Granada*, ed. *Biblioteca de Autores Españoles*, 21 (Madrid, 1852), p. 70.

[7]See Esperabé Artega, *Historia Pragmática é Interna de la Universidad de Salamanca* (Salamanca, 1914), 1: 356–361. For more about Galíndez de Carvajal, see Beltrán de Heredia, *Cartulario de la Universidad de Salamanca* (Salamanca, 1971), 3: 283–96.

[8]See AGS: NC. leg. 1 and Roxas y Contreras, *Historia del Colegio Viejo de San Bartolomé* (3 vols., Madrid, 1766), vol. 1, which lists San Bartolomé's students and the offices they held.

[9]Cited in Reynier, *La Vie Universitaire dans l'Ancienne Espagne* (Paris, 1902), p. 182.

Council were obliged to prepare the consultas alone, although during much of the reign of Philip II, Mateo Vázquez, one of the king's favored secretaries, frequently intervened in this work.[10]

Although the basic criteria of recruitment set by the Catholic kings were never formally altered during the reigns of Charles V and his son, they narrowed as the letrado officials who gained control of appointments sought to recruit men of backgrounds similar to their own. This quest for homogeneity, so typical of sixteenth-century Castilian life, tended to sacrifice appointments made solely upon individual merits and skills without regard to birth, blood, or social origin; indeed, in the long run, this quest gradually undermined the ideals set by the Catholic kings.

One of the first results of this contraction was a "Castilianization" of letrado government in Castile. Following the disruptive series of revolts known as the *Comunero* risings (1520–21), disturbances which were themselves partially directed against the presence of Flemish officials at the Castilian court of Charles V, "foreigners" from Spain's eastern kingdoms and other parts of the empire were excluded from the central government of Castile.[11] Completed by the 1540s, this policy of territorial segregation remained in effect over the following centuries, helping to promote mutual suspicion and distrust within the kingdom of Spain, particularly in the years leading up to the revolts of Catalonia and Portugal in 1640.

Parallel with the drive against territorial "foreigners" was that against "foreigners" of religion and blood. The reign of Charles V brought the century-old persecution of conversos to a head, and this problem mingled with fears of Lutheran infiltration in Spain. First those whose forefathers were brought before the inquisition were excluded from official posts,[12] then a movement to ban from public office anyone of converso lineage, by guilt of ancestry alone, gathered strength. Despite opposition, Spain's cathedrals, beginning with Toledo's ruling of 1547, barred conversos from their offices.[13] In secular posts, custom rather than statutes had the same effect.[14] Though individuals of questionable lineage, or those who had managed to hide that fact, still received appointments from time to time, by the end of the century such officials were few and re-

[10]See Kagan, "Education and the State," chap. IV and Escudero, *Secretarios*, vol. I, pp. 187–93.

[11]One of the leading proponents of this policy was the president of the chancillería of Valladolid, Diego Ramírez de Villaescusa, Bishop of Málaga, who advised the new monarch to fill the posts of each of his kingdoms with natives of the region, "Castile for the Castilians, those of Aragon for the Aragonese, those of Flanders for the Flemish, and those of Germany for the Germans, because this conforms with reason . . ." (Olmedo, *Diego Ramírez de Villaescusa 1459–1537* [Madrid, 1944], p. 118).

[12]See Kamen, *Spanish Inquisition*, pp. 120–21.

[13]Ibid., p. 123. Also useful is A. A. Sicroff, *Les Controverses des Statuts "Pureté de Sang" en Espagne du XVe au XVIIe Siècle* (Paris, 1960).

[14]"Purity of blood" became a vital qualification for office, as the following exerpt from a *consulta* of Cardinal Tavera, president of the Royal Council (1534–39), to Charles V suggests: "It is essential to have Old Christians as Councillors of the Indies because *conversos* will not give good counsel" (AGS: EE, leg. 13, folio 43).

garded with suspicion and distrust. In 1590, for example, Philip's secretary, Mateo Vázquez, reviewing a consulta on openings in the Royal Council, advised: "It is a pity that Agustín Alvarez is not considered to be pure of blood because . . . I consider him the best of all possible candidates."[15] Needless to say, Alvarez did not receive the post.

The triumph of *limpieza de sangre* within the royal administration was only one manifestation of the general contraction in the criteria of appointment. Educational requirements faced a new, more stringent interpretation as well. As more and more letrados clamored for office, standards were raised, turning most of the applicants away. There were, of course, exceptions and oversights as the following petition, read in the Cortes of 1548, suggests: "We beg Your Majesty to enforce the laws which stipulate that no letrado shall receive an office unless he has studied ten years in a university, because, by not enforcing it, the nation suffers when young men of little experience and letters hold important posts of justice."[16] And though it may be true that a few letrados entered government posts with less than the required training, especially in the lesser temporal offices of justice, most evidence suggests that the standards for recruitment were on the rise. During the reign of the Catholic kings, for example, *bachilleres*, that is, students holding a first degree, were fairly common in important letrado posts,[17] but in the course of the following century they disappeared; advanced graduates, licentiates, and doctors, enjoyed a monopoly.[18] Such a change was indicative of a "professionalization" of letrado government that was introduced largely at the initiative of the letrados themselves. Those in high office made sure that the king appointed only the advanced and supposedly competent students from the swelling crowd of university graduates. And, consequently, as men with these qualifications reached positions with a say in the distribution of office, they made certain that new recruits were of backgrounds similar to their own.

Such considerations led to a preference for university instructors. Throughout the Middle Ages professors of law in Castile had served as legal advisors for the crown, but after the development of the letrado hierarchy, they were at a premium. More and more professors, lured by the lucrative offices offered by the crown, abandoned the universities. During the reign of Charles V ex-professors constituted approximately one-fifth of the letrados named to the Royal Council of Castile and the

[15]BM: Add. 28,263, folio 544.
[16]Cortes de Valladolid, 1548, pet. 38.
[17]For lists of these officials see AGS: NC, leg. 1; CMC, 1ª época, leg. 1587. Between 1480 and 1517 there were at least 18 bachilleres who served on the Royal Council of Castile and the chancillerías of Granada and Valladolid.
[18]In 1529 a Bachiller Miranda appeared as an *alcalde de crimen* on the chancillería of Valladolid for five months, probably in the absence of another magistrate. Two years later Miranda was officially named to this post, but on this occasion he was listed as a licentiate; ACV: Libros de Acuerdos.

chancillería of Valladolid, and by the reign of Philip II they accounted for as many as 40 percent of the men elected to the *plazas de asiento* of Castile.[19]

On a par with the professors were the graduates of the colegios mayores. These communities, famous for their rigid purity of blood statutes and high academic standing, must have been an ideal source for royal officials, and their reputation was enhanced by the large number of university instructors included among their members. Such credentials assured the colegiales of a high place on the monarchy's list of preferred graduates, and former members of the colegios mayores, already in government offices, provided an extra push (Table 4). Those in important positions served as living examples of the high-caliber officials the colleges could produce, and, in addition, they openly praised their *almae matres* while actively favoring fellow colegiales in the distribution of office. An incident of this nature took place in 1543 when Pablo de Talavera, a member of the Colegio Mayor de Santa Cruz (Valladolid), accepted the see of the Puebla de los Angeles in the New World. He was said to have received this appointment when he was still a student "by his own merits and the favor of our colegial, don Sebastian Ramírez, Bishop of Cuenca, who had much influence in the business of the Indies."[20] The College of Santa Cruz had another influencial graduate—Toribio Alfonso Mogrovejo, Archbishop of Lima. His letter in 1589 to his old college reads: ". . . please inform me . . . about the appointments which the college receives and employ me in your service for that will give me great satisfaction as a son of that Holy House whose prosperity I much desire. Licentiates Salinas and Carillo who have come to these regions and about whom I received letters from the college, I have accommodated with visitations in this archbishopric worth 500 pesos apiece."[21] This service, however, was not rendered without strings. Mogrovejo went on to thank the college for admitting his relative, the Licentiate Villagómez, to a scholarship.

The powerful presidents of the Royal Council of Castile also extended their favor to colegio mayor graduates. The Marquis of Mondéjar, neither a colegial nor a letrado, supposedly advised Philip II to appoint colegiales,[22] and Cardinal Espinosa maintained close ties with his old College of Cuenca in Salamanca, which sent him lists of colegiales available for office.[23] Espinosa's affection for the colegios mayores was also put

---

[19]I arrived at these estimates by matching my own lists of tribunal and counciliar magistrates in Habsburg Spain (Kagan, "Education and the State," chap. V) with published lists of instructors at the universities of Salamanca (Esperabé Artega, *Universidad de Salamanca*, vol. 2) and Valladolid (Alcocer Martínez, *Historia de la Universidad de Valladolid* [6 vols., Madrid, 1918–31], vol. 3). Since similar lists of instructors for Castile's other universities are generally not available; these estimates may well be too low.
[20]BSC: Ms. 174, no. 176.
[21]Ibid., folios 31–31v.
[22]Roxas y Contreras, *Colegio Viejo*, 2: 319.
[23]BM: Add. 28,352, folios 61–62.

Table 4. Colegio Mayor Graduates on the Chancillerías

Years (by reign)		Oidores Appointed	Colegiales Mayores	%
Granada				
(Charles V)	1517–56	61	32	52.5
(Philip II)	1556–98[a]			
(Philip III)	1599–1621	55	30	54.5
(Philip IV)	1621–65	110	68	61.8
(Charles III)	1665–1700	80	49	61.3
Valladolid				
1517–56		77	39	50.7
1556–98		82	46	56.1
1599–1621		65	38	58.5
1621–65		122	75	61.5
1665–1700		108	72	66.7

Colegio Mayor Graduates on the Councils

	Oidores Appointed	Colegiales Mayores	%
Castile			
1517–56	37	16	43.3
1556–98	75	44	58.6
1599–1621	38	22	57.9
1621–65	92	63	68.5
1665–1700	104	75	72.1
Cámara			
1588–98	7	4	57.1
1599–1621	12	6	50.0
1621–65	17	13	76.5
1665–1700	18	12	66.7
Indies[b]			
1517–56	24	11	45.8
1556–98	39	24	61.5
1599–1621	34	16	47.1
1621–65	56	30	53.6
1665–1700	48	28	58.3
Military Orders			
1598–1621	24	17	70.8
1621–65	52	38	73.1
1665–1700	36	31	86.1
Inquisition			
1517–56[a]	28	13	46.4
1556–98[a]	46	23	50.0
1599–1621[a]	32	19	59.4
1621–65	69	24	36.2
1665–1700	49	22	44.9

[a]Incomplete data.
[b]The figures for this council do not include *capa y espada* councillors.

Sources: ACV: libs. 1–6; AHN: Cons., legs. 13515–18, 13529, 51708; libs. 724–32; AHN: Inq., libs, 246–49, 356–61, 366–408, 426–30, 489–95, 572, 1232, 1246; AGS: CMC, 1 época, leg. 1587; NC: legs. 1–4; QC, legs. 1–40; Schäefer, *Consejo de Indias*, 1: app. 1, sections 2, 3.

into practice; during his presidency, eleven of the sixteen letrados named to the Royal Council and nearly one-half of the letrados named to the tribunals at Granada and Valladolid—stepping stones to the higher councils—were colegiales. Shortly after his death, an anonymous author, commenting upon favoritism in royal appointments, reported that "it also appears that when former colegiales become councillors or presidents, they are inclined to favor colegiales in the appointments to office they make."[24] A 1585 *consulta* of the president of the Council of the Indies illustrates this author's words. In this memo, Hernando de Vega y Fonseca, a graduate of San Bartolomé, tells the king that ". . . it would be very good for your Royal Service if colegiales wish to serve in those regions [the Indies] because they are commonly well-born, virtuous, and letrados; they would govern well and even for the places in this council [of the Indies] they would be most appropriate."[25]

A glance at the number of colegiales reaching offices influential in the recruitment of new crown officials helps to explain the advantage they held over ordinary graduates. Six of the fourteen presidents of the Royal Council of Castile who served under Charles V and Philip II were former colegiales, and over one-half of the presidents of the Indies were of similar backgrounds.[26] Moreover, the presidencies of the chancillerías of Granada and Valladolid, key offices in appointments, since their reports were usually the bases for promotions to the upper councils, were also monopolized by colegiales mayores; eighteen of the twenty-eight officials to occupy these two offices during the sixteenth century were of this background.[27]

Thus through a mixture of merit and achievement, past example and patronage, members of the colegios mayores continually moved from the universities into government posts. By the close of the sixteenth century, their representation in the important *plazas de asiento* was routine (see Table 4).

Under the later Habsburgs the recruitment practices initiated by the council presidents of the sixteenth century remained more or less the same. Dissatisfied with the quality of the consultas which the overworked presidents of Castile prepared and with the apparent short-comings of many of the letrado officials he had himself appointed, Philip II in 1588 organized a new council, the Real Cámara de Castilla, to handle the work of royal patronage, both clerical and lay.[28] Appointments in Castile re-

[24]AGS: DC, leg. 5–106, "Memorial para el Rey Don Felipe II . . ."

[25]AGI: IG, leg. 741, ramo 1, no. 6, *consulta* of 4.V.1585.

[26]See Kagan, "Education and the State," p. 131.

[27]Ibid.

[28]The only appointments outside its jurisdiction were those of the Inquisition, which were handled by the Inquisitor General, offices within the estates of the Military Orders which belonged to the Council of the Military Orders, certain financial charges that were filled by the president of the Council of Finance, military offices which were the work of the Council of War, and posts in the New World which remained the prerogative of the president and Council, and later of the Cámara, of the Indies.

mained under the Cámara's jurisdiction until the eighteenth century, when its work was centralized in the office of the Secretary for Grace and Justice. Previously, the Cámara, composed of the president and the most senior members of the council of Castile, had jealously guarded its prerogatives, and under the pressure of work, its membership grew from an original complement of four to seven or eight. It remained, however, the preserve of the senior letrado officials in Castile, men who had spent their lives in the service of the crown. With this experience their competence over the business of appointments developed rapidly; meanwhile, the influence of the royal secretaries and other court officials in the business of patronage declined, while the king's dependency upon the Cámara to make just and meritous appointments increased. The *camaristas* were, of course, expected to be above corruption of any form, but such expectations were never realized; ties of blood and fraternity proved too strong for even the most senior and devoted of the crown's servants to overcome. In spite of these shortcomings, the Cámara, virtually independent in its judgments, contributed a greater degree of continuity and uniformity to the selection of letrado officials than the council presidents and the royal secretaries of the past. This "bureaucratization" of appointment procedures fixed the type of individual nominated to office, and in this manner the second century of Habsburg rule created a civil service with a common blood, background, and, above all, education.

It would be superfluous to discuss the continuing importance of the requirements of age, purity of blood, and territorial origin for appointments to letrado offices; they each remained in force. The letrado hierarchy also remained a hidalgo hierarchy, even though the average social rank of its members was on the rise. Letrados of "peasant stock" disappeared, and those from the other end of the social scale were more numerous,[29] but on the whole the letrado hierarchy remained just that—the one sector of royal government dominated by families who owed their wealth and importance to the study of law. By the opening of the seventeenth century many of these families had a history of letrado officials which dated back to Ferdinand and Isabel. In the course of time they had intermarried time and time again, and sons of these alliances followed letrado careers. In this manner great letrado dynasties gradually emerged, among them the Arce y Otalora, Blanco de Salcedo, Corral y Arellano, Camporredondo y Rio, Manso de Zúñiga, Marquez de Prado, Queipo de Llano, Quiroga, Ronquillo y Briceño, Santos de San Pedro, and Trejo y Paniagua. Often in control of the Cámara and the Royal Councils, officials from this core of families were anxious for the appointment of new

---

[29] *Títulos* in the letrado hierarchy included Baltasar de la Cueva y Enríquez, councillor of the Indies; Antonio de Aragón y Córdoba, Alonso de Aguilar y Córdoba, and Carlos de Borja, all of whom served on the Council of the Military Orders; and Gerónimo de Portacarrero y Nozama and Antonio de Sarmiento y Luna, members of the Royal Council of Castile. In order, their titles are listed on p. 86.

letrados from their own caste. Under these circumstances, family connections and services became essential criteria in appointments, contributing to the formation of a restricted social class from which the letrado
hierarchy drew a majority of its new recruits.

The consultas of the Cámara clearly reflect this development.[30] The
importance of family ties, especially those concerned with the services and
offices of relatives, past and present, grew considerably in the short
biographies about each candidate these memos contained. The same
family names appear again and again in the consultas, consequently, in the
offices, suggesting the growing consolidation of the letrado class, but the
lack of precise knowledge about family ties among the leading letrado officials does not allow more than a few examples of how certain clans managed to occupy a wide variety of offices. One was the Santos de San Pedro
family which had at least nine members in important offices in the seventeenth century alone. Among them were two councillors of Castile, one of
the Indies, two of the Military Orders, two who served on the chancillería
of Valladolid, two bishops, and another who acquired a canonry in the
cathedral of León. Four other Santos de San Pedro presumably would
have received similar appointments had they not died while still at university.[31]

Rivaling the Santos de San Pedro were the Ronquillo y Briceño.
Antonio Ronquillo, son of an alderman in Arevalo, was an oidor on the
Royal Council of Castile in the time of Philip IV. Pedro de Ronquillo y
Briceño, either the son or nephew of Antonio, occupied a number of
audiencia posts before being named to the Royal Council. He eventually
became the second Count of Grasnedo, while his brother, Antonio, oidor
on the Supreme Council of the Inquisition, married the third Countess of
Francos. She was the daughter of Gerónimo Miguel Ramos de Mançano,
a councillor of Castile, and granddaughter of the first Count of Francos,
Francisco Ramos de Mançano, who had been a member of the Royal
Council of Castile as well. This alliance created a vast letrado clan whose
members regularly appeared thereafter in important government posts.[32]

But these are only two of the many families and clans spread throughout the letrado hierarchy. To discover all of the links and connections that
existed among the letrado families and that were so important to appointments, the structure of court factions, and policymaking itself would be
an immense undertaking, one that would require a detailed prosopography
of the leading letrados in Castile. Without this kind of information, merely
to list those families who seem to have captured a particularly large or

---

[30]These can be found in the AHN: Cons., legs. 13489, 13494, 13500–01, 13515–18,
13529, 51708.
    [31]I have drawn this information from the student registers of the Colegios Mayores of
Arzobispo, Oviedo, San Ildefonso, and Santa Cruz; cf. chap. VI, note 23.
    [32]The above is taken from the student registers of the Colegio Mayor de Oviedo (BNM:
Ms. 940, esp. nos. 297,305).

wide variety of offices would give a distorted, perhaps inaccurate and certainly incomplete picture of the whole. Nevertheless, it would be correct to assume that family ties in the course of the seventeenth century played an increasingly important, indeed, crucial, role in the distribution of letrado offices.

Family ties, however, never superseded a university background in jurisprudence as the primary requisite for letrado posts. If the monarch, as he did on occasion, saw fit to appoint an official who lacked the necessary academic credentials, the Cámara usually reacted with a strong protest. Such an incident occurred in 1611 when Philip III named Licentiate Luis Pardo de Lago to an office in the audiencia of Seville.[33] The ostensible reason for this appointment was Pardo's forthcoming marriage to an important woman at court. But Pardo had never been recommended by the Cámara, which argued that the concession of letrado office via the "marriage road" set a very bad precedent; it would dissuade the nation's youth from attending universities and colleges when it became apparent that other means to obtain valued letrado posts existed. In subsequent incidents of this nature, the Cámara's arguments remained unchanged.[34] Its members were not inherently opposed to allowing considerations such as marriage and family ties to influence their appointments, but as officials with defined duties they resented the king's ability to ignore their carefully prepared consultas at will. The camaristas were experienced professionals, intent on making appointments according to plan and equally intent on keeping the educational requirements for office intact. In this way they could limit the number of applicants and also have a weapon to use against the king's occasional caprice. Accordingly, the consultas of the seventeenth century continued to place a heavy emphasis on the academic credentials of potential office-holders, including those referring to senior positions where other considerations might be expected to carry more weight. The result was that even candidates from the most influential letrado clans were obliged to have the necessary university background.

This was unmistakable. Notwithstanding the rise of new universities since the time of the Catholic kings, graduates from Salamanca and Valladolid, and to a lesser degree, from Cisneros's University of Alcalá de Henares, commanded the greatest respect, almost to the total exclusion of graduates from other institutions.[35] Though existing appointment records are incomplete, it would appear that as many as 90 percent of Castile's

[33]AHN: Cons., leg. 13500, consulta of 13.VIII.1611.

[34]For example, see AHN: Cons. leg. 13500, consultas of 11.VI.1652, 4.XII.1662, 9.VIII.1670; leg. 13515, no. 113; leg. 13517, nos. 20, 45; leg. 13529, consulta of 17.X.1663; leg. 51708, consultas of 11.XI.1675, 18.I.1678.

[35]Among 103 *oidores* appointed to the *chancillería* of Valladolid between 1588 and 1633, only seven can be positively identified as graduates from other universities and four of these had taken a first degree either at Alcalá, Salamanca, or Valladolid (AHN: Cons. leg. 13529). At Granada, only nine of the 94 oidores apointed during these years graduated from other universities (AHN: Cons. legs. 13515–18).

plazas de asiento went to graduates of these three universities, and even this figure could be raised slightly if one included those who attended but did not graduate from these institutions. So lop-sided was the distribution of office that the Count-Duke of Olivares, a patron of the College of Santa Maria de Jesús in Seville, asked Philip IV in 1622 and again in 1628 to remind the Cámara to recommend graduates from that college for *corregimientos* and *plazas de asiento* in Castile.[36]

Alcalá, Salamanca, and Valladolid owed their success primarily to a reputation for excellence which none of the other universities could match. Also in their favor was the sheer weight of numbers. Together Salamanca and Valladolid produced more advanced graduates in civil law than all of the other universities combined, although in canon law this was not the case.[37] But tradition also worked in favor of the major universities; the officials influential in appointments were graduates of Alcalá, Salamanca, and Valladolid, and they selected new officials for the same reasons. Under these circumstances it was difficult for graduates from other institutions to compete.

As in the sixteenth century, the graduates most in demand were those in university teaching posts. Instructors from Alcalá, Salamanca, and Valladolid accounted for at least one-half and probably more of the appointments made to the two chancillerías between 1599 and 1700.[38] Instructors from other universities no doubt represented a proportion of the remaining officials, but owing to a shortage of faculty lists for these institutions it is impossible to know exactly how many.

Graduates of the colegios mayores also maintained their strong positions in the plazas de asiento (see Table 4). They were aided in this by their continuing success in the competitions for university teaching posts,[39] but, as in the past, other considerations were at work to allow these small communities to produce so many university instructors and, consequently, letrado officials for the crown. The case of Licentiate Egas Vanegas de Girón, graduate of the College of Cuenca, later *alcalde de crimen* in Valladolid, is instructive. In 1589 Mateo Vázquez requested the president of Valladolid's chancillería to prepare a report on Girón, who was then *alcalde*. Vázquez commented that Girón could not "construe two phrases of Cicero" and that he had heard other things about the alcalde's lack of "qualities," but he wanted to know about Girón's work as a magistrate. The president answered: "I do not believe he knows much

---

[36]See AHN: Cons. leg. 4422, consulta of 22.XII.1622; leg. 13490, consulta of 21.VIII. 1628. I would like to thank Dr. Charles Jago for bringing the consulta of 1622 to my attention.

[37]See below, p. 201.

[38]This figure was reached by matching names of professors on the law faculties of the universities with those of letrados serving on the royal chancillerías. For the professors, see Alcocer Martínez, *Universidad de Valladolid*, vol. 2, and Esperabé Artega, *Universidad de Salamanca*, vol. 2. The lists of chancillería officials, drawn from the AHN: Cons., Libros de Plazas, are my own.

[39]See below, pp. 136–40.

about letters."[40] Girón apparently tried to make up for his scholarly shortcomings through hard work, but he still could not merit a recommendation. Nevertheless, he was promoted to the Council of the Military Orders in 1600.

A 1645 report by the Bishop of Salamanca on the university of that city gives some further hints about the actual academic qualifications of some *colegiales*.[41] One licentiate from the college of San Bartolomé, according to the bishop, "has studied very little and has almost never attended lectures." The following year this student, don Carlos de Vargas y Heraso, son of the head groom of the royal princess, was appointed oidor in Seville. Another "mediocre student without any luster" from San Bartolomé, don Pedro Gamarra, became *alcalde de hijosdalgo* in Valladolid in 1649, while a student of "few qualifications and letters," don Gabriel Meléndez, also a member of San Bartolomé, was subsequently appointed alcalde in the audiencia of Seville in 1656. He was the son of the governor of la Florida, a fact not unrelated to his appointment. Although many colegiales merited promotions to office in terms of talent, others, like the above, were eased into important positions through a variety of questionable means.

Past example and the prestige of former graduates bolstered the reputation of qualified and unqualified colegiales alike. The seventeenth century in Castile marked an age in which family, confraternity, college, and faction were every bit as important to one's identity (let alone qualifications for office) as the person himself. Reputation, therefore, was largely a product of time; the past weighed heavily on the present; and under these conditions the colegios mayores could not fail to reap considerable rewards. In their correspondence with the Royal Council, seldom did they neglect to refer to the string of councillors, magistrates, bishops, and other officials they had produced in the past.[42] The glories of yesterday implied superiority today, and to a monarchy which looked more to the past than the future for inspiration, this technique brought about satisfactory results.

The influence and help afforded by old graduates was more direct. Once in office, former colegiales generally kept in close touch with their old community, informing them of their promotions and offering aid if ever it was required.[43] A number of graduates served as court agents for their colleges, attempting to influence appointments, law-suits, and other business in which the colleges had a stake.[44] Considering the fact that the

[40]BM: Add. 28,349, folio 225.

[41]AUS: Ms. 1925, folio 144, "Memoria de los Colegiales, 4.II.1645."

[42]See, for example, AHN: Cons., leg. 7138, "Memorial de los Cuatro Colegios Mayores de Salamanca al Rey Felipe IV," 17.X.1636, and in this same *legajo*, a similar memorial directed to Philip V. See also BUS: Ms. 2266, folio 4, a letter of the colleges of 8.IV.1659.

[43]Examples of these letters can be found in the AHN: Univs., leg. 23².

[44]The most clearcut admission of such services took place in 1628 at a time when the colleges were threatened by possible reforms. The College of Santa Cruz wrote to that of

presents of the royal councils and tribunals, as well as the councillors themselves, were colegiales mayores more often than not,[45] the University of Salamanca was probably correct when it complained to Charles II that "the judges of Your Council . . . are partisans, . . . solicitors and agents for the Colleges."[46]

Little wonder then that the Cámara de Castilla in 1608 could inform Philip III that "when a colegial wins a professorship his qualifications are outstanding."[47] A few days later, the Cámara in a similar vein noted "that the colleges are filled with subjects worthy of appointment because of their qualifications, studies, letters, and exemplary lives and customs."[48] A list of eight colegiales available for office followed and, even though none had been specifically proposed in the consulta, two received offices immediately. Support of this nature continued throughout the century, with the Cámara acting to protect the interests of younger colegiales whenever their positions on the ladder of promotion were threatened by the king. Just such an incident occurred in 1679 when Charles II challenged the Cámara on its decision to favor two inexperienced students resident in the colegios mayores for a vacant position of alcalde de crimen in Valladolid ahead of Diego de Vaquerizo, an experienced alcalde de hijosdalgo in the same tribunal. Adopting a defensive tone, the Cámara replied: "We have always taken into consideration the manner and circumstances under which some subjects entered ministerial positions and upon occasion we have proposed to Your Majesty others who have excelled in academic titles, professorships, and literary skill within their colleges and universities. To the latter we give preference."[49]

In part, the Cámara's open support of the colegios mayores dated from the time when the councillors of Castile received the right to appoint university instructors at Alcalá, Salamanca, and Valladolid. This task first came to the council in 1623 after corruption in the elections through which students elected their instructors had become intolerable, although it was handed back to the students nine years later, since the council had shown itself equally corrupt, openly distributing university chairs to relatives, friends, and fellow colegiales.[50] The following years brought an extended debate on the best means to appoint instructors; in the meantime, the power of appointment shifted back and forth between the students and the Council of Castile. The latter, controlled by colegio mayor graduates

San Ildefonso advocating a plan in which "our colegiales in Madrid . . ." would contact San Ildefonso's representatives, "making use of the colegiales we have on the councils." Cf. AHN: Univs., leg. 23², no. 32. In this same legajo, see also nos. 23, 27–29.

[45] See Table 4 and Kagan, "Education and the State," p. 142.
[46] AHN: Cons. leg. 7138, letter of 28.IV.1694.
[47] AHN: Cons. leg. 13529, consulta of 1.IX.1608.
[48] AHN: Cons. leg. 13529, consulta of 6.IX.1608.
[49] AHN: Cons. leg. 13529, consulta of 2.VIII.1679.
[50] For details of these maneuverings, see Kagan, "Education and the State," pp. 246–50.

and partisans, in alliance with the colleges themselves, fought persistently to keep the vote away from the students; if the councillors could control appointments to teaching posts, they could also control entrance to important letrado offices. Relatives and protégés could therefore be guaranteed a secure career. The outcome of these debates was the permanent return of the power to appoint university instructors to the Royal Council in 1641, and by this act colegio mayor domination of university teaching posts and, consequently, of the plazas de asiento was assured. The colegio mayor "faction," perhaps the best term to describe those who exercised influence on behalf of these communities, had emerged victorious, and this victory was to have important results for the subsequent history of the colegios mayores as well as the Castilian government and society itself.

Exploiting their friends on the Royal Council, colegiales moved regularly into teaching positions and official posts. Promotion was almost automatic, and it was common knowledge that the son or nephew of a government official who obtained a *beca* (a scholarship in a college) would have a secure political future. But becas were few, while the colleges controlled elections to their ranks, giving them the power to bargain. So it was even common among those councillors and officials who were not party to the colleges to back colegiales for professorships and jobs, since this support might improve the chances of their sons in the competition for becas. Conversely, the colleges could not afford to be too independent of the council which possessed the keys to promotion. This mutual dependency grew stronger and stronger. The council and the Cámara moved colegiales into jobs in order to acquire becas, hence future jobs for their families and friends.[51] But inasmuch as admission to the valued letrado posts was regulated largely by colegio mayor membership and professorships, letrados also needed close connections with families influential at court or with officials high in the letrado hierarchy to obtain promotions. Those who lacked the necessary ties of family and college found themselves hard-pressed to secure either a beca, a teaching post, or an important job. In the course of the seventeenth century this intricate web of obligations was perhaps the most significant contribution toward the consolidation of the families and clans in control of letrado government, indeed, toward the consolidation of a "nobility of the robe" in Castile. At the same time it transformed the colegios mayores, communities designed to harbor the university's academic elite, into institutions which catered for an elite of power and wealth who were more interested in future jobs than in scholarly excellence and the university routine.

The close links between the Royal Council and the colleges attracted both the attention and the criticism of contemporaries. One of the first to consider the impact of these ties was the Count-Duke of Olivares. He

[51]On this point see Sala Balust, *Constituciones*, 1:35–40. Francisco Pérez Bayer, *Por la Libertad de la Literatura Española* (Palacio Real de Madrid, Mss. 27–28) also describes this mutual dependency and its results.

recognized that the colegio mayor monopoly served only to dampen the zeal of ordinary students for study and that this in turn was damaging not only to the universities but the monarchy as well, since it tended to reduce the number of graduates who were qualified to enter government office.[52] Yet it was an anonymous author, writing in the early eighteenth century, who best elucidated the nature of these ties. He claimed that ever since the colegiales had gained control of the Royal Council, "they have regularly offered professorships, and, consequently, offices to men from their own colleges who were also their sons, relatives, countrymen, or friends . . . and from this has resulted a situation in which the councils and tribunals as well as bishoprics, canonries, and other letrado offices are filled with Colegiales Mayores."[53] He added that "the councillors need the colegiales so that the latter can give becas to their sons, relatives, and friends, while the colegiales need the former for their posts." Although slightly exaggerating the extent of colegio mayor control, this author outlined the means by which the ordinary university student, the *manteista*, was excluded from the important positions in the letrado hierarchy.

As long as the colegios mayores preserved their close ties with the Royal Council, criticism of their power and influence continued unabated. Then, toward the middle of the eighteenth century, a movement to abolish the colegios mayores gathered strength. Influential critics such as Francisco Pérez Bayer, tutor to the royal *infantes*, subsequently exposed the colleges' close connections with the officials of the letrado hierarchy, but no author described this situation more clearly and succinctly than Melchor de Macanaz, *fiscal* of the Royal Council of Castile in the reign of Philip V. He wrote that

. . . all the officials in the Councils and the Chanceries make their posts not only perpetual but also hereditary in their house and family. The method of it is this. In the three leading universities of Spain there are six colegios mayores where the young enter to study. Those who enter are the sons, nephews, brothers, and cousins of officials. The student who applies himself manages after several years to get a lectureship. For every one who succeeds, twenty fail and obtain posts outside. As many as enter the university, therefore, leave with an official post in the Audiencias or Chanceries, and from there they go on to the councils. There is no instance of anyone, however ignorant he may be, being refused an official post.[54]

Furthermore, these same family ties aided those colegiales who were interested in ecclesiastical careers, since the Cámara maintained the right to appoint a wide range of ecclesiastical offices, including those of the episcopacy itself. In practice, the camaristas extended their criteria of appointment to the church with only a minimum of changes, allowing the

[52]BUS: Ms. 2064, folio 8.
[53]BNM: Ms. 18,055, folio 131v, "Papal Curioso en punto de Colegios."
[54]Cited in H. Kamen, *The War of Succession in Spain, 1700–1715* (London, 1968), p. 41.

Table 5. Colegio Mayor Graduates in the Bishoprics of Castile

Archdiocese and diocese	Bishops appointed 1474-1600	Colegiales	Bishops appointed 1601-1700	Colegiales
Toledo				
Ávila	12	4	12	7
Cartegena	12	5	16	12
Córdoba	18	5	11	2
Cuenca	14	7	5	2
Osma	13	4	15	2
Palencia	15	4	8	2
Segovia	13	5	21	7
Sigüenza	12	3	16	8
Toledo	11	4	6	3
Sevilla				
Cadiz	6	1	15	2
Canarias	17	5	11	4
Jaen	12	4	10	6
Malaga	10	2	11	4
Sevilla	9	2	14	1
Santiago				
Astorga	16	4	13	3
Badajoz	13	5	16	5
Ciudad Rodrigo	22	7	17	8
Coria	7	4	16	6
Lugo	16	7	15	8
Mondoñedo	16	9	14	4
Orense	12	7	14	5
Plasencia	10	3	20	7
Salamanca	15	4	18	9
Santiago	13	6	13	3
Tuy	15	5	19	7
Zamora	12	2	18	6
Granada				
Almeria	—	—	—	—
Granada	10	3	13	4
Guadix	11	3	17	4
Burgos				
Burgos	8	2	11	6
Calahorra	16	4	14	5
Pamplona	17	2	15	8
Valladolid	1	—	13	4
Papal Jurisdiction				
León	16	7	15	8
Oviedo	17	10	16	5

Source: P. B. Gams, *Series Episcoporum Ecclesiae Catholicae* (Ratisbonae, 1873).

colegiales mayores to capture nearly 40 percent of the Castilian sees in the seventeenth century (Table 5), while the remaining appointees were primarily law graduates from Alcalá, Salamanca, and Valladolid.[55] The inquisition, although outside the Cámara's patronage and jurisdiction, was headed by generals who were colegiales as often as not and by a Supreme Council that was often under colegio mayor control.[56] Consequently, college graduates were able to obtain magisterial positions in the Holy Office without difficulty.[57]

This chapter has been an attempt to outline the openings available to university graduates in sixteenth- and seventeenth-century Castile and to trace the changes in the standards of recruitment these positions demanded. In the royal administration, as in the inquisition and the church, the sixteenth century had coincided with a rapid expansion in the number of positions open to graduates. This was followed by an era of stagnation or marginal growth. Simultaneously, the "bureaucratization" of these ruling hierarchies, particularly in terms of recruitment, led toward a narrowing of standards which made it increasingly difficult for the majority of job-seeking graduates to qualify. The economic problems of the seventeenth century, coupled with increased nepotism, closed off many opportunities for advancement and led to a tightening of the letrado labor market which affected not only the ruling hierarchies but the learned professions as well. It would be wrong to assume that all of the students at Castile's universities were interested in or cared about such developments. Many, particularly nobles and members of the religious orders, came to university for other reasons; changes in the letrado hierarchy had little to do with their lives. But for the majority of students these developments were crucial to their education and to their future professional careers.

[55]As Professor Curtis Noel has demonstrated, these three universities gave to the church 66 percent of its bishops between 1700 and 1725, 62 percent between 1759 and 1765, but only 50 percent in the closing decades of the century (see "Campomanes and the Secular Clergy in Spain, 1760-1780: 'Enlightenment vs. Tradition'," Ph.D. dissertation [Princeton University, 1969]). The declining representation of the graduates of these universities among the episocopacy after 1765 is best attributed to the suppression of the colegios mayores which had provided, in certain epochs, nearly one-half of Castile's bishops.

[56]Cf. Table 4 and AHN: Inq. lib. 323, "Relacion del personel y sus servicios en las diferentes tribunales del Inquisición, 1666-67." Meanwhile, between 1516 and 1600, four of eleven *Generales* of the Inquisition were colegiales, and in the seventeenth century, six of fourteen. See M. Alcocer Martínez, "El Consejo Real de Castilla," *Revista Histórica* 5 (1925): 67-73.

[57]Colegiales, however, frequently refused appointments to the local tribunals of the inquisition, preferring instead to hold either ecclesiastical or secular charges before assuming a position within the Holy Office, usually in the Supreme Council itself. This explains why in 1666-67 only 9 of the 37 inquisitors on Spain's tribunals were colegiales, whereas they represented about 45 percent of the members of the Supreme Council.

The remainder of this book is an attempt to assess how the evolution of the letrado hierarchy, superimposed on the ups and downs of early education, the economy, and other aspects of Castilian life, affected the evolution of Castile's universities in the years between 1500 and 1808. This survey intends to present on the one hand a picture of university life and on the other, an investigation into the wider problem of the relationship between education and social change. This is a huge topic; consequently, it is perhaps best to begin with the colegios mayores, a small sector of the academic world but the part that was linked most directly with the world of office and honor and whose history was crucial to that of the universities themselves.

part III
THE UNIVERSITIES
OF CASTILE

chapter 7
THE COLEGIOS MAYORES

In an earlier chapter reference was made to the establishment of Castile's six colegios mayores, but until now these institutions have only been considered in relation to letrado appointments. The mutual relationship which existed between the colleges and the letrado ministers has been described, and suggestions have been made about some of the possible effects of this relationship upon the royal administration. By definition, however, a mutual relationship is a reciprocal arrangement; changes in the status of one partner invariably affect the other; thus the colleges, in the face of changes within the royal administration and its criteria of appointment could not remain static. As a result the colleges followed a path far removed from that laid down by their founders.

The original constitutions of the colegios mayores obliged their students to conform to certain immutable conditions of age, education, geographical origin, poverty, and purity of blood.[1] In return each community, endowed with ecclesiastical rents, provided a set number of worthy but impoverished scholars with dress, food, lodgings, and expenses for a fixed length of time, enabling them to work toward the costly university degrees. In addition, most of the colegios mayores, on account of the supposed poverty of their members, obtained special privileges which allowed their scholars to graduate at reduced cost.[2]

The aim of this program was to produce an academic elite. Only *bachilleres*, a group which was already a small minority within the university, were admitted. Each was elected after an open competition in which he was asked to demonstrate not only his academic skills but also his proofs of Old Christian blood, and the college he entered constituted a small, highly disciplined, almost monastic community. Inside, the way of life was designed to be wholly academic, consisting of long hours of practice and study along with daily readings and practice sessions designed to supplement the regular university curriculum.[3] Moreover, this routine was

[1]The constitutions of Salamanca's four colegios mayores have been published in Sala Balust, *Constituciones, Estatutos, y Ceremonias de los Antiguos Colegios Seculares de la Universidad de Salamanca* (4 vols., Madrid, 1962–66). For those of San Ildefonso, see AHN: Univ., leg. 674 F or 1086 F. The constitution and statutes of the Colegio Mayor de Santa Cruz are located in the Biblioteca Santa Cruz, Valladolid.
[2]See below, p. 153.
[3]For details about life in the colegios mayores, see M. A. Febrero Lorenzo, *La Pedagogía de los Colegios Mayores en el Siglo de Oro* (Madrid, 1960); E. Madruga Jiménez,

coupled with a minimum of comfort in order to prevent extrascholastic attractions.[4] The colleges also enjoyed a considerable degree of autonomy, selecting their own members and managing their financial affairs, yet they were never wholly independent of the universities of which they formed a small part. Colegiales attended university lectures, competed for university professorships, and remained subject to the jurisdiction of the university rector.

The College of San Ildefonso at the University of Alcalá de Henares stood apart from colegios mayores at Salamanca and Valladolid both in organization and design. Whereas the others formed semiindependent communities within the larger institution, Cardinal Cisneros intended this college to act as the head of the university which he created.[5] The rector of the college, elected by his fellows, was automatically the rector of the university, and, together with a number of other colegiales, he administered the affairs of the entire institution. In contrast, the colegios mayores of Salamanca and Valladolid, grafted onto existing universities, constituted only a small segment of the academic community. They were subject to regulations made by the university council and in most cases colegiales were officially excluded from positions in university government.[6]

San Ildefonso differed also in its total dedication to the study of theology. Cisneros, concerned about the disregard for this subject among the Spanish clergy, barred jurists from his college, presumably to prepare its members for the purely spiritual needs of the church. The other five colleges admitted law students, canon and civil, as well as theologians, medical students, and others in the liberal arts; consequently, they allowed some of their members to prepare for more worldly careers.

The ultimate goals of the colegios mayores were rather vague. To a certain degree, they were simply charitable institutions intended to allow "poor" bachilleres who could not otherwise pursue advanced studies

---

Crónica del Colegio Mayor del Arzobispo de Salamanca (Salamanca, 1957); and J. Puyol, *El Colegio Mayor de Santa Cruz y los Colegios Mayores* (Madrid, 1929), who gives a daily schedule of the students in the colegios mayores (p. 21). At least nine hours a day were devoted to study. Beltrán de Heredia, *Cartulario de la Universidad de Salamanca* (Salamanca, 1971), 3: 371–478, provides additional details concerning the establishment of the colleges of Cuenca and Oviedo.

[4]The college of San Ildefonso was somewhat of an exception in this regard, since about half of its scholarships were in the gift of various important personages, families, and towns; see J. de Rujula y Ochotereña, Marqués de Ciadoncha, *Índice de los Colegiales del Mayor de San Ildefonso y Menores de Alcalá* (Madrid, 1946), p. xvii.

[5]Ajo y Sainz de Zúñiga, *Historia de la Universidades Hispánicas* (8 vols., Madrid, 1957–72), 2: 300–01.

[6]The 1538 statutes of the University of Salamanca debarred colegiales from the office of university rector and councilor; see Esperabé Artega, *Universidad de Salamanca* (Salamanca, 1914), 1: 141–42. At Valladolid the colegiales of Santa Cruz were granted special

to remain at university. Thus Pérez Bayer, writing in the eighteenth century, claimed that the colleges were "to help virtuous and diligent youths in their studies who, because of poverty, could not continue at the universities; and the goal is that remaining at the universities and continuing their studies, the fruit of their talents will be put towards the benefit of Religion and the State."[7] The colleges' founding statutes were somewhat more precise. Those of the Colegio Mayor del Arzobispo stated that its purpose was "the intellectual and moral formation of poor and ignorant clerics,"[8] while the original constitutions of the other colleges noted the need for "education" and "science," particularly in canon law and theology, with an eye toward raising the cultural level of the clergy. More specifically, the colleges were designed to produce trained officials; they were, after all, with the sole exception of San Bartolomé, established at the precise moment when the ruling hierarchies of Castile initiated demands for letrados with advanced degrees and, apparently, their founders had created them in order to produce just such men. This professional alignment is demonstrated in the colleges' initial bias toward the study of law and theology, the subjects leading to official appointment, instead of literature and philosophy, the subjects touted by the humanist authors of the time.

Such arrangements made certain that the colegios mayores, almost from the time of their inception, were going to command special attention from those in charge of recruitment to ecclesiastical and governmental posts. In practice, the colleges quickly became schools for officialdom, and they themselves confessed that in spite of their dedication to scholarship, they had "another, and even more noble goal, which is that of the education and the political and moral training of their students for the wise management of the highest posts of the monarchy."[9] Students who entered the colleges looked forward to an office-holding career,[10] and nearly every scholar, upon completion of his university course, moved into an ecclesiastical or secular post. A scholarship or beca in one of the colegios mayores was in fact tantamount to an office, with only time separating the two. The effects of this special relationship upon the nature and membership of these communities is the theme of this chapter.

---

permission by the crown in 1500 to be able, if elected, to hold the rectorship of the university; see F. Arribas Arranz, "El Colegio Mayor de Santa Cruz en sus primeros anos," Santa Cruz 21 (1961): 6. For some of the problems to which this particular privilege led, see AGS: DC, leg. 5-106.

[7]Pérez Bayer, Por la Libertad de la Literatura Española (Palacio Real de Madrid), vol. I, folio 5.

[8]Angel Riesco Terrero, Proyección Histórico-Social de la Universidad de Salamanca a Través de sus Colegios (siglos XV y XVI) (Salamanca, 1970), p. 50.

[9]See Olmedo, Diego Ramírez de Villaescusa 1459-1537 (Madrid, 1944), p. xii.

[10]See pp. 131-34 and Febrero Lorenzo, Los Colegios Mayores, pp. 155-62.

COLEGIALES AND COLLEGES[11]

In an inquiry of this type the term college and colegial—the Spanish is preferable to collegian—will be used almost interchangeably. The history of the colegios mayores 'was in large part the history of the interrelationship between the institution and its students. To separate the two would be impossible.

GEOGRAPHICAL ORIGINS

The founders of the colegios mayores distributed becas on a fixed, well-balanced geographical basis. According to the original constitutions of each college, students from within the Crown of Castile were preferred, but not more than two colegiales from one diocese nor one colegial from any town were allowed in college at the same time.[12] "Foreign" kingdoms such as Galicia, Asturias, Navarre, Vizcaya, Aragón, Catalonia, and Portugal were generally restricted to one student each.[13] Thus the colegios mayores were not to be monopolized by one specific region, but aimed at establishing an academic elite from all parts of Castile.

Once the founders had died, elections to becas passed to the colegiales, and the delicate geographical balance of each community broke down. This change was partly an attempt by the colleges to adapt to the general geographical distribution of students at their respective universities; the colleges, consequently, grew to reflect the regional biases of the institutions of which they were part.[14] But the breakdown in the geographical balance of these communities was also the result of the rise of regional factions or *bandos* among the colegiales, each of which supported candidates from their own area.[15] "Gallegos," "vizacainos," "manchegos," or some other bando struggled for mastery; the strongest were able to regulate college membership in their own favor and to manipulate the system through which the colegiales competed for university teaching positions. Luis Curiel, for instance, commented in 1714 that García de Haro y Abellaneda, later President of Castile and Count of Castrillo, lost his turn to compete for a university lectureship in the name of his Colegio Mayor de Cuenca because he belonged to a minority bando.[16] The problems related to the bando system within the colleges, however, are perhaps best sum-

---

[11]As a reminder to the reader: the colleges of Arzobispo, Cuenca, Oviedo, and San Bartolomé belonged to the University of Salamanca; Santa Cruz was in Valladolid and San Ildefonso in Alcalá de Henares.

[12]See Sala Balust, *Constituciones*, 3: 14, 68, 209. The college of San Ildefonso was unique in that it preferred students from one diocese—Toledo.

[13]In the college of Oviedo, Galicia and Asturias were allowed two colegiales each.

[14]See below, pp. 203–10.

[15]See L. Sala Balust, *Colegios de Salamanca, 1623–1770* (Valladolid, 1956), pp. 15–26.

[16]AGS: GJ, leg. 959, "Discurso sobre los Colegios Mayores de Salamanca y Valladolid . . . 1714," folio 4.

marized in an anonymous report about Salamanca's colegios mayores in the mid-seventeenth century. It referred to "The passion of some 'nations' against others, each trying to elect persons of its own as often as possible to the offense, insult, and exclusion of the rest, and against the express intentions of their founders."[17]

Across the sixteenth and seventeenth centuries the bando system distorted the geographical distribution of college places and allowed students from particular regions to dominate each community (Tables 6.1– 6.4). In every college, becas became heavily weighted in favor of a few regions, often to the total exclusion of areas originally granted representation. At San Bartolomé, for example, the dioceses of Old Castile retained over one-third of all college becas after 1450, while other areas, notably León, steadily lost ground. San Bartolomé allowed this development to take place officially by passing a statute in 1534 which permitted three, rather than two, students from the same diocese to be in college at one time.[18] Navarre, originally classified as a "foreign" kingdom, was designated part of Castile in 1524 and allotted one college scholarship. Its representation, however, steadily increased until *navarros* accounted for nearly 20 per cent of the college's scholars.

Correspondingly, San Bartolomé, in a description not far from the truth, was noted for the following *bandos*: *vizcainos*, *montañeses*, and *navarros*. The other colleges earned their own regional reputations: Arzobispo was known to be controlled by *manchegos*, Cuenca by *andaluces*, Oviedo by *campesinos* although *castellanos* might have been more correct, Santa Cruz by *riojanos*, and San Ildefonso by *toledanos*, *manchegos*, and *alcareños*.[19]

While each college acquired its own particular geographical coloring, the colegios mayores together favored scholars from the north of the peninsula. With the exception of San Ildefonso where New Castile enjoyed a strong representation, students from Old Castile, particularly the region around Burgos and Calahorra, along with Navarre, accounted for the largest share of colegio mayor becas. This situation suggests that top letrado places in Castile, a majority of which were held by colegiales, went also to "northerners" to the detriment of graduates from other parts of the Crown of Castile.

These tables also indicate the growing representation of the diocese of Toledo in the colegios mayores during the seventeenth century. This development can in large part be attributed to the increasing attraction which the colegios mayores held for the sons of ministers and noblemen

[17]BM: Add. 24,947, folio 96.
[18]The colleges of Arzobispo and Santa Cruz later passed similar statutes.
[19]See Pérez Bayer, *Literatura Española*, vol. I, folios 82–101. For a geographical breakdown of the colleges in the 1630s, see AHN: Cons., leg. 7138, "Información de los Colegios Mayores," 19.I.1636.

Table 6.1 Students in the Colegio Mayor de
Oviedo: Geographical Origins by Diocese

	1524–40	1550–99	1600–49	1650–99	Total[a] 1524–1699
CROWN OF CASTILE					
Andalucia:					
Córdoba	—	3	—	—	
Granada	—	—	3	—	
Guadix	—	—	—	—	
Jaen	2	—	—	1	
Malaga	—	—	—	—	
Seville	3	5	—	—	
Total	5	8	3	1	17 (4%)
Asturias:					
Oviedo	1	5	13	14	
Total	i	5	13	14	33 (7.8%)
Castile (New)					
Cuenca	—	—	—	—	
Sigüenza	1	4	—	—	
Toledo	3	9	8	15	
Total	4	13	8	15	40 (9.4%)
Castile (Old)					
Avila	3	2	3	9	
Burgos	5	9	6	3	
Calahorra	5	12	9	2	
Osma, Burgo de	1	5	4	3	
Palencia	4	6	9	18	
Segovia	2	4	10	7	
Valladolid	—	—	6	9	
Total	20	38	47	51	156 (36.7%)
Extremadura:					
Badajoz	2	1	—	—	
Coria	—	—	—	—	
Plasencia	—	6	1	—	
Total	2	7	1	—	10 (2.4%)
León:					
Astorga	1	2	1	1	
Ciudad Rodrigo	—	—	—	—	
León	4	7	9	20	
Salamanca	3	4	1	2	
Zamora	3	1	5	4	
Total	11	14	16	27	68 (16%)
Galicia:					
Lugo	—	2	4	5	
Mondoñedo	—	—	2	2	
Orense	—	1	1	1	
Santiago	6	4	4	7	
Tuy	—	—	4	2	
Total	6	7	15	17	45 (10.6%)

Table 6.1   (continued)

	1524–40	1550–99	1600–49	1650–99	Total[a] 1524–1699
Murcia:					
Albacete	—	—	—	—	
Almeria	—	—	—	—	
Cartagena	—	—	—	—	
Murcia	—	—	—	1	
Total	—	—	—	1	1 (0.2%)
Total Crown of Castile	49	92	103	126	370 (87%)
Kingdom of Navarre:					
Pamplona	5	4	6	3	
Total	5	4	6	3	18 (4.2%)
Basque Provinces:					
Alava	—	—	—	—	
Victoria	2	—	—	—	
Total	2	—	—	—	2 (0.4%)
CROWNS OF ARAGON					
Aragón:					
Albarracín	—	—	—	2	
Barbastro	—	—	—	—	
Calatayud	—	—	—	—	
Huesca	—	—	—	—	
Jaca	—	—	—	—	
Tarazona	1	1	1	2	
Teruel	—	—	1	—	
Zaragoza	—	1	—	—	
Total	1	2	2	4	9 (2%)
Catalonia:					
Barcelona	—	—	1	—	
Gerona	—	—	—	—	
Lérida	—	1	—	—	
Mallorca	—	—	—	—	
Tarragona	—	—	—	—	
Tortosa	—	—	—	—	
Urgel	—	—	1	—	
Vich	—	—	—	—	
Total	—	1	2	—	3 (0.7%)
Valencia:					
Orihuela	—	—	—	—	
Segorbe	—	—	—	—	
Solsona	—	—	1	—	
Valencia	1	1	2	1	
Total	1	1	3	1	6 (1.4%)
Total Crowns of Aragón	2	4	7	5	18 (4.2%)

Table 6.1   (continued)

	1524–40	1550–99	1600–49	1650–99	Total[a] 1524–1699
Miscellaneous:					
Nullius diocese	1	1	—	1	
Indies	—	—	1	—	
Italy	—	—	1	—	
Portugal	2	3	—	—	
Unkown	6	—	1	—	
Total Misc.	9	4	3	1	17 (4%)
GRAND TOTAL	67	104	119	135	425

[a]Figure in parenthesis is the percentage of the grand total represented by this region.

Table 6.2.   **Students in the Colegio Mayor de San Bartolomé: Geographical Origins by Diocese**

	1450–99	1500–49	1550–99	1600–49	1650–99	Total[a] 1450–1699
CROWN OF CASTILE						
Andalucia:						
Córdoba	—	3	6	1	2	
Granada	—	—	—	—	3	
Guadix	—	—	—	—	—	
Jaen	—	4	2	1	1	
Malaga	—	—	1	1	—	
Seville	3	7	4	3	2	
Total	3	14	13	6	8	44 (7.8%)
Asturias:						
Oviedo	—	3	2	5	3	
Total	—	3	2	5	3	13 (2.3%)
Castile (New)						
Cuenca	9	8	8	1	—	
Sigüenza	4	4	1	—	—	
Toledo	6	10	14	16	18	
Total	19	22	22	17	18	99 (17.5%)
Castile (Old)						
Avila	9	9	7	1	1	
Burgos	14	10	11	15	23	
Calahorra	8	16	12	15	21	
Osma, Burgo de	6	5	5	2	2	
Palencia	8	5	9	1	1	
Segovia	5	1	4	—	—	
Valladolid	—	—	—	2	6	
Total	50	46	48	36	54	234 (41.7%)

Table 6.2 (continued)

	1450–99	1500–49	1550–99	1600–49	1650–99	Total[a] 1450–1699
Extremadura:						
Badajoz	—	—	—	1	—	
Coria	—	—	—	—	—	
Plasencia	2	1	—	4	—	
Total	2	1	—	5	—	8 (1.4%)
León:						
Astorga	1	1	—	—	—	
Ciudad Rodrigo	1	2	—	—	—	
León	9	1	4	—	1	
Salamanca	8	5	2	2	—	
Zamora	—	—	—	—	—	
Total	19	9	6	2	1	37 (6.6%)
Galicia:						
Lugo	1	1	—	—	—	
Mondoñedo	—	—	1	1	—	
Orense	1	2	—	1	1	
Santiago	2	—	3	4	—	
Tuy	—	—	1	1	—	
Total	4	3	5	7	1	20 (3.6%)
Murcia:						
Albacete	—	—	—	—	—	
Almeria	—	—	—	—	—	
Cartagena	—	—	—	—	—	
Murcia	1	—	—	—	—	
Total	1	—	—	—	—	1 (0.1%)
Total Crown of Castile	99	98	97	78	85	457 (81.5%)
Kingdom of Navarre:						
Pamplona	5	3	4	14	22	
Total	5	3	4	14	22	48 (8.6%)
Basque Provinces:						
Alava						
Victoria						
Total	—	—	—	—	—	—
CROWNS OF ARAGÓN						
Aragón:						
Albarracín	—	—	—	—	—	
Barbastro	—	—	—	—	—	
Calatayud	—	—	—	—	—	
Huesca	—	1	—	—	—	
Jaca	—	—	—	—	—	
Tarazona	4	1	1	2	3	

Table 6.2 (continued)

	1450–99	1500–49	1550–99	1600–49	1650–99	Total[a] 1450–1699
Teruel	1	—	—	—	—	
Zaragoza	2	4	3	2	1	
Total	7	6	4	4	4	25 (4.4%)
Catalonia:						
Barcelona	—	—	—	1	—	
Gerona	—	—	—	—	—	
Lérida	—	—	—	1	—	
Mallorca	—	—	—	—	—	
Tarragona	—	—	—	—	—	
Tortosa	—	1	—	—	—	
Urgel	—	—	—	—	—	
Vich	—	—	—	—	—	
Total	—	1	—	2	—	3 (0.5%)
Valencia:						
Orihuela	1	—	—	—	—	
Segorbe	—	—	—	1	—	
Solsona	—	—	—	—	—	
Valencia	2	—	1	—	—	
Total	3	—	1	1	—	
Total Crowns of Aragón	10	7	5	7	4	33 (5.9%)
Miscellaneous:						
Nullius diocese	—	—	2	—	4	
Indies	—	—	1	1	—	
Italy	—	—	—	1	—	
Portugal	3	4	3	1	—	
Unknown	—	—	2	1	—	
Total Misc.	3	4	8	4	4	23 (4.1%)
GRAND TOTAL	117	112	114	103	115	561

[a]Figure in parenthesis is the percentage of the grand total represented by this region.

Table 6.3. Students in the Colegio Mayor de San Ildefonso: Geographical Origins by Diocese

	1508–49	1550–99	1600–49	1650–99	Total[a] 1508–1699
CROWN OF CASTILE					
Andalucia:					
Córdoba	2	2	4	—	
Granada	2	—	1	—	
Guadix	—	1	—	—	

Table 6.3   (continued)

	1508–49	1550–99	1600–49	1650–99	Total[a] 1508–1699
Jaen	2	3	4	—	
Malaga	—	—	—	—	
Seville	6	—	1	2	
Total	12	6	10	2	30 (3.2%)
Asturias:					
Oviedo	—	1	3	17	
Total	—	1	3	17	21 (2.2%)
Castile (New)					
Cuenca	14	12	30	9	
Sigüenza	3	12	18	11	
Toledo	35	45	59	57	
Total	52	69	107	77	305 (32%)
Castile (Old)					
Avila	2	1	—	4	
Burgos	15	13	9	33	
Calahorra	12	25	18	19	
Osma, Burgo de	5	4	4	6	
Palencia	8	16	4	10	
Segovia	4	7	10	3	
Valladolid	—	—	2	7	
Total	46	66	47	82	241 (25.3%)
Extremadura:					
Badajoz	1	—	—	—	
Coria	—	—	—	—	
Plasencia	1	—	1	—	
Total	2	—	1	—	
León:					
Astorga	—	—	—	2	
Ciudad Rodrigo	—	—	—	—	
León	—	1	5	13	
Salamanca	2	1	—	1	
Zamora	5	1	—	3	
Total	7	3	5	19	34 (3.6%)
Galicia:					
Lugo	—	—	—	2	
Mondoñedo	—	—	—	1	
Orense	—	—	—	—	
Santiago	—	—	—	1	
Tuy	1	—	—	—	
Total	1	—	—	4	5 (0.5%)
Murcia:					
Albacete	—	—	—	—	

Table 6.3   (continued)

	1508–49	1550–99	1600–49	1650–99	Total[a] 1508–1699
Almeria	—	—	—	—	
Cartagena	1	—	3	1	
Murcia	—	—	—	—	
Total	1	—	3	1	5 (0.5%)
Total Crown of Castile	121	145	176	202	644 (67.6%)
Kingdom of Navarre: Pamplona	5	24	15	19	
Total	5	24	15	19	63 (6.6%)
Basque Provinces: Alava	—	—	—	—	
Victoria	—	—	1	—	
Total	—	—	1	—	1 (0.1%)
CROWNS OF ARAGÓN Aragón: Albarracín	—	—	—	—	
Barbastro	—	—	—	—	
Calatayud	—	—	—	—	
Huesca	—	—	2	1	
Jaca	—	—	1	2	
Tarazona	7	7	9	7	
Teruel	—	—	1	—	
Zaragoza	10	5	9	7	
Total	17	12	22	17	68 (7.1%)
Catalonia: Barcelona	2	1	—	—	
Gerona	—	—	—	—	
Lérida	—	—	—	—	
Mallorca	—	—	—	—	
Tarragona	2	—	—	—	
Tortosa	—	—	—	—	
Urgel	—	—	—	—	
Vich	—	—	—	—	
Total	4	1	—	—	5 (0.5%)
Valencia: Orihuela	—	—	—	—	
Segorbe	—	1	—	—	
Solsona	—	—	—	—	
Valencia	—	—	1	1	
Total	—	1	1	1	3 (0.3%)
Total Crowns of Aragón	21	14	23	18	76 (8%)

Table 6.3   (continued)

	1508–49	1550–99	1600–49	1650–99	Total[a] 1508–1699
Miscellaneous:					
Nullius diocese	4	6	11	9	
Bayonne	2	—	—	1	
Flanders	—	—	1	—	
Indies	—	—	1	3	
Italy	—	1	1	—	
Portugal	1	—	—	—	
Unknown	78	17	21	11	
Total Misc.	85	24	35	24	168 (17.6%)
GRAND TOTAL	232	207	250	263	952

[a] Figure in parenthesis is the percentage of the grand total represented by this region.

Table 6.4.   Students in the Colegio Mayor de Santa Cruz: Geographical Origins by Diocese

	1484–99	1500–49	1550–99	1600–49	1650–99	Total[a] 1484–1699
CROWN OF CASTILE						
Andalucia:						
Córdoba	1	3	4	2	—	
Granada	—	1	2	1	1	
Guadix	—	—	—	—	—	
Jaen	1	2	3	—	2	
Malaga	—	—	1	—	—	
Seville	2	4	4	1	6	
Total	4	10	14	4	9	41 (6.9%)
Asturias						
Oviedo	—	2	5	9	7	
Total	—	2	5	9	7	23 (3.9%)
Castile (New)						
Cuenca	5	7	3	4	2	
Sigüenza	2	3	6	6	11	
Toledo	3	13	13	12	18	
Total	10	23	22	22	31	108 (18.3%)
Castile (Old)						
Avila	4	11	5	2	1	
Burgos	5	10	14	12	12	
Calahorra	6	14	11	10	21	
Osma, Burgo de	2	3	5	4	12	
Palencia	4	8	11	6	2	
Segovia	5	5	4	2	—	
Valladolid	—	—	—	1	3	
Total	26	51	50	57	51	235 (39.8%)

Table 6.4   (continued)

	1484–99	1500–49	1550–99	1600–49	1650–99	Total[a] 1484–1699
Extremadura:						
Badajoz	—	—	—	1	—	
Coria	—	—	—	—	—	
Plasencia	—	1	1	—	—	
Total	—	1	1	1	—	3 (0.5%)
León:						
Astorga	—	—	1	2	2	
Ciudad Rodrigo	—	—	2	—	1	
León	4	8	6	10	1	
Salamanca	2	9	5	2	—	
Zamora	2	4	2	2	3	
Total	8	21	16	16	7	68 (11.5%)
Galicia:						
Lugo	—	2	1	1	5	
Mondoñedo	—	—	—	1	1	
Orense	—	—	—	3	—	
Santiago	1	—	3	3	5	
Tuy	—	—	—	3	—	
Total	1	2	4	11	1	29 (4.9%)
Murcia:						
Albacete	—	—	—	—	—	
Almeria	—	—	—	—	—	
Cartagena	—	—	—	—	—	
Murcia	—	3	—	1	—	
Total	—	3	—	1	—	4 (0.6%)
Total Crown of Castile	49	113	112	99	116	489 (82.7%)
Kingdom of Navarre:						
Pamplona	3	7	4	10	12	
Total	3	7	4	10	12	36 (6.1%)
Basque Provinces:						
Alava	—	—	—	—	—	
Victoria	—	—	1	—	—	
Total	—	—	1	—	—	1 (0.2%)
CROWNS OF ARAGON						
Aragón:						
Albarracín	—	—	—	—	—	
Barbastro	—	—	—	—	—	
Calatayud	—	—	—	—	—	
Huesca	—	—	2	—	—	
Jaca	—	—	—	1	—	
Tarazona	3	5	4	4	6	

Table 6.4 (continued)

	1484–99	1500–49	1550–99	1600–49	1650–99	Total[a] 1484–1699
Teruel	—	—	—	—	—	
Zaragoza	3	4	1	2	1	
Total	6	9	7	7	7	36 (61%)
Catalonia:						
Barcelona	—	—	—	—	—	
Gerona	—	—	—	—	—	
Lérida	—	—	—	—	—	
Mallorca	—	—	—	—	—	
Tarragona	—	—	—	—	—	
Tortosa	—	—	—	—	—	
Urgel	—	—	—	—	—	
Vich	—	—	—	—	—	
Total	—	—	—	—	—	—
Valencia:						
Orihuela	—	—	—	—	1	
Segorbe	—	—	—	—	—	
Solsona	—	—	—	—	—	
Valencia	—	3	1	—	2	
Total	—	3	1	—	3	7 (1.2%)
Total Crowns of Aragón	6	12	8	7	10	43 (7.3%)
Miscellaneous:						
Canary Islands	—	—	—	—	1	
France	1	—	—	—	—	
Portugal	—	2	—	—	—	
Nullius diocese	—	2	—	—	—	
Unknown	—	2	1	4	7	
Total Misc.	1	6	1	4	8	20 (3.4%)
GRAND TOTAL	59	138	126	122	146	591

[a] Figure in parenthesis is the percentage of the grand total represented by this region.

resident in Madrid as well as the growth of the capital as a center for wealthy letrado clans.

AGE

Except for the Colegio Mayor de Santa Cruz at Valladolid, there is little exact or continuous information available about the ages of students entering the colegios mayores. By statute each college had a minimum age of

Table 7. Mean Entrance Age of Students: the Colegio Mayor de Santa Cruz
(Based upon Ten-Year Averages)

Decade	Mean age (in years)
1510–19	32.0
1520–29	29.7
1530–39	29.9
1540–49	29.4
1550–59	29.3
1560–69	30.8
1570–79	30.5
1580–89	30.0
1590–99	29.6
1600–09	29.5
1610–19	29[a]
1620–29	28.5
1630–39	29.4
1640–49	28.6
1650–59	26.1
1660–69	26.8
1670–79	25.7
1680–89	25.5
1690–99	24.3

[a] Excluding one beca awarded to an old official, aged fifty-four years, who was admitted solely for honorary reasons.

entrance. This varied between twenty and twenty-four.[20] At Santa Cruz, for example, twenty-one was the youngest at which a student could be admitted, although, as Table 7 illustrates, the mean entrance age for students in this college stood well above the statutory minimum throughout the Habsburg era. The advanced age of the students at this and the other colegios mayores reflected the stiff entrance requirements these communities upheld; only mature scholars working at an advanced level qualified for college places, and this in turn helped to guarantee the colegios mayores an important place within their respective universities.

There was, however, an unmistakable drop in the age of the students admitted into Santa Cruz after the middle of the seventeenth century. This occurred less by design than as a result of a general decline in the age of university students in Castile, a situation which forced the colleges to admit younger students and to break statutes which had previously remained inviolate.[21] Yet it is also true that the youngest entrants into the colegios mayores almost invariably had close family ties with former colegiales or with influential government officials, considerations which became increasingly important for elections to college becas. The first

[20]See Febrero Lorenzo, Los Colegios Mayores, p. 54.
[21]See below pp. 175–79 for changes in the age of university students.

twenty-two-year-old elected to Santa Cruz, for example, was Rodrigo Vázquez, son of Martin Vázquez, a graduate of Santa Cruz serving as a member of the Royal Council of Castile.[22] And in general it appears that age was always less of a consideration than family connections in the elections to college scholarships.

The drop in the age of entrance, however, had little effect upon the age at which students left the college. The increasing amount of time spent at university by a majority of colegiales more than compensated for their earlier start.[23] Waiting their turn to compete for university lectureships, then teaching for a number of years, most students in the seventeenth century left the college between the ages of thirty-five and forty.

FAMILY TIES

The lack of adequate genealogical records for the colegios mayores prevents any detailed analysis of their students' family backgrounds. This short section is based upon the limited biographical information supplied by the "admission books" of the various colleges and a few published sources, such as J. Roxas y Contreras, *El Colegio Viejo de San Bartolomé* (Madrid, 1766).[24] The capsule biographies published in this volume have many shortcomings, since the work was itself a polemic intended to embellish the backgrounds and careers of San Bartolomé's members. Moreover, the admission books, available only in manuscript, are sketchy, and only a small proportion of the students are identifiable by more than place of birth and the names of their parents. If a student was related to an important official or a former colegial this was often, but not always, noted; consequently, there exist many more links among the colegiales themselves and between colegiales and court officials and important noblemen than a superficial inquiry by nomenclature alone could uncover.

In any case, the repetition of family names in replica and in varying combinations is immediately striking in the colleges' entrance lists. Though not especially common during the sixteenth century, after 1600 the recurrence of names increases to a point where blood ties between past colegiales and new entrants were no longer an exception but almost a fixed rule; sons, nephews, grandsons, brothers, and cousins of former members abound. San Bartolomé, for example, admitted in the seventeenth century alone four students from the Juaniz de Echalaz family, while three others with Echalaz as part of their surnames were probably members of the same

---

[22]BSC: lib. 22, no. 195.
[23]See below, pp. 140–43.
[24]For those of Arzobispo, see Ferrer Ezquerra and Misol García, *Catálogo de Colegiales del Colegio Mayor de Santiago del Cebedeo, del Arzobispo de Salamanca* (Salamanca, 1956); for Cuenca, see BSC: Ms. 285 and BUS: Ms. 2424; for Oviedo, see BSC: lib. 174, BNM: Ms. 940; for San Ildefonso, AHN: Univs., lib. 1233 F; and Santa Cruz, BSC: lib. 22.

clan.[25] The Queipo de Llano, an important Asturian family, had three
representatives in Santa Cruz, six in Oviedo, and another at San
Bartolomé,[26] but the one family who appeared most frequently in the
colleges was the Santos de San Pedro. Miguel Santos de San Pedro, who
entered Santa Cruz in 1615 only to die the following year, was apparently
the first member of this Leonese family to enter a colegio mayor. He was
followed by sixteen other Santos de San Pedro: one in Santa Cruz, six in
Oviedo, five in San Ildefonso, and four in Arzobispo.[27]

A number of other families appeared almost as frequently in the colleges' rolls, and by the end of the century it is difficult to identify those who
were not related in some fashion to a colegial of the past. Since the entrance
books often fail to take note of blood ties among colegiales, let alone those
of marriage, a simple matching of surnames is not sufficient to catch all of
the various relationships. Nevertheless, it can be established that nearly one-
fourth of the students who entered the college of Oviedo during the first half
of the seventeenth century belonged to established "colegio mayor"
families. At Santa Cruz relatives accounted for over 20 percent of the
students (34 of 137) admitted between 1650 and 1699, and during this same
period no less than 35 percent of San Bartolomé's students had similar
ties. In actuality, however, the number of relatives was far higher than these
figures would suggest, owing to the shortcomings of the colleges' entrance
lists.

In some instances college scholarships virtually became a private,
family preserve, as brother replaced brother. Thus when Bartolomé Sierra
left the college of Santa Cruz in 1689, his brother, Lope de Sierra Ossorio,
entered into his beca. Lope left the college ten years later to take up a
canonry in Toledo, and his place was taken by his younger brother,
Fernando.[28] In much the same way a number of other colegiales assumed
places left vacant by their siblings.[29]

Father-son successions within the colleges were even more frequent. An
early example of such an occurrence is that of Martin de Vázquez, a
member of Santa Cruz late in the fifteenth century, who placed two of his
sons in his alma mater and a third in the Colegio Mayor del Arzobispo.[30]
Likewise, Fernando de Chumacero y Sotomayor, a colegial in San

[25]Roxas y Contreras, *Historia del Colegio Viejo de San Bartolomé* (3 vols., Madrid, 1766), 1: no. 497; 2: nos. 23, 33, 42, 63, 85, 105.
[26]Ibid., vol. I, no. 473; BSC: lib. 22, nos. 488, 513, 579; BSC: lib. 174, nos. 180, 256, 368, 346, 362, 378.
[27]BSC: lib. 22, nos. 356, 397; BSC: lib. 174, nos. 271, 290, 312, 331, 411, 416; AHN: Univs., lib. 1233 F, nos. 727, 758, 890, 914, 937; Ferrer Ezquerra, *Colegio del Arzobispo*, nos. 232, 334.
[28]For the Sierra family in this college, see BSC: lib. 22, nos. 533, 565, 587.
[29]See BSC: lib. 22, nos. 511, 517, 526, 551. In a few cases, the nephew of the out-going colegial was admitted to the empty place; cf. BSC: lib. 22, nos. 500, 501.
[30]BSC: lib. 22, nos. 58, 170, 195. For the third son, see Ferrer Ezquerra, *Colegio del Arzobispo*, p. 35.

Bartolomé, sent three sons to three different colegios mayores: Juan to San Bartolomé, Francisco to Arzobispo, and Antonio to Cuenca.[31] Similar incidents abound. By the seventeenth century it is evident that the colegios mayores, acting more or less as a single unit, drew their members from a shrinking number of families with close ties to at least one of the six. More and more, family replaced academic expertise as the entrance key to these privileged colleges, and when Carlos and Francisco de Borja, both sons of the Duke of Gandía, entered the college of San Ildefonso in 1679, the colegios mayores had gone as far as to ignore statutes which precluded the presence of more than one member of the same family in college at the same time.[32] By the close of the Habsburg era and continuing into the eighteenth century, these academic institutions, originally intended to recruit students on the basis of scholarly merit, were primarily serving the interests of a relatively small number of families and clans.

These families, moreover, comprised the great letrado families who controlled senior offices in the ruling hierarchies. After the late sixteenth century, royal councillors, tribunal magistrates, prelates, and other important officials, colegial and noncolegial, sent their kin to the colegios mayores whenever possible. The result was the increased representation of sons of important letrado officials within the colleges, almost as if such parentage had guaranteed admission. For instance, no fewer than nine colegiales in San Bartolomé during the seventeenth century had a father who sat on the Royal Council of Castile.[33] If other councils and tribunals and other family relationships are included, examples of influential connections among the members of San Bartolomé proliferate, and the same is true for the five other colleges.

Approximately 10 percent of the students admitted to the colegios mayores in the seventeenth century can positively be identified as relatives of royal councillors and of members of the royal households, but this figure is far too low owing to the shortcomings of the colleges' admission books. A thorough investigation of the families of the letrados who served on Castile's councils and tribunals would further demonstrate the close connections between these officials and the colegiales, but such an undertaking is beyond the scope of this book. It would not be an exaggeration, however, to state that the families who controlled the colleges controlled the royal councils as well, or as Pérez Bayer put it: "Rare are the present-day colegiales who do not have or had a father or uncle or close relative on the [Royal] Council, Cámara, or in other tribunals, a Bishop, Archbishop, or important dignity in one of the cathedrals; and rare, on the other hand, are the Camaristas,

---

[31]Roxas y Contreras, *Colegio Viejo*, vol. I, no. 362. His sons were Juan Chumacero y Sotomayor, colegial of San Bartolomé; Francisco Carrillo Chumacero, colegial of Arzobispo; and Antonio Chumacero, colegial of Cuenca.

[32]AHN: Univs., lib. 1233 F, nos. 862–63.

[33]Roxas y Contreras, *Colegio Viejo*, vol. I, nos. 457, 499; vol. II, nos. 5, 27, 34, 72, 74, 78, 106, 131, 138.

Councillors, and Bishops who do not have in the colleges sons, nephews, or relatives."[34]

In spite of the frequency with which the letrado clans made use of the colegios mayores, sons of grandees and *títulos* were not excluded, particularly during the seventeenth century when more and more of Castile's aristocracy sought to prepare their sons for office-holding careers. The Duke of Cardona, a grandee of Spain, sent three of his sons to the College of San Bartolomé, and no fewer than twenty-one other titled families of ancient lineage placed one or more of their off-spring into colegio mayor becas.[35] Normally, it was the younger sons, but occasionally the eldest enrolled as well. Mateo Ibáñez de Mendoza y Segovia, for example, heir to the Marquisate of Mondejar, was a student in the Colegio Mayor de San Ildefonso.[36] Never numerous, sons of old aristocratic families accounted for less than 5 percent of the colegiales, but they were joined by the sons of Castile's newly promoted letrado nobility, and together sons of the titled nobility represented at least 10 percent of the entrants to the colegios mayores in the seventeenth century.

In sum, colegiales with blood relations to other colegiales, living and dead, to the nobility, and to letrado officials constituted a minimum of one-half, and probably more, of the membership of the colegios mayores after 1650. These connections help to demonstrate the new role these communities had assumed. Formerly the preserve of the professional scholar, home of the university's academic elite, these colleges, serving as training grounds for important letrado offices, catered more and more for sons of Castile's ruling families who sought to follow office-holding careers. Important officials, using as a lever the patronage at their command, pushed their sons and relatives into becas which in time would give these youths a definite advantage in the race for public office. The colleges, on the other hand, eager to accommodate influential students whose family connections might benefit the community as a whole, altered or simply overlooked many of their original statutes regarding standards of admission in order to welcome these new members. Across several generations it is apparent that robe officials and noblemen, obtaining becas for their kinsmen again and again, practically forced the colleges to close their doors to students who lacked important family ties. In this manner the original academic elite lodged in the colegios mayores gave way to a new elite based on family and political connections as well as social rank. Meanwhile, the colleges exchanged their scholarly role for one that eventually bound them to the letrado families upon whom they depended for new members and for jobs.

[34]Pérez Bayer, *Literatura Española*, vol. I, folio 66, note 49.

[35]These colegiales are spread throughout the admission books of the six colleges. For a list of *colegiales ilustres* from these communities, see Roxas y Conteras, *Colegio Viejo*, 2: 44 ff.

[36]AHN: Univs., lib. 1233 F, no. 872.

THE END OF POVERTY

One of the first sacrifices made by the colleges in recognition of their changing role was the relaxation of their statutes on poverty. The founders of these communities had initially intended to aid poor students lacking the means to pursue the higher university degrees, and to implement this program they imposed restrictions on the personal income members of the college would be allowed. Depending on the individual college, this figure hovered between twenty and thirty ducats or florins a year.[37]

These restrictions soon lapsed. In 1505 San Bartolomé received a papal bull allowing its members to alter college statutes as they saw fit,[38] and subsequently, in 1534, the 1,500 mrs. limit on personal income was raised to 12,000 mrs.[39] The other colleges followed suit. Arzobispo in 1552 raised its poverty limit from 30 to 50 ducats; Santa Cruz went from 25 to 50 florins; and Oviedo lifted its 6,000 mrs. restriction for one of 15,000 mrs.[40] In the seventeenth century the official poverty line went even higher. Reformers of the colegios mayores in 1635 and 1641, referring to violations of existing poverty statutes, suggested that a limit of 300 ducats (112,500 mrs.) be maintained.[41] But these new restrictions, like the earlier ones, were something of a joke. For years students with more than the permissible income had been admitted to the colleges. Oviedo, for instance, confessed a few years after its foundation when a 6,000 mrs. limit on income was still in effect that "already, by special pardon, those with 2,000 ducats (750,000 mrs.) and more have been admitted."[42] And in 1580 this same college made reference to "meals paid for by the colegiales who have more money than that permitted in the constitutions."[43] Indeed, the fact that the colleges of Arzobispo and Oviedo charged up to 800 *reales* (28,000 mrs.) and more as entrance fees is ample proof that these communities were no longer restricted to impoverished students.[44] By the opening of the seventeenth century the image of the "poor" colegial had faded, while the concept of the colegios mayores as charitable institutions had almost been forgotten.

To a limited extent the inflation plaguing the Castilian economy necessitated the redrawing of the poverty line, and in order to justify their altered statutes the colleges repeatedly invoked this argument.[45] But their case is dubious if one considers seventeenth-century reports about the

---

[37]See Febrero Lorenzo, *Los Colegios Mayores*, pp. 60–63; Sala Balust, *Constituciones*, 3: 15, 209; 4: 15, 176; Pérez Bayer, *Literatura Española*, vol. I, folio 8.

[38]Sala Balust, *Constituciones*, 3: 95.

[39]Ibid., 3: 128.

[40]See ibid., 4: 212; Pérez Bayer, *Literatura Española*, 1: 16.

[41]AGS: GJ, leg. 959, *visita* of 18.1.1635; BM: Add. 24, 947, folio 91. See also Sala Balust, *Colegios de Salamanca*, pp. 13, 102.

[42]Sala Balust, *Constituciones*, 4: 48.

[43]Ibid., 4: 83.

[44]Ibid., 4: 146–47, 296.

[45]See the 1534 statute of San Bartolomé which raised the college's poverty limit from 5,000 to 12,000 mrs.; cf. ibid., 3: 128.

nature of college life.[46] Totally absent is the impression of impoverished scholars struggling for the barest necessities of life. They note, rather, an abundance of private servants, horses, coaches, sedan chairs, and hunting dogs, along with lavish furnishings and dress, luxuries which the original statutes of the colleges had expressly prohibited. Certainly, the problems of the national economy had contributed to the abrogation of the poverty statutes, but far more important was the steady rise in the wealth and the social position of the average colegial.

It should also be remembered that only *bachilleres* secured becas in the colegios mayores. This meant that students entering the colleges had already supported themselves for a number of years at the university, either independently or with the help of a clerical prebend or a scholarship in an undergraduate college. Aspirants to colegio mayor scholarships were also asked to cover the costs of the extensive *limpieza de sangre* investigations which were required for entrance. Such inquiries entailed numerous paid testimonials and journeys for the colegiales performing the task, and the total expenditure involved was substantial. In view of these initial expenses, few colegiales, even in the early sixteenth century, could have been truly classified as paupers. Moreover, in an inflationary era wealthy applicants, better able to meet the preliminary costs and entrance fees, enjoyed a considerable advantage over their poorer competitors. Thus the colleges, facing financial difficulties of their own and solicited by students whose incomes surpassed the limits laid down in the statutes, did not find it very difficult to relax their restrictions on poverty.

Yet the underlying reason for the end of poverty within the colegios mayores was their identification with the social and political elite of Castile. As long as becas constituted an important aid to office-holding as well as a mark of considerable prestige, the letrado dynasties, along with a few members of the old aristocracy, would continue to seek colegio mayor places for their sons. To make room for these wealthy and influential students the colleges loosened their restrictions on poverty, since colegiales with powerful court connections would bring patronage and prestige to the community as a whole. With this aim in mind, San Ildefonso in the seventeenth century admitted fee-paying pensioners (*porcionistas*) from notable families, among them Fernando Moscoso y Osorio, nephew of Baltasar Moscoso y Sandoval, Archbishop of Toledo (1646–65), Carlos and Francisco de Borja, sons of the Duke of Gandía, and Luis de Haro y Paz, son of the Viceroy of Naples, the Count of Castrillo.[47] The other five colleges, though officially excluding pensioners until later in the century, openly welcomed

    [46]See the reports of seventeenth-century visitations to the colleges in AGS: GJ, leg. 959. These have been published in Sala Balust, *Colegios de Salamanca*; see esp. the 1665 report of don Matías de Rada, pp. 106–16. See also AHN: Cons. leg. 7138, letter of the *maestrescuela* of Salamanca, 9.XI.1701.
    [47]See AHN: Univ., lib. 1233 F, nos. 640, 675, 862–63. For accounts of this college's *porcionistas*, see AHN: Univs., lib. 911 F.

the sons of the high nobility. And to make its own position clear, the Colegio Mayor de Cuenca in 1586 passed the following statute: "We order that, given parity between the competitors, he with the best lineage be elected [to the College] because Aristotle 'ex bestis bestiam et ex bonis bonum, putat generari'."[48]

However eager the colleges were to admit sons of the aristocracy, the relaxation of their poverty statutes had less to do with the grandees than with the growing wealth and importance of the letrado families who dominated college scholarships. Letrado ministers, steeped in a legal tradition, sought becas for their sons and nephews. To meet this demand, the colleges altered their statutes in violation of their founders' charitable designs but in conformity with the educational demands of Castile's letrado elite. Simultaneously, the interests of the letrados and those of the colleges became one.

CAREERS

Changes in the family backgrounds of the colegiales mayores also found expression in the careers which these students elected to follow. In the early sixteenth century graduates of the colleges, with the exception of those from Arzobispo, tended to follow ecclesiastical careers rather than those in secular office. Colegiales who became churchmen included the famous Archbishop of Toledo, Juan Martínez Siliceo, a San Bartolomé graduate, notorious for his campaign against Spain's conversos. But toward the end of this century colegiales displayed the beginning of a marked preference for secular careers, either in the letrado hierarchy or the inquisition (Table 8), signaling a reorientation of their professional goals.[49]

This evolution can be partly explained by the increasing prestige of secular office. Convention now states that during the Middle Ages, in Spain as elsewhere, the renunciation of the world for the life of the cloth was considered, with the possible exception of war, as the ideal vocation for all men. Such ideas began to change, however, in the course of the fifteenth and sixteenth centuries, when the growing popularity of Italian ideas on "civic humanism" helped to support the position that worldly careers, particularly those in government, were virtuous and honorable in their own right. Moreover, new opportunities created by the expansion of the monarchy offered respectable alternatives to both the church and the military; consequently, sons of noble families who once would have prepared for the battlefield or the altar in an either/or fashion turned increasingly to offices. By the seventeenth century, office-holding as a

---

[48]Sala Balust, Constituciones, 3: 234.

[49]San Ildefonso is somewhat of an exception. Expressly designed to train churchmen, all of its graduates in the sixteenth century entered the church. However, by the reign of Charles II, nearly 20 percent rejected ecclesiastical careers for those in government.

Table 8. Careers of Colegio Mayor Graduates [a]

Reign	Let.	Ecc.	Let.-Ecc.	Inq.	Inq.-Ecc.	Med.	Univ.	Other	Dead	?	Total
Ferdinand & Isabel	51 (25.4)	66 (32.8)	12 (6.0)	17 (8.5)	3 (1.5)	9 (4.5)	3 (1.5)	1 (0.4)	15 (7.5)	21 (10.4)	201
Charles V	107 (31.7)	105 (31.1)	24 (7.1)	10 (3.0)	24 (7.1)	8 (2.4)	1 (0.3)	6 (1.8)	28 (8.3)	25 (7.4)	338
Philip II	113 (30.3)	120 (32.2)	13 (3.5)	15 (4.0)	20 (5.4)	3 (0.8)	3 (0.8)	2 (0.5)	35 (9.4)	49 (13.1)	373
Philip III	78 (35.5)	61 (27.7)	14 (6.4)	3 (1.4)	6 (2.7)	—	2 (0.9)	4 (1.8)	27 (12.3)	25 (11.4)	220
Philip IV	188 (41.0)	103 (22.5)	10 (2.2)	14 (3.1)	10 (2.2)	—	2 (0.4)	9 (2.0)	60 (13.1)	62 (13.5)	458
Charles II	124 (31.0)	78 (19.5)	8 (2.0)	24 (6.0)	11 (2.8)	—	4 (1.0)	19 (4.8)	64 (16.0)	68 (17.0)	400

Key:

Let.   A career in the letrado hierarchy.
Ecc.   A church career.
Let.-Ecc.   A career with positions in the letrado hierarchy and the church.
Inq.   A career in the tribunals of the inquisition.
Inq.-Ecc.   A career with positions in the church and the inquisition.
Med.   A career as a physician.
Univ.   A teaching career at a university.
Other   Capa y espada positions at the royal court, an army career, a life outside government, etc.
Dead   Student died before leaving the university.
?   Career unknown because of insufficient data.

[a]Figures represent the aggregate total of four colegios mayores: Arzobispo, Oviedo, San Bartolomé, and Santa Cruz. Cuenca is omitted because of insufficient data. For San Ildefonso, see p. 131. Figures in parentheses represent percent of the total.

career had come into its own, although this is not to say that important families in the years after 1600 shied away from the church. On the contrary, it remained a tradition among many families to have at least one son take ecclesiastical vows, but at the same time, careers in secular offices became a part of family tradition as well. Among the letrados, the goal to be achieved was the wealth, status, and life-style of the aristocracy, and royal offices appeared as the ideal means of achieving such ends. Furthermore, in an era when worldly success had itself become a mark of public notoriety and prestige, these same families worked to secure lucrative public charges for their sons. Though pious in their daily lives and dedicated to the service of the crown, the "office" and the social and monetary rewards it promised served as the guiding force in their lives.

To explain the growing preference among the colegiales mayores for secular careers only in terms of their aspirations is insufficient. As important were changes in their family backgrounds. During the seventeenth century Castile acquired an "administrative nobility" as letrado families with a long tradition of service to the crown took control of key positions in royal government. In the meantime, graduates of the colegios mayores acquired a permanent, often dominant place in the letrado hierarchy. These two phenomena, loosely connected in the past, merged rapidly after 1600, marking the first era of mutual dependency between colegiales on the one hand and letrado officials on the other. The colegiales wanted professorships and jobs; the letrados—becas. And this convergence of interests allowed the offspring of the letrado dynasties to enter the colleges on a regular basis. These students, eager for wealth, prestige, and titles of nobility, followed their fathers into the world of office and honor.

There were a few students, however, particularly those with influential family ties, who eschewed letrado careers for those of a more aristocratic bent. The increase at the end of the seventeenth century in the "other" category of Table 8 represents those colegiales who, despite their legal training, entered the military, acquired capa y espada charges at the royal court, or lived idly as *rentiers*. A number of these were younger sons of the aristocracy, such as Luis de Benavides y Aragón, son of the Count of Santisteban del Puerto, who left his college of San Bartolomé to become Gentleman of the Chamber to King Charles II and, subsequently, viceroy of Navarre.[50] Others, like Manuel de Arce y Astete whose father was president of the Council of Finance, were sons of letrados. After earning his licentiate in law, Manuel left his college either to "inherit his house" or to contract a favorable marriage.[51] Similar temptations led other colegiales to abandon letrado careers. Therefore, it would appear that in spite of the prestige and importance that the study and profession of law had acquired in the two cen-

[50]Roxas y Contreras, *Colegio Viejo*, vol. II, no. 98.
[51]Ibid., vol. II, no. 138.

Table 9. Distribution of Becas by Faculty in the Colegios Mayores

Years	Theology	Canon Law	Civil Law	Arts	Medicine	?	Total
			Colegio Mayor de Oviedo				
1524–49	8 (11.3)	9 (12.7)	7 (9.9)	—	5 (7.0)	42 (59.2)	71
1550–99	26 (24.8)	43 (41.0)	14 (13.3)	—	4 (3.8)	18 (17.1)	105
1600–49	30 (25.6)	75 (64.0)	11 (9.4)	—	—	3 (2.6)	117
1650–99	28 (27.5)	102 (75.0)	1 (0.7)	—	—	5 (3.7)	136
			Colegio Mayor de Arzobispo				
1528–50[a]	4 (12.9)	11 (35.5)	6 (19.4)	1 (3.2)	—	9 (29.0)	31
1551–1600	16 (15.2)	45 (42.9)	27 (25.7)	—	—	17 (16.2)	105
1601–50	30 (19.4)	92 (59.4)	19 (12.3)	1 (6.4)	—	15 (9.7)	155
1651–1700	23 (14.8)	90 (58.1)	23 (14.8)	—	—	30 (19.4)	155
			Colegio Mayor de San Bartolomé				
1450–99	15 (12.6)	71 (59.7)	7 (5.9)	23 (19.3)	—	3 (2.5)	119
1500–49	30[b] (25.4)	60 (50.8)	23 (19.5)	5 (4.2)	—	—	118
1550–99	36 (31.3)	45 (39.1)	23 (20.0)	5 (4.3)	—	6 (5.2)	115
1600–49	19 (18.6)	53 (52.0)	27 (26.5)	3 (2.9)	—	—	102
1650–99	27 (23.3)	33 (28.4)	55 (47.4)	—	—	1 (0.8)	116
			Colegio Mayor de Santa Cruz				
1500–49	35 (25.2)	61 (43.9)	21 (15.1)	3 (2.2)	16 (11.5)	3 (2.2)	139
1550–99	38 (30.2)	58 (46.0)	12 (9.5)	5 (4.0)	6 (4.8)	7 (5.6)	126
1600–49	33 (28.4)	73 (62.9)	13 (11.2)	1 (0.9)	—	—	116
1650–99	22 (15.1)	64 (43.8)	27 (18.5)	2 (1.4)	—	31 (21.2)	146

[a] Data incomplete.
[b] One switched to canon law.

Note: Figures in parentheses represent percent of the total.

turies of Habsburg rule, the land and its titles remained the ultimate goals of the university graduate. A life as a letrado, an end in itself, was also an efficient means to achieve these higher aims.

With these exceptions, the majority of colegiales prepared for careers in public office. Rare was the college student who, if he outlived his stay at university, did not assume an administrative post. In this sense, the colegios mayores remained true to the ideal of service to the state their founders had originally devised. Destined to harbor the academic elite of the universities to which they belonged, the colegios mayores were also to be the training schools for the university-trained officials of the Spanish crown.

REALLOCATION OF THE BECAS

One result of the sustained interest in secular careers among the colegiales was the increase in the number of college students studying jurisprudence. The popularity of this subject, necessary for letrado offices as well as the inquisition and the church, is another illustration of the close relationship of the colegios mayores with careers in the king's service.

The founders of the colleges had allocated a set number of becas to each of the higher university faculties: law (canon and civil), the arts, theology, and medicine, but the balance between the faculties was short-lived.[52] A redistribution of becas took place; theology and medicine were excluded, while canon law, and in some colleges, civil law, came to the fore (Table 9), a change that was effected by the illegal transference of becas from one faculty to another. Santa Cruz, for example, although permanently endowed with three places for *médicos*, admitted its last student of medicine in 1578 and elected jurists to the places left vacant.[53] The colleges del Arzobispo and Cuenca also had provisions for medical students, but they apparently filled these places with jurists from the start.[54]

Royal visitations in the seventeenth century demanded that the colleges return to their original allocation of becas among the faculties, but projected reforms brought no results.[55] In the case of Santa Cruz, where the proportion of theologians within the college fell from the mandatory one-third to approximately 15 percent in the later seventeenth century, the Royal Council in 1668, angered at the college's refusal to correct this imbalance, temporarily suspended that community's right to elect new members.[56] Theologians in the other colleges were also in short supply; the popularity of

---

[52]Sala Balust, *Constituciones*, 3: 14, 209; 4: 14. See also AHN: Cons., leg. 7138, "Información de los Colegios Mayores," 19.I.1636.

[53]Francisco Bartolomé, admitted to this college on 6.VIII.1578, was Santa Cruz's last student of medicine; cf. BSC: lib. 22, no. 274.

[54]In 1580 the Royal Council ordered these two colleges to explain why they had never admitted *médicos*; cf. Esperabé Artega, *Universidad de Salamanca*, 1: 571.

[55]See Sala Balust, *Colegios de Salamanca*, pp. 24, 32, 102, 111.

[56]BSC: Caja 31, no. 416.

the study of jurisprudence had left the "science of sciences" only a minor, subsidiary place within the colegios mayores.[57]

The College of San Ildefonso offers a striking example of the growing importance of the law within these communities. Its original statutes barred the admittance of law students, and this regulation throughout the sixteenth century was treated with respect.[58] But on October 17, 1617 don Alvaro de Ayala, son of the Duke of Fuensalida and licentiate in canon law, became San Ildefonso's first *colegial jurista*.[59] On the same day two other jurists were elected to becas, marking the start of a new era; by the reign of Charles II canon lawyers accounted for more than 40 percent of the students elected to the college.

The reallocation of the becas constituted a direct response to pressures placed on the colegios mayores from above and below. Confronted by a monarchy demanding jurists and influential families seeking law degrees for their sons, the colleges, eager to maintain their favored position on the Cámara's lists, needed to switch some becas to the law. At the same time students seeking admittance to the colleges were increasingly interested in office-holding careers and, consequently, in legal studies. Caught between the two, the colleges, not unwillingly, elected lawyers to places formerly reserved for students of theology and medicine.

The development of a juridical spirit among the colegios mayores was in this sense unavoidable. Catering both to students seeking office-holding careers and to the letrado officialdom, the colleges sacrificed the balance of the faculties in order to fulfill their social and bureaucratic obligations. Reform was virtually impossible, since a return to their original state demanded more than a rigid imposition of their founding statutes. It called for an alteration of the social classes and the institutions which the colleges had come to represent.

INSTRUCTORSHIPS

Another manifestation of the colleges' adhesion to Castile's letrado elite was the rate at which colegiales became university lecturers and professors. As we already know, the colegios mayores, admitting only students with a first degree, were originally intended to provide a small number of promising scholars with the time and the facilities to study and to obtain advanced degrees. But the latter were expensive and their recipients relatively few. On the other hand, members of the colegios mayores, owing to their special graduation privileges, could obtain licenses

---

[57]See Sala Balust, *Colegios de Salamanca*, p. 25; AHN: Cons., leg. 7138, "Información de los Colegios Mayores," 19.I.1636; and Pérez Bayer, *Literatura Española*, vol. I, folio 154.

[58]On 15 December 1576 the Royal Council debated whether there should be "colegiales juristas" in San Ildefonso, probably after a previous request by that college for permission to admit such students; see AHN: Cons., Consultas de Viernes, leg. 7043.

[59]AHN: Univs., lib. 1233 F, no. 536.

Table 10. Colegiales Mayores with University Teaching Posts

Reign	Total admitted	Number of Lecturers & Professors	%
ARZOBISPO			
Charles V	55	4	7.3
Philip II	81	11	13.6
Philip III	59	13	22.0
Philip IV	148	45	30.4
Charles II	110	36	32.7
Total	453	109	24.1
OVIEDO			
Charles V	84	30	35.7
Philip II	86	32	37.2
Philip III	54	19	35.2
Philip IV	108	49	44.8
Charles II	97	28	28.9
Total	429	158	36.8
SAN BARTOLOMÉ			
Catholic Kings	87	22	25.3
Charles V	95	49	51.6
Philip II	96	44	45.8
Philip III	47	21	44.7
Philip IV	92	45	48.9
Charles II	84	34	40.5
Total	501	215	42.9
SANTA CRUZ			
Catholic Kings	116	20	17.2
Charles V	100	54	54.0
Philip II	109	84	77.1
Philip III	48	40	83.3
Philip IV	104	43	41.4
Charles II	117	84	71.8
Total	594	325	54.7
GRAND TOTAL	1,977	807	40.8

and doctorates at bargain rates. This, in turn, put them in an excellent position to become university instructors, since the majority of teaching positions were awarded only to scholars with advanced degrees.

Table 10 illustrates their success. At Salamanca between one-third and one-half of the students in the colegios mayores were regularly named to university instructorships and in Valladolid nearly all of the colegiales of Santa Cruz taught at the university. San Ildefonso's record at Alcalá was probably similar to that at Santa Cruz, but, unfortunately, existing documents do not provide the information upon which its success in obtaining teaching posts for its members can be measured.

To a large extent scholarly excellence was responsible for this outstanding record. As graduate students enjoying financial support, colegiales could devote their lives to study, while weekly review and practice sessions within the colleges readied them for the public lectures and examinations they would have to face in order to win a chair. Few ordinary students enjoyed such opportunities, and this difference helps to explain the ability of the colegiales to win so many teaching posts. Yet study and academic achievement alone were not sufficient to assure the colegiales of continued success in the increasingly turbulent and corrupt elections in which university students named their instructors. So, in addition, the colleges employed a variety of special tactics designed to secure victories for their members and thus to enhance their own prestige.

Toward this end the college of Santa Cruz collected from each of its members an annual tax of one hundred reales for the express purpose of buying student votes.[60] Depending on the chair in question, the sums distributed by this college among the students rose as high as 400 reales.[61] This practice, if employed on a regular basis, might help to explain this community's extraordinary record of success in the *oposiciones*, the open competitions for university chairs. Indeed, so formidable was the presence of Santa Cruz in these contests that the defeat of one of its candidates was considered a rare and unusual event. Fabio Nelli de Espinosa, writing on April 3, 1599, to the famous merchant of Medina de Campo, Simón Ruiz, commented on a recent miracle at the University of Valladolid: a "poor" student had taken a chair from a certain Docotor Soria, a colegial, in spite of "the great negotiations of the College and of Soria himself."[62]

At Salamanca the four colegios mayores used equally unsavory methods to collect the necessary student votes. From the 1550s until the king called a permanent halt to student elections in 1641, the history of appointments to the chairs at this university is a never-ending tale of bribery, corruption, and violence.[63] The Royal Council, backed by the king, repeatedly issued orders and threatened stiff fines to stop the abuses, but matters grew continually worse, reaching a climax in the 1630s. The colegios mayores, which together provided a steady stream of competitors, stood at the center of these events. Gifts, dinners, and money distributed by the wealthy

[60]Bennassar, *Valladolid au Siècle d'Or* (Paris, 1967), p. 360.

[61]Ibid., p. 360.

[62]Ibid., p. 361.

[63]See U. González de la Calle, *Oposiciones a Catédras en la Universidad de Salamanca, 1550–60* (Madrid, 1933). Orders of the Royal Council to stop corruption in the student elections appeared in 1558, 1561, 1565, 1567, 1580, 1584, 1586, 1592, 1595, 1598, 1602, 1604, and 1621; cf. Esperabé Artega, *Universidad de Salamanca*, vol. 1. See also AHN: Cons., leg. 7138.

colegiales helped influence votes in their favor, even though colegiales were occasionally caught in the act, as in 1592 when Alvaro de Arellano, a student in Cuenca, and Alonso Yañez de Lugo, a student in Oviedo, were accused of buying votes.[64]

As leaders of the various "nations" or regional groups among the university students, the colegios mayores had additional leverage upon the student elections. Through the bando system, each college identified itself with one of the university "nations," and a letter to the Royal Council written in 1636 confirmed that the colegios mayores were "the heart of the nations."[65] Two years later, in a *memorial* to Philip IV, the colleges admitted their leadership over the regional groups within the university.[66] While student elections lasted, each "nation" supported its own candidate, and he was ordinarily a colegial mayor.[67]

At Salamanca, there were also older graduates who made a regular business out of rounding up with certain promises penniless students from their own region and province and then selling them en masse as blocs of votes to prospective candidates for university chairs.[68] As heads of the nations, the colegios mayores were intimately involved in such practices, and, exploiting their followers, they regularly provoked violence in the days leading up to the elections in order to intimidate voters to their side. So intense was the competition for instructorships that colegiales, as representatives of opposing nations, were even known to fight among themselves. In 1636, for instance, a rivalry arose over the chair of Old Digest between Juan de Góngora, a colegial of Arzobispo, and Francisco de Vergara, colegial of San Bartolomé. Fighting broke out among the armed followers of both candidates, the *gallegos* representing Góngora, while the *vizcainos* took the part of the latter.[69] Intercollegiate hostility, however, was infrequent; the four colegios mayores at Salamanca, conscious of their equal status and prestige, similar organization, and shared family lineages, did little to incite one another. On most questions they joined together against the university as a whole.[70]

In 1641 the corregidor of Salamanca, Francisco de Vera, decried the violence of student elections and the armed groups of students going in and out of the colegios mayores. He wrote: "The Colleges favor this practice because it perpetuates the success they desire and because they have no other alternative. We have put strict prohibitions on the possession of

---

[64]Esperabé Artega, *Universidad de Salamanca*, 1: 607.
[65]AHN: Cons. leg. 7138, Fernando de Ibarra al Consejo Real, 19..I.1636.
[66]Ibid., "Memorial de los Colegios Mayores," 9.XI.1638.
[67]González de la Calle, *Oposiciones*, p. 71.
[68]Ibid., p. 77.
[69]AHN: Cons. leg. 7138, letters of 16 and 17.I.1636 and 2.II.1636 describe this clash.
[70]See Pérez Bayer, *Literatura Española*, vol. II, folios 207 ff. The solidarity of the colegios mayores is also evident in the numerous joint memorials they sent to the Royal Council. Several of these can be found in AHN: Cons. leg. 7138.

pistols and guns but these are not enough."[71] That same year the
Royal Council, weary of student disorders and the "wars of the nations,"
which gave the kingdom's leading universities the appearance of armed
camps, assumed the appointment of university instructors on a permanent basis. But this move, so far from weakening the position of the
colegios mayores, in fact enhanced their opportunities in the competition
for university chairs. The favor and the influence of family members and
former colegiales on the Royal Council were much more helpful than the
bribery, gifts, and intimidation of the past. Now nearly every colegial
who desired a teaching post secured his reward, and later in the century
what had become a recognized fact was institutionalized through an administrative device known as the *turno*. "The *turno* means that when a
vacant chair is about to be filled, the [Council] recommends, for example, a
member of the Colegio Mayor of San Bartolomé; for the next chair to
vacate, one from Cuenca; for the next, one from Arzobispo; for the next,
one from Oviedo; and for the last, a *manteísta* graduate. Then it returns to
nominate a colegial of San Bartolomé, and the *turno* begins again in the
same way."[72]

That the proportion of colegiales securing teaching posts declined in the
later seventeenth century is indicative of the job-security these students
had come to possess (Table 10). With more and more colegiales belonging
to important letrado and noble families, qualifications which alone were
sufficient in the nepotistic world of Habsburg Spain to secure appointment
to royal office, many found it unnecessary to compete for university chairs
and relied upon their personal connections to obtain the desired posts. The
career of Andrés de Medrano y Mendizaval, a member of San
Bartolomé, exemplifies this new security. Son of García de Medrano, a
former San Bartolomé student and a member of the Royal Council and
Cámara of Castile, Andrés left the college four years after he had
entered, and without any teaching experience whatsoever, to become
Juez Mayor de Vizcaya in the chancillería at Valladolid.[73] Other colegiales
exploited family ties of their own, and, in the end, nepotism proved far
more effective than corruption and violence as a means of acquiring both
lectureships and chairs.

TIME IN COLLEGE

One result of the competition for teaching posts and letrado offices among
the colegiales was the lengthening of the average student's college career.
These positions were relatively scarce, and the would-be competitors far
too many. Thus waiting first for chairs, and then for offices, colegiales frequently remained at university fifteen or twenty years.

[71]AHN: Cons., leg. 7138, letter of 30.XI.1641.
[72]AGS: GJ, leg. 943, "Relacion del Turno en la Universidad de Salamanca."
[73]Roxas y Contreras, *Colegio Viejo*, vol. II, no. 72.

The college beca, implying room, board, gown, and expenses, was originally intended to last only a limited period of time, after which the student was obliged to leave the community. Depending on the college, this period stretched from seven to nine years, sufficient time for a *bachiller* to earn one or more of the higher university degrees.[74]

For the first three-quarters of the sixteenth century these statutes remained in force; students left the college when obliged to do so, although several colleges had received permission to extend the allotted stay by one or two years.[75] But the following examples show that by the middle of the seventeenth century, colegiales remained within their communities well beyond the statutory limit.

Student	College	Years in College[76]
Jorge de Cárdenas y Valenzuela	Arzobispo	1674–95
Garcia Pérez de Araciel	Arzobispo	1667–88
Andrés Doriaga	Cuenca	1676–96
Juan Francisco de Hierro	Santa Cruz	1651–69

The matriculation books of the Universities of Salamanca and Valladolid record numerous examples of other college students with seventeen, eighteen, even nineteen years of residence in their colleges; to remain in college beyond the expiration of one's beca was no longer an exception but the general rule.

An extrastatutory device known as the *hospedería* or lodging house made possible these extended college careers. Erected by each of the colleges in the course of the sixteenth century, they received official recognition in a statute passed by the College of Cuenca in 1585:

"After finishing their time in the college, the colegiales may move into the rooms designated for *huéspedes* [lodgers] and remain there for the space of one year, and this may be extended for a further year . . . but from now on no additional extensions shall be granted except for great and very urgent reasons upon which the colegiales must unanimously decide. Furthermore, the *huésped* must pay to the College 40 ducats per annum for his sustenance."[77]

In practice, the huéspedes of Cuenca and the other colleges stayed on well past the two-year limit, and by the later seventeenth century nearly every

---

[74]Sala Balust, *Constituciones*, 3: 15, 218; 4: 20, 176.

[75]Arzobispo extended its beca from eight years to nine in 1581; cf. E. Madruga Jiménez, *Crónica del Colegio Mayor del Arzobispo*, p. 28. Oviedo and Santa Cruz also added another year or two to their scholarships; cf. Pérez Bayer, *Literatura Española*, vol. I, folio 138.

[76]See AUS: *Libros de Matrículas*, for the appropriate years. Colegiales are listed separately at the front of each of these volumes. The same applies for the college of Santa Cruz: cf. AUV: Libros de Matrículas.

[77]Sala Balust, *Constituciones*, 3: 269.

colegial at the end of his beca, moved into the hospedería, paying the college the stipulated fees.[78] A 1666 visitation to the College of San Ildefonso by a graduate of San Bartolomé gave such practices official consent; subsequently, time restrictions in the hospederías were lifted.[79] Now it was possible for colegiales like Jorge de Cárdenas y Valenzuela, noted above, a paying lodger for eleven of his twenty-one years in the college of Arzobispo, to live in the hospederías for extended periods of time without violating college statutes and rules.

The need for those lodging houses arose after the colleges instituted a seniority system which regulated the candidacies of their members for university teaching posts. The college of San Bartolomé was the first to develop such a system after it ruled late in the fifteenth century that not more than one of its members would compete for a vacant university chair.[80] Soon this statute, and it was copied by the other colleges, came to mean that the college was to elect only one student—the statute stipulated the one who was judged most capable—to compete in the oposiciones in the community's name.[81] But as chairs became increasingly valuable for their salaries and prestige, more and more colegiales sought to compete. Problems arose when several qualified colegiales fought for the right to represent the college in the oposiciones; consequently, the colleges passed new statutes giving priority to the eldest colegial.[82] This rapidly developed into a seniority system whereby each student, according to the faculty in which he was enrolled and his time in the community, earned the right to enter the competition for chairs and to receive the full support of his college. But, as a 1552 statute in the college of Oviedo stipulated, "there cannot be an appointment of a new opositor until the one who has already been named pursues his oposiciones [successfully]";[83] so if one colegial had difficulty in obtaining a chair, his juniors were obliged to wait for his appointment before they could begin to compete for posts in that faculty. Complications ensued, since so many of the colleges' students were registered in the faculties of law where competition for teaching positions was ex-

[78]It is also known that colegiales moved into the *hospedería* before their regular scholarship was up. This was done to free themselves from certain restrictions—poverty limits, prohibitions on the possession of clerical prebends, curfews, etc.—which applied to students with becas.
[79]See Pérez Bayer, *Literatura Española*, vol. I, folio 139. Previously, the Royal Council had opposed extended stays in the *hospederías*; cf. Sala Balust, *Colegios de Salamanca*, p. 32.
[80]See Roxas y Contreras, *Colegio Viejo*, vol. I, no. 143.
[81]BSC: caja 2, statute no. 28; Sala Balust, *Constituciones*, 3: 118, 247; 4: 31, 192.
[82]BSC: caja 2, statute of 1.VIII.1580; Sala Balust, *Constituciones*, 3: 139. At the College of Fonseca in Santiago de Compostela a statute was passed in 1583 which allowed only one colegial to compete for a chair at the same time in order to prevent "partialities and differences" within the community. The privilege of representing the college went to the eldest member; cf. Antonio Fraguas Fraguas, *Historia del Colegio de Fonseca* (Santiago de Compostela, 1956), p. 53.
[83]Sala Balust, *Constituciones*, 4: 66, 221.

ceptionally stiff. Appointments to these chairs often took years to obtain, therefore, a waiting-list, based upon year of entrance into the college, had to be compiled and hospederías organized so that the colegiales could wait their turn to compete for a university chair.

But there is another reason for the growth of the hospederías and the long university careers of many colegiales. In 1714 Luis Curiel, a former colegial and a member of the Royal Council of Castile, explained the situation in these terms: "The reason for the long years spent by the colegiales in their communities is their belief that it is permissible to leave the beca only for the toga.[84] It offends their vanity only to imagine one of their members as a lawyer, a local judge, prebendary, or a parish priest; they say that they will burn the gown of a colegial who plans to enter one of these posts, and at various times, such a threat has been carried out."[85] Although students had always been reluctant to leave their college without a secure position, a small number of colegiales before the late sixteenth century had been content to become lawyers, corregidores, or some other minor judicial officer. Santa Cruz, for example, produced at least eight students who left the college as lawyers before 1600, while another five became corregidores, and it is likely that these figures are much too low.[86] In the seventeenth century fewer colegiales left the security of the college for one of these lesser positions.[87] Instead they preferred to remain in the hospederías, preparing for oposiciones or merely waiting for an appointment as a cathedral canon or tribunal magistrate.

The students' reluctance to leave their colleges for anything but a prestige post is simply another manifestation of changes in their family backgrounds. The humble origins of many of the early colegiales was not incompatible with a career as a lawyer or parish priest, but few of the seventeenth-century colegiales would have followed such "clerkly" careers. Furthermore, pampered by their friends and relatives on the councils, the colegiales possessed what contemporaries called a "security of promotion" with the knowledge that the sought-after offices would eventually be forthcoming. Under these conditions colegiales lived luxuriously in the hospederías, awaiting the offices that favoritism would eventually bring their way.

[84]*Toga*, or judicial robe, implies a position in one of the tribunals or councils of the crown; in other words, a *plaza de asiento*.

[85]AGS: GJ, leg. 959, "Discurso sobre los Colegios Mayores . . .," folio 1v.

[86]In the sixteenth century, three of San Bartolomé's graduates became lawyers, while another three entered into the corregimientos of the crown. However, Roxas y Contreras, author of the biographies of this college's graduates, frequently avoided mention of jobs other than *plazas de asiento* that were held by San Bartolomé students in order to enhance the prestige of the college's record. It is likely, therefore, that more of San Bartolomé's students entered "temporal" offices during the fifteenth and sixteenth centuries than Roxas y Contreras admits.

[87]For the seventeenth century I have not been able to find reference to any student who left a colegio mayor as an abogado, and in all six of the colleges, only five students left for a corregimiento.

INCREASE IN SIZE

One final result of the colleges' position as training schools for the sons of important letrado and noble families destined for office-holding careers was an increase in size. As the colleges' reputation for excellence grew, numerous students, eager for the prestige and the patronage a beca would confer, clamored for admission. The colleges responded by increasing the number of college scholarships, nearly all of which were reserved for students in law.

The original constitutions of the six colegios mayores allowed for no more than a total of 141 becas. Each college had a limited number of places regulated by the size of its endowment and its founder's desires for a small community that would supposedly foster a spirit of fraternity among the colegiales. San Bartolomé was the smallest with fifteen becas and two places for chaplains; San Ildefonso was the largest with a total of thirty-three places. Santa Cruz, though officially endowed with twenty-seven places, never reached more than 20 or 21 because of financial difficulties. For similar reasons, the other colleges remained quite small, usually well short of their allotted number of places, although gifts of plate and money left to them in the wills of former students and the fees received from incoming students and pensioners enabled them to survive.

Gradually, the situation improved. After 1620, as Figure 2 illustrates, each of the colleges grew sharply in size. This expansion, beginning at a time when the economic situation can hardly have been very favorable to college rents, reflected the increased demand for becas, as well as the growing wealth of the average colegial. The private means of the students supplemented the colleges' income, while the increased acceptance of

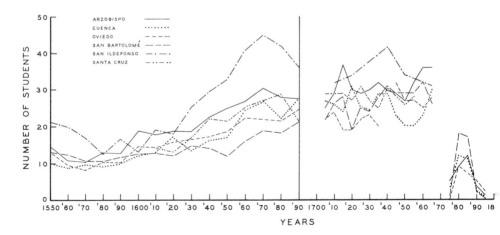

Fig. 2. Growth of the colegios mayores. Thanks to privilege and patronage, the colegios mayores prospered in the seventeenth and eighteenth centuries, while the total student population of the universities declined (see Fig. 8).

fee-paying pensioners helped also to improve college revenues.[88] So, in spite of their financial difficulties, the colleges were in a position to add new scholarships, while their students maintained an increasingly sumptuous style of life commensurate with their personal means and their aspirations to live as gentlemen. In 1714 Luis Curiel admitted that every colegial, upon entrance to the community, paid his college a certain sum to cover the costs of his "meat and bread."[89] Apparently, the beca no longer carried with it full support, but the wealth of individual members had allowed the colleges to increase their numbers without having to tap their revenues for the necessary funds. In other words, the original intention of the college founders to use the beca as an instrument of charity was dismissed as the colleges adapted themselves to the service of the kingdom's ruling elite.

In the decade 1670–79 the six colegios mayores possessed a total of approximately 170 places, a figure which is roughly 21 percent above their original, statutory size and about two and one-half times larger than that of a century before. By the middle of the eighteenth century, the colleges were even larger; in 1740 they had close to two hundred becas. And it was during this period that the colleges, in order to accommodate these students, acquired new, more sumptuous buildings. Salamanca's elegant Palacio de Anaya, the eighteenth-century quarters of San Bartolomé, stands today as a reminder of the prosperity the colegios mayores enjoyed.

THE FAILURE OF REFORMS

The colegios mayores' lack of respect for the constitutions and statutes their founders had originally established did not go unnoticed. Beginning with the reign of Philip II, gradually there emerged a movement aimed at collegiate reform, designed in the first instance to eliminate many of the extrastatutory practices that the colegiales had implemented. Castilians in the sixteenth and seventeenth centuries had a special reverence for tradition; constitutions, charters, and other legal documents were supposed to be fixed and immutable; to ignore or to alter what was duly set down in writing at some time in the past was a wrong that had to be set right, regardless of the merits or demerits of the change. Thus to reform the colleges meant to restore them to their "original lustre," to set back the clock of change, and the critics called for effective royal visitations to review the colleges' present situation and to recommend the corrections deemed essential.

The founders of the colegios mayores made allowances for annual "visits" by local clerics to ensure that the constitutions and statutes were

---

[88]On other occasions library books were sold, while San Ildefonso resorted to the sale of university offices in order to make ends meet; see AHN, Univ., leg. 387, letter of 25.V.1648, and Sala Balust, *Colegios de Salamanca*, pp. 33, 108.

[89]AGS: GJ, leg. 959, "Discurso sobre los Colegios Mayores . . .," folio 4v.

being properly observed. Little evidence survives to suggest that these in-spections ever took place on a regular basis,[90] and by the reign of Philip II *visitas* to the colleges were rare. The colegiales, jealous of their autonomy, opposed interference in their affairs and extended their "purity of blood" regulations to the "visitors" in an effort to discourage such inspection tours. This ploy met with some success, since potential "visitors" were reluctant to risk an examination of their ancestors' lineage by colegiales bent on discovering traces of "tainted" blood.[91] Furthermore, when visitations did occur, they were often carried out by former graduates sympathetic to the colleges' position;[92] accordingly, the whole process degenerated into a farce.

The first call for truly effective visitations was presented to Philip II by an anonymous author in the 1570s or early in the 1580s.[93] Recognizing the importance of the colegios mayores as training schools for crown officials, he wanted university graduates who were not colegiales to "visit" these communities. They were to restore college life to its original, quasi-monastic tone and to make sure that the colleges' students were letrados in more than name alone. His call for thorough reform was followed in 1587 by another presented jointly by a Licentiate Mantilla and García de Loaysa, soon to be Archbishop of Toledo, both of whom agreed on the importance of effective visitations to the colleges.[94]

These early scemes came to naught. For the most part, the colegios mayores were left on their own, except on those few occasions when a protest from a student wronged by the colleges evoked a royal decree de-signed to end a specific abuse.[95] Such laxity ended, however, when Philip IV in 1623 created a *Junta de Colegios* entrusted with the supervision of college affairs.[96] Subsequent investigations revealed the thoroughly uncon-stitutional character of the colleges; the reallocation of the becas, the re-laxation of poverty statutes, the bando system, the luxury of college life, and the improper maintenance of academic standards were ample proof of the colleges' deviation from their pristine state. The colleges, while ad-

---

[90]For the college of San Bartolomé, there are references to visitations in 1490, 1497, 1526, 1561, and 1565–66; see Sala Balust, *Constituciones*, 3: 85, 93, 121, 139, and Esperabé Artega, *Universidad de Salamanca*, 1: 520.

[91]San Bartolomé passed a statute of this nature in 1507; see Sala Balust, *Constitu-ciones*, 3: 101.

[92]The 1561 *visita* to San Bartolomé was carried out by Doctor Matías Rodríguez, a former student. The names of previous "visitors" are not known.

[93]AGS: DC, leg. 5–106.

[94]IVDJ: Envio 90, folios 706 ff, "Coll[egi]os de Sala[man]ca . . . 15.IX.1587"; García de Loaysa a Mateo Vázquez, 15.IX.1587.

[95]Such an occurrence took place in 1603, when two Latin students at Alcalá complained that San Ildefonso's becas went only to "friends and relatives [of the colegiales] and those from their own regions and factions." Subsequently, the crown demanded an inquiry into these accusations. See AHN: Univ., leg. 387, *cédula* of 3.IX.1603.

[96]AHN: Cons., leg. 7138, letter to the four colegios mayores of Salamanca, XII.1623. This was the first letter of the junta asking the colleges to conform to their original statutes. In this same legajo, a letter, dated 23.XII.1623, of the rector of the college of Oviedo also refers to the "*Junta.*"

mitting to some minor faults, fought against a proposed royal visitation, using their representatives and agents in Madrid to head off any reforms which, as the College of San Bartolomé warned, have "such grave consequences for us all."[97] But the fever for reform ran high, and the Royal Council, ostensibly to preserve the reputation of the colleges, recommended a visita in 1634. The king, welcoming this suggestion, asked the council to advise him on a suitable "visitor" by secret vote.[98] The following year don Mendo de Benavides, Bishop of Segovia, royal councillor, and graduate of Santa Cruz, performed the first of a series of seventeenth-century visitations aimed at restoring the four colegios mayores at Salamanca to their original state. He presented the Royal Council with an extensive list of reforms, but his suggestions, debated in a council controlled by former colegiales, brought few results.[99]

In 1646 the Royal Council proposed the establishment of a permanent *Junta de Colegios* composed of six former colegiales chosen from among its own members.[100] According to the president of the Royal Council, Juan Chumacero y Carrillo, the junta was to maintain high academic standards within the colleges "in order to train subjects who are to serve Your Majesty as always."[101] In operation by 1648, the junta immediately drew up a list of reforms similar to those of Benavides in 1635. These included everything from the prohibition of private servants and private dinner parties among the colegiales to an end to the bando system which, as one member of the junta had expressed, allowed "each nation to attempt to elect as many of their own students as they possibly can to the detriment and exclusion of the others."[102] Five years later, yet another visitation was begun, indicating that the proposals of 1648 had been frustrated.[103]

The major stumbling-block to effective reform was the close relationship between the colegios mayores on the one hand and the Royal Council and the Junta de Colegios on the other. The latter, controlled by former colegiales, displayed open sympathy toward their old colleges, and they no doubt listened to their sons' and nephews' arguments against unwarranted reforms. Moreover, in spite of violations of college statutes and the visitors' demands for change, the royal councillors continued to reward colegiales with important posts whereas their refusal to do so could have been used as an important spur toward reform. As long as the councillors needed the

[97]AHN: leg. 23², no. 28.

[98]AHN: Cons., leg. 7138, consulta of 4.VII.1634.

[99]Sala Balust, *Colegios de Salamanca*, pp. 10–26; AGS: GJ, leg. 959, "Visita of Don Mendo de Benavides . . ." AUS: MS 1925, folio 188 deals with this same *visita*.

[100]BM: Add. 14,947, folio 71, cédula of 8.VII.1646.

[101]Ibid., folio 91.

[102]Ibid., folio 95.

[103]Subsequent visits and lists of proposed reforms were little different; see Sala Balust, *Colegios de Salamanca*, pp. 31–37, 106–16; AGS: GJ, leg. 959; AUV: lib. D–7; BSC: caja 31, nos. 413–15.

colegiales to secure becas for their children, little headway could be made against corrupt college practices. Reform after reform was suggested, but these were never put into effect. Indeed, because of their common interests, it seems likely that the Royal Council and the Junta de Colegios gave tacit consent to the existing state of the colleges and blocked any attempts by outsiders to implement the projected reforms. The reallocation of the becas, for example, benefited the councillors in that it enabled their sons to study jurisprudence in preparation for letrado careers. The lifting of the poverty statutes allowed the wealthy councillors' sons to enter the colleges, while the bando system permitted letrado officials, many of whom were from the Basque provinces, Navarre, and the northern parts of Old Castile, as well as Madrid, to acquire college scholarships for their offspring. Moreover, the luxurious life of the colleges was certainly more in accordance with the ostentation of court life and in line with the ambitions of "robe" families to live in the sumptuous, expensive fashion of the aristocracy. In short, the Royal Council, although hesitant about some aspects of college life, rarely enforced reforms, since the colegios mayores suited their personal ambitions and goals.

Under these circumstances the colleges, adapting to the requirements of the letrado hierarchy and its officials, moved further and further away from their original design. Their place within the university and in the society had altered; they recognized this, making the necessary changes along the way. Thus attempts to uphold the sanctity of the old constitutions and to return the colleges to their original states were largely unrealistic, and, consequently, fruitless. To deny the realities of the present, to set back the clock of change was impossible, and this tended to make the reforms suggested by the "visitors" nothing more than a waste of time.

In the early eighteenth century, Philip V, first of the Spanish Bourbons, attempted a major reform of the colegios mayores, but once again, the powerful allies of these communities at the royal court frustrated the intentions of the crown.[104] The colleges, more prosperous and more influential than ever before, defended their position, emphasizing their unique contribution to the monarchy in terms of generations of archbishops, bishops, councillors, magistrates, and noblemen they had educated and trained.

In spite of this eloquent defense, their critics were not to be silenced, and in the 1760s the need for a thorough overhaul was being seriously considered. This time the attack on the colleges included influential court figures such as the Count of Campomanes, *fiscal* of the Royal Council, Manuel de Roda, Minister of Grace and Justice, Francisco Pérez Bayer, ex-professor of Hebrew at Salamanca and tutor to the royal *infantes*, as

---

[104]Sala Balust, *Colegios de Salamanca*, pp. 45–62. See also Pérez Bayer, *Literatura Española*, vol. I, folios 106–26, 134; BNM: Ms. 18.055, folios 130–36, "Papel Curioso en punto de Colegios."

well as Felipe Beltrán, Bishop of Salamanca.[105] As partisans of the ideas and principles of the Enlightenment, they hoped to sweep away the archaic institutions of the *antiguo régimen* which they saw as roadblocks to change, innovation, and prosperity in Spain. And in their eyes, the colegios mayores were no longer simple communities of scholars, but bastions of the privileged orders which stood in the way of effective reforms. Pérez Bayer led the assault, and in his famous polemic, *Por La Libertad De La Literatura Española*, he attributed the "general ruin of the universities" as well as many of the backward traditions of Spanish government and law to the "reign of the colleges."[106] As might be expected, the colleges fought back, sending a stream of petitions and memorials to the monarch, while their supporters at court, among them the Marquis of Aliventos, composed lengthy histories of their *almae matres* to demonstrate the extent to which the colleges had aided the monarchy in the past. The debate continued for nearly a decade, but in accord with the "enlightened" spirit of Charles III's reign, the critics won out. In 1777 reforms were introduced which attempted to recast the colleges in their original mould, ending two centuries of statutory abuse. The colleges, though dealt a crippling blow, managed to survive; and their critics, still not content, called for abolition—the only solution in their minds which could put an end to the many problems which the colleges were said to have spawned. Gaining the support of a monarchy interested in assuming control of the lands and revenues the colleges had come to possess, the reformers prevailed. The decisive act came during the reign of Charles IV. First, the Count of Floridablanca ordered an end to elections to becas, and by 1793, the colleges stood empty. Then, in 1798, the colleges were officially suppressed, and the revenues from their properties were put toward the amortization of the national debt.

THE COLEGIOS MAYORES AND THE UNIVERSITIES

The suppression of the colegios mayores was largely a political act, yet it was also a measure for educational reform. In a sense, it marked a day of liberation for the universities to which the colleges had belonged, universities which had been long awaiting the decree of 1798. This is so because the colleges, though housing only a tiny fraction of the students, housed those students who represented at first the academic and later the social elite of their respective institutions. And in both roles, the colleges, bolstered

[105]On this attack and the reforms which were later enacted, see L. Sala Balust, *Visitas y Reformas de los Colegios Mayores de Salamanca en el Reinado de Carlos III* (Valladolid, 1958). Also useful is George M. Addy, *The Enlightenment in the University of Salamanca* (Durham, 1966), esp. chap. 10.
[106]Pérez Bayer, *Literatura Española*, vol. II, folios 19, 212. See also BNM: Ms. 18,377, *Diario Histórico de la Reforma de los Seis Colegios Mayores . . . desde . . . 1771 . . . hasta . . . 1777* by the same author.

by their friends and supporters at the royal court, had been able to set the tone of university life.

As Table 11 illustrates, colegiales throughout the sixteenth and seventeenth centuries were able to win continuing success in the competitions for university teaching posts. The combination of money, merit, and manipulation of the "nations," and, later, the favoritism of the Royal Council which has been already described, was largely responsible for this extraordinary achievement, but at the same time it created a situation in which a small body of colegiales occupied a disproportionate number of the universities' chairs, particularly those in the faculties of law. The imbalance between colegial and *manteista* professors at Salamanca was cited in 1714 in a complaint registered by that university to the crown. It claimed that ever since the Royal Council had assumed for itself the appointment of university professors, that is, in the previous seventy-three years, only 39 of the 180 individuals named to the chairs of law at Salamanca had been manteistas even though manteistas constituted the vast majority of applicants for these positions. The university added that in the current year, only two of its twenty law professors were manteistas; the others claimed membership in a colegio mayor.[107]

Mastery over teaching positions constituted only one facet of the power of the colegios mayores within the universities. In open violation of university statutes, colegiales regularly held the office of *maestrescuela* and university rector.[108] They were also in frequent control of university magistracies, the offices of *juez escolástico* and *juez del estudio*, regardless of rules which prohibited colegiales from occupying these important posts.[109] As a result, university disputes involving the colegios mayores rarely went counter to their interests.

Rich, self-confident, and secure, the colleges, using the social prestige of their members to enhance their position, also attempted to upset the traditional ceremonial order of the universities to which they were attached. Disputes over precedence in one procession or another led to friction and even fistfights and brawls between the heads of the colegios mayores and the university rector and the heads of other colleges. Just such an incident occurred in 1637 when a member of one of the colleges apparently mistreated or verbally abused the rector of the University of

[107]AHN: Cons., leg. 7294, letter of 21.II.1714.

[108]On 19 and 30 October 1655 the Royal Council reaffirmed university statutes barring colegiales from the offices of rector and *maestrescuela* of Salamanca; cf. AGS: GJ, leg. 942.

[109]In 1567 the Royal Council first ordered that the office of Juez del Estudio was to be closed to colegiales; cf. Esperabé Artega, *Universidad de Salamanca*, 1: 520. This ruling, however, was repeatedly ignored; see BM: Add. 28,349, f. 227, "Los inconvenientes que ay que en Sala[man]ca tengan Colegiales en los oficios de provisor, juez metropolitano, y juez del estudio, 14.XI.1589." In the 1660s the Council was forced to reaffirm the original statute and this action was repeated in 1689; cf. AGS: GJ, leg. 942, no. 1 and Esperabé Artega, *Universidad de Salamanca*, 1: 677.

Table 11   Colegiales Mayores as Lecturers and Professors in
the Faculties of Canon and Civil Law

Chairs	Years	No. of instructors	Colegiales	%
The University of Salamanca				
Canon Law:				
Prima (a)	16th C.	6	1	16.7
	17th C.	16	3	18.6
Prima (b)	16th C.	10	—	0
	17th C.	17	5	29.4
Decreto	16th C.	10	—	0
	17th C.	29	12	41.4
Vísperas (a)	16th C.	14	1	7.1
	17th C.	52	29	55.8
Vísperas (b)	16th C.	10	—	0
	17th C.	23	10	43.5
Sexto	16th C.	11	11	100.0
	17th C.	61	35	57.4
Civil Law:				
Prima (a)	16th C.	8	1	12.5
	17th C.	16	4	25.0
Prima (b)	16th C.	8	1	12.5
	17th C.	15	6	40.0
Vísperas (a)	16th C.	7	1	14.3
	17th C.	33	23	89.6
Vísperas (b)	16th C.	6	—	0
	17th C.	25	13	52.0
Instituto (a)	16th C.	37	15	40.5
	17th C.	62	47	75.8
Instituto (b)	16th C.	42	21	50.0
	17th C.	60	49	81.7
Código (a)	16th C.	25	8	32.0
	17th C.	60	43	71.7
Código (b)	16th C.	37	16	43.2
	17th C.	52	40	76.9
Digesto Viejo	16th C. (1534 ff.)	15	4	26.7
	17th C.	62	42	67.7
Volumen	16th C. (1551 ff.)	21	7	33.3
	17th C.	65	50	76.9
The University of Valladolid				
Canon Law:				
Prima	16th C. (1523 ff.)	11	8	72.7
	17th C.	31	16	51.

Table 11   (continued)

Chairs	Years	No. of instructors	Colegiales	%
	The University of Salamanca			
Vísperas	16th C.			
	(1533 ff.)	17	15	88.2
	17th C.	27	19	70.4
Decreto	16th C.			
	(1517 ff.)	11	5	45.5
	17th C.	22	14	63.6
Sexto	16th C.			
	(1545 ff.)	12	7	58.3
	17th C.	38	20	52.6
Clementinas	16th C.			
	(1529 ff.)	15	11	73.3
	17th C.	64	40	62.5
Civil Law:				
Prima	16th C.			
	(1502 ff.)	9	7	77.8
	17th C.	29	18	62.1
Vísperas	16th C.	12	9	75.0
	17th C.	26	17	65.4
Digesto Viejo	16th C.			
	(1541 ff.)	23	23	100.0
	17th C.	65	43	66.2
Código Antigua	16th C.			
	(1529 ff.)	23	20	87.0
	17th C.	43	31	72.1
Código Moderna	16th C.			
	(1548 ff.)	18	15	83.3
	17th C.	43	24	55.8
Instituto Antigua	16th C.			
	(1568 ff.)	12	9	75.0
	17th C.	42	30	71.4
Instituto Moderna	16th C.			
	(1529 ff.)	23	20	87.0
	17th C.	43	23	53.5

Source: Esperabé Artega, Universidad de Salamanca, vol. II; Alcocer Martínez, Universidad de Valladolid, vol. III.

Salamanca. Upon learning of the squabble, Philip IV, in an irate note to the Royal Council, wrote:

"any colegial who injures a university rector will lose his beca and be debarred from serving me in all the posts of these kingdoms. . . . Neither will he be able to compete for the position of Doctoral or Magistral canon nor be recommended for a bishopric because the pretension of these colegiales who are neither older nor better letrados than others is highly irregular."[110]

Another point of friction between the University of Salamanca and the colegios mayores was the graduation ceremony. Pointing to special papal privileges which enabled students of the Colegio Mayor of San Bartolomé to take their examinations and degrees in ceremonies independent of those of the university, Salamanca's other colegios mayores secured similar privileges, since they would cut sharply the cost of degrees for college students.[111] The university, fearful of a loss of revenue as well as the loss of control over the examinations and degrees of all the colegiales mayores, protested, declaring these privileges to be null and void. The result was a battle that raged on throughout the sixteenth century and ended only in the 1620s when the university abandoned its fruitless fight.[112]

But hostilities between the colleges and the university did not cease at that point. In the disputes of the 1630s over appointments to professorships, the colegios mayores and the Universities of Salamanca and Valladolid were consistently at odds.[113] The former, seeking the patronage of the Royal Council, campaigned against student elections, while the latter, for the opposite reason, favored the continuance of the student vote. No doubt bitterness arising from these disputes had something to do with the mistreatment of Salamanca's rector by a colegial in the incident cited above.

As the colegio mayor share of Salamanca's teaching posts increased in the course of the seventeenth century, relations between the colleges and the university deteriorated. In 1681, 1685, and 1692 the University of Salamanca protested that doctors from the colleges boycotted examinations and degree ceremonies to the detriment of the students.[114] Meanwhile, the Royal Council, always eager to promise an investigation but partial to the colegio mayor cause, did little to correct the situation. Enmity between the two sides continued into the eighteenth century, coming to a head during the debates of the 1760s and 1770s over the projected reform of the colegios mayores. The disputes ended only with the final dissolution of the colleges in 1798.

[110]AHN: Cons., leg. 7138, letter of 28.IX.1637.
[111]See Beltrán de Heredia, *Bulario de la Universidad de Salamanca* (3 vols., Salamanca, 1966–67): 195, 204, 243. The College of Santa Cruz had similar privileges at the University of Valladolid; cf. BSC: caja 4, letter of 2.IV.1647.
[112]Disruptions occurred in 1535, 1539, 1549, 1552, 1563, 1581, 1585, 1588, 1592, and 1613; see Esperabé Artega, *Universidad de Salamanca*, 1: 413, 420, 488, 595, 633. By 1613 the president of the Royal Council, apparently weary of this endless feud, was said to be on the verge of ending all special graduation privileges for college students, including those of monks belonging to the religious colleges; cf. AUS: Ms. 2969, letter of 23.III.1613.
[113]See AHN: Cons. leg. 7138 and Kagan, "Education and The State," pp. 247–49.
[114]AUS: Ms. 2287, no folio; AHN: Cons., leg. 7138, letter of 25.I.1692.

The other major rivals of the colegios mayores at Salamanca were the three Colleges of the Military Orders. Founded in the sixteenth century by the crown for the offspring of knights belonging to the orders of Alcantará, Calatrava, and Santiago, these communities enjoyed considerable wealth and prestige.[115] Their feud with the colegios mayores centered on questions of ceremonial precedence.[116] In 1659 Philip IV, probably under pressure from the Royal Council and its colegial-president, the Count of Castrillo, ruled in favor of the four colegios mayores.[117] This decree served only to increase the bitterness between the two rival groups of colleges, and in 1659, 1666, 1678, 1679, and 1680 armed clashes took place between them.[118] The Colleges of the Military Orders appealed to Charles II for retribution, alleging that the maestrescuela of Salamanca, the Royal Council, and even their own Council of the Military Orders were partisan to the colegios mayores. But the king replied by reaffirming the ceremonial leadership of the colegios mayores in 1680, and violence between the rivals erupted that same year. These clashes continued into the eighteenth century, coming to a halt only when the colegios mayores were suppressed, an action which did not go unsupported by the Colleges of the Military Orders.

The strong influence of the colegios mayores within the universities and the rivalries this fostered need not be considered only in a negative light. If the colleges had provided for their students a curriculum that was more innovative than that offered in the "schools," or had the colleges managed to supply the university with skilled, imaginative, and responsible instructors, then their control of teaching posts could be interpreted with favor. But as we shall see, the colegios mayores offered relatively few advantages to the universities, particularly with regard to teaching.

College instruction was limited to review sessions and mock exams designed to prime colegiales for the formal public examinations that they would have to face in order to gain their degrees.[119] Informal lectures may also have been delivered within college walls, but in any event this instruction was intended to supplement, not supplant the regular university curriculum. That the college of San Ildefonso early in the eighteenth century rejected a royal request to teach national law at Alcalá de Henares

[115]For their history, see Sala Balust, *Constituciones*, 1: 15; Ajo, *Universidades*, 2: 228.

[116]See AHN: Cons., leg. 7138, "Memorial de los Tres Colegios Militares, 1659"; BUS: Ms. 2266, folios 10, 29; RAH: Ms. 9-31-8-7120, "Memorial de los Cuatro Colegios Mayores . . ."; AUS: Ms. 1925, folios 196 ff., "Apologia por la affeción de las vecas de los Colegios Mayores."

[117]BUS: Ms. 2266, folio 4, cédula of 8.IV.1659.

[118]BUS: Ms. 2266, folio 29 ff.; RAH: Ms. 9-31-8-7120; AUS: Ms. 939, folios 149, 165.

[119]Although teaching chairs were provided for in the original constitutions of the colleges, these, for the most part, remained a dead letter. Febrero Lorenzo, *Los Colegios Mayores*, pp. 115-24, claims that chairs were being read in the colleges, but in support of her claim cites only the original college statutes. Closer to the truth was Pérez Bayer, *Literatura Española*, vol. II, folio 195, who attests that the colegios mayores lacked the teaching chairs for which their founders had provided.

is a good indication that the other colegios mayores were equally conservative in their classes.[120] Nevertheless, the colleges could have contributed to teaching at the universities by offering high quality instructors to serve in the faculty chairs, and there is no doubt that many colegiales were exceptional scholars.[121] But it must also be remembered that the colegiales, owing to special graduation privileges they had fought for and won, received their academic titles within the walls of their own community after an examination conducted by professors largely of the college's own choosing. In view of the high proportion of colegial professors, it is not surprising that many of these examinations lost all pretense to objectivity. Little information about the academic caliber of these students survives, but an impression that colegiales, particularly in the years after 1600, neglected both their studies and their teaching duties for more pleasurable pursuits and private concerns can easily be obtained.

In 1618, for instance, the Royal Council of Castile ordered an investigation into the College of Cuenca after reports that the college was awarding academic degrees with "little ceremony" to men lacking the necessary qualifications.[122] And in 1637, in a document already cited, the king himself expressed the opinion that colegiales were not necessarily superior letrados to those who were not.[123] A report conducted in 1645 by the Bishop of Salamanca, Juan de Valençuela, on the academic merits of university scholars also suggests that the colegiales were not all they were made out to be. For example, Toribio de Santos, a student in Oviedo and reader of the university chair of Institutes in the faculty of civil law, merited only the following comment: "He has little reputation for letters or intelligence; he is a nephew of the President of Castile, Santos."[124] It would be difficult to argue that ability alone had earned Toribio de Santos his chair.

Another reference to the academic qualifications of the colegiales mayores lies in a memorial sent by the Colleges of the Military Orders to Charles II. These colleges, admittedly the sworn enemies of the colegios mayores, presented the following, rather derogatory picture:

"The Colegios Mayores are totally ignorant communities, since of the 120 who are now resident in them, one hundred are idiots and so incapable that they do not even know Latin; the chairs they read are without listeners; they study with dissolution and liberty . . . because they know their defects and excesses will not

[120]BNM: Ms. 18,657³, "Respuesta de la Universidad de Alcalá a un decreto de Felipe V sobre el estudio de leyes patrias, 1713."
[121]Members of the Colegios Mayores who were authors have been catalogued and their works noted in José Rezábal y Ugarte, *Biblioteca de los Escritores que Han Sido Individuos de los Colegios Mayores* (Madrid, 1805).
[122]Esperabé Artega, *Universidad de Salamanca*, 1: 712.
[123]See p. 153.
[124]This refers to Miguel Santos de San Pedro, president of the Royal Council of Castile from 1629 to 1633; see BUS: Ms. 1925, folio 144 ff., "Memoria de los Colegiales . . .," 4.II.1645.

come before your eyes but only before those of the royal ministers, their fellow colegiales, who disregard their faults."[125]

This statement is of course exaggerated, but it may indicate that not all colegial-professors were worthy of the chairs they read. Pedro Abarca, though an apologist for the colegios mayores, admitted in 1685 to the President of Castile that the Royal Council's favoritism allowed many undeserving colegiales to obtain teaching posts.[126] And in the early eighteenth century the following comment was made about the performance of the colegiales in the competitions for university chairs in law:

"What is certain is that in all of the chairs for which colegiales compete, the oposiciones are . . . almost familiar in tone and in all those in which there are no Colegiales Mayores, the oposiciones are carried out with the necessary rigor as in the case of the chairs of medicine and in those of Latin, Rhetoric, Hebrew, and Greek."[127]

During the oposición itself, which was supposed to last one hour, this author added that the colegiales mayores were never criticized even though "many read in a whisper (or in a low voice) so that no one can understand them; others have the invocation to the Saints last almost one-half hour."[128]

Hints and suggestions that many colegiales were students of questionable academic ability appear more credible when compared with the reports of the royal visitors who inspected college life. Their comments about the need to maintain high academic standards in the elections to becas lasted throughout the century, and these are good indications that geography and family had as much, if not more, to do with selection than merit. Furthermore, their descriptions of the luxury and the pleasurable appurtenances of college life does not suggest that colegiales lived in total dedication to academic pursuits. Yet these same students, using patronage to obtain university chairs, controlled teaching in the major faculties and brought their personal standards of scholarship into the schools. To compare the relative merits of colegial and manteista professors would be an impossible task, but one might venture the hypothesis that, especially in the seventeenth and eighteenth centuries, the academic ability and scholarly distinction of the colegiales frequently fell below that of other instructors.

If colegiales did not injure teaching standards through lack of ability, they certainly endangered them by a lack of dedication to their work. Absenteeism among all university instructors, colegial and manteista alike, was common throughout the seventeenth and eighteenth centuries.[129]

[125]RAH: Ms. 9-31-8-7120.
[126]BUS: Ms. 761, ff. 80–87, "Informe del Estado de los Colegios Mayores . . . 1685." See also Febrero Lorenzo, *Los Colegios Mayores*, p. 24.
[127]AGS: GJ, leg. 943, "Relacion del turno. . . ."
[128]Ibid.
[129]See below, pp. 171–73.

Aside from illness, the major cause of this problem was personal business which interfered with university duties. For many professors the conflicts arose especially from negotiations for public office which necessitated extended trips to Madrid. The colegiales, keenly interested in these appointments, readily abandoned their chairs, or so a comment made in 1648 about the arts faculty at Salamanca suggests: ". . . it is very rare that a chair in arts held by a Colegial Mayor is read continuously for a year; some do not even read for a month, others two days."[130] The anonymous author of this report noted further that in previous years "every colegial professor vacated his chair in the middle of the academic year to compete in oposiciones for other positions, thus leaving his students temporarily without a teacher."

In the law faculties, where colegial professors were the most numerous, problems multiplied. Colegiales often spent less time in the lecture halls than in oposiciones for higher chairs and in Madrid. In the meantime, their chairs were either left unattended or placed in the hands of substitutes, usually fellow colegiales, who were no more diligent in their classroom duties. As a result many of the chairs in these faculties suffered from exceptionally high rates of absenteeism and a rapid turnover of instructors. Teaching, moreover, was sporadic and discontinuous, while the Royal Council's reluctance to punish negligent colegiales served only to make matters worse.[131]

The indifference of colegial professors toward teaching stemmed from a belief that the university chair was not an end in itself but a passport to public office. The University of Salamanca in a letter to Philip V explained the colegiales' attitude this way:

"The colegiales regard their chair as a honorary title and as a step to the Office, and they neglect their instruction. It happens that today among the six professors of law (three chairs are vacant), it can be said that only one, Doctor Bernardino Francos Militar, a manteista, teaches; . . . the others, who are Colegiales Mayores, some for lack of ability, others for various pretexts, do not attend their classes."[132]

To enhance their reputation the colegiales sought out university posts only to leave as quickly as possible for a *plaza de asiento*. The professorship constituted only a means to that end rather than a position worthy of serious attention of its own.

[130]AHN: Cons. leg. 7138, "Memorial de 17.III.1648."

[131]When the University of Salamanca protested in 1694 that Ambrosio Bernal, a colegial in San Bartolomé, had vacated his chair of Decreto but continued to collect his salary, Bernal, backed by the Bishop of Salamanca, a graduate of the Colegio Mayor de San Ildefonso, the *maestrescuela* of Salamanca, and the four colegios mayores of that city, appealed to the Royal Council. The partisan council upheld Bernal's position and ordered that his salary be paid. Furthermore, they threatened to fine the university for its vindictive action. For these proceedings, see AHN: Cons., leg. 7138, "Pleitos de la Universidad de Salamanca sobre la renta de don Ambrosio Bernal."

[132]See Pérez Bayer, *Literatura Española*, vol. II, folio 107.

In addition to the disruption of university instruction, contemporaries charged that the colegios mayores were responsible for a decline in student matriculations, a problem common to all universities in seventeenth-century Castile.[133] The Colleges of the Military Orders explained that "with advancement in the colleges regulated more by seniority than excellence in their studies, many colegiales are idle because of the security of eventual promotion, while for those who are not colegiales, the result is a despair which urges them to abandon the university, as they see that the door to offices is closed and that it will open only to a few accredited lawyers who are considered necessary in the tribunals."[134] The *"falta de premios"* or shortage of offices was said to discourage university study, and the colegios mayores, because of their dominant position within the universities and their monopoly of letrado posts, were obliged to take much of the blame for the decline in the number of students. It is possible that the colegiales, famous for the ease with which they received professorships and public offices, did indeed keep a number of potential students away from the universities. The six colegios mayores, consequently, must be seen as one, but by no means the only, reason for the depopulation of Castile's universities during the seventeenth and eighteenth centuries.

Supporting the colegios mayores, however, were the letrado and noble families who monopolized the leading positions in church and state. The educational interests of this class, combined with the Cámara's biased methods of appointment, helped turn the colleges into schools for the sons of court families and brought about the abandonment of charitable and academic goals set down in the colleges' founding statutes. The beca became merely a wedge to pry open the office door, the entrance to Castile's ruling elite. But in this sense the colegios mayores fulfilled at least one of their original aims. Generation after generation of colegiales dedicated their careers to the service of the crown, to the fulfillment of the Renaissance goals of service set by their founders. The changes which had taken place within the colleges were therefore responses to the growth, ideals, and interests of a letrado class created by the development of the absolute monarchy in Castile. And this was a world from which none of Castile's universities could remain immune.

---

[133]See below, pp. 219–21.
[134]AHN: Cons., leg. 7138, "Memorial de los Tres Colegios Militares, 1659."

chapter 8
TEACHERS AND STUDENTS

Teaching at Castile's universities in the sixteenth and seventeenth centuries was a stiff and formal affair. Instruction consisted mainly of lectures delivered daily at appointed times by university instructors. Lasting up to two hours, these classes involved the explication and interpretation of selected passages from well-known texts; meanwhile, the students, known archaically as "listeners," took notes, a tradition which was said to have begun in 1539 when Francisco de Vitoria, Prima professor of theology at Salamanca, told his pupils that they "must write down what we say."[1] During these sessions good instructors like Vitoria might innovate, contributing their ideas and outlooks of their own; poor ones would not, relying instead upon the hackneyed commentaries of the past. Question and discussion, moreover, were generally unknown except after the hour when the teacher went "against the post" outside the lecture hall. Not all instructors were so accommodating, but those who were earned their students' esteem. Fray Luis de Miranda, professor of theology at Santiago de Compostela in 1584, was considered an excellent teacher in part because "after the hour, he is at the door, waiting for whatever questions the students wish to ask him."[2]

Regular university lectures were supplemented by "extraordinary" classes presented by advanced students and visiting lecturers. These extra sessions, however, differed from the scheduled classes only in content, not form. They were intended to examine in a more detailed fashion topics either neglected or glossed over in the regular course.[3] More intimate were the review sessions provided by some colleges and the graduates in charge of the student boarding houses. Since the latter were supposed to be made

---

[1]On Vitoria's teaching and pedagogy at Spanish universities in the sixteenth century in general, see Demetrio Eparraguirre, "Quelques Aspects De L'Enseignement Dans Les Universités Espagnoles A L'Epoque De La Renaissance," in *Pedagogues et Juristes* (Paris, 1963), pp. 72–85.

[2]S. Cabeza de León, *Historia de la Universidad de Santiago de Compostela* (Santiago de Compostela, 1945), 1: 430.

[3]Typical of such instruction was a special class on the writings of Hippocrates offered in 1626 at the University of Seville by Diego Matheo Capino, a medical student; cf. AUSA, lib. 862, folio 72. See also Cabeza de León, *Universidad de Santiago*, 1: 329–30. Not all "extra-ordinary" instruction, however, stuck to the regular curriculum. The University of Alcalá de Henares, for instance, admitted in the mid-seventeenth century that Roman Law, a subject which was not officially taught at the university until the 1660s, had for many years been offered in an "extra-ordinary" fashion; cf. AHN: Univ., lib. 1222 F, folio 234.

up of students belonging to a single faculty, this lodging-house instruction could have been rather effective. But in practice this uniformity of students was never obtained and the heads of the houses were known to skimp on their obligations.[4] In the colleges these sessions did take place, but that was the only formal instruction provided within the walls of these communities. Wealthy students often brought with them a tutor of their own or, alternatively, paid university instructors for private lessons, but for the vast majority of university students instruction was centered in the "Schools."

The one exception was the lectures provided by the religious colleges attached to the universities. These convents and monasteries, many of which antedated the universities themselves, always provided instruction in grammar, the arts, and theology for their members. This situation changed during the sixteenth century, when a number of the more prosperous convents opened their classes to outsiders and began to compete with the universities for students.[5] The latter, jealous of their prerogatives, fought back, attempting to quash this unwanted competition, but the religious orders persisted, particularly the Society of Jesus which posed the gravest threat. The root of the problem was a privilege granted to the Society in 1584 by the Papacy which allowed students from Jesuit colleges to qualify for university degrees.[6] The universities balked, among them Granada, which in 1585 refused to honor courses taught by the Society after complaining that this competition was the cause of its own shortage of students.[7] Squabbles between the two sides continued until 1609 when a bargain was struck. Granada agreed to allow the Society to teach but only at hours which did not conflict with university lectures and on topics different from those covered by the regular instructors. The university also agreed to allow Jesuit students to take degrees, but on no condition would these students be allowed to graduate in another university.[8] Though their lecture halls may have been empty, Granada's instructors wanted their examination fees.

Other universities were less easily placated, notably, Salamanca. One of its major concerns was what it called the "depopulation of the universities," said to be caused by Jesuit competition.[9] The classes in grammar offered by the Society had undercut instruction in that subject at Sala-

[4]See p. 191.

[5]The University of Salamanca, for example, complained in 1593 and again in 1601 about the instruction offered by the Benedictine, Dominican, and Jesuit colleges of that city; cf. Esperabé Arte20, *Historia Pragmática é Interna de la Universidad de Salamanca* (Salamanca, 1914), 1: 610, 648.

[6]See Montells y Nadal, *Historia de la Universidad de Granada* (Granada, 1870), 1: p. 117. This privilege was originally granted in 1571.

[7]Ibid., p. 118.

[8]Ibid., pp. 120, 122, 152.

[9]Ibid., p. 196. The University of Santiago used the same phrase in 1694 when it referred to the effects upon the university of the instruction in the liberal arts that was offered by the Jesuit and Dominican colleges of the city; cf. AUSC: lib. A 126, folio 3v.

manca and other institutions which refused to allow the Jesuits to teach in the university's name, and, to a lesser extent, the same was true in the arts and theology. The University of Valladolid in 1686 sent a strong protest to the Royal Council, asserting that "students . . . attended the Colleges of San Gregorio (Dominican) and San Ambrosio (Jesuit), leaving the university with only a few listeners for its professors." It added: "it is well known that the University of Salamanca is suffering from the same problem."[10] University requests for redress, however, went unheeded until after the Jesuits were expelled. Then, in 1771, the crown ordered that courses heard in a religious convent or seminary could not be applied toward a university degree, and the following year this edict was strengthened by another, making regular attendance at university lectures mandatory for a degree.[11]

These decrees marked an important step in the emergence of the modern university in Castile, since they finally brought university-level instruction under university supervision and control. Previously, teaching, particularly in the arts and theology, had been offered by a number of competing agencies, each with approaches, interpretations, and standards of its own. The universities, though strongly opposed to this outside teaching, could do little to root it out. The religious colleges were independent, outside the university's control. Furthermore, the friars' argument that they had to provide their own classes, since university instructors did not adequately treat questions and topics of especial importance to the regular clergy could never be challenged. But that the classes of the religious proved such a success among the students was related to the failure of the universities, interested above all in law and its *premios*, to provide adequately for instruction in the liberal arts. The religious orders, in other words, filled a pedagogical gap that the universities had left behind. When this competition was ended, students returned to "Schools," while the universities themselves could begin to direct the nature, content, and quality of instruction in areas long outside their effective control. In this changeover, some variety of approach may have been lost, but order and uniformity were deemed more important.

What the universities sought to protect was their monopoly of instruction in five faculties: the arts, medicine, theology, and law (canon and civil). Their problem was that teaching in these disciplines revolved around set texts, readily accessible to any individual qualified to read and interpret the Latin prose in which they were written. Civil law, for example, was based wholly upon the study of Justinian's *Corpus Juris Civilis* and its medieval glossators, while canon law was simply the interpretation of papal bulls and church decrees amassed over the ages. In both of these faculties, the subject matter changed but little over the years. Though historical and

[10]AUV: lib. D 6, no. 9.
[11]Ajo y Sainz de Zúñiga, *Historia de las Universidades Hispánicas* (8 vols., Madrid, 1957-72), 5: 47-49.

philological interpretations of the law were introduced early in the six-teenth century by humanist scholars such as Antonio Agustín, the legal curriculum did not take another major step forward until the middle of the eighteenth century when the study of "national law" was added to it, an innovation which involved instruction in the *Siete Partidas* of Alfonso X, the Leyes de Toro (1505), and subsequent codifications of royal promulga-tions and decrees. Readings in medicine were equally static: Avicenna, Galen, and Hippocrates remained the standard fare throughout the Habs-burg era, and it was only at the end of the eighteenth century that the writings of the ancients were supplemented by more up-to-date medical tracts and new courses in botany, pharmacology, and experimental medi-cine.

Theology and the liberal arts were only slightly more flexible. The former, rooted in the writings of the scholastics, was advanced early in the sixteenth century at the University of Alcalá de Henares with the introduc-tion of sacred texts in their original languages. El Pinciano, Hernan Núñez de Guzman (1475?-1533), author of a Greek edition of the New Testa-ment, was in the forefront of this movement, along with his colleagues, Aires Barbosa and Antonio de Nebrija. Meanwhile, at the University of Salamanca, the teaching of theology was also in flux. Francisco de Vitoria broke with tradition by substituting Acquinas's *Summa* for the *Sentences of Peter Lombard*, a change consistent with the interest of humanist theology in questions relating to the interrelation of morality and politics. This was a theme upon which Vitoria dwelt for most of his life, forging in his lectures many of the fundamental principles governing the law of na-tions, the right of war, freedom of the seas, and other topics dealing with the origin, nature, and limits of political power. His teachings, published posthumously by another Salamancan theologian, Melchor Cano, are often said to form the basis of modern international law.[12] And in keeping with this spirit aimed at studying the various problems of mankind, a number of theologians in sixteenth-century Salamanca, including Martin de Azpilcueta, Domingo de Soto, and Tomás de Mercado, concerned with the economic impact of the importation of American silver into Castile, gradu-ally developed ideas which which later became known as the Quantitative Theory of Money, a theorem which postulates that the rate of inflation at a given moment is in direct ratio with the size of the money supply.[13] Such creativity, however, was not destined to last. By the seventeenth century the religious orders which dominated Salamanca's faculty of theology were more interested in propagandizing their own versions of religious truth than in developing new theories and ideas, the sole exception being the

[12]See L. Pereña Vicente, *La Universidad de Salamanca, Forja del Pensamiento Político Español en el Siglo XVI* (Salamanca, 1954).
[13]See M. Grice-Hutchinson, *The School of Salamanca: Readings in Spanish Monetary Theory* (Oxford, 1962), and Pierre Vilar, "Les Primitifs espagnols de la pensée economique. Quantitavisme et bullionisme," *Mélanges Marcel Bataillon* (special number of the *Bulletin Hispanique*, 1962): 261-84.

Jesuits, who pioneered instruction in moral theology, the basis of which was the explanation of the human conscience and such themes as redemption and guilt.

Similarly, the arts curriculum, flexible in the early sixteenth century, suffered from progressive ossification and decay. The basis of this program from the Middle Ages to the late eighteenth century was Aristotle and a number of chairs—physics, metaphysics, logic, etc.—concentrated on different aspects of his philosophy. Otherwise, the program was subject to alteration. Studies in the literature and language of classical Greece and Rome were added in the years around 1500, and chairs in Arabic, Chaldean, and Hebrew were established as well. Contemporary authors, among them Valla and Copernicus, were also taught while instruction in astronomy, mathematics, and music, none of which was very popular among students, completed the program.[14] In the seventeenth century the arts curriculum, frozen in time, stood still, the only addition being moral philosophy, a course designed to counter the Jesuits, who had pioneered the subject. And it was only in the 1790s that the universities, under orders from "enlightened" reformers in Madrid to reform their curriculum, expanded the arts program to include instruction in modern languages and other subjects with a more scientific bent: algebra, experimental physics, natural history, etc.

Why the university curriculum stagnated after an epoch of change and innovation in the sixteenth century is a question yet to be solved. The Spanish Inquisition, fearful of heretical influence, was partly at fault, but more significant was the general spirit of the times: innovation, in all walks of life, was frowned upon, difficult to introduce, whatever the merits of change. Moreover, as institutions geared increasingly toward the professional certification of the young, the universities were slow to adapt to changing concepts and ideas, particularly in the realm of science and philosophy. Fundamentally, the universities were guilds of medieval origin and like many craft guilds, entrants were obliged to pass certain stock tests which were considered valid for all time. Deviation was the equivalent of heresy, a dangerous evil in itself. The immutable nature of the university curriculum in the seventeenth and eighteenth centuries is therefore best attributed, not to any external force such as the inquisition or Spain's "supposed" intellectual isolation from Europe, but to the ideas and aspirations of university teachers themselves.

TEACHERS

Teachers at Spain's universities can be roughly divided into two broad groups. At the top stood the senior professors whose chairs carried tenure

---

[14]The teaching of the liberal arts at Spain's universities is described in A. F. G. Bell, *Luis de León (A Study of the Spanish Renaissance)* (Oxford, 1925). More specialized is José Lopez Rueda, *Helenistas Españoles del Siglo XVI* (Madrid, 1973) which examines the study and teaching of Greek.

for life.[15] Every university faculty had at least two individuals of this rank, although Salamanca's large legal faculties each had four. At the bottom were the junior, nontenured lecturers who read in the "temporal" chairs— the *regencias* and *catedrillas*—so-called because their terms lasted no more than three or four years.[16]

The division of each university into tenured and nontenured members, that is, professors and lecturers, was not universal. Many of the newer universities were established during an epoch when the concept of life-tenure was under attack; consequently, even the distinguished Prima and Vísperas professorships at universities like Granada and Seville were "temporal" chairs.[17] Indeed, the furor over this question was sufficiently strong to bring the following petition before the Cortes of 1528:

We ask Your Majesty that the chairs at the estudios of Salamanca and Valladolid be granted not for life but only temporarily as they are in Italy and other places, because when they are life-tenured many problems and troubles arise, especially among those professors who, once they have taken possession of their chair, do not care to study nor to help the students. But when the chairs are temporary, there are many benefits because the readers seek to be returned to the chair, to increase their salaries and to have larger student attendance. They work to aid the students, and they write and make the students take examinations and other exercises in letters.[18]

Despite the king's promise to investigate the possibility of reform, nothing changed. Life-tenured positions, for better or for worse, survived at the older universities until 1771 when they were transformed into short-term regencias.[19]

At those universities where lecturers and professors were not distinguished by tenure, the two groups were set apart by pay, power, and, above all, prestige. Professors enjoyed ceremonial precedence, the right to belong to the university council, and the opportunity to participate in all examinations and degree ceremonies, a privilege which allowed for considerable income, thanks to student fees. Furthermore, their regular sti-

[15]The top positions were the Prima and Vísperas professorships, so named because the former met in the morning, the latter in the late afternoon.

[16]The number of these lower chairs varied from university to university. Salamanca had close to sixty, while Baeza, Oñate, and Osuna had no more than one or two. Each was named after the subject matter upon which the reader was supposed to lecture. The chair of Instituto in the law faculty, for example, dealt with Justinian's Institutes; Biblia in the theology faculty concentrated upon the Holy Book, etc.

[17]Requests from the readers of these chairs that their positions be "perpetual" were usually denied; see Cabeza de León, *Universidad de Santiago*, 2: 367.

[18]Cortes de Madrid, 1528, pet. 49. The President of the Royal Council took a similar stand in 1648. For his comments, see BM: Add. 24,947, folio 101–02.

[19]See *Collección Universal de Todas las Reales Ordenes que para el Régimen del Estudio General de la Real Universidad de Valladolid se ha Servido Cominicar . . . en . . . el . . . Reynado de . . . el Señor Carlos III Hasta el Presente Julio de 1771* (Valladolid, 1771), pp. 183–85.

pends were on average two or three times above that of lecturers, and at a few universities, particularly Salamanca, even more, owing to a privilege which entitled professors to share in the university's annual income.[20] Consequently, professors at this university, followed by those of Alcalá and Valladolid, were men of comfortable means. For example, the earnings of Valladolid's instructors in the sixteenth century ranged between 300 and 700 ducats a year, with 500 ducats (187,500 mrs.) as the mean.[21] This was a substantial sum, five times the income of a master artisan and nearly as much as a magistrate in one of the royal courts. Salaries at the other universities, however, lagged behind, especially during the difficult years of the seventeenth century, when a number of institutions forced their instructors to take cuts in pay. Teaching positions at Alcalá, Salamanca, and Valladolid, consequently, were the prizes of the academic world, but to win one was no easy task.

University teaching posts required a minimum of a baccalaureate, although most institutions had additional rules obliging newly appointed teachers to graduate licentiate or doctor within six months to a year. But these degrees were costly and increasingly so; at Salamanca, for instance, a license and doctorate early in the eighteenth century was said to involve an expenditure of as much as 20,000 reales.[22] And with the prices so high, degrees served not only as stumbling blocks to teaching posts but they also forced many new instructors to go into debt.[23] On top of this, new professors were required to pay installation fees which could amount to as much as 20 percent of a year's salary.[24]

Money was not the only thing which stood between a talented graduate and a teaching post. More problematical was the competition, since the universities regularly produced more graduates than they could absorb. Whenever a chair fell vacant through death or promotion, university officials were obliged by statute to post edicts at other universities and in

[20]In 1739, the Prima professor of canon law at Salamanca earned over 650,000 mrs., a very substantial salary indeed. Cited in Addy, *The Enlightenment in the University of Salamanca* (Durham, 1966), p. 24.

[21]Bennassar, *Valladolid au Siècle d'Or* (Paris, 1967), p. 359.

[22]Esperabé Arteaga, *Universidad de Salamanca*, 2: 824. One reason for the elevated price of university degrees was the guild-like nature of the university teaching staff. A degree, especially the doctorate, was much less of a test of one's knowledge than an entrance card into the professors' guild. Membership entailed special privileges: ceremonial precedence, a share in university revenues and graduation fees, and access to important letrado offices. And it was precisely because of these privileges that the costs of advanced university degrees rose quickly in the seventeenth century, since the professors' sought to keep their guild as small and restricted as possible in order that every member could reap the maximum benefits.

[23]Frequently, new instructors petitioned the university for loans and advances in pay in order to meet the cost of the required degrees. For example, Baltasar de Céspedes, appointed Prima professor of grammar at Salamanca in 1597, asked the university shortly thereafter for a loan of 400 ducats so that he could pay for the license and doctorate he needed to keep his post; cf. Andrés, *El Maestro Baltasar de Céspedes y su Discurso de las Letras Humanas* (El Escorial, 1965), pp. 80–81. For a similar request, see AHN: Univs., leg. 48; Esperabé Arteaga, *Universidad de Salamanca*, 2: 816–17, 884.

[24]Ibid., vol. I, statutes of 1567.

Madrid announcing the vacancy and inviting qualified scholars to apply.[25] Not all openings were announced nor were edicts posted; competition was easily sacrificed for convenience and corruption or both, and in 1627 the Royal Council rebuked the University of Granada for condoning this very practice.[26] But when edicts were posted and applications filed, the chair was filled after a series of public examinations known as oposiciones. Candidates prepared a commentary of a text agreed upon in advance, and the one judged most competent took the prize.

The means of selection varied. At the college-universities the power of appointment generally belonged to the members of the core community, but at Castile's larger universities, most of which remained loyal to the Bolognese tradition, teachers were elected by student votes.[27] The pitfalls of these elections were many. In the first place, it was difficult to decide which students could vote for a position in a particular faculty, although this was solved by allowing them to participate only in elections held in the faculty in which they were enrolled. More troublesome was the problem of deciding who was a student and who was not. Matriculation books were inaccurate, since many students registered late[28] while others never bothered to matriculate at all.[29] The task of delineating the student population was further complicated by the mass of part-time students and hangers-on who drifted in and around the universities, among them servants of wealthy students, university employees, pícaros, and thieves, as well as former students who never left the university town. Together they constituted an informal student body, ready to take part in elections regardless of rules to the contrary. Officials attempted to prevent this illegal participation by declaring that only those students who had been matriculated for six months could vote, but infractions continued, since it was impossible to check the eligibility of every student on election day. Even then there was no indication that the names in the matriculation books were students. The University of Santiago noted the presence of "doctors, masters, and others who had finished studying but matriculated each

[25]As an example, see that posted by the University of Santiago in Valladolid: AUV: lib. 514, "Edicto de la Universidad de Santiago de Compostela, 1647."

[26]AUG: leg. 1462, letter of 29.VII.1627. See also AHN: Univ., leg. 42, letters of 19.V.1691, 16.IX.1708.

[27]There were exceptions, however. At Seville the students were empowered to select every teacher except those competing for the Prima professorships in theology and canon law. These were entrusted to the College of Santa Maria de Jesús. At Salamanca, the regencias in grammar and certain minor chairs in the arts faculty—astrology, music, and oriental languages—were specifically designed to be beyond student control; cf. AUS: leg. 2109, carpeta 3, folio 15.

[28]The University of Santiago de Compostela was obliged in 1594 to order that all students studying at the university have their names inscribed in the matriculation book promptly at the beginning of each academic year. See Cabeza de León, Universidad de Santiago, 2: 506.

[29]Manuel Sagado, a student at Salamanca's college of Pan y Carbón, never matriculated officially at the university; cf. Nogaledo Alvarez, El Colegio Menor de 'Pan y Carbón,' primero de los antiguos Colegios Seculares de Salamanca, 1386-1780 (Salamanca, 1958), p. 92.

year,"[30] and it was mentioned that professors at Salamanca had used as voters "the absent and the dead."[31] Even the religious orders were not immune to electoral chicanery, and at Salamanca they were known to import brothers from distant convents to serve as voters when an election threatened to be close.[32] Furthermore, nothing prevented an enterprising contender from hiring groups of street urchins, bribing the university secretary to inscribe their names in the university rolls, creating for himself a hired voting claque.[33]

Once the votes, legitimate or illegitimate, were counted, the candidate receiving a plurality won the chair. But counting was not so simple, especially at Salamanca, where the work was complicated by a system of weighted ballots which awarded first-year students one vote, graduates four or five.[34] Elections, however, were not decided by votes alone. Bribery, corruption, violence and terrorism each played an important part. And despite attempts by university officials and the Royal Council to bring such practices to a halt, one seventeenth-century witness to the chaos of Salamanca's student elections wrote: "there is not a life-tenured chair without one million mortal sins."[35]

The salaries and prestige enjoyed by instructors at the leading universities were partly responsible for these tactics, but the mounting corruption that was evident in the oposiciones after the late sixteenth century has also to be connected to the ease with which teachers from Alcalá, Salamanca, and Valladolid entered letrado posts. Chairs at these universities, particularly those in law, were nothing less than guarantees of letrado office; by the second half of the seventeenth century approximately 80 percent of the law instructors at Salamanca who outlived their teaching careers left the university for positions in government, the inquisition, or the church.[36] Accordingly, competition for the teaching posts among the job-hungry students grew intense. In the mid-sixteenth century a vacant

[30]Cabeza de León, *Universidad de Salamanca*, 3: 507.

[31]BM: Eg. 439, folio 164v.

[32]The famous Augustinian friar, Luís de León, leveled this very charge against the Dominicans at Salamanca in 1565. See Gregorio de Santiago Vela, *Ensayo de una Biblioteca Ibero-Americano de la Orden de San Agustín* . . . (Madrid, 1917), 3: 425.

[33]In a related situation a Master Juan García, *opositor* to a chair in the arts faculty at Alcalá in 1583, was known to have "by himself and through third persons bribed some of the votes." An investigation revealed that he had promised to "students and friends from his land and nation" good marks in their examinations if they voted for him. García was subsequently ousted from the competition and stripped of his university degrees. See AHN: Univ., leg. 43, folio 22.

[34]AUS: lib. 955 lists the results of a number of these contests.

[35]AHN: Cons., leg. 7138, letter of 18.VIII.1632. The following year the Royal Council threatened to have excommunicated any opositor found to have purchased student votes (AHN: Univs., leg. 43, folio 79). Bribery had long been a common tactic in these elections. As early as 1419, investigations revealed that sums up to 50,000 mrs. had been distributed in the name of a single *opositor*; cf. Riesco Terrero, *Proyección Histórico-Social de la Universidad de Salamanca a Través de Sus Colegios* (Salamanca, 1970), p. 103. See also pp. 138–39.

[36]This estimate is based upon my own lists of officials on Castile's councils and tribunals.

chair in the law faculty might attract five or six contenders; by 1700, rarely less than thirty, in spite of a sharp decline in the total number of university graduates.[37] Little wonder then that the oposiciones became so corrupt; the teaching chair, created originally as a pulpit from which professional scholars could teach the young, had developed into a mandatory stop-over for letrados on their way up.

This change had serious consequences for the university, the most important of which was the disappearance of the professional scholar. The faculties of the arts and theology, staffed increasingly by religious little interested in worldly careers, were in this respect better off than the faculties of law, whose instructors were more in demand. Here, instructors, once installed, changed teaching positions rapidly in the hope of reaching the prestige professorships, only to leave the university as quickly as possible for an outside post. This phenomenon first manifested itself within the universities through the disappearance of a ceremony known as the *jubilación*, which rewarded professors who had taught for twenty years with retirement at half pay. Common during the fifteenth and sixteenth centuries, when scholars frequently remained at the university for a life-term, the jubilación, at least in its formal sense, ended during the last century of Habsburg rule.[38] Salamanca's last true *jubilado* in the faculty of canon law, Cristóbal Gutierrez de Moya, retired in 1591, while civil law at this university in the seventeenth century gave rise to only one true professional scholar: Pablo de Maqueda de Castellano who was Prima professor from 1625 to 1648.[39] Though other professors continued to earn the jubilación, it was only a watered-down version of the ancient ceremony, since the requirement of two decades of service was repeatedly waived.[40]

In the meantime, the concept of a university chair as something of permanence was forgotten. Table 12 illustrates this change. The increasing frequency of appointments to chairs at the universities of Salamanca and Valladolid means that these positions were less and less able to keep their readers for more than a short period of time.[41] The Vísperas professorship in canon law at Salamanca is an excellent example of how frequently these appointments could take place. Between 1670 and 1676, this life-tenured chair was in the possession of six different readers, almost one a year.[42]

[37]See Alcocer Martínez, *Historia de la Universidad de Valladolid* (6 vols., Madrid, 1918–31), vol. 3.

[38]Canon and civil law at Salamanca during these centuries gave rise to sixteen *jubilados*, eight apiece. Gonzalo Gomez de Villasmedina, Prima professor of canon law from 1481 to 1532, had the longest teaching career.

[39]Esperabé Artega, *Universidad de Salamanca*, 2: 285, 436.

[40]As examples, see ibid., 1: 790, 802.

[41]This point has also been made by Addy, *Enlightenment at Salamanca*, pp. 22–23. Figures he publishes demonstrate the sharp decline in the average stay of instructors at the University of Salamanca between 1650 and 1750. He notes, for example, that the average tenure of the Prima professors of canon law dropped from twelve years in the period 1650–1700 to a little more than four years in the succeeding half century.

[42]Esperabé Artega, *Universidad de Salamanca*, 2: 436.

Table 12.   Appointments to Teaching Posts

Chair	Number of appointments		
	15th C.	16th C.	17th C.
University of Salamanca			
Prima Canones (a) (1447 ff.)	2	6	16
Prima Canones (b) (1444 ff.)	2	10	17
Decreto (1447 ff.)	2	10	29
Vísperas Canones (a) (1471 ff.)	3	14	52
Vísperas Canones (b) (1464 ff.)	3	10	23
Sexto (1450 ff.)	1	11	61
Prima Leyes (a) (1468 ff.)	2	8	16
Prima Leyes (b) (1447 ff.)	2	8	15
Vísperas Leyes (a) (1468 ff.)	3	7	33
Vísperas Leyes (b) (1468 ff.)	3	6	25
Instituto (a) (1519 ff.)	—	37	62
Instituto (b) (1519 ff.)	—	42	60
Código (a) (1520 ff.)	—	25	60
Código (b) (1519 ff.)	—	37	52
Digesto Viejo (1534 ff.)	—	15	62
Volumen (1551 ff.)	—	21	65
Prima Teologia (1461 ff.)	5 (4)*	8 (8)	15 (12)
Vísperas Teologia (1436 ff.)	5 (2)	7 (4)	17 (13)
Biblia (1449 ff.)	2	10 (4)	19 (12)
Prima Medicina (1445 ff.)	4	9	12
Vísperas Medicina (1469 ff.)	3	5	13
Filosofía Moral (1457 ff.)	4	8 (4)	19 (15)
Filosofía Natural (1456 ff.)	2	6	13 (5)
Prima Lógica (Súmulas) (1484 ff.)	2	7 (2)	18 (12)
Lógica Magna (1464 ff.)	4	5 (3)	17 (9)
University of Valladolid			
Prima Canones (1523 ff.)	—	11	31
Vísperas Canones (1523 ff.)	—	17	27
Decreto (1517 ff.)	—	11	22
Sexto (1545 ff.)	—	12	38
Clementinas (1529 ff.)	—	15	64
Prima Leyes (1502 ff.)	—	9	29
Vísperas Leyes (1499 ff.)	1	12	26
Digesto Viejo (1541 ff.)	—	23	65
Código Antigua (1529 ff.)	—	23	43
Código Moderna (1548 ff.)	—	18	43
Instituto Antigua (1568 ff.)	—	12	42
Instituto Moderna (1529 ff.)	—	23	43
Sagrada Escritura (1542 ff.)	—	7	23 (6)
Prima Teologia (1500 ff.)	—	18 (1)	17 (12)
Vísperas Teologia (1498 ff.)	1	9	15 (9)
Durando (1554 ff.)	—	7 (1)	37 (9)
Vísperas Medicina (1505 ff.)	—	7	17
Prima Avicenna (1486 ff.)	1	8	10

Table 12. (continued)

| Chair | | Number of appointments | |
	15th C.	16th C.	17th C.
Prima Filosofía	—	16 (2)	44 (9)
Lógica (1504 ff.)	—	14	33 (5)
Arts (1) (1542 ff.)	—	19	22[a]
Arts (2) (1552 ff.)	—	14	32[b]

*Figures in parentheses represent the number of instructors who belonged to a religious order.
[a] Suppressed in 1652 because of a lack of students and rents.
[b] Suppressed in 1692 because of a lack of students and rents.

Source: Esperabé Artega, Universidad de Salamanca, 2; Alcocer Martínez, Universidad de Valladolid, 3.

Not surprisingly, the rate of turnover in the short-term "temporal" chairs was the highest, but even then it was relatively common for a lecturer in the sixteenth century to read for his full term and perhaps even stay on for another. In the following century, rare was the lecturer who bothered to teach for his full term. Frequently, one post had two, even three, different lecturers every year. The chair of Code at Valladolid set the record: five readers in two years.[43]

To a certain extent the rapid turnover of instructors in the seventeenth century was exacerbated by an administrative practice, instituted by the Royal Council, known as the acenso. Based on the letrado hierarchy's own practice of promotion by seniority, the acenso created an academic ladder in each faculty, ranging from the lowest catedrilla to the chairs of Prima. In order to avoid time-consuming competitions and vacancies during the oposiciones, instructors were simply moved up the ladder one rung at a time as their superiors vacated their positions through death or promotion. Enacted officially into law in 1716, the ascenso served mainly to diminish the time each instructor served in a single chair, while creating a situation in which instructors were promoted by seniority rather than merit. One critic expressed the view that "In order to be a professor at Salamanca, it is not necessary to study but to live longer than the others; years make catédraticos, not merits."[44]

As instructors busied themselves with promotions, oposiciones, and appointments to letrado jobs, the quality of university instruction suffered. According to primitive evaluations of teachers' classroom performances, students reacted to their professors as they always do, running the gamut from enthusiasm to harsh complaints.[45] The worst marks on the

[43]See Alcocer Martínez, Universidad de Valladolid, vol. 3.
[44]AGS: GJ. leg. 943.
[45]The earliest and, incidentally, the most objective of these are published in Antonio de la Torre, "La Universidad de Alcalá. Estado de la Enseñanza, según las Visitas de Catédras

instructors' records were their absences and lack of interest in their teaching. This problem was as old as the universities themselves, but it grew progressively worse. As early as the 1520s a student at Alcalá de Henares, in reference to Miguel Carrasco, a professor of theology, claimed that "his absences are so frequent that it would almost be better if he did not read at all," while another remarked: "I do not go to hear [the lesson on] St. Thomas because there is no continuity."[46] Complaints of this nature abounded as similar problems affected nearly every university in sixteenth- and seventeenth-century Castile.[47] Professorial absences were frequent and often prolonged, as more and more of the day-to-day work of instruction was left to young, inexperienced substitutes. Meanwhile, criticism of university teaching mounted. Gregorio de Portilla, professor of civil law at Salamanca for ten years, wrote in 1638 that "in former days there were no lecture halls for the masters, now there are no masters for the lecture halls."[48] He also believed that because of professorial neglect university examinations were "diminishing both in quality and in quantity."[49] Soon the Royal Council, "recognizing the great harm caused by the absences of professors and the reading of chairs by substitutes," obliged the instructors to read daily and imposed strict fines for those who did not.[50] But subsequent rulings, including those which threatened negligent professors with dismissal, brought few results.[51] Teaching continued to deteriorate, and toward the end of the century the University of Salamanca was obliged to admit that lectures in the religious colleges were well-attended, since the friars taught with regularity, while its own instructors attracted few students because they did not.[52] Such problems were not corrected until late

---

de 1524-25 a 1527-28," *Homenaje ofrecido a Menéndez Pidal* (Madrid, 1925), 3: 360-78. Later ones for this university can be found in Juan Urriza, *La Preclara Facultad de Artes y Filosofía de la Universidad de Alcalá de Henares* (Madrid, 1942), pp. 123 ff. See also AUSA: lib. 939; AUSC: lib. A 115; AUS: lib. 940-41; and Cabeza de León, *Universidad de Santiago*, 1: 427, 431.

[46]La Torre, "Universidad de Alcalá."

[47]A report sent to the Royal Council in 1610 about the work of Granada's professors states: "there has been so much neglect in teaching that some [instructors] have not read two lessons in two years" (AHN: Libros de Iglesia, no. 8, folio 3). See also Montells y Nadal, *Universidad de Granada*, pp. 86, 104, 106, 118, 159, 167, 201, 211, and 252. Teaching problems at Santiago are noted in AUSC: lib. A 36, folio 38 ff., *visitas* of 1600 and 1611, and Cabeza de León, *Universidad de Santiago*, 1: 348; 2: 392, 449. For other universities, see AUSA: lib. 862, folio 78; AHP Toledo: lib. I/429, folios 80, 99v.

[48]AUS: Ms. 1925, letter of 2.X.1638.

[49]Ibid.

[50]AUV: lib. D-6, no. 2.

[51]Esperabé Artega, *Universidad de Salamanca*, 1: 767; AUV: lib. D-6, no. 8; BM: Add. 24,947, folio 103. See also AHN: Cons., leg. 7138, "Arbitrio y Discurso del Modo que puede aver para remediar la facultad de Artes en la Universidad de Salamanca," 17.III.1648. This report noted that "all the troubles in this faculty stem from those instructors who enter its chairs but fail to remain in them. Among the opositores there are none willing to read a three-year course, only those wishing to leave the chairs for oposiciones, canonries, or parishes as soon as they can." Furthermore, "for the major part of the year the chairs are left completely unread because the professors leave their chairs deserted when they go to the oposiciones."

[52]AHN: Cons., leg. 7138, "Impreso memorial de la Universidad de Salamanca . . .," 1694.

Table 13. University of Santiago de Compostela: Daily Absences of Instructors

Chair	1634	1635	1649	1656	1670	1685	1692	1699	1701	1702	1703	1720	1730
Prima Canons	19	16	absent Feb.–June	0	77	26	15	48	7	18	16	26	33
Vísps. Canons	33	41	54	6 wks.	29	5	5	63	19	23	9	21	0
Institutes	—	—	—	—	49	—	—	11	6	22	15	—	0
Prima Laws	—	—	6	1 mo.	29	79	9	60	4 mos.	31	31	40	28
Vísps. Laws	—	—	6	—	21	—	16	28	27	12	45	45	51
Prima Theology	33	16	5	5	44	13	30	—	12	35	28	0	53
Vísps. Theology	21	34	3	—	0	15	—	—	14	—	14	12	0
St. Thomas	—	—	—	—	—	"ill all year"	—	—	10	—	9	24	—
Prima Medicine	—	—	—	35	19	103	12	16	29	35	12	43	—
Vísps. Medicine	—	—	—	—	—	"very ill"	—	9	16	—	7	66	—
Method	—	—	—	—	—	12	43	6	18	—	8	—	35
Súmulas	121	27	—	62	—	24	30	24	19	31	13	42	—
Logic	41	33	—	93	89	26	30	16	—	33	15	12	27
Philosophy	62	47	—	56	22	—	8	23	16	51	79	22	32
Average	47.1	30.6	37.3	39.6	37.9	25[a]	18.7	27.6	24.1	29.0	21.5	29.4	25.9

[a] Excludes the chairs of Prima Medicine and Method.
Source: AUSC: leg. 383.

in the following century, but by then whatever prestige had been attached to university instruction had already been lost.

A more accurate assessment of how much teaching time was wasted is possible through an examination of the registers of professorial absences kept by the universities, but, unfortunately, very few of these have survived. The earliest are those for the University of Alcalá de Henares in the mid-sixteenth century.[53] They list the fines or *multas* levied upon each instructor, and the accounting was done three times a year. Between January and April 1559, Alcalá's 27 instructors missed a total of 383 classes, an average of approximately 14 absences each, although individual records ranged from a low of 2 absences to a high of 60. In the following decade, however, absences for Alcalá's staff averaged only 434 for each academic year, that is, 16 absences for each instructor. Considering the high incidence of illness and disease at the time, Alcalá's teachers appear to have been comparatively mindful of their duties.

The only comparable records are those for Santiago in the seventeenth century, and these suggest that the diligence of university professors had deteriorated (Table 13). On average, a teacher at Santiago between 1634 and 1720 was absent a little more than one month out of each academic year. Overall figures, however, tell us little about the change-over of instructors from week to week. Constantly coming and going, professors taught one month but were absent the next, often, but not always, leaving substitutes in their place.[54] But the substitutes were no more reliable than the professors, and substitutes even had substitutes of their own. Consequently, many chairs were subject to a teaching circus, a merry-go-round of different instructors that undoubtedly affected the pace and quality of the course.

Busy with personal business, oposiciones, and letrado appointments, professors in seventeenth-century Castile neglected their teaching as they loitered about the royal court, hoping to influence officials in charge of royal patronage. This practice became so troublesome that it was necessary for Philip IV to prohibit university graduates from traveling to Madrid without special license.[55] Similarly, it was Philip IV, perhaps on the advice of Olivares, who questioned the Cámara's policy of appointing university instructors to government posts without concern for its effect on the universities. In 1627, for example, the Cámara recommended don Melchor de Valencia, Vísperas professor of civil law at Salamanca, for a position on the *audiencia* in Galicia. Philip responded:

Since Salamanca has lost so many great teachers . . . , I hesitate at taking Doctor Valencia away from it, but I also hesitate at leaving a person of his great merits and

---

[53] AHN: Univs., leg. 49.
[54] AHN: Univs., lib. 417 F illustrates this problem at the University of Alcalá de Henares in the late seventeenth century.
[55] AUS: Ms. 939, folio 135.

skills unrewarded. The Cámara will consider what I have said here and advise me whether it is feasible to have him read several more years but with the promise of a future place on one of the *chancillerías*; a solution through which everyone's needs can be met without anyone suffering. But above all the Cámara must advise me on what it thinks.[56]

Later *consultas* carried no response to the king's request, but the Cámara presumably ceded to his wishes, since Valencia remained at Salamanca until 1631, when he left for a position on the *chancillería* in Valladolid.

Melchor de Valencia was an exception. When the Cámara recommended lecturers and professors for government posts, it generally elicited no other reaction but that of agreement from the king. In practice, the *camaristas* were free to nominate whomever they pleased. Rarely did they flinch at stripping the universities of their instructors, even those newly appointed to their chairs. So teachers were named to letrado posts with increasing frequency, heedless of the injuries caused to the universities themselves.[57]

But the Cámara was not wholly at fault. Lecturers and professors represented Castile's academic elite, and to the Cámara they represented excellence amidst the swell of university students and graduates. Although it is true that the Cámara did little to ameliorate the universities' loss of experienced teachers, this exodus was spurred by falling professorial incomes, the result of a decline in university rents and a drop in the student population which in turn reduced the professors' fees.[58] The Cortes of 1627 explained the situation in these terms: "Nowadays the lack of *premios* for letters, the expenses of the times, and the shortage of students in the universities are so notable, and the stipends and salaries of the professors so much below what they used to be, that, as a result, wise, serious scholars cannot persevere in the universities but look for other positions more suitable to their support."[59] Certainly, the rate of departure was highest in the short-term, lower chairs of law, whose occupants were poorly paid in comparison with the tenured professors. But the entire problem of professorial absenteeism, neglect, and departure was also linked to the "careerism" of

[56]AHN: Cons., leg. 13494, consulta of 4.II.1627.
[57]The Cámara did make one isolated gesture at correcting the universities' teaching woes. This occurred in 1648 when it recommended that Toribio de Santos Risoba, a student in the Colegio Mayor de Oviedo and a substitute instructor at Salamanca, be named to a tribunal post so that his position could be filled "in property," that is, on a life-tenured basis (AHN: Cons. leg. 13494, consulta of 11.II.1623). One must suspect the true motives of the Cámara, however. In this case it probably acted in the best interests of Santos, the dull nephew of a former President of Castile, rather than in those of the university.
[58]The diocese of Salamanca, one-third of whose revenues supported the university, lost over 40 percent of its recorded laborers in the first two decades of the seventeenth century; the result may have been a drop in university revenues, and consequently, in professorial incomes. Records of this nature, however, do not exist. See Domínguez Ortiz, *La Sociedad Española en el Siglo XVII* (Madrid, 1963, 1970), 1: 119.
[59]Cortes of Madrid, 1627, p. 334.

the instructors themselves; lucrative and promising opportunities beckoned, they accepted. The Cámara, charged with securing the best of the university graduates for government positions, was merely doing its job. At the center of this development lay the colegiales mayores. Dominating the faculties of law, their eyes trained on letrado office, these graduates had few reservations about leaving their chairs unattended as they searched for official posts, then to abandon the university as quickly as possible. Accordingly, the students, deprived of adequate instruction, boycotted the lecture halls despite repeated attempts to make attendance mandatory.[60] In sum, the university had lost many of its teachers and until the monarchy altered its policies of recruitment and professors developed a sense of dedication to their students lectures went unread while the classrooms remained practically deserted. In Castile such changes were more than a century away. In the meantime, scholarly excellence and curricular innovation were neglected; instructors who put little faith, let alone effort, into their teaching were content to leave things as they were. Such lassitude, no doubt, does much to explain the conservative nature of the curriculum in Castile's universities. Indeed, it is the teachers themselves who must bear most of the responsibility for Spain's removal from the mainstream of European intellectual life. Much more than the inquisition, it was the professors, interested more in profit and prestige than speculative research, who choked off whatever possibilities existed for the development of a rational philosophical and scientific culture in seventeenth-century Spain.

STUDENTS

Owing to the limited biographical information contained in the matriculation registers of Castile's universities, students are not a readily identifiable group.[61] Generally, their age and geographical origins are listed, but their family backgrounds are not. Therefore, any discussion about the students who attended institutions of higher learning in Castile between the sixteenth and eighteenth centuries is largely a matter of guesswork.

AGE

Although in many cases the ages of university students listed in the matriculation registers may not be exact,[62] it is clear that students in the sixteenth century were, in comparison with later decades, relatively advanced in age (Table 14). Young teenagers were few while men in their twenties

---

[60]See AGS: CJ. leg. 942, cédula of 12.X.1650; AHN: Cons., leg. 7138, cédula of 24.IX.1656; AUV: lib. 1, no. 10, cédula of 25.II.1685.
[61]Available matriculation registers for Castile's universities are listed in appendix II.
[62]See appendix B.

Table 14. Mean Age of University Students: the University of Alcalá de Henares

Faculty	Years				
	1550	1610	1650	1690	1771
Arts	20.7	19.42	19.39	17.96	17.06
Canon Law	24.12	21.64	19.85	18.32	19.38
Medicine	23.58	24.82	23.78	22.96	24.8
Theology	25.24	23.33	23.40	21.95	21.14

Source: AHN: Univs. Libros 431 ff.

were common, but the median age at which students first matriculated was approximately eighteen. In subsequent years the median age of incoming students dropped as teenagers became increasingly numerous, older men less so. In the arts faculty at Alcalá de Henares, for example, the median age of first-year students fell to sixteen in 1771, a figure two years below that of the mid-sixteenth century (Fig. 3). This decline undoubtedly contributed toward the evolution of the arts faculty at this and other universities from a sophisticated degree program in philosophy to nothing more than a grandiose grammar school. By the opening of the nineteenth century this evolution had run its course; the arts faculty, catering for boys who were often no more than thirteen or fourteen years of age, lost university rank.

The advanced, professional faculties taught boys who were several years older than those registered in arts, but here too the median age was on the decline. Most dramatic was the drop in the age of law students. The median age for canon lawyers at Alcalá—first-year students through those in the fifth—was twenty-four in 1550 but only eighteen in 1700, a swing of six years in a century and one-half. One reason for this drop was the rising rate of attrition among students in the course of the seventeenth century (Figs. 4 and 5).[63] This meant that proportionally fewer and fewer students remained at university beyond their first or second year, automatically reducing the median age for the faculty as a whole. But in order to account for these "drop-outs," it is necessary to keep in mind the changing place of legal studies in Castile. A faculty catering largely for future professionals in the Middle Ages, law (both canon and civil) toward the latter part of the sixteenth century became an increasingly "popular" subject in that it attracted more and more students who were little interested in university degrees. The "legal-mindedness" of Castile's propertied and office-holding classes brought to the law faculties boys fresh from grammar schools, who substituted legal training for advanced studies in the liberal arts. For these students law was important for reasons of practical knowledge rather than career; consequently, degrees were redundant, long years of university un-

[63]See below, p. 178.

necessary, and this in turn helped to lower the age of students registered in that faculty.

If this hypothesis helps to explain the new youthfulness of law students in the seventeenth century, it cannot account for the general decline in the age of university students in Castile after 1600. Lower standards of admission certainly contributed to this change, although it is true that university entrance in the sixteenth century, that is, when the students' age was at its peak, posed little or no difficulty for anyone with a modicum of Latin schooling. But why were students in the sixteenth century so much older? One reason is that entrance into university for many boys was "artificially" delayed. Military, religious, or vocational training interrupted their schooling; hence, matriculation at university was postponed. University violence, so common at that time, may also have kept younger boys away until they were old enough to look out for themselves. Parental concern for their sons' security also required many older brothers to defer university until their

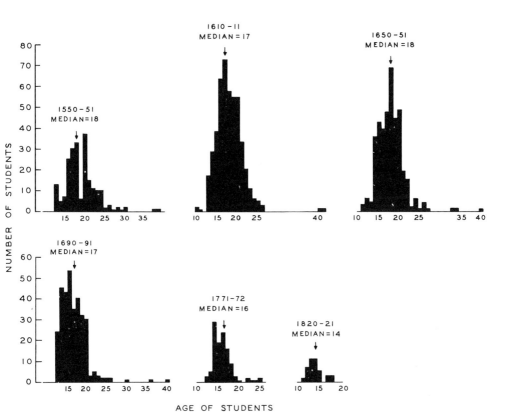

Fig. 3. Age of students: first year of the arts, University of Alcalá de Henares. The median age of arts students, following that of students of grammar, drops quickly after the sixteenth century. By 1820, most of the students are in their early teens, while the arts faculty has degenerated into nothing more than a grandiose grammar school.

younger siblings reached the age of thirteen or fourteen, the youngest at which students were accustomed to matriculate. In this way, the older could look after the younger, costs could be cut, and a single tutor could care for them both.

Yet another reason why matriculation at university was so frequently postponed in the sixteenth century was the loose connection between

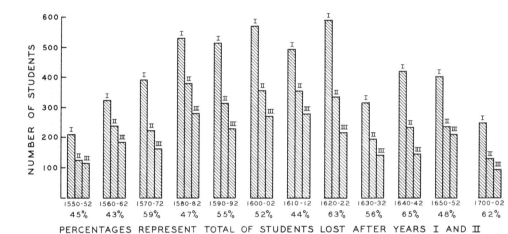

Fig. 4. Attrition among university students: the arts faculty of the University of Alcalá de Henares. The first year of study took a heavy toll, but those students who made it through the second year generally manage to earn a degree. On average, more students abandoned the faculty during the seventeenth century than in the more prosperous and promising years of the sixteenth century.

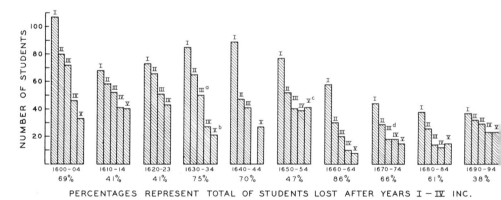

Fig. 5. Attrition among university students: canon law faculty, of the University of Santiago de Compostela. The difficult middle years of the seventeenth century were the worst. Some improvement followed since the faculty was left with a reduced number of professionally oriented students bent on earning degrees. a. Total includes 3 "transfer" students. b. Total includes 1 "transfer" student. c. Total includes 2 "transfer" students. d. Total includes 1 "transfer" student.

physical age on the one hand and school or university class on the other. No urgency then existed to advance a boy's education as regularly as he advanced in age, and it was not thought unnatural to mix old and young together in a single classroom and have them taught the same subject in a similar way. By the eighteenth century, however, such ideas were out of fashion. Age-mixing, as such, was regarded as evil; children and adolescents were now thought to be very different from one another (as well as from adults), and, therefore, they were each in need of special attention, discipline, and care. Simultaneously, school age and physical age were linked together for the first time, and this meant that upper- and middle-class children, as they matured, were passed directly from class to class with little interference or delay. Consequently, the age-spread at both school and university was reduced, while more and more students clustered around a single, more youthful, modal age (Figs. 1 and 3).

One important consequence of this decline was the gradual erosion of many of the rights and responsibilities which had been entrusted to the mature students characteristic of the Middle Ages.[64] The first to go was the students' privilege to select their own instructors; this occurred in 1641 when the Royal Council appropriated this responsibility for itself. And then, in the later eighteenth century, the students' right to participate in university administration was also revoked.[65] Age was not the only factor which contributed to these developments, but at a time when adults began to fix in their minds that adolescents were different than adults and not to be treated as such, age cannot be easily dismissed.

GEOGRAPHY

One thing that Castile's students, young and old, had in common was their geographical background. The vast majority were originally town-dwellers rather than residents of rural hamlets and villages.[66] This was certainly the case at Alcalá de Henares in the sixteenth century where only a tiny proportion of students hailed from small, village communities (Table 15). And this was also true at the University of Seville in 1570, where over 60 percent of the students living within the archdiocese of Seville came from eleven towns each of whose inhabitants numbered 5,000 or more.[67] Though smaller communities had their representatives at the university, few were able to contribute more than one or two students each; thus Seville's student

[64]It has recently been asserted that one of the reasons why students at medieval universities in the south of Europe gained so much power was their relative maturity; cf. Cobban, "Medieval Student Power," *Past & Present* 53 (1971): 28–66.

[65]See below, p. 227.

[66]"Intellectuals" during the Habsburg era were also products of the towns; cf. Juan J. Linz, "Intellectual Roles in 16th and 17th Century Spain," *Daedalus* (Summer, 1972): 70–74.

[67]AUSA: Libros de Matrículas. There were 275 students from the archdiocese of Seville registered at the university that year. Similar distributions were recorded in 1610 and 1660.

Table 15.   University of Alcalá de Henares: Faculty of Canon Law Geographical Origins of
Students

		1550		
Community size		Number	Number of students	%
0–99 vecinos		3	3	3.1
100–499		11	17	17.3
500–999		6	8	18.2
1,000		7	43 ‖	43.8
?		21	27	27.6
	Totals	48	98	100.0
		1610		
Community size		Number	Number of students	%
0–99 vecinos		2	2	1.9
100–499		21	28	12.3
500–999		19	39	17.2
1,000		9	85	37.4
?		41	73	32.2
	Totals	92	227	100.0

Source: AHN: Univs. Libros 431 ff.

population was overwhelmingly "urban" in character. Two centuries later, little had changed. In 1750, for instance, 100 students from the archdiocese of Seville were registered at Seville's faculty of canon law. Owing to faulty population statistics, it is possible to determine the size of the home-town of only seventy-five of these students, but among them, sixty-seven, or 90 percent, came from towns with populations surpassing 5,000.[68]

Students at Castile's other universities were of similar geographical origins; city and town boys were numerous, whereas, village boys were relatively few. The towns, after all, harbored those families· with sufficient wealth and interest to send their sons to university, while those living in the countryside—poor, illiterate, backward, and immobile—did not. Training in Latin, essential for university entrance, was also restricted.[69] There were only a few grammar schools in the small villages and these were expensive

[68]Ibid. Six students (8 percent) came from towns with a population between 2,500 and 5,000; two from communities with 500 to 2,500 inhabitants; and none from villages with a population under 500.
[69]See p. 48.

and available only to a few; higher education, therefore, was almost an impossibility except for those able to obtain sponsorship from an outside source. Boys living in the towns, on the other hand, had an opportunity to learn Latin and to qualify for university. And across the centuries this difference may help to explain the continuing political impotency of the rural areas of Spain. Country boys learned only literacy, if that, while city boys, partly as a result of their advanced education, were able to obtain positions of power and prestige.

Among the cities from which students hailed, Seville and, above all, Madrid, stood out.[70] The wealth and dynamism of the former, the latter's position as capital and court, attracted to them families likely to seek a university education for their sons. Thus Madrid, lacking a university of its own, was able to provide those of Castile with more students than many whole provinces could muster. At the end of the seventeenth century, for example, Madrid had as many as 500 of its youths enrolled in universities each year, a figure approximately equal to 3 to 4 percent of its boys of university age[71] and one that was well above the national mean for university attendance at that time.[72] Together with other graduates who chose to make the capital their home, this reserve of university-educated manpower helps to explain why Madrid, the political core of the empire, the economic heart of New Castile, was also a capital of culture, the arbiter of Spain's artistic and literary tastes.

On a regional basis, most of the university students in Castile came from the north and center of the peninsula, in particular, Asturias, the Basque provinces, León, Navarre, Old Castile, and the parts of New Castile surrounding Cuenca, Toledo, and Madrid. On the other hand, Extremadura and Andalucia, save for cities like Córdoba, Granada, and Seville, contributed relatively few students.[73] This distribution should come as no surprise. In the sixteenth century, the former were wealthy, well-populated regions, well-stocked with Latin schools. Furthermore, and especially in comparison with the southern and western parts of the kingdom, they contained a relatively high concentration of *hidalgo* families, a group among whom university attendance was commonplace. It follows that thirteen of Castile's nineteen universities were situated in these same regions, while the hidalgo- and Latin-poor lands to the south supported only a few, none of which attained a size comparable to their northern counterparts. Clearly,

[70]Again, this is comparable to the geographical origins of Spain's "intellectuals"; cf. Linz, "Intellectual Roles," pp. 73–74.

[71]For the mathematics involved in this estimate, see chap. IX, note 13. I have put the capital's population at approximately 150,000.

[72]This was approximately 2.5 percent.

[73]This distribution differs from the regional distribution of "intellectuals" in that relatively few of the former were from the south, while few of the latter were from the far north. However, the center of the kingdom (i.e., Old Castile) was well-represented in both groups.

universities in Castile followed in the wake of privilege and of wealth, not to mention an abundance of primary and secondary schools.

Beyond age and geographical origins, very little can be known about the students at Castile's universities. There are some exceptions, but owing to the shortcomings of the matriculation registers, a systematic analysis of student backgrounds is next to impossible unless one were to search through local and parish records, an endeavor which could easily consume several lifetimes of labor. Nevertheless, a more impressionistic approach is still valuable.

THE NOBILITY

As in England, the nobility of Castile in the sixteenth and seventeenth centuries matriculated at universities in growing numbers, but to compare the experiences of the two countries is difficult.[74] England had a small, easily recognizable aristocracy and a somewhat larger gentry class which together represented not more than 2 percent of the total population. In Castile nobles of one sort or another accounted for as many as 10 percent of the kingdom's inhabitants, that is, about 600,000 persons. So large is this group that it is often difficult to determine who was noble and who was not. By strict, legal definition, anyone who was not a clergyman and who did not pay direct taxes was a nobleman, but among those who could be classified as noble through this definition, the differences were huge. In the Basque provinces privileges granted to the local population by medieval kings exempted everyone from direct taxation; consequently, the entire population was "noble," including those who tilled the soil and practiced manual crafts technically prohibited for members of a privileged class whose major occupation was supposed to be war. Similarly, the kingdom of Navarre was awarded "noble" status, and throughout the north of Castile there were countless "nobles" who had little more than such status to their names.

Simple noblemen such as these were known as hidalgos, a term derived from those individuals who had been traditionally able to keep a horse and who had also participated in the *Reconquista* against the Moors. By the sixteenth century, however, hidalgo referred broadly to the poor, often landless, noblemen who constituted the bulk of Castile's "noble" class. In addition, there were six higher rankings of nobility of which only two, *títulos* and *grandes*, the equivalent of the English aristocracy, resembled a coherent, easily-definable group. In 1520 only sixty Castilian families boasted titles, although royal generosity in subsequent years quadrupled this number by 1641. Likewise, grandee families, set apart from títulos by their greater wealth, prestige, and certain ceremonial privileges, were limited to twenty in 1520 by order of Charles V, but by 1707 their number

---

[74]See Lawrence Stone, "The Educational Revolution in England, 1560 to 1640," *Past & Present* 28 (1964): 41–80.

had passed one-hundred and the class was divided into three ranks so that grandees of ancient vintage could be distinguished from those of recent creation.[75]

The matriculation registers of the University of Salamanca make note of students with aristocratic backgrounds, but as these begin only in 1546, it is impossible to know how many sons of the aristocracy attended this university before that date. To be sure, the younger male offspring of Castile's titled houses who were destined for ecclesiastical careers had attended this and other universities since the Middle Ages, but it would have been unlikely for a young título or grandee who was preparing for a worldly career to attend university much before the opening of the sixteenth century. Then the university's acceptance of humanist studies helped to attract the aristocracy's interest, while the Catholic kings openly encouraged the sons of their courtiers to attend university by offering special subsidies.[76] Writers of the time also mention the presence of young nobles at university during the reign of Ferdinand and Isabel, but they could not have been very numerous.[77] Even in the middle of the sixteenth century, there were only a few at the University of Salamanca (Table 16).[78] Other, less renowned universities proved no more popular, and in total, it does not appear that more than 5 or 10 percent of the sons of Castile's aristocracy were registered at university at any given time. The others, like the commander of the Spanish Armada, the seventh Duke of Medina-Sidonia, were educated at home.

Among those members of the aristocracy who did attend university, many belonged to families who were in the habit of doing so generation after generation. Notable in this regard were the Dukes of Gandía, the Counts of Benavente, Monterrey, and Santisteban, and the Marquises of Cerralbo. Otherwise, university matriculation among the aristocracy was a chance affair, almost a whim. The Duke of Infantado sent a son to Salamanca in 1570, but never again did a scion of this famous house appear in this university's books. And the same is true for most of the other magnates; except for a handful of interested families, Spain's aristocracy had little use for the universities.

[75]On Spain's nobility, see Domínguez Ortiz, *Sociedad Española*, 1: 209–22.

[76]The crown, for example, granted 100,000 mrs. a year to the sons of the Court of Haro "who are studying at Salamanca" in 1498, 1499, and 1500. Previously, they had awarded 30,000 mrs. to two sons of the royal councillor, Doctor de Madrigal, "so that they could remain at university." Cited in M. A. Ladero Quesada, "La Hacienda Castellana de los Reyes Católicos (1493–1504)," *Moneda y Credito* 103 (1967): 99, 107–08, 110.

[77]Known to be university students at this time were sons of the Duke of Alba, the Count of Paredes, and Pedro Fernandez de Velasco, who subsequently became Condestable de Castilla; see Antonio Gil y Zarate, *De la Instrucción Pública en España* (Madrid, 1855), p. 10.

[78]The first members of this class recorded in Salamanca's matriculation books were Alonso de Fonseca, son of the Count of Toledo, and Sancho de Avila y Toledo, son of the Marquis of Velada. Both were enrolled in grammar in the year 1555–56. See AUS: Libros de Matrículas, 1555–56.

Table 16.   "Nobles, Generosos, y Dignidades" at the University of Salamanca

Decade	No. of years for which information is available	Títulos + Grandees	Nobles
1540–49	1	—	32
1550–59	8	4	115
1560–69	8	10	50
1570–79	10	11	41
1580–89	5	5	13
1590–99	6	5	64
1600–09	4	9	45
1610–19	9	13	34
1620–29	9	18	11
1630–39	10	9	20
1640–49	10	5	—
1650–59	10	12	—
1660–69	10	15	—
1670–79	10	3	—
1680–89	10	3	—
1690–99	10	4	—

Source: AUS: Libros de Matrículas.

One should note, however, that among those grandees and títulos who did matriculate, law was the favorite subject for study, although only a few went so far as to take a degree.[79] The university provided them, on the other hand, with an opportunity to acquire a smattering of useful knowledge as well as a chance to have a good time before they assumed the responsibilities of inheritance, marriage, and the offices of state.

More numerous at the University of Salamanca, but with interests similar to those of the grandees, were the sons of *caballeros* and other important, though untitled, noble families (Table 16). Relatively common in the sixteenth century, their presence diminished in the next century, although the decline in their numbers is exaggerated by apparent flaws in the matriculation books. Sons of these families continued to enroll at Salamanca, particularly as members of the colegios mayores.[80] But it does appear that many important noble families had altered their educational habits in the course of the seventeenth century, preferring to educate their children at home or in a local college rather than send them to the universities, notorious for their riotous and undisciplined student life.

In spite of their scant representation—less than one percent—among Salamanca's students, the sons of Castile's leading families were not without influence at this university. The office of university rector was almost

[79]One who did was Juan de Mendoza, son of the Duke of Infantazgo, who was a *bachiller* in canon law in 1570. The other aristocratic students who earned degrees were primarily those belonging to the colegios mayores; see p. 128.

[80]As colegiales, they would not appear in the special section of the matriculation books reserved for nobles and dignitaries.

theirs for the asking, nor were those who applied for a place in one of the colegios mayores often turned away. Moreover, as a privileged group among the students, they imparted to the university a culture of wealth and extravagance which it otherwise would have lacked. The young grandees existed almost in a world of their own, living apart from the ordinary students in rented houses and surrounded by luxuries few of the others could enjoy. How many students could afford to live in the style of the young Count of Olivares who, when he came to Salamanca in 1600, had a retinue which included one tutor, one preceptor, eight pages, three house servants, four lackeys, a chef, a butler, various house servants and their helpers, plus additional staff to care for his horses?[81] Dressed in brightly colored silks, the grandees stood out from the mass of students clad in dull, black scholars' gowns, and whereas most of the students went about on foot, the wealthy noblemen rode on horseback or in coaches; a few were reputed to be carried in litters to class. Even in academic matters they were set apart, since their degree course was one year shorter than that of the other students, a privilege accorded them in the fifteenth century on account of their supposedly superior preparation for university study. Thus with a lightened load, tutors, and servants to reserve the best seats in the lecture halls or even to attend lectures and take notes in their place, sons of the aristocracy, few of whom were interested in advanced scholarship or degrees, led an easy, pleasurable student life.

Their lifestyle, moreover, was infectious. Other students, many of whom aped noble status, sought to acquire for themselves the fanciful trimmings and dress of their more privileged counterparts. The Royal Council reacted by demanding that students must wear only the prescribed academic gown and lead a modest, scholarly life. Moreover, their "excessive spending" had to stop, and in 1606 the crown decreed that "students of every quality and condition are not permitted to have carriages, coaches, litters, mules, or horses."[82] But violations of this ruling continued, and it had to be proclamated anew in 1608.[83] Yet this decree and others like it, based on aged statutes and rules, were out of step with the times. Most students in the seventeenth century had little interest in the monkish regulations of the past. Aristocratic students, however few, had brought to the universities new standards of behavior and dress which students of lesser rank adopted for their very own.

With regard to teaching, on the other hand, the leading noblemen at university were practically without influence, except for the few who, as members of the colegios mayores, obtained professorial rank. Had it been otherwise one could imagine that the academic routine, already in decline by the seventeenth century, would have been further sacrificed to light-

[81]See J. García Mercadal, *Estudiantes, Sopistas, y Pícaros* (Madrid, 1934), p. 116.
[82]Esperabé Artega, *Universidad de Salamanca*, 1: 673.
[83]Ibid., p. 762.

headedness, superficial learning, and play. As it was, the absence of the aristocracy from the teaching chairs helped to preserve in the university a professional milieu in which students interested in scholarship and others seeking letrado careers worked to obtain their degrees.

THE CLERGY

These students included the clergy, regular and secular. Among the latter those most in evidence were priests holding a cathedral office: a canonry, deanship, chaplaincy, etc. The University of Salamanca's registers listed seventeen of these dignitaries in 1546–47, although in the following years their numbers decreased.[84] By 1600 it was rare to find more than one or two members of the cathedral clergy at the University in any year. Paradoxically, this disappearance suggests that the educational attainments of the priests who were entering the upper echelons of the Catholic hierarchy was on the rise, rather than the reverse. Before the Council of Trent (1545–63) many ecclesiastics received cathedral appointments and were subsequently sent to university to acquire academic titles and degrees. Then the church made degrees mandatory for members of the cathedral clergy, and this meant that clerics elected to canonries and other cathedral offices had to be graduates. It appears, therefore, that the decline in the number of church dignitaries studying at Salamanca in the course of the sixteenth century had something to do with improved standards of recruitment among the cathedral clergy in Castile, standards which were in part strengthened by the orders of the Council of Trent.

Whether similar improvements occurred in the training of the lesser clergy is difficult to ascertain. Ordinary priests, holders of benefices, and simple clerics ordinarily merited no special distinction in the matriculation books, consequently, it is impossible to know how many received university training. The universities of Seville and Valladolid made an effort to note the presence of a *clérigo* or *presbítero* among their students, but many went unnoticed. At Valladolid, for example, less than 12 percent of the students matriculating in 1570 were listed as clergymen, and at Seville the percentage was even less.[85] Such figures are misleading, since they are certainly too low, but they do emphasize the overwhelmingly secular character of the student population at Castile's major universities in the sixteenth century. In Seville clerics preferred the Dominican University of Santo Tomás, and clerics elsewhere may have attended the convent-universities instead of larger, more expensive and more turbulent institutions. But in general the rank-and-file churchman was educated in a Jesuit college, cathedral school, or in a seminary, while only the intellectual elite of the

---

[84] These clergymen are listed along with nobles in the "Nobles, Generosos, y Dignidades" section of Salamanca's matriculation books.

[85] In 1570 clergymen at the University of Seville accounted for 4 percent of the 244 matriculants. In 1599 they represented 5.3 percent of the students (14 of 299).

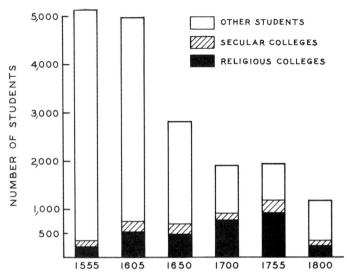

Fig. 6. College students at the University of Salamanca. By the mid-eighteenth century, over one-half of Salamanca's students belonged to a college. Those in the religious colleges were especially numerous, underscoring the "christianization" of Spain's most important university. (*Source*: Appendix A, Table II.)

clergy—bishops, canons, urban priests, etc.—bothered to pursue advanced training at the university level.[86] To understand this division in the education of Spain's churchmen is also to understand why the secular clergy made such a poor showing at Seville and Valladolid in the sixteenth century, although it would be wise to repeat that there were many more clerics at these universities than the matriculation books, rife with omissions during that epoch, reveal.

More in evidence and clearly noted as such were students who belonged to the regular clergy.[87] At universities in which the religious orders had colleges of their own, the followers of each order matriculated en masse, usually in the faculties of arts and theology and, to a lesser degree, in medicine and canon law. The largest of the religious colleges attached to the universities was San Esteban at Salamanca, a Dominican house which at its peak counted well over 150 members. In addition, the University of Salamanca by the seventeenth century incorporated eighteen other religious colleges.

Before 1600, however, only the larger orders had built university colleges; consequently, the total number of religious studying at the university was relatively few (Fig. 6).[88] Then as the total population of the university

[86]On this point see Domínguez Ortiz, *Sociedad Española*, 2: 11.

[87]They are noted in the matriculation registers by the Fray or Fr. preceding their names.

[88]In comparison, the University of Valladolid incorporated fewer than ten religious colleges, the largest of which was the Dominican college of San Pablo. Alcalá had six religious colleges, while Granada and Santiago each had two or three.

declined in the course of the seventeenth century, more religious colleges were built while existing ones expanded in size. By the middle of the eighteenth century the religious orders at Salamanca, with a total membership of over 900, accounted for nearly one-half of the university's students. That the religious studying at Salamanca practically disappeared thereafter is something of a mystery. Partly, it was precipitated by the expulsion of the Jesuits in 1767 and then by a 1771 ruling that denied university credit to courses taken at a religious college. But for other reasons which are not yet understood, the 1760s and 1770s coincided with a sharp decline in the membership of nearly all of Salamanca's religious colleges, almost as if the head of each order had transferred the religious to convents located elsewhere. San Esteban, for one, had 175 members in 1765 but only 36 in 1775, and that same year the regular clergy's total share of the university population was less than 20 percent. An era—was it the Counter Reformation?—had come to an end.

Nor was Salamanca's experience with the religious orders unique. In Alcalá de Henares and Valladolid the membership of the religious colleges incorporated within the universities grew sharply throughout the seventeenth century, reaching a peak around 1750. By then, the religious represented approximately 40 percent of the students registered at Valladolid[89] and nearly as many at Alcalá.[90]

Increases in the number of religious studying at the universities between the sixteenth and eighteenth centuries were matched by their appearance in university teaching posts (Table 12). Before the sixteenth century the convents surrounding the universities were independent institutions of learning. Correspondingly, the religious, either as teachers or students, occupied a relatively small place within the universities proper. But in subsequent years they adapted to the general demand for university degrees and began to matriculate on a regular basis. Those who earned degrees competed for and often obtained university chairs, with the result that instruction in the arts and theology fell increasingly under their sway, since secular scholars preferred the more lucrative teaching positions in the faculties of law. But the religious were also dedicated instructors, while the lay teachers, busy with promotions, appointments, and letrado careers, were not. This alone may help to explain why the regular clergy met with such success in the oposiciones for university chairs, although it is true that they were not above the bribery and corruption practiced by other graduates.[91]

[89]The students belonging to Valladolid's religious colleges numbered 234 in 1755, of whom 161 were members of the College of San Pablo.
[90]In 1750 the religious colleges at Alcalá enrolled 182 students, that is, approximately one-fourth of all the students at Alcalá.
[91]In 1608, for example, "the corrupt voting practices of the religious" were criticized; see AUS: lib. 2109, folio 5 v. Apparently, each order arranged to have its members vote as a solid bloc for their particular candidate, a procedure which was in violation of university rules.

The presence of the regular clergy as teachers within Castile's leading universities was also assured by a number of chairs especially reserved for members of particular orders. The first of these, created for the Dominicans in Salamanca's faculty of theology in 1605, was a gift from the Duke of Lerma who, a few years later, awarded this order a second chair.[92] The Dominicans also acquired special chairs at Alcalá de Henares and Santiago de Compostela, while similar privileges were extended to the Augustinians, Benedictines, Franciscans, and Jesuits.[93] Soon every major Spanish university had a number of chairs attached to one or more of the religious orders, since each was thought to deserve a special pulpit from which it could expound its particular version of philosophical and theological truth. With similar reasoning in mind, an administrative procedure known as the *alternativa* was instituted at a number of universities. In operation, for example, at Alcalá by 1673, it made certain that new instructors in the arts faculty alternated among the religious orders represented at that university.[94] Consequently, nearly all of the teaching in the arts as well as that in theology was handed over to the regular clergy.

The infiltration of Castile's universities in the seventeenth and eighteenth centuries by the religious orders stands in apparent contradiction to what is generally conceived to be a "secularization" of higher education in Europe after 1650 or 1700. In Castile, the tide flowed the other way. Overwhelmingly secular in the sixteenth century, the universities were "christianized" in the centuries that followed. This evolution, led by the Dominicans and Jesuits and aided by the inquisition, seems to have helped to keep new ideas in science and philosophy out of the curriculum at a time when universities in the north of Europe gradually absorbed the discoveries of Descartes, Galileo, Leibniz, and Newton. Castile's universities, bent on orthodoxy, protested loudly against any "perversion" of the traditional course.[95]

It would be wrong to attribute the intellectual torpor of these universities to the conservatism of the religious orders alone. The professorate's antipathy toward innovation and their general distaste for teaching are no doubt sufficient to explain why the universities of Castile failed to keep abreast of European ideas. But it is also true that curricular innovation in Castile only took place in the 1770s annd 1780s, that is, after the religious orders had all but abandoned the universities and the governance of these institutions had been assumed by "enlightened" reformers at the royal court. By 1800 the universities of Castile manifested a secular spirit. Akin

[92]Esperabé Artega, *Universidad de Salamanca*, 1: 659, 667–68.

[93]At Salamanca the Jesuits received a chair of theology in 1665, the Franciscans in 1734; cf. ibid., 1: 822, 899.

[94]Ibid., 1: 873; Addy, *Enlightenment in Salamanca*, p. 21; and AGS: GJ, leg. 941, "Relacion del turno. . . ."

[95]Typical was the University of Seville's complaint about new Dutch and English ideas "perverting" Aristotle, Hippocrates, and Galen; see Ajo, *Universidades*, 5: 235.

to their counterparts in the Golden Age, they again stood open to the intellectual currents of the world. It seems tempting, therefore, to speculate that the interim, a period of general stagnation and decay for the universities and an epoch in which the influence of the religious orders was at its height, brought about a severance of many of the links which the universities in the early sixteenth century had forged with the wider world. A popular, open, innovative spirit was superseded by another grounded upon tradition, orthodoxy, and resistance to experimentation and change. In this regard the universities only mirrored wider changes within Castile itself, but retrenchment and withdrawal were exactly what so many of Spain's religious, as teachers and students, so solemnly espoused.[96]

MANTEISTAS AND COLEGIALES

The remaining students at the universities, the vast majority by far, are little more to us than names. One can be sure that they were literate in the vernacular and had probably been introduced to the rules of Latin grammar; therefore, it can be presumed that they belonged to that minority of the population able to acquire such skills. Beyond this, however, the scanty information provided in the matriculation books reveals nothing about students' family backgrounds.

It was not expensive to register at a university in sixteenth- and seventeenth-century Castile. A fee was required, but it was so small—only four or five mrs. a year—as to be well within the reach of most literate Castilians.[97] Costs spiraled, however, when it came to living in a university town, or this is at least what surviving records of the *pupilajes* or licensed student lodgings at the University of Alcalá de Henares would indicate.[98] These houses, subject to university jurisdiction, were inspected annually by officials who questioned lodgers about living conditions and costs and then challenged the *pupilero*, the head of the pupilaje, if any violations of university rules had occurred. The results of only two of these inspection tours

[96]In this perspective, the contribution of the Benedictine friar Benito Jerónimo Feijóo (1676-1764) at the University of Oviedo is indeed remarkable. Speaking out for the need to reform the universities and to modernize their curriculum at a time when the intellectually conservative religious orders were gaining in strength, Feijóo stood alone. Perhaps this is the reason why his ideas had little influence until he was nearing his death. For Feijóo's contribution, see Gaspard Delpy, *L'Espagne et l'Esprit Européen, l'Oeuvre de Feijóo* (Paris, 1936); Ramón Ceñal, "Feijóo, hombre de la Ilustración," *Revista de Occidente* 2 (December 1964): 312-24; and the collective work, *Feijóo y Su Siglo* (Oviedo, 1961). Addy, *Enlightenment in Salamanca*, pp. xiv, 104-05, also discusses his contributions.
[97]Santiago charged four mrs. a year (cf. Cabeza de León, *Universidad de Santiago*, 3: 65), while Salamanca, according to its statutes of 1561, declared that students of grammar must pay 3 mrs., ordinary students 5, graduates 7, and nobles 17 (Esperabé Artega, *Universidad de Salamanca*, 1: 311).
[98]What proportion of this university's students lived in such dwellings as opposed to private houses, colleges, and rented rooms is unknown. Presumably, the *pupilajes* catered for quite a substantial number.

have survived; the first, dating from 1557, covers 24 pupilajes serving over 200 students—all of whom studied the arts or grammar—while the second, made in 1567, is more fragmented and involves only 5 pupilajes and 83 students.[99] Nevertheless, together these reports are sufficient to paint a picture of what life for a university student in the sixteenth century was like.[100]

In the first place, the pupilajes were small. The largest belonged to a Master Segura who had twenty-eight students under his charge, the smallest were those of two masters named Peña with only four students apiece. The average pupilaje, however, housed between ten and fifteen students: small enough to allow the pupilero to conduct the weekly review sessions required by university rules, although complaints by students indicate that such classes did not always take place.

Fees in the pupilajes varied. In 1567 the cheapest was that run for six students of grammar by Francisco de Orillano, who charged 24 ducats for eight months. The most expensive, those of the masters Beltran, Espejo, Morales, and Segura, cost each student 60 ducats for the academic year, although lodgers who were accompanied by a servant paid up to 100 ducats each. But students accompanied by servants were rare; the majority came to university alone, and for them the average cost of a pupilaje was 40 to 50 ducats a year.[101]

For such a sum each student was entitled to a bed, bed-clothes, food, soap, and candles for light,[102] but students frequently claimed that the pupileros skimped on what university regulations required. They protested that the water in one house was "very dirty," that the sheets in another were "unclean," and in a third that the bread was "very bad and very black." Others grumbled about the insufficient quality and quantity of the meat provided at meals and about the lack of candles. In one instance a pupilero who was charged with having substituted oil lamps for candles defended himself, answering that candles would not last the six or seven

[99]For the first, see AHN: Univs., leg. 65, no. 18. The second can be found in the ACM: leg. 3, no. 1.

[100]For a literary picture of university life, the picaresque novels are excellent, especially Mateo Aleman, *Guzman de Alfarache* (1599), Francisco de Quevedo, *La Vida del Buscón* (1626; written ca. 1604), Jerónimo de Alcalá, Yañez y Rivera, *El Donado Hablador o Alonso Mozo de Muchos Anos* (1625), and the *Novelas Exemplares* of Cervantes, particularly "El Licenciado Vidriera" and "Colloquio de los Perros." Also interesting are García Mercadal, *Estudiantes, Sopistas, y Pícaros*; Reynier, *La Vie Universitaire dans L'Ancienne Espagne* (Paris, 1902); and Marcellin Defourneaux, *Daily Life in Spain in the Golden Age*, trans. Newton Branch (New York, 1971), chap. 9.

[101]These prices are comparable to the forty ducats which the University of Salamanca, in its statutes of 1561, allowed its *pupileros* to charge; cf. Esperabé Artega, *Universidad de Salamanca*, 1: 552. Ten years later, prices of *pupilajes* in Alcalá had not changed very much. In 1567, for example, Master Segura collected 100 ducats a year from students who were accompanied by a servant. In 1577 the charge was only ten ducats more.

[102]A pupilero in Salamanca was required to provide each of its students with one pound of meat daily except on Friday, fish day, although servants of students were entitled only to a half portion. In addition, regulations called for a good bed, two clean sheets weekly, and a three-hour candle daily. See Esperabé Artega, *Universidad de Salamanca*, 1: 552.

hours [sic] his students were accustomed to study each night. Other masters, criticized for charging different prices to individual students, replied that they had to charge more to those who wanted single rooms than those who shared doubles. Ambrosio de Morales defended his high prices on the grounds that he catered only for wealthy students. He tried to make clear that "It is well known that the students I have in my house are all distinguished gentlemen and from the principal families of the kingdom; consequently, they have to be treated well and presented with more amenities than the rest of the students."[103] Others claimed they charged higher prices only to those students who learned Latin with difficulty, justifying this practice on the basis of the increased time that they had to spend with dull students in comparison to those who learned quickly. Furthermore, the masters were quick to cite inflation as the reason why they had raised prices above the levels the university had set.

Regardless of the merits or demerits of each pupilaje, it is clear that such lodgings were expensive and certainly beyond the means of all but a small proportion of families in sixteenth-century Castile. Therefore, it is safe to presume that the poorer classes of Castile contributed relatively few students to the universities, with the exception of those lucky enough to be a servant to a wealthy student, a *familiar* at a university college,[104] a local resident, or the recipient of either church support or a college scholarship. For the majority of the poor, university was simply out of the question. These families, living at the edge of subsistence, were predominantly illiterate and ignorant of Latin, and, therefore, technically unable to qualify for university. Moreover, their immediate interests, necessities, and goals had little to do with universities and academic degrees. Thus to eliminate the 80 percent of Castile's population who worked on the land and in small shops and to concentrate on the 20 percent who are left is to place most of the universities' students within the proper social context. Although there were sharp differences of wealth and culture within this minority, these people represented the literate members of society, a portion of whom had also been trained in Latin. Here was centered most of Castile's wealth in the form of land ownership, banking, finance, commerce, and offices. Here were the families of sufficient means, interest, and ambition to launch their sons into professional and office-holding careers and into the upper ranks of the church, occupations which required a number of years at university, if not a degree. And here too were those families sufficiently well-placed that a university education could serve as an informative and pleasurable preface for their sons' adult years. To recognize these limitations is to understand that the universities lived by means of an extremely limited clientele.

[103]AHN: Univs., leg. 65, no. 18.
[104]A *familiar* was a student, akin to a sizar at Cambridge, who worked as a house servant in a college.

This minority encompassed the nobility, above all the large hidalgo class interested in improving their fortunes through crown offices and the church, officers in government and in the military, members of the liberal professions, and Castile's small but wealthy merchant class. Among the latter, the family of Diego de Espinosa, an early sixteenth-century merchant who emigrated to the New World, may be typical.[105] While many of his sons, grandsons, and nephews entered into the world of business and commercial enterprise, others entered the university in order to qualify for offices and the liberal professions. They in turn sent their offspring to university in order to prepare them for careers similar to their own. Along with the wealthier members of the artisan class, these were the families who provided the bulk of the university students in Castile.

In sum, the university lived off the top, if not the peak, of Castilian society, and its fortunes rested largely with their changing educational tastes. The popular classes were far more concerned with food and survival than with higher education. For these people, the university was often no more than a prospective employer, a landowner, a tax-collector, an official who claimed to buy wheat, wine, and meat free of tax. It was also a monumental stone building, an imposing array of stately gentlemen in long black gowns parading through the streets, a bunch of rich and rowdy young nobles carousing late into the night. Otherwise, the university was generally aloof from their world and its goals.

The exceptions were those members of the popular classes who, thanks to a college scholarship, managed to attend university and benefit from the opportunities conferred by its degrees. Every Castilian university had a number of colleges, each with its own rules and statutes but which shared a common charitable goal. By imposing a limit on the private income their members could enjoy (a figure which rarely exceeded 40 to 50 ducats a year) the founders of these communities had hoped to allow sons of families who could not otherwise meet the costs of higher education to attend university. Outside of the church, therefore, the colleges were the only organized source of financial aid available for students of modest means and thereby provided a few students of humble origin access to elite jobs and positions that they could otherwise never have hoped to reach.

In practice, however, the colleges never lived up to these exalted goals. Like the colegios mayores, their limitations on income were open to increasingly generous interpretation, especially during periods of financial difficulty when the colleges' survival depended on their ability to attract rich boys. Furthermore, the rents promised by the college founders frequently fell short, and the fiscal problems that resulted allowed only a few of the colleges to attain their statutory size. Matters grew worse during the financially disastrous years of the seventeenth century. By then, a number

---

[105]See Guillermo Lohmann Villena, *Les Espinosa, une famille d'hommes d'affaires en Espagne at aux Indies à l'époque de la colonisation* (Paris, 1968).

of the university colleges had folded, while others struggled along with no more than two or three students apiece. The charitable intentions of the founders, in other words, had been frustrated by a combination of economic circumstances and statutory abuse, and this situation further restricted the opportunities for the "poor" to attend universities in Castile.

The experience of the University of Salamanca demonstrates how difficult the colleges' position became. Ostensibly, Salamanca allotted to the "poor" the largest number of scholarship places in all of Castile. In addition to the religious colleges, the colegios mayores, and those of the Military Orders, this university early in the seventeenth century incorporated approximately twenty colleges known commonly as *colegios menores*.[106] They differed from the colegios mayores in that they admitted students of grammar and undergraduates, and they differed from one another in terms of their entrance requirements.[107] Most were small—less than ten places each—but taken together with the colegios mayores these scholarship students formed a sizable proportion of Salamanca's students (Fig. 6).

Between 1550 and the opening of the eighteenth century, the number of college students was on the rise, but this increase belies the fact that the majority of the colegios menores were in financial straits which forced them to reduce either the number or value of their scholarships. Indeed, the increase in the collegiate population at this university can largely be accounted for by the colleges' willingness to accept fee-paying *huéspedes* and *porcionistas* whose contributions helped to defray mounting debts. The problems faced by Salamanca's oldest college, Pan y Carbón, were not atypical. After a relatively prosperous period in the fifteenth and sixteenth centuries, the college, despite the presence of pensioners paying 80 ducats a year, closed its doors in 1628 because of diminishing revenues. It reopened in 1650, but within a few years, Pan y Carbón attempted to unite with other colleges in an effort to stay alive.[108] The Colegio de la Concepción de Teólogos, established in 1608, was in more serious trouble. It closed down permanently in 1665, while Santa Catalina, created in 1594, left the university's records in 1652, although it was not officially disbanded until 1780.[109] A number of other colegios menores, faced with a financial pinch and a lack of scholarships, amalgamated, pooling students and rents. The first of these unions took place in 1624 when Santa Cruz de Cañizares merged with San Adrian.[110] Encouraged by the Royal Council which regarded the existence of these small, impoverished colleges as useless, the

---

[106]See Sala Balust, *Constituciones, Estatutos, y Ceremonias de los Antiguos Colegios Seculares de la Universidad de Salamanca* (4 vols., Madrid, 1962–66), 1: Introduction; Riesco Terrero, *Salamanca a Través de Sus Colegios*, p. 14.

[107]See p. 66.

[108]See Nogaledo Alvarez, *Pan y Carbón*, pp. 44, 72.

[109]See Sala Balust, *Constituciones*, 1: 27; Francisco Borraz Girona, *El Colegio de Santa Catalina de la Universidad de Salamanca, 1594–1780* (Salamanca, 1962).

[110]Sala Balust, *Constituciones*, 1: 25.

process of union continued into the eighteenth century, when six of the colegios menores banded together because of their mutual problems.[111] Amalgamation, however, was not sufficient to rescue them from their plight; in 1780 the surviving colegios menores at Salamanca were suppressed and what rents, goods, and buildings they possessed were put toward the establishment of a seminary for the church.[112]

So even though the proportion of college students at Salamanca increased sharply between the sixteenth and eighteenth centuries, this rise cannot be interpreted as an increase in the number of "poor" students at the university. The financial difficulties of the colleges ensured their takeover by students whose incomes far exceeded the limits imposed at the time of their creation. Aided by Castile's economic decline and a widely felt unwillingness to allow the "poor" access to Latin education, the exclusion of students of modest origins from the colleges meant that the number of students who could be truly said to qualify as paupers probably diminished at Salamanca at this same time.

Meanwhile, students of noble background were siphoned off into the privileged colegios mayores, leaving the universities to the religious and the preprofessionals seeking letrado careers. Cloistered behind college walls, these students were hard-working and industrious, little given to raucous violence and play. The open street brawls and the "wars of the nations," the last of which occurred in the 1640s and 1650s, became a thing of the past. Concurrently, change in the curriculum came to a halt. During an era of economic decline and an uncertain labor market, these job-seekers, as students and teachers, were content to leave things as they were, to satisfy the requirements of a program sanctioned by time in the hope that perseverance would bring its just rewards. Thus the universities of Castile in the seventeenth and eighteenth centuries lost their flexibility and with it their ability to adapt to changing conditions, to a changing world. In time this inelasticity contributed to the institution's ultimate decay.

---

[111]Ibid., vol. 1: 32. In 1713 the colleges of Pan y Carbón, Monte Olivete, Santa María de los Ángeles, Santa Cruz de Cañizares, San Millán, and Santo Tomás united.

[112]See Nogaledo Alvarez, *Pan y Carbón*, p. 75.

chapter 9
CHANGE AND DECAY

In recent years the analysis of student matriculations across a given period of time has become a convenient means of assessing the changing place and importance of schools and universities in the societies of which they were part. Traditionally, however, the success and the failure, the prosperity and the decline of academic institutions were linked more often than not to the reputation of famous teachers, curricular reform, pedagogical innovation, and the like. Though not without value, such methods have many pitfalls, the deepest of which is measuring the performance of a school of university in the past with the pedagogical yardstick of the present. But rather than criticize the many educational histories which have been written in this fashion, the aim of this chapter is to begin where these studies leave off. Its purpose is, therefore, to examine changes in the pace and nature of student matriculations at Castile's universities between 1500 and 1808. Though not without dangers of its own, in particular that of the reliability of the materials upon which the statistics are based,[1] there is perhaps no better nor more accurate method of measuring how past societies put their institutions of learning to use.

Fortunately, matriculation registers for the universities have survived, occasionally in long, unbroken series, but rarely do they begin much before the middle of the sixteenth century.[2] Any attempt to estimate student population before that time is fraught with difficulty. Medieval chroniclers provide vague reports about various universities, noting that there were "many students" at Salamanca or a "great crowd of students" assembled to hear a lecturer speak, but in the main these descriptions are not of very much use. One of the first reporters to give a numerical estimate of the number of students at a university was Jerónimo Münzer. A German traveling through Spain in 1494, he put the number of students studying at Salamanca at 5,000.[3] Though exaggerated, his report may serve as evidence that this university had attained a considerable size by the end of the fifteenth century. It would also be reasonable to assume that after a depressed period during the civil wars of the fourteenth and fifteenth centuries,

---

[1]See appendix B. In this chapter I have omitted as many references to matriculation registers as possible. The statistical material for various universities is available in appendix A while archival references to these registers are noted in appendix C.

[2]See appendix B.

[3]Cf. García Mercadal, *Viajes de Extranjeros por España y Portugal* (Madrid, 1962), 1: 392

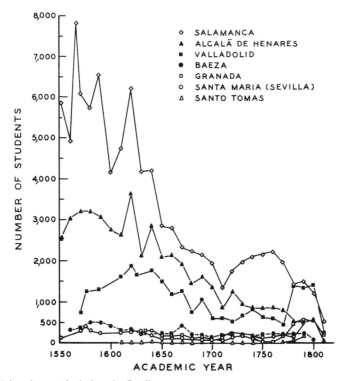

Fig. 7. University matriculations in Castile.

matriculations were on the rise during the reign of Ferdinand and Isabel. This expansion, moreover, was still underway in the middle of the sixteenth century when the first matriculation registers appear. Though some form of matriculation records had undoubtedly existed before that time, the swelling student population seems to have forced the universities to take record-keeping more seriously than in the past.

The half century which followed was a period of almost uninterrupted growth for the universities of Castile, and toward the end of the sixteenth century many acquired a total student population that they were not to match until the later nineteenth century. Though the names in the matriculation registers were not all students,[4] matriculants at Salamanca hovered between 5,000 and 7,000 a year, a figure which made this university the peninsula's largest (Fig. 7).[5] In second place was the new university of Alcalá de Henares which boasted between 3,000 and 4,000 students

[4]See p. 166. Approximately 100–150 signatures in the matriculation registers were those of instructors, university officials, etc.

[5]Possibly the largest university in Europe as well. No precise estimates for the number of students at the University of Paris, the largest of the French universities, exist for this epoch. Germany's largest university, Leipzig, had well under 1,000 students throughout the sixteenth

a year (Fig. 7), and it was followed by the University of Santiago de Compostela whose students in some years topped the 3,000 mark. Close behind was the University of Valladolid. Though its matriculation records are fragmentary for this period, there are indications that its students numbered 2,000 and more (Fig. 7).[6]

Ranged behind these larger institutions were a number of medium-sized universities, most of which were located in the south. Baeza supported a total of 600 students a year (Fig. 7), and this figure was probably matched and possibly exceeded by the universities at Granada, Osuna, and Seville (Fig. 7). Incomplete matriculation records for this period, however, do not allow for an exact indication of their size. At bottom were small universities such as Sigüenza, suffering from the competition of nearby Alcalá, which never attracted more than 100 students,[7] and Ávila which had enrolled even fewer (Fig. 7). In similar straits were Almagro, Burgo de Osma, Irache, and Oñate, although in the latter in some years there were 300 students.[8]

The severe plague of 1596–1602, particularly devastating in the north of the peninsula,[9] kept students away from university towns for a number of years and cut short the century-long rise in matriculations. But most of the universities recovered quickly, and by 1620 student populations neared their previous record levels (Fig. 7). The resilience of the universities in the years following the plague is best attributed to the relatively high social rank of their students. They came from among Castile's more prosperous families, groups normally removed from the worst ravages of plague, famine, and disease. Otherwise, one would have expected that a severe demographic crisis, such as this plague, a period of low birth rates, should be followed by a negative response in university matriculations fifteen to twenty years later. One would be unwise, therefore, to attribute changes in matriculations to population trends alone;[10] in many instances the two

---

century; cf. F. Eulenburg, *Frequenz der Deutschen Universitäten* (Leipzig, 1903), p. 289. In Italy, the University of Naples, the largest on the peninsula, had approximately 5,000 students in 1607; see Francesco Terraca, *Storia della Universitá di Napoli* (Napoli, 1924), p. 255. In England, a 1577 estimate put the joint student population of Oxford and Cambridge at 3,000 although Oxford, alone, in the sixteenth century had a resident population which regularly topped 2,000, cf. W. R. Prest, *The Inns of Court under Elizabeth I and the Early Stuarts, 1590–1640* (London, 1972), p. 16, and Stone, "The Size and Composition of the Oxford Student Body," in *The University in Society*, ed. Lawrence Stone (Princeton, 1974), 1: 3–110.

[6] The Cámara de Castilla noted that students at Valladolid numbered c. 2,400 in the year 1584–85; cf. Bennassar, *Valladolid au Siècle d'Or* (Paris, 1967), p. 358.

[7] On 6.I.1714 Sigüenza complained: "those students who have the means to do so go to the University of Alcalá since it is so close by" (AHN: Cons., leg. 7294).

[8] The estimate for the University of Oñate is that of Ignacio Zumalde, *Historia de Oñate* (San Sebastián, 1957), p. 615.

[9] For estimates of losses caused by the plague, see Bennassar, *Valladolid*, p. 205, and by the same author, *Recherches sur les Grandes Epidémies dans le Nord de l'Espagne a la Fin du XVIe Siècle* (Paris, 1969).

[10] There were a number of contemporaries who made this same observation. Pedro de Amezqueta, corregidor of Salamanca in 1638, wrote: "If there is a shortage of students it

curves show little or no relation to one another, or how else could one explain the later seventeenth century, a period in which matriculations at the universities were falling rapidly but the population of Castile was stable.

Despite the flaws and shortcomings of the matriculation registers, it appears that Castile's universities at their peak during the last quarter of the sixteenth century supported as many as 20,000 students annually (Fig. 8). Inadequate population figures for the era make it difficult to know what proportion of Castile's youth of university age this figure represented. But with some statistical reservations one can estimate that in Castile, with a population of 6.9 million and a student population of 20,000, about 3.2 percent of its males aged fifteen to twenty-four attended university each year.[11] It is important to note, however, that since these students stemmed largely from Castile's populous *hidalgo* class, perhaps as many as one-fourth to one-third of the kingdom's young noblemen attended university. Such estimates, crude though they may be, suggest that Castile in the later sixteenth century ranked among Europe's most highly educated nations, a position which in part accounted for her cultural florescence as well as her ability to create and to staff a bureaucratic empire which stretched around the world.

Lawrence Stone has estimated that in seventeenth-century England, approximately 2.5 percent of seventeen-year-olds entered university each year.[12] To compare this figure with Castile's statistics is troublesome, first because Spanish matriculation books are usually arranged so that it is

---

does not necessarily correspond to the general shortage of people in the Kingdom. This cause is important but not accurate . . ." (AHN: Cons. leg. 7138, letter of 11.XII.1638).

[11]To obtain this figure, the percentage of males, aged fifteen to twenty-four, has been estimated at 9 percent of Castile's population. Using the recent figures offered by Antonio Domínguez Ortiz, *The Golden Age of Spain 1516–1659* (New York, 1971), p. 174, Castile, along with Navarre and the Basque provinces, had a total population of 6.9 million; therefore, youths of university age numbered approximately 620,000. It was on the basis of this figure that the percentage of youths attending university was calculated.

One must recognize that the 9 percent figure is not intended to be exact, but only a rough approximation of the number of university-aged males in Castile's population. It is based upon the application of the birth and death rates of the province of Valladolid during the sixteenth century (see Bennassar, *Valladolid*, pp. 171–99) to the age distribution tables in Ansley J. Coale and Paul Demeny, *Regional Model Life Tables and Stable Populations* (Princeton, 1965). The stable population, Model South, Mortality Level 4 with a growth rate standing between 0/1000 and 5/1000 (ibid., p. 782) may apply to sixteenth-century Valladolid and, by extension, to all of Castile. In a previous article (Richard L. Kagan, "Universities in Castile, 1500–1700," *Past & Present* 49 (November 1970): 48, footnote 11) a number of difficulties posed by this estimate have been raised. It should also be noted that the discrepancy between the estimate presented there and in this volume has two causes: (1) In the earlier version, a misreading of Coale and Demeny, *Regional Model Life Tables*, resulted in a faulty calculation for the number of males aged 15–24 in Castile. They represented 9 percent of the total population, not the 18 percent noted there, a figure which included both boys and girls; (2) an upward revision of the population of Castile, Navarre, and the Basque Provinces to 6.9 million.

[12]Stone, "The Educational Revolution in England, 1560 to 1640," *Past & Present* 28 (1964): 57.

difficult to know what proportion of the university's total matriculants constituted new, first-year boys. Second, the entrance age of Castilian students varied widely from faculty to faculty, although the mean age in the sixteenth century was in the neighborhood of eighteen. If we allow for these differences and remove the students of grammar from Castilian university matriculations in order to improve the bases of comparison be-

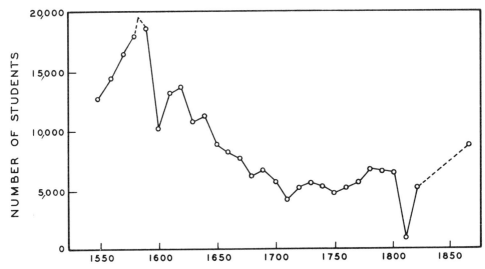

Fig. 8. Total estimated university matriculation in Castile. The educational revolution of the sixteenth century was followed by two centuries of stagnation and decline.

tween the two nations, Castile in the last decades of the sixteenth century is left with a university population of about 15,000. Of these, approximately one-quarter were newcomers, and such a figure would allow us to estimate that at least 5.43 percent of male eighteen-year-olds entered university each year.[13] If this figure is correct,[14] then Castile was far, far ahead of England in terms of access to university and, even though similar estimates do not yet exist for other nations, Castile was possibly the most educated society in Western Europe at that time.

[13]This estimate presumes, again on the basis of the life tables for stable populations, that male eighteen-year-olds constituted c. one percent of Castile's total population, or c. 69,000 persons. One-fourth of the university population of 15,000 was c. 3,750 students. 3,570/69,000= 5.43%. Once again, this figure represents only a guide. My thanks go to Professor Lawrence Stone for advice on these calculations.

[14]Possible flaws in this estimate are several. The matriculation books may be either wildly exaggerated or our estimates of what proportion of the population represented eighteen-year-old males may be far off, but neither of these two possibilities is very likely. Alternately, the replacement rate at the universities, that is, the figure which represents the length of time the average student remained in residence, allowing us to calculate what percentage of students were new each year, may be incorrect. "Drop-outs" were common to the universities in the sixteenth and seventeenth centuries (see above, p. 178), and the high attrition rates among the students complicate our estimate of the number of first-year stu-

If students were numerous, graduates were relatively few. In the late sixteenth century less than one-third of the students who began their course took a degree, and in the succeeding decades, the proportion dropped.[15] Mistaken aptitude and the high cost of living in university towns were mostly to blame for this high rate of attrition, inasmuch as preliminary examinations to weed out weaker students did not exist. If a student lasted beyond his first or second year, chances were good that he would earn a degree, since very few ever failed the final examination. But the early years of study had exacted a heavy toll, so even at their peak, Castile's universities never awarded more than 1,200 *baccalaurea* in one year.[16] Assuming that the average age of these students was twenty-two, this meant that less than 1.73 percent of males at this age had earned a university degree.[17]

Of these, only a handful managed to obtain one of the advanced degrees of master, licence, and doctor. One reason for this was cost. At the smaller universities a licence or doctorate in one of the professional faculties demanded an expenditure of as much as 500 or 600 reales, owing to the fees and gifts, banquets and parades that the successful candidate was required to provide. Similar titles at Alcalá, Salamanca, and Valladolid cost many times more.[18] Indeed, so onerous were these charges that by the later sixteenth century requests for university loans to help defray the costs of graduation were commonplace.[19] And aside from students who were clergymen and members of the colegios mayores, all of whom

---

dents at the universities, since one does not know whether drop-outs really dropped out or if they returned the following year, matriculated in another faculty, or even in another university. It would appear plausible, however, that the average stay for most students approached four years, even though the four years may not have been consecutive or at the same institution.

[15]This figure has been calculated by comparing the number of students in the four years of the arts course at Alcalá de Henares over consecutive years with graduation records. By the mid-seventeenth century only one in four first-year students managed to earn degrees, and in the following century it was only one in five. The law faculties at the universities of Granada and Santiago recorded similar rates of attrition.

[16]Seventy to 80 of these degrees were in medicine, and about 100 were in theology. The remainder were divided more or less evenly between the arts and the law. The universities of Alcalá, Salamanca, and Valladolid awarded close to 80 percent of the baccalaureates in Castile.

[17]Males, aged twenty-two, like those of seventeen or eighteen, presumably accounted for about one percent of the total population. The arithmetic used in this estimate is outlined in footnote 13.

[18]University statutes regulated the fees which graduates were required to pay; see AUBA: Estatutos de 1609; Montells y Nadal, *Universidad de Granada* (Granada, 1870), Statutes of 1542, tit. xxxi; Cabeza de León, *Historia de la Universidad de Santiago de Compostela* (Santiago de Compostela, 1945), 2: 150. The expenditures outlined by the statutes, however, represented only the minimum of what a student had to pay since they failed to include the mounting expenses of the ever more elaborate degree ceremonies that were demanded of a new graduate. Petitions by students for university loans to cover degree expenses give a more accurate indication of the total cost of these titles; cf. the following note.

[19]See AHN: Univs., leg. 48, nos. 16, 17, 23, 24, 26. It was about this time that Baltasar de Céspedes asked the University of Salamanca for a loan of 400 ducats (4,400 reales) he needed to pay for license and doctorate; cf. p. 165, note 23.

graduated at a bargain rate, the cost of advanced degrees may have presented an obstacle that was difficult to overcome.

Another reason for the scarcity of advanced degrees was time. If a baccalaureate required three to four years, a doctorate demanded a minimum of seven or eight. There were only a few students willing and able to persevere in the hope of achieving the prestige and opportunities such a degree could bring. Thus the law faculty of the University of Salamanca at the end of the sixteenth century graduated as many as 400 *bachilleres* each year, but conferred fewer than twenty advanced degrees in the same period of time.[20] In total, Castile's universities never turned out more than 150 to 175 licentiates and perhaps 50 to 60 doctors annually, the majority of whom were in the arts faculty where these honors were both cheaper and easier to obtain than in medicine, theology, or law.[21] In other words, out of a university population which numbered in the thousands, only a small percentage of students became fully-licensed professionals, with the privilege of putting the valued abbreviation *Lic.* or *Doc.* before their name. Yet it was this small group who staffed Castile's cathedrals, law courts, and councils and who, in these positions, directed much of the administrative and religious policy of the empire, while shaping the education of the kingdom's young.

Total matriculation and graduation figures, however valuable, do not tell very much about the character of the universities themselves. Thanks to the geographical information provided about students in the matriculation registers, it is clear that except for Alcalá, Salamanca, and Valladolid, each of which attracted students from across the peninsula and even from abroad, Castile's universities drew the vast majority of their students from the regions in which they were situated. Small universities, Avila or Baeza for instance, attracted students only from the university town itself and one or two others located nearby. Other universities, like Santiago de Compostela, Granada, or Seville, had a more regional pull. The first served Galicia and the Cantabrian coast; the latter, Andalucia. Seville took its students mainly from the west of that region, Granada from the east, although the former, located in a busy, cosmopolitan port city, also attracted a number of students from the Canary Islands and the center of Castile.

The major reason for the local and regional character of Castile's universities was that many lacked the popular faculties of law as well as the prestige which the larger institutions enjoyed. Outsiders, therefore, had few incentives to travel to these lesser-known universities. Meanwhile,

---

[20]See AUS: Libros de Grados.

[21]According to the statutes of the University of Santiago de Compostela, a master of arts degree, the equivalent of a doctorate in this faculty, required a total of five years of study. A baccalaureate in law took as long, a license in law another year or two. Meanwhile, a master of arts degree at this university cost 150 reales in 1610 while a doctorate in law required a minimum expenditure of 300 reales. See Cabeza de León, *Universidad de Santiago*, 1: 246–47; 2: 113.

difficult and hazardous travel conditions worked to keep many boys close to home. It was also cheaper to live at home or with relatives in a nearby town or to receive weekly provisions from one's family than to pay the costs of room and board at a distant university. Furthermore, universities in the sixteenth and seventeenth centuries, particularly the larger ones, were notorious for their riotous life; drinking, gambling, and whoring were common distractions, and parents were understandably concerned lest their sons be led astray.

Yet another cause for worry is illustrated in the baptismal registers of university towns where the listing "son of a student and an unmarried girl" was not infrequent; it has been demonstrated that in one parish close to the university in Salamanca, nearly 60 percent of the infants baptized in 1558 were illegitimate.[22] Perhaps more disturbing for parents and certainly more dangerous for their sons were the armed clashes and street brawls that occurred at the major universities before the mid-seventeenth century. Repeated prohibitions on guns and swords proved utterly useless, and the results were "tumults and feuds, with arms and without," brawls involving "sticks and swords," "disrupted classes," "wounded" students, students "stabbed with swords," and even occasional deaths.[23] Under these circumstances, it is easy to understand why parents might not allow their sons to study far from home, or, if they did, they make certain that he lived with relatives, in a college, or a supervised lodging house.

Such considerations can also help to explain why sixteenth-century Spain acquired such a multitude of small universities rather than concentrating its educational resources in one or two larger institutions. Spain was a kingdom divided against itself: by mountains, by languages, by customs, and even by political boundaries. The concept of the *patria chica* was strong; local pride, combined with parental interests in economy and the security of their sons, demanded that every region have a university of its own.

But, as mentioned above, the universities at Alcalá, Salamanca, and Valladolid were able to escape from this local and regional pattern of recruitment. Valladolid, the most limited of the three in terms of its area of geographical attraction, was a university serving all of the north of Spain (map 3). Alcalá, although heavily dependent upon the large and populous archdiocese of Toledo, of which it was part, managed to attract students from every corner of the peninsula, students who could have easily matriculated at institutions closer to home (map 4). And Salamanca, with students from almost every part of the kingdom, could also be said to be Spain's only international university, thanks to the large contingent of Portuguese who matriculated every year (map 5). The ability of these in-

[22]Riesco Terrero, *Proyección Histórico-Social de la Universidad de Salamanca a Través de sus Colegios* (Salamaca, 1970), p. 88.
[23]Cf. AUSA: lib. 862, folios 25–26, 31, 45–45v, 48, 63, 116, 170.

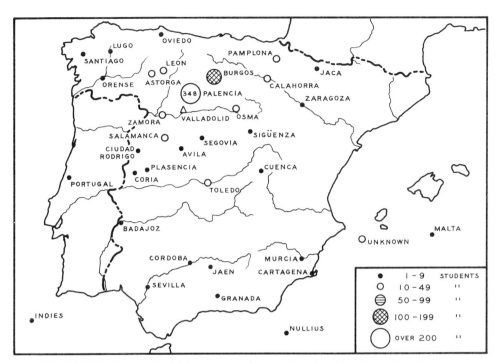

Map 3.1. University of Valladolid: geographical origins of students (1570—number of students by diocese).

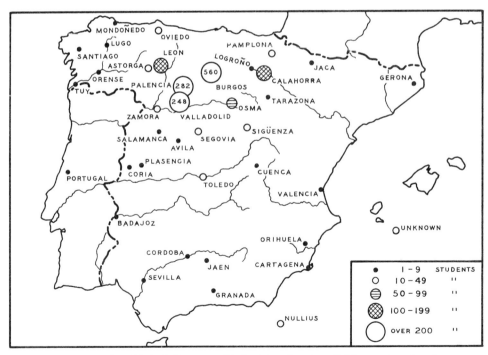

Map 3.2. University of Valladolid: geographical origins of students (1620—number of students by diocese).

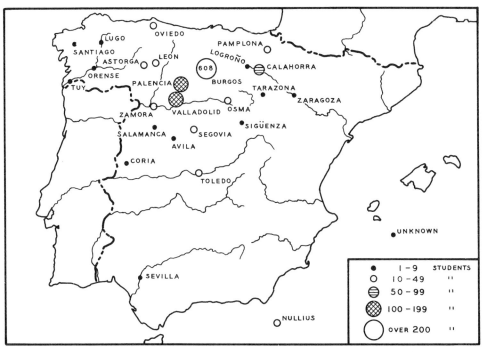

Map 3.3. University of Valladolid: geographical origins of students (1671—number of students by diocese).

Map 3.4. University of Valladolid: geographical origins of students (1700—number of students by diocese).

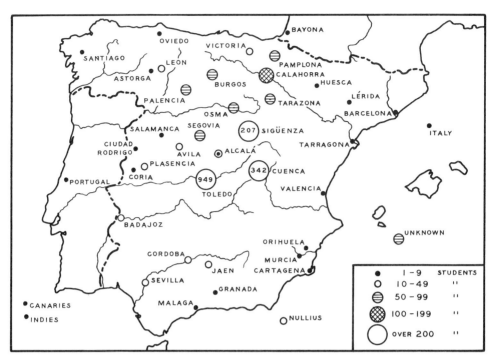

Map 4.1. University of Alcalá de Henares: geographical origins of students (1550—number of students by diocese).

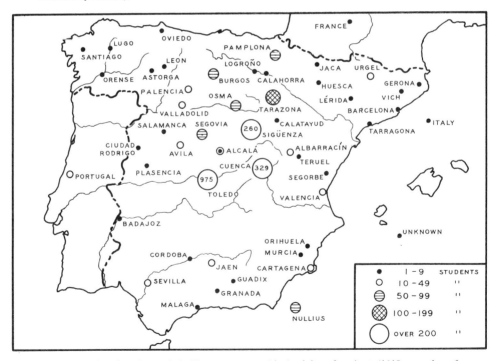

Map 4.2. University of Alcalá de Henares: geographical origins of students (1610—number of students by diocese).

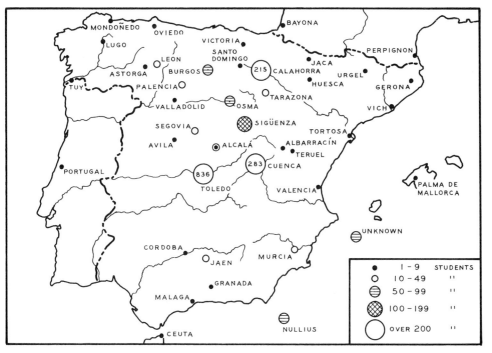

Map 4.3. University of Alcalá de Henares: geographical origins of students (1650—number of students by diocese).

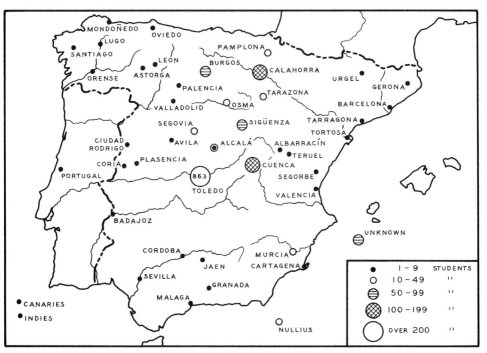

Map 4.4. University of Alcalá de Henares: geographical origins of students (1690—number of students by diocese).

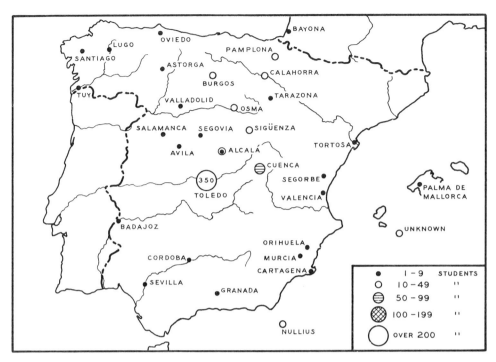

Map 4.5. University of Alcalá de Henares: geographical origins of students (1750—number of students by diocese).

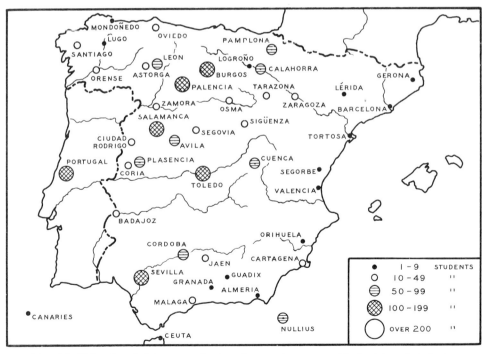

Map 5.1. University of Salamanca, faculty of canon law: geographical origins of students (1570—number of students by diocese).

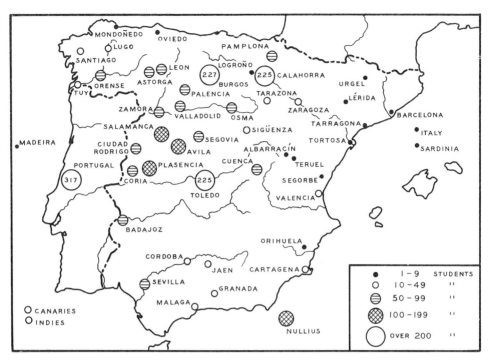

Map 5.2. University of Salamanca, faculty of canon law: geographical origins of students (1620—number of students by diocese).

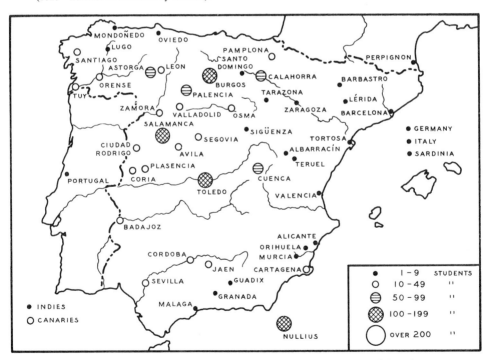

Map 5.3. University of Salamanca, faculty of canon law: geographical origins of students (1650—number of students by diocese).

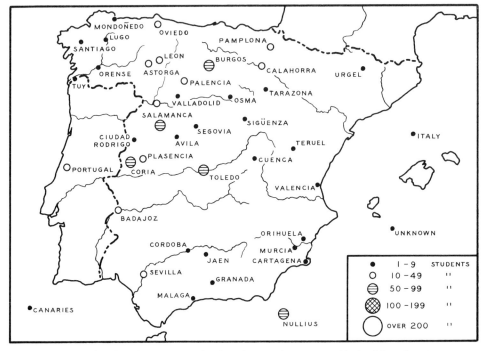

Map 5.4. University of Salamanca, faculty of canon law: geographical origins of students (1690—number of students by diocese).

stitutions to serve a wider clientele sprang from the fame of their instructors and the prestige of their degrees. Since it was obvious that graduates of these universities commanded the best letrado positions in the empire, students from all parts of Spain, eager for such prizes, enrolled at the institutions which offered the best chances for success. Though financial difficulties forced the majority of these students to abandon these universipies, perhaps to return to institutions closer to home, Alcalá, Salamanca, and Valladolid acted as magnets strong enough to overcome the local and regional forces which would have otherwise created a far more static system of higher education. Students from outlying areas, trained in grammar and perhaps with a first degree from a provincial university, transferred to one of these three, generally to study in the professional faculties for which they were famous.

The movement of students about the kingdom, however, was not always toward the center, toward the universities at Alcalá, Salamanca, and Valladolid. The high costs of these universities, particularly the elevated costs of their degrees, forced many students to abandon their studies or to graduate at a cheaper "provincial" university. Suárez de Figueroa, an early seventeenth-century author, wrote: "the costs of degrees at Salamanca are excessive, and for this reason, the poor flee from it and we go to where it is cheap."[24] Thus isolated Santiago de Compostela was able to attract each year a number of advanced "transfer" student from Salamanca and Valladolid.[25] Oñate, a small university in Navarre, did much the same. It made a regular practice of incorporating bachilleres from other universities on one day and conferring higher degrees upon them the next.[26] Since the professors at Oñate earned a substantial portion of their income from graduation fees, it was always in their interest to condone such practices, and by the eighteenth century a number of universities, among them Oñate, Osuna, Irache, and Almagro, were known to have sold their degrees.[27]

Since most universities failed to list their "transfer" students, it is impossible to get a complete picture of where students were coming from and going to. Presumably, the regional universities lost more than they gained. Though a few students graduated from the cheaper universities, many more headed toward the major institutions, drawn by their professional faculties and the fame of their degrees. This influx assured Castile of a pool of highly educated manpower, perhaps to the detriment of those regions from which these students had originally come. And though it can be assumed that many of them returned to their native regions to take up local jobs, others, perhaps the most talented and ambitious of the lot, stayed on in Castile, competing for the prestige positions offered by the crown. The large numbers of Basques, *navarros, riojanos*, and other letrados originally from the northern fringes of the peninsula, who served on the royal *chancillerías* and councils, is good evidence of such a migration.[28] One other sign is Philip II's order in 1588 sending the office-seekers crowding about the court back to their homes, while a similar decree issued by Philip IV in 1639 had much the same intention.[29] Provincials at Alcalá, Salamanca, and Valladolid undoubtedly heightened competition within Castile's letrado labor market; the skilled, the fortunate, and above all, those with family and collegiate ties in Madrid, left home for good, adding to the bureaucratic population of the court. But whether this internal "brain-drain" aided Castile to the detriment of other regions is not yet clear, and the net results of this back and forth movement of students remain unknown.

[24]Cited in Valbuena Prat, *La Vida Española en la Edad de Oro Según sus Fuentes Literarias* (Barcelona, 1943), p. 47.
[25]1637 was a record year: five students from the University of Salamanca transferred into the fifth year of Santiago's course in canon law.
[26]See AUV: Universidad de Oñate, Libros de Grados.
[27]See Ajo, *Historia de las Universidades Hispánicas* (8 vols., Madrid, 1957–72), 5: 34–36. As early as 1597, Almagro had its right to grant degrees temporarily revoked because of such practices; see A. Javierre, "La Universidad de Almagro, Fundado por Fernando de Córdoba, Clavero de la Orden de Calatrava," *RABM* 68 (1960): 622.
[28]This information can be garnered from the biographical information assembled in the consultas of the Cámara; cf. p. 96, note 30.
[29]AHN: Cons. lib. 666, folio 3v; AUS: Ms. 939, folio 135.

What is certain is that Alcalá, Salamanca, and Valladolid attracted men from diverse geographical regions and then trained them for the highest posts in Spain and the empire. In other words, these served as the true "imperial" universities of the Habsburgs, and it is no accident that a motto carved into the University of Salamanca's elaborate sixteenth-century façade should read: "Kings for Universities, Universities for Kings." The provincial universities, on the other hand, remained relatively small institutions, serving local, probably clerical, needs. In the long run, Castile's biased and tradition-bound system of royal patronage failed to include the provincial universities in the distribution of national and imperial offices, and this problem, on top of other difficulties with the recruitment of students and finance, meant that these universities had to contend continually with instructors and students who were often mere transients, ready to transfer to the large universities or to leave for higher rewards. Thus Castile may have lost an opportunity in the sixteenth and seventeenth centuries to develop and maintain a broad-based, pluralistic university system which could offer possibilities for competition, variety, and change. As it was, the "imperial" universities, so vital to the monarchy, gradually lost their autonomy and independence to the crown, preventing Castile from developing a tradition of university learning independent of royal interest and control.

The influx of students interested in letrado jobs and professional training also had profound effects within the universities themselves. In every institution which offered instruction in all of the major faculties there was a steady shift, beginning in the middle years of the sixteenth century, away from the study of the arts and theology to the study of law, particularly canon law, gateway to both clerical and secular careers (Figs. 9–11).[30] At Seville and Granada, law became the most popular and important faculty and the same was true at Alcalá de Henares. A university originally dedicated to the study of the arts and theology with a curriculum limiting studies in canon law, the number of law students at Alcalá equaled those studying theology in 1550, and by the opening of the seventeenth century, jurists outnumbered theologians almost two to one, a ratio which doubled before the century was out. Moreover, under pressure from the Cortes of Castile, Alcalá, in violation of her original statutes, began instruction in civil law, while making canon law into a regular degree course.[31] At Salamanca and Valladolid, neither of which had any curricular restrictions, theology fared even worse; by the end of the seventeenth

[30]In 1563 the Cortes asked Philip II to establish two or three chairs of civil law in order to make Alcalá "perfect"; cf. Cortes de Valladolid, pet. CXIX.

[31]A major problem in attempting to measure the number of students in each faculty is to decide whether those students who signed up in one faculty actually came to study that subject. There exists, for example, the disturbing case of Alonso, hero of the picaresque novel *El Donado Hablador o Alonso Mozo de Muchos Años*, by Jerónimo de Alcalá y Yañez. He moved about from faculty to faculty; at times he heard laws, at times medicine, and on other days attended lectures in philosophy and theology, all without leaving his assigned place in the class of Greek and Latin rhetoric. How many Alonsos there were it is impossible to say al-

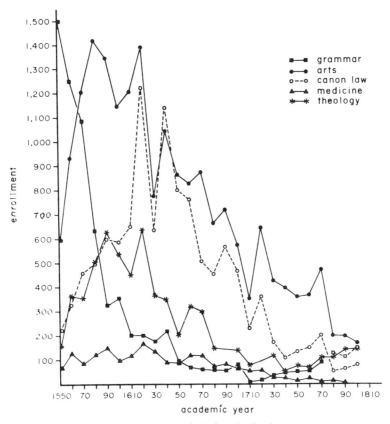

Fig. 9. University of Alcalá de Henares: matriculations by faculty.

century law students at both institutions outnumbered theologians over twenty to one, while their arts faculties suffered from a "lack of listeners," a shortage of instructors, and declining prestige. Thus while the legal faculties prospered, one seventeenth-century critic, in reference to the University of Salamanca, claimed that the arts faculty was "totally lost."[32] This sustained emphasis on juridical studies seems also to have prejudiced those provincial universities which lacked the popular faculties of law, and this in turn contributed to the influx of students at the universities of Alcalá, Salamanca, and Valladolid.

though it is certain that in the faculties of canon and civil law, students regularly studied both "laws and canons," although they were registered in only one faculty, usually the former.

[32]AHN: Cons., leg. 7138, "Memorial de 22.VII.1648 a Antonio Camporredondo y Rio." That same year the suppression of a number of chairs, among them, Greek, rhetoric, Hebrew, astrology, and mathematics, none of which attracted very many students, was advised; cf. ibid., *memoriales* of 17.III, and 22.VII.1648. The combined Greek-rhetoric faculty for instance, matriculated its last students in the year 1557–58, while Hebrew had disappeared from the matriculation books in 1555. It did not appear again until 1800.

The drift is unmistakable. Students at Castile's universities eschewed the liberal arts and theology for law (canon and civil) either to prepare for a professional legal or office-holding career or to acquire a brief introduction to the subject for practical reasons. Most of these abandoned their studies, turning alternatively to the army, the church, offices not requiring university training or degrees, or independent lives as financiers, merchants, and rentiers. But those who did graduate, perhaps only one-third of those who matriculated initially, competed for scarce professorships and letrado jobs. In this light the old, popular assertion that a one-sided, conservative preoccupation with theology thwarted educational and scientific progress in Spain and her universities is not borne out by the matriculation lists; the almost exclusive pursuit of law, legal studies, and letrado careers would be a more credible answer. Experimental sciences, modern languages, history, and studies in political economy had little place in an institution

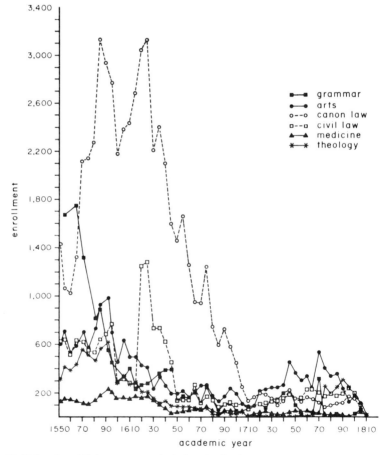

Fig. 10. University of Salamanca: matriculations by faculty.

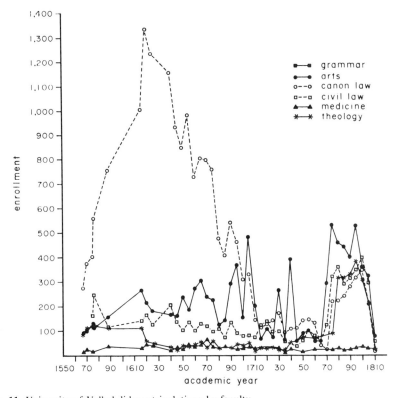

Fig. 11. University of Valladolid: matriculations by faculty.

which was, and which regarded itself as, a professional training school for lawyers and legally trained clerics and noblemen. Law degrees, crown offices, and the prestige these conferred were the ultimate goals of the Castilian universities in the sixteenth and seventeenth centuries, not the advancement of medicine nor the scientific understanding of the world. Thus it is perhaps no surprise that the first sharp break from this legalistic university tradition which occurred in eighteenth-century Spain came not from Castile but from Valencia, whose university led the way toward a modern medical curriculum.[33]

The decline in the study of the arts and theology, as well as in Latin grammar, at the universities was accelerated by the rise of municipal schools along with Jesuit and other religious colleges. Safety and an opportunity to save on the costs of educating their sons were two reasons why parents preferred to have their teenage sons study close to home, but there is also evidence to suggest that the major universities, geared primarily toward professional training, allowed these faculties to fall into decay,

[33]See Richard Herr, *The Eighteenth Century Revolution in Spain* (Princeton, 1958), p. 166.

thus contributing to the rise of Jesuit colleges and local schools. Shortages of qualified teachers in the arts and grammar began in the middle of the sixteenth century and continued unchecked into the next.[34] Salaries, which were among the lowest at the universities, were partly responsible for this,[35] but the failure of the universities to pay higher stipends to these instructors is perhaps an indication of their relative lack of concern. Yet even the well-financed trilingual colleges at Alcalá and Salamanca, both of which offered scholarships in the classical languages, suffered from a lack of student interest, and in 1597 the Colegio Trilingüe at Salamanca, without students, was missing from the matriculation books nor did it reappear there for over fifty years.[36] Thus with trained teachers in short supply, dwindling numbers of interested students, and an apparent lack of cash to raise teachers' salaries, a number of universities heeded their critics' demands and allowed the Jesuits and the other religious orders to take over teaching in the arts, grammar, and even theology. In perspective, therefore, the Jesuits seem to have filled an educational vacuum left behind by the professionally oriented universities.

If this vacuum existed, it had been many years in the making. During the Middle Ages jurists occupied the leading place in Spain's universities. Doctors of law were especially revered, having been awarded many of the fiscal and ceremonial privileges of nobility. The other disciplines could not compete until the later fifteenth century, when Spain's blossoming interest in Italian humanism and classical studies, though adding a new historical and philological dimension to law, favored the study of the liberal arts and theology. The new universities of the era, Sigüenza, Alcalá, and Santiago, reflected this trend and awarded these disciplines the leading place in their curriculum, while the new interest in literary philology and classical antiquity breathed fresh life into faculties of the arts and theology at existing institutions. Though law remained popular, humanist theology and the liberal arts won the day. Lectures on classical topics by noted humanists such as Peter Martyr and Marineo Siculo reportedly drew large crowds of students at Salamanca,[37] and this university, in imitation of Alcalá, acquired a Colegio Trilingüe of its own to pursue studies in Greek, Hebrew, and Chaldean. Moreover, Salamanca, at the insistence of its medical faculty which was interested in Arabic texts of the Middle

[34]In 1578, for example, a complaint was registered at the University of Salamanca that the chairs of astrology and mathematics had been vacant for over three years without any candidates except for one under youth lacking in qualifications; cf. Esperabé Artega, *Historia Pragmática é Interna de la Universidad de Salamanca* (Salamanca, 1914), 1: 568. For similar problems in the faculties of grammar, see p. 43.

[35]At Salamanca, chairs in arts and grammar frequently received less than one-half the slary of those in law; cf. AUS: Libros 1027–28.

[36]In 1648 one reformer urged the abolition of this college, since its rents "served no purpose"; cf. AHN: Cons., leg. 7138, Memorial de 22.VII.1648.

[37]See p. 35.

Ages, created a chair of Arabic in 1542 and added it to its faculty of arts.[38] Records for the period are scarce, nevertheless, it appears that the study of the arts and theology won a new popularity in the late fifteenth and early sixteenth centuries, with the need for trained clerics to convert the heathen in Granada, North Africa, and the New World sustaining this interest well into the Habsburg era.

But the challenge offered by the Renaissance did not last long. Religious controversy abroad, troubles with suspected heretics and religious fanatics at home, and the monarchy's new emphasis on censorship combined to put a halt to the free inquiry typical of Renaissance scholarship, particularly that connected with matters of theology and faith. Though the study of classical languages and humanist theology remained popular among the religious orders and within the literary circles of the rich, the medieval legacy of law proved triumphant within the lecture halls. The decade of of the 1550s, heralded by the famous debates between Las Casas and Sepúlveda over the sensitive moral and theological issues connected with the problem of slavery and capped by the end of Erasmian influence in Spain at the great *auto da fe* staged for the new king, Philip II, at Valladolid in 1559, was the symbolic era of change. After that decade, the study of the arts and theology at the universities began to languish, while students increasingly favored studies in the law. Though these students received preliminary training in the arts before studying a jurisprudence imbued with the critical, historical elements which the jurists of the Renaissance had bestowed upon it, by the end of the century Castile's universities had a new intellectual configuration, at once conservative, traditional, and overwhelmingly dedicated to the study of law.

After all, other subjects had their liabilities. In general, they suffered from what contemporaries called the *"falta de premios"* at a time when the arbiters of patronage in Castile favored students who had studied law. One seventeenth-century author, writing in reference to the University of Salamanca, claimed: "In the faculty of theology, experience has shown that the lack of *premios* and competition has abetted its fall."[39] And in a similar vein, the University of Salamanca wrote that its Colegio Trilingüe had no students either in Greek or in Hebrew "partly because of the absence of masters, but, above all, because the study of the Holy Languages has no *premio* afterwards."[40] Potential students, so the university claimed, transferred to other faculties, since the only premios for graduates in these subjects were a handful of underpaid university chairs. There were other drawbacks as well. To matriculate in theology involved a long and difficult university career which led almost automatically into the church and the

[38]On the establishment of this chair, see Marcel Bataillon, "L'Arabe A Salamanque Au Temps De La Renaissance," *Hesperis* 20 (1935): 1–16.
[39]BM: Eg. 439, folio 163.
[40]AHN: Cons., leg. 7294, report of the University of Salamanca, 20.I.1714.

religious orders; consequently, in the course of the seventeenth century, this faculty became more and more the preserve of the religious, as secular students turned to other courses of study. In addition, the inquisition's activity against prominent theologians accused of emending or tempering with scriptural texts and sacred doctrines may have frightened some students off, though it is difficult to say how many.

An alternative course with medicine: profitable, able to bring its most successful practitioners to permanent positions at the royal court,[41] but a faculty that was shunned by most students, perhaps on account of a long-standing association of the medical profession in Castile with the stigma of converso blood. Finally, to remain in the arts meant either school-teaching or the church or heavy reliance on the influence of family and friends to help secure an important secular or military charge.

Considering the limitations of other subjects and the doors to which legal training could lead, most of the students who attended Castile's universities matriculated in one of the two faculties of law although, in practice, they studied in both. With court letrados achieving positions of influence and power, membership in the Military Orders, and titles of noble rank, legal study quickly shed whatever remained of its old "clerkly" reputation, attracting to it young men in search of wealth, power, and rank.

Yet it would be wrong to insist that the popularity of this subject depended only upon its value as a basis for a career. Owing in part to the Habsburgs' insistence upon domestic peace and tranquillity, Castile in the sixteenth century was an increasingly litigious society, willing to settle its differences before a judge. To accommodate this new business, existing courts expanded in size and new magistrates were added to the royal bench. Even then, the backlog of cases was enormous and increasing year by year.[42] In a society in which most people, directly and indirectly, lived off the land, litigation was a daily fact of life. Suits involving boundaries, *mayorazgos*, seigneurial rights, dues and taxes involved individuals from every social class. Expansion in the world of commerce and trade was yet another source of legal haggling, while the growth of the royal bureaucracy itself led to lawsuits involving overlapping jurisdictions, demands for special privileges, and countless other administrative details on an unprecedented scale. Thus a knowledge of law and legal procedure was essential not only for those seeking letrado careers but also for noblemen, ecclesiastics, merchants, and officials, anyone for that matter who had some attachment to the land, trade, or government. Contemporaries, too, were well aware of the law's popularity. Francisco de Torquemada,

---

[41]The successful career of one sixteenth-century medical doctor is outlined in Luis S. Granjel, *Vida y Obra del Doctor Cristóbal Pérez de Herrera, 1558–1618* (Salamanca, 1959).

[42]The litigiousness of sixteenth-century Castile is reflected in the numerous petitions of Cortes of Castile directed toward the expansion and improvement of the royal bench; cf. Kagan, "Education and The State," chap. 3.

author of the *Monarchía Indiana* (1615), remarked that this subject was
"the most universal science for those who pursue the secular life of the
gentry [*de capa y espada*],"[43] and he could have added that it was also commonplace among those who were preparing to enter the church. In short,
the "rule of law" imposed by the Habsburg monarchy was gradually taking
hold, sparking new interest on the part of Spaniards to acquire a knowledge
of difficult legal texts.

Under these circumstances, the universities, the sole organized
source of legal training, were filled with youths eager for an education in
law. Consequently, these institutions, beginning in the years following
the decade of the 1550s, were dominated increasingly by legists. As this
change came about, they discarded their pluralistic Renaissance spirit for
one that was more strictly professional and vocational. Medieval Salamanca and Valladolid had also concentrated on the study of jurisprudence,
but with an eye toward ecclesiastical careers. In the Habsburg era, law
again dominated these institutions, but now the production of lawyers
and legally trained amateurs was their primary goal, and the universities
neglected those studies which did not directly serve such ends. Overcon-
centration on the law, moreover, helped to diminish interest in mathematics and natural history along with philosophy and the classics, thus
effectively cutting off Castile's universities from contemporaneous developments in European philosophical and scientific thought.

By the opening decades of the seventeenth century, university expansion in Castile had run its course. The rise in matriculation gave way to a
period of stagnation during the 1620s and 1630s, followed by a period of
steady decline lasting well into the eighteenth century (Figs. 7 and 8).
Contemporaries noted this phenomenon, attributing it variously to population decline, the sagging economy, changes in the methods by which
professors were selected, university violence, the colegios mayores, and
what they called a "*falta de premios.*" To a certain extent, each of their ex-
planations was correct, some being more logical than others. Violence
among the students, for example, had almost certainly given the universities
a bad name. The competition and rivalries associated with the student election of professors had been a festering sore for decades, a source of constant
violence and disruption until the Royal Council intervened in 1623. The
resumption of these contests in the years 1632–36 and 1638–41, however,
renewed the fighting on an unprecedented scale, as the famous "wars of
the nations" erupted. The number of brawls and violent clashes multiplied;
students brandishing clubs and sticks and guns were said to be a common
sight; and armed, menacing bands of students roamed the streets of
Salamanca and Valladolid at night. In an epoch which began to stress strict
surveillance of the young, especially when the economic squeeze rendered

---

[43]Cited in *Hernan Cortes Letters from Mexico*, ed. A. R. Pagden (New York, 1971),
p. xlvii.

every son more valuable because of his potential to bring to his family a dowry of considerable size, fathers may have been reluctant to send their offspring into the troubled and dangerous atmosphere of the universities. Such considerations undoubtedly influenced the sharp fluctuations in matriculations at Alcalá, Salamanca, and Valladolid during the 1630s. Furthermore, as the *corregidor* of Salamanca, Pedro de Amezqueta, attested, they probably contributed to university decline as a whole.[44]

Amezqueta, however, also believed that the "rising cost of living and the probable lack of wealth among fathers" contributed to what he called the "shortage of students."[45] It seems likely that inflation and mounting taxation, in addition to the other financial problems which beset seventeenth-century Castile, influenced the downward trend in university matriculations, but the extent of their impact will remain an open question until something more is learned about the effects of Spain's general economic decline upon private pocketbooks, particularly among those families most likely to send their sons to university. For example, although it is true that the years between 1620 and 1640, perhaps the most severe period of economic instability for Castile during the seventeenth century, coincided with a drop in the total student population of the kingdom, in the half decade between 1635 and 1640, the most bitter years of all, matriculations were on the rise.[46] Even in the worst of times there are those who earn profits and reap their rewards, and in seventeenth-century Castile it is likely that letrados and office-holders, that is, groups among whom a university education was common, were getting rich on the spoils of office and their investments in tax-farming and land. Thus, before any simple economic explanation of matriculation patterns can be offered, detailed studies of family incomes and resources, especially among hidalgos, letrados, and crown officials, are essential.

In the long range, however, the economic situation had its effect. Castile's economic advance during the sixteenth century had helped to finance the spread of education at all levels; conversely, economic problems in the seventeenth century did much to bring such progress to a halt. University costs, particularly those for degrees, were on the rise, and many families were undoubtedly unable to finance an advanced education for their sons. At the same time clerical prebends, a popular means of student support, must have declined in either number or value, or possibly both, depriving would-be students of financial aid. Finally, this era of hard times undoubtedly persuaded many families to cut their costs by educating their children at a local school or a Jesuit college instead of at a university.

If this was indeed the case, these families had good reason to do so. The demands of a new monarchy, a militant Catholic church, and a pros-

---

[44]See AHM: Cons., leg. 7138, letter of 11.XII.1638.
[45]Ibid.
[46]For the economic history of this period, see A. Domínguez Ortiz, *Política y Hacienda de Felipe IV* (Madrid, 1960), esp. chaps. 2–4.

perous society for letrados and other trained officials had helped bring about university expansion in the sixteenth and early seventeenth centuries. But as the number of students and graduates climbed, competition grew stiff and jobs increasingly scarce. Moreover, the requirements for official appointments narrowed. University study in law came to mean study at certain universities, advanced degrees, and then teaching experience or a place in one of the colegios mayores. But to earn a teaching post or a colegio mayor beca, family connections and personal ties with royal officials were increasingly essential. High letrado offices, consequently, became the almost exclusive preserve of colegiales and university instructors, while ordinary students, particularly those lacking influential personal ties, were crowded out of the market for letrado jobs.[47]

Castilians in the seventeenth century were quick to cite the "falta de premios" as a major cause of university decline, although in most instances they put the blame for this situation upon members of the colegios mayores, who they saw occupying an extraordinary number of university teaching posts and letrado jobs. While this argument has some validity, to maintain that the colegios mayores, acting alone, caused university decline in seventeenth-century Castile would be untrue. The colegiales, after all, were relatively few in number, and the posts they monopolized represented only a fraction of the total number of places usually reserved for letrados. Their influence, however, was far greater than their numbers would indicate. The offices that they, along with other university instructors, did control represented the important, prestigious, most sought-after places. Apparently, many students, frustrated by such overwhelming competition in a shrinking, overcrowded labor market, believed that promotion and advancement were almost impossible for those lacking the requisite family and collegiate ties. This was certainly the position of a Licentiate Gregorio Tovar y Pizarro, a student at Valladolid in 1576, who abandoned his hope of winning a university chair because

"in the *oposiciones* they [the colegiales] enter with great advantages and many votes from their fellow-*colegiales*, *huéspedes*, servants, and the friends of all of these. Thus it is only by a miracle that a chair escapes them."[48]

And on a wider scale this was also the position of the colegios militares in 1659 as well as that of the University of Salamanca in 1713, when it referred to the extraordinary number of colegiales and the shortage of its own *manteista* graduates in university teaching posts and on the councils and tribunals of Castile. It emphasized that "this inequality produces little or no ambition [among the students]," and added that declining opportunities for advancement had persuaded many students to abandon the uni-

---

[47]See pp. 101–02.
[48]G. de Tovar y Pizarro, "Un Jurisconsulto del Siglo XVI Pintado por sí mismo," *RABM*, 18 (1903): 21.

versities, others to become frustrated in their goals, while causing the universities themselves considerable harm.[49]

The almost complete lack of contemporary diaries and letters makes any statement about possible student frustrations difficult to prove,[50] but it is very likely that student hopes in the seventeenth century were shattered by a diminution in the number of letrado places available, which in turn tended to sharpen competition for scarce jobs and offices. While more and more of the top positions were controlled by colegiales, professors, and other letrados with influential family ties, the average student was forced to look elsewhere for employment.[51] Although evidence is often lacking, population loss, economic decline, and the atrophy of Castile's industrial and mercantile cities may have combined to reduce the number of local letrado offices and to deprive many lawyers of their careers; certainly, at the chancillería of Valladolid, the number of registered attorneys fell sharply during the seventeenth century from a peak of around fifty in the 1590s to an average of approximately fifteen after 1640.[52] It is also possible that the economic squeeze led to a change in litigation habits which resulted in more cases being either settled privately out of court or at a local level, circumstances which may have thrown the lawyers at the chancillería out of work and encouraged them to practice elsewhere. Letrados may have also been shut out of local magistracies, since many of these positions, particularly in the large towns, came under the control of one or two powerful families and were subsequently removed from the open, competitive market. Even school-teaching as a career suffered as Jesuit influence grew and municipal schools, after having their subsidies cut, were obliged to trim their staffs and in some cases close completely.[53]

All such estimates require statistical proof, but there seems to be sufficient evidence to suggest that the letrado's world was shrinking at a time when the costs of university attendance were rising and the important posts remaining open to him were blocked by a favored minority. This contraction of the labor market served only to exacerbate Castile's long-standing problem of too many graduates competing for jobs which were always in short supply. Degree-holders, although never numerous in absolute terms, constituted a group too large for Castile's professional labor market to absorb. For these students preferment was not absolutely impossible, but the promise of promotion and advancement undoubtedly waned

[49]AHN: Cons. leg. 7294, report of Salamanca, 21.II.1713.

[50]One student who kept a diary was the Italian, Girolamo de Sommaia, son of a Florentine senator, who was enrolled at Salamanca between 1602 and 1607. I have not been able to consult this diary, which is housed in Florence, but reference is made to it in George Haley, "The Earliest Dated Manuscript of Quevedo's Sueño Del Juicio," *Modern Philology* 67 (February 1970): 242.

[51]It was also at this time that the century-old expansion in the letrado hierarchy came to a halt; cf. pp. 82–83.

[52]See p. 84.

[53]See pp. 45, 50–51.

during a period when the investment demanded by a long letrado education no longer brought a sound return. Indeed, as the costs of the advanced
degrees required for the important offices in the church, the royal administration, and the legal profession, spiraled out of control, more and more
students may have been encouraged to abandon their studies, while others
were forced to earn hollow diplomas at the cheap degree mills.[54] Combined
with the poor and irregular instruction in the lecture halls, such conditions
allowed the pampered colegios mayores to prosper while university matriculations steadily declined.

The colegios mayores, however, were not the only successful colleges
in seventeenth-century Castile. The communities of the religious orders,
particularly the Jesuits, offered alternatives to university education and,
since the late sixteenth century, the number of their students was on the
rise.[55] Faced by a world of war, disease, famine, and uncertain employment, the instruction offered by the religious, deeply ingrained with lessons of Christian doctrine and example, offered for many of these students
not only an alternative to a university education but also a new ideal and
way of life. Given the special economic and social conditions of the time,
the expansion of the regular clergy in seventeenth-century Castile possibly
represented one facet of a general reaction against university education
and the competitive, office-holding world.[56] It appears, therefore, that the
church in Spain may have channeled the energies of frustrated students
in a way that seventeenth-century England was not able to achieve.

But falling university attendance was connected with other circumstances, the most important of which was the rapid rise of capa y espada
offices in the seventeenth and eighteenth centuries. These positions,
many of which were up for sale, rarely required a university education, let
alone a degree. So rather than sending their offspring to potentially dangerous universities, where the quality of instruction was known to be inferior,
wealthy families could educate their children at home or in a local school
and then purchase a fee-paying office, the income from which could support a son for life. Indeed, it is tempting to connect the drop in the number
of nobles studying at Salamanca, as well as the first signs of stagnation in
university matriculations, with the increase in the sales of offices beginning in the reigns of Philip III and Philip IV. What may have occurred is
that potential letrados shunned the universities for venal offices and capa
y espada careers, but until more information is collected about office-
buyers and the total volume of offices sold, this particular hypothesis must
remain untested. Yet it is likely that among those families who, in the
sixteenth century, would have automatically directed one or more of their

---

[54]See p. 211, note 27.
[55]See p. 55.
[56]On the growth of the regular clergy in seventeenth-century Spain, see Domínguez
Ortiz, *La Sociedad Española en el Siglo XVII* (Madrid, 1963, 1970), 2: 70.

sons into letrado careers, the university in the course of the following century became an increasingly superfluous institution.

On another plane, there is the possibility that the great international conflicts of the 1630s and 1640s and the coming of war to the Iberian peninsula itself after the Catalan and Portuguese revolts of 1640, together with Olivares's complaints about the "lack of leaders" among the court aristocracy, may have persuaded sons of hidalgo families to shun offices for military careers.[57] The declining interest in university education after 1640, therefore, could also have been related to the spread of traditional aristocratic ideas and chivalric values among the sons of the wealthy, particularly those of royal officials, merchants, and members of the liberal professions who aspired to noble status and a genteel style of life. Such a change would probably have fostered a movement away from the traditional school-college-university education common among society's middle and upper ranks toward training of a more private, literary, and chivalric nature. A systematic study of educational and career patterns among hidalgo and office-holding families would be necessary to confirm (or refute) this assertion, but there is some evidence which suggests that colegiales mayores, toward the end of the seventeenth century, began to shy away from letrado offices in order to become military officers, dignitaries in the royal households, and rentiers living off their estates.[58] Thus it is possible that Castile's educated classes, eager for the rank and titles of the aristocracy, attempted to live "nobly" and that this practice, perhaps akin to the well-noted *trahison de la bourgeoisie*, hindered university as well as economic development in seventeenth-century Castile.

Whatever the exact cause, the outcome is clear—the general decline of the university in Castile. After more than a century of new foundations, Castile after 1620 would not receive another new university until the 1830s, when the moribund university at Alcalá de Henares was moved and reorganized to become the Central University of Madrid.[59] Similarly, after 1620 the establishment of a new university college was a rarity while existing ones, suffering from lack of interest, Jesuit competition, and

[57]Certainly, there were more opportunities for military officers in seventeenth-century Spain, since the number of these places doubled after the size of army companies was halved; see N. G. Parker, *The Spanish Road and the Army at Flanders 1567–1659* (Cambridge, 1972).
[58]See p. 133.
[59]In 1693 the Bishop of Astorga, concerned about the "great ignorance of the clergy" and the fact that the closest universities to his diocese, Santiago and Valladolid, were too far away for many local youths to attend, expressed interest in the creation of a new university, but his ideas came to naught (AHN: Cons., leg. 7138, letters of 26.II. and 12.III.1693). In the eighteenth century two universities were added; the first, Cervera in Catalonia, was established in 1714 with the revenues from the six existing Catalan universities which Philip V had suppressed; and La Laguna, an Augustinian convent-university in the Canary Islands. This institution received papal approval in 1701 and the *jus ubique docendi* in 1744, only to be suppressed in 1747 and turned into a seminary. A small university emerged in Murcia in 1771 out of an existing *estudio particular*, but its foundation does not appear to have gone very far.

financial difficulties, either disappeared completely or amalgamated.[60] Moreover, by 1660, Alcalá, Salamanca, and Valladolid attracted less than one-half of the students they had had a century before (Fig. 7). Matriculations continued to fall even after the end of the seventeenth century, while graduations, hurt by increases in the rate of attrition among students, followed suit. At the provincial level, where universities had begun to languish even before the major institutions, the number of students at Santiago and Seville fell to less than 300 per annum.[61] Granada and Baeza barely managed the same (Fig. 7), and poor Sigüenza after mid-century could never muster more than thirty students in any one year. In overall terms, many of Castile's smaller universities by the close of the seventeenth century were close to extinction and the major ones were rapidly losing their influence and prestige.

Despite the accession of the Bourbons to the Spanish throne, the history of Castile's universities for the next seventy-five years merely confirmed those trends begun the century before. Matriculations at the major universities stagnated at relatively low levels: Salamanca attracted between 1,500 and 2,000 students a year; Alcalá rarely had more than 1,000; Valladolid, even fewer (Fig. 7). At the regional level, the smaller universities continued to decay, and a few, notably Granada and Sigüenza, temporarily dropped out of sight, while others stayed alive by selling their degrees, a practice which the larger universities, aided by the crown, attempted to stamp out.[62] By the middle of the eighteenth century the universities of Castile could together attract no more than 5,000 to 6,000 students a year, a figure less than one-third of the total two centuries before (Fig. 8). In relative terms, this decline meant that Castile around 1750 sent only 2.2 percent of its seventeen-year-olds to university each year.[63] In other words, since 1600 Castile had lost only a small fraction of her population and by the mid-eighteenth century demographic recovery was well under way, but during this same period her professionally trained, university-educated population had diminished by over one-half, while the number of students earning degrees had declined at a similar rate.[64] Once the educa-

[60]See p. 194. Salamanca's last college was established in 1608, Granada's in 1611. Alcalá acquired five colleges in the seventeenth century, one of which was reserved for Irish Catholic émigrés, but only three of these rent-poor foundations survived.

[61]In 1626 the University of Santiago, alarmed at the disastrous fall in its number of students, implored fathers to make their sons attend university and exhorted its instructors to continue to give their lectures, even though the professors had complained that their classes were empty; see Cabeza de León, *Universidad de Santiago*, 2: 449.

[62]This campaign, sparked by the University of Salamanca during the 1730s "against the multiplicity of universities without standards or many students and in which degrees are awarded in a manner which prejudices those who achieve them legitimately," led in 1771 to the invalidation of degrees from Avila, Irache, and Osma. See Ajo, *Universidades*, 5: 34, 49.

[63]Castile's population at this time was about 6.3 million. For the mathematics involved in this estimate, see footnote 13 in this chapter.

[64]In comparison with the 1,000–1,200 baccalaureates they awarded at their peak, Castile's universities in the eighteenth century rarely awarded more than 400 to 500 of these in a

tional leader of Europe, Castile in the middle of the eighteenth century was well on the road that in the course of the next hundred years would turn her into one of the educational backwaters of the European continent.

In the meantime, the universities changed profoundly. Now that many of the law's attractions had faded, students were distributed more or less evenly about the various faculties, although the arts were slowly becoming the university's most popular discipline (Figs. 9–11). Students were also younger,[65] but more of them belonged to one of the religious orders or lived behind college walls, a situation which helped to bring streeet violence to an end.[66] Nevertheless, the universities continued to languish and decay. The curriculum stagnated, money was short, and the monarchy did relatively little to rescue them from their plight. The Royal Council, for example, was generally more concerned with protecting the colegios mayores than aiding the universities and by doing so contributed to the latter's decay. After the reconstitution of Salamanca's Colegio Trilingüe in 1648, a measure partly designed to bolster sagging interest in the study of the liberal arts by creating new premios toward which talented graduates in the arts could aspire,[67] the council did little more than issue stop-gap orders designed to end statutory abuse.[68] Though reforms of a more general nature were often suggested,[69] few were put into effect until Philip V ascended the Spanish throne. In his opinion the University's mission was to "educate youth and to provide ministers for the government."[70] Toward this end Philip worked in the opening years of his reign to aid the troubled arts faculties and colegios menores. He also instituted instruction in Spanish law, "since it is by this and not by Roman Law that future judges must decide and substantiate legal cases," and put an end to the corrupt and

---

single year. The output of advanced graduates was also halved, although at some universities the decline was more pronounced. At Alcalá de Henares, for example, the number of licences in arts awarded annually went from a high of 110 to 120 in the late sixteenth century to about 25 by 1700; cf. AHN: Univ., libs. 400–413.

[65]See pp. 175–79.

[66]See pp. 188, 195.

[67]Sala Balust, *Constituciones, Estatutos, y Ceremonias de los Antiguos Colegios Seculares de la Universidad de Salamanca* (4 vols., Madrid, 1962–66). In 1659, however, four of this college's becas were switched from the faculty of arts to medicine; cf. Esperabé Artega, *Universidad de Salamanca*, 1: 779. Sixteen hundred and forty-eight also marked a year of proposals to revive the entire arts faculty at Salamanca; see AHN: Cons. leg. 7138, "Arbitrio y Discurso del Modo que puede remediar la facultad de Artes en la Universidad de Salamanca"; Francisco Chumacero y Carrillo a Antonio Camporredondo y Río, 22.VII. 1648. See also BM: Add. 24,947, folio 101.

[68]Many of these are recorded in Esperabé Artega, *Universidad de Salamanca*, vol. 1.

[69]One ingenious plan, noting that there are "few friends of early rising because Salamanca is such a cold place," advocated that the chairs of Prima at this university be read at 9 or 10 a.m. instead of the usual 7:30. Otherwise, the lecture halls would remain "almost completely deserted," the professors "crippled," and youth "benefited" but little; see AHN: Cons. leg. 7138, letter of 13.V.1684.

[70]Cited in Ajo, *Universidades*, 5: 32.

nepotistic methods the Royal Council had used to fill university professor-ships.[71]

But Philip's early enthusiasm for university reform, followed by an un-successful attempt in the 1720s to curb the influence of the colegios mayores, waned by the later years of his reign. Sweeping change had been blocked by inertia and tradition, and with the exception of piece-meal changes, the issue of wholesale university reform was not raised again until the 1760s, when it emerged as part of a campaign to weaken the power and independence of the colegios mayores. With the advice and encourage-ment of influential court officials such as Campomanes and Jovellanos, Pablo de Olavide's plan to overhaul the structure and curriculum of the Uni-versity of Seville in 1768 spread in the course of two decades to Castile's other universities.[72] Consequently, these institutions, with the crown's help, achieved a new look. The colegios mayores were suppressed, the *turno*, along with other procedures thorough which instructors had been able to advance to important university chairs by means of seniority alone, was abolished, and the government of each university was handed over to the senior professors, working under the supervision of a royal minister in Madrid. In addition, degree costs were reduced by ending the elaborate pomp of the degree ceremonies, diplomas from the cheap degree mills were invalidated, and competition from the religious colleges brought to an end, all in the hope of encouraging students to attend the major univer-sities. Meanwhile, the curriculum was modernized along European lines; medicine shed many of its classical vestiges for studies of a more empiri-cal bent; the works of Newton and Galileo as well as algebra and experi-mental physics were added to the faculty of arts; and in jurisprudence new emphasis was given to Spanish as opposed to Roman and canon law.

Together these changes were designed to kindle a new enthusiasm for university study and in some respects they did. Students who a few years earlier would have eschewed the university for a Jesuit college turned to the *estudios generales*, and their return helped to raise ma-triculations at many universities in the late eighteenth century. The most popular faculties were the arts and theology although students in the for-mer displayed little interest at first in "modern" subjects such as experi-mental physics (App. A, Table ix). On the whole, they preferred Aristotle; science, even in the late eighteenth century, was still a pastime for gen-tlemen dilettantes, whereas the traditional course offered the meal-

[71]Ibid., pp. 31–33. Philip began his campaign to reform the universities after conducting an inquiry into their problems; see AHN: Cons., leg. 7294.

[72]See F. Aguilar Piñal, *El Plan de Estudios de la Universidad de Sevilla* (Barcelona, 1969), and by the same author, *La Universidad de Sevilla en el Siglo XVIII. Estudio sobre la Primera Reforma Universitaria Moderna* (Sevilla, 1969); Addy, *The Enlightenment in the Univer-sity of Salamanca* (Durham, 1966); Ajo, *Universidades*, 5: 60–73; and A. Alvarez Morales, *La Ilustración y la Reforma de la Universidad en la España del Siglo XVIII* (Madrid, 1971).

ticket the job-hungry students of the eighteenth century had in mind. For
this reason it would be unwise to attribute the renewed enthusiasm for
university study at this time to administrative and curricular changes
alone. Equally important were advances in the population and the economy
and an expanding labor market now freed from colegio mayor control.
Although the history of this period in Castile is still relatively unknown, it
seems likely that the late eighteenth century brought to the kingdom new
places for university graduates in schools, government, and law. It also
coincided with the emergency of a class of new families with fortunes
rooted in the commercial expansion of the epoch, who were interested in
university education for their sons, since such training would help them
to escape or at least to disguise their mercantile past. And it was developments such as these, together with curricular reform, changes in university
rules, and the end of competition from the religious colleges, which formed
the bases of the recovery for Castile's universities after 1770.

In many instances, this recovery was remarkable. The University of
Sigüenza, moribund for much of the previous century, now enrolled 100
students and more; Avila, which had only 5 students in 1740, had close to
200 in 1790; and the University of Osuna in 1790 enrolled close to 300 students, nearly 6 times as many as it had attracted in the century's opening
decades. Similar advances were recorded at Granada, Oviedo, Seville,
Toledo, and Valladolid. In fact, the only major universities not to share in
this epoch of prosperity were Alcalá de Henares and Salamanca, but
their failure to take part was significant. Though matriculations at the
smaller universities were up, losses at Alcalá and Salamanca caused
total university attendance in Castile to rise marginally, if at all (Fig. 8).
And now that Castile's population was rapidly on the rise,[73] the overall
position of the university at the opening of the nineteenth century was
weaker than at any time since the early years of the reign of Ferdinand
and Isabel.

What actually seems to have happened to university matriculations
in the last quarter of the eighteenth century was a shift away from the
established universities of Castile toward smaller, less renowned institutions in the provinces. Years of colegio mayor domination, inordinately
expensive degrees, and resistance to innovation and change had gradually
weakened the reputations of the famous universities. For many of these
same reasons, Alcalá and Salamanca after 1700 resembled the other
universities in that they too had become "regional" institutions, drawing
the bulk of their students from the province in which they were located
(Maps 4 and 5). For much of the Habsburg era these two universities, along

[73]Massimo Levi-Bacci, "Fertility and Population Growth in Spain in the Eighteenth and
Nineteenth Centuries," *Daedalus* (Spring, 1968): 523–35, deals with the question of rising
population in late-eighteenth-century Spain.

with Valladolid, had helped to unite the kingdom, mixing together intellectuals and professionals from every province and region. But by the eighteenth century no university, Alcalá and Salamanca included, was serving more than a local clientele. This situation no doubt helped to keep the nation's educated populace apart, perhaps reinforcing the deep cultural and political divisions of Spain.[74]

When interest in university study revived, would-be students from outlying areas, rather than trek to Alcalá or Salamanca, universities which could no longer guarantee either scholarly excellence or a secure future, attended the cheaper, sometimes more flexible and innovative institutions closer to home. Accordingly, Alcalá and Salamanca lost ground, but their inability to keep pace with the other institutions coincided with the weakening of Castile itself. The region's economic and demographic preponderance within the peninsula had long been eroded; its political leadership was under attack; and its empire in the Americas, increasingly independent of the mother country's control, was soon to fall apart. It was only fitting that in educational, perhaps even in intellectual, terms, Castile's leading universities, linked closely to the royal government in Madrid, would give way to institutions located in more prosperous and dynamic parts of the kingdom. Barcelona and Valencia, along with Oviedo, Seville, and the medical faculties of Cadiz, were to be the intellectual leaders of Spain during the next generation. And it was not until the establishment of the Central University in Madrid in 1836 that Castile and its monarchy attempted to renew its educational mastery over the kingdom as a whole.

At the opening of the nineteenth century, the fortunes of higher education in Castile were relatively bleak. Though some gains had been made in the last twenty years, matriculations continued to languish, the quality of instruction was poor, and most of the universities were almost bankrupt. To improve matters Charles IV in 1807 pushed through a new series of administrative and curricular reforms,[75] and three years later, he suppressed the majority of Castile's universities, leaving only seven behind.[76] This measure, designed to concentrate the remaining financial and intellectual resources of the universities and to ensure graduates of a superior and more uniform caliber than before, had no immediate chance of proving itself. The Napoleonic invasion of Spain in 1808 and the bitter civil war which ensued closed the universities education for nearly a decade. The 1820s brought the beginnings of recovery, but it would take most of the

---

[74]To some degree the advent of scholarly journals with a national distribution had rendered this function of the university obsolete. On journals, see Herr, *Eighteenth Century Revolution*, chap. VI.

[75]See Addy, *Enlightenment in Salamanca*, pp. 228–43, app. II.

[76]Cf. Ajo, *Universidades*, 5: 90. The survivors were Alcalá, Granada, Oviedo, Salamanca, Santiago, Seville, and Valladolid.

nineteenth century before Castile's universities could rival the position and importance they had enjoyed three centuries before.[77]

The dynamic shift in the importance of the university within Castilian society in the century between 1550 and 1650, the year which signaled the beginning of a long century of stagnation and decay, was perhaps more of a readjustment than an absolute decline. One could postulate that in the sixteenth century the university, despite its numerous students, rested upon weak foundations. Elementary and secondary education in Castile was primarily limited to a small elite within the towns and cities, and the university, dependent upon this wealthy, educated elite, was sensitive to its interests and tastes. When, in the course of the seventeenth century, these apparently changed, the universities were stripped of their larger clientele and were left to the religious orders, scholarship students, and hard-core professionals. In other words, by the mid-seventeenth century the university, after passing through a phase—we may call it the "Renaissance"—somewhat resembled its medieval counterparts: small, dominated by churchmen, highly vocational, and overwhelmingly legalistic. Matriculations, however diminished, may have reflected the kingdom's actual demand for lawyers, theologians, and physicians, rather than the social and cultural interests of the elite. Thus the university regained its purely professional spirit, while its popular, pedagogical, "Renaissance" element passed into the hands of the regular clergy. Not until late in the nineteenth century would the two be reunited under university auspices, and then matriculations in every faculty were rapidly on the rise.

[77]The history of student matriculations at Castile's universities in the nineteenth century is difficult to trace. Mysteriously, most of the matriculation registers after the 1830s have either been lost or misplaced or they are in such a state of disarray as to render their use almost impossible. Madrid's few remaining registers, for example, have suffered from a recent archival flood, and as of the summer of 1970, they were damp, covered with mold, and soon to fall apart. Moreover, no university archive or library has in its possession a complete set of the *annuarios*, many of which contain summaries of student matriculations, that every university published annually.

CONCLUSION

The Renaissance goal of placing education in the service of the state triumphed in the universities of Castile, but not through the medium the humanist authors had originally envisaged. They had regarded the study of the liberal arts as the ideal preparation for the "*vita activa e civile*," but for the majority of students in the *estudios generales*, the classics served only as a background for professional training. Law, the subject with the widest opportunities for advancement and prestige, was also the subject most in demand.

Tied to the interests of lawyers, the universities gradually acquired a highly conservative bent. As centers for the training of important officials, Castile's rulers attempted to make certain that the universities would be free from all heretical and revolutionary ideas, a policy which led to the active discouragement of curricular innovation and change.[1] Before these considerations reigned supreme, however, that is, before the second half of the sixteenth century, scholarship at the universities had been relatively dynamic and free. The universities, in fact, stood at the forefront of Spanish intellectual life. Adaptable to the new ideas which the Renaissance had spawned, they also met head-on the intellectual problems posed by the emergence of imperial Spain. So it was that Salamanca, late in the fifteenth century, welcomed the proposals of Columbus, who sought a new route to the East, and later taught the theories of Copernicus on the place of man in the universe. Alcalá, responding to the humanists' call for studies of sacred texts in their original languages, gave Europe its first institution— the Colegio Trilingüe—wholly dedicated to the study of classical languages, an effort that resulted in that monumental piece of scholarship, the Polyglot Bible, with parallel texts in Latin, Hebrew, Greek, and Chaldaic. Habsburg expansion overseas also found an original legal and philosophical base in the writings of university scholars such as Martin de Azpilcueta, Domingo do Soto, and Francisco de Vitoria. At the same time the fundamental questions which this expansion raised—the enslavement of the Amerindians, church policy toward peoples who had never heard of Christ, and the natural rights of sovereign states—and the problems created by it (including the relationship of bullion imports to

---

[1]On the standardization of texts, see Esperabé Artega, *Historia Pragmática é Interna de la Universidad de Salamanca* (Salamanca, 1914), 1: 536, 553-54, 613, 661.

inflation) were readily discussed and debated in the lecture halls.[2]
Classical scholarship was also advanced by masters such as Nebrija,
Hernán Núñez, "El Pinciano," and Francisco Sánchez "El Brocense,"
while Spanish theologians, headed by Melchor Cano, a professor at
Salamanca, led the forces of a resurgent Catholic church at the Council of
Trent.[3] Then too the arts found a home at the university; Fray Luís de
León, one of Spain's greatest poets, was a professor at Salamanca for many
years.[4]

But the most significant contribution of the universities during these
early years, at least for the subsequent history of Castile, was the formation
of a new social class: the letrados, serving as the mainstay of the new
Habsburg state. Yet in this class also lay the seeds of the universities'
decay. Legally trained prelates, councillors, magistrates, and statesmen
remained at the core of Castilian government for over three centuries.
Concomitantly, there emerged a bureaucratic elite, comprised of the
letrado dynasties who occupid key posts in the monarchy, and these families, governing the universities through their positions on the Royal
Council and their control of the colegios mayores, were in a position to
fashion higher education as they saw fit. Their goal of office-holding as a
means to obtain and to preserve power, riches, and prestige became that
of the university, particularly as students and professors from other backgrounds sought to emulate the letrados' spectacular careers. Thus the study
of law inundated the lecture halls, forcing other disciplines into retreat or
into the hands of the regular clergy and the circles of gentlemen
dilettantes.

Left only with the interests of the letrados, the universities gradually
lost contact with the wider context of Castilian life, and with it they lost
their ability to absorb new ideas, teach new theories, and devise new
social and academic goals. The universities were in this sense consumed
by an overriding passion for the study of law and the formation of letrados,
blind to whatever additional contributions they could have made. Accordingly, the advancement of the liberal arts, of scientific learning, practical
and pure, studies in political economy, modern languages, and the like
escaped the universities' ken. And just as the letrados hankered back to
the aristocratic ideals of ages past, the universities were unable and unwilling to rid themselves of medieval statutes and a curriculum that was
long out of date, totally mindless of those who, like Diego de Torres Vil-

[2]See above, pp. 162–63.
[3]Biographies of these and other famous professors exist, but they are far too numerous to
list here. Many are listed in the bibliographies provided in Bell, *Luis de León*, and volume 1
of Ajo, *Historia de las Universidades Hispánicas* (8 vols., Madrid, 1957–72). Beltrán de Heredia, *Cartulario de la Universidad de Salamanca* (Salamanca, 1971), vol. 3, contains a number
of brief sketches of the lives and writings of Salamanca's most notable sixteenth-century
scholars. Spanish theologians at Trent are listed in C. Gutiérrez, *Españoles en Trento* (Valladolid, 1951).
[4]See Bell, *Luis de León*.

larroel, professor of astronomy and mathematics at Salamanca, warned that they must change, since "The world is of a different character from that when the University of Salamanca was established. The men of this epoch aspire to other maxims and studies that are more in conformity with the temper of this century."[5]

But change, they did not with the result that as early as the middle of the sixteenth century, critics began to attack their outmoded teaching and antiquated methods of instruction. Pedro Simón Abril, a noted grammarian, suggested that the universities teach in the vernacular and provide training in "practical" subjects such as mathematics, agriculture, architecture, and the techniques of war.[6] But the universities held tight to their ancient ways; Simón Abril's suggestions for reform were just as valid two centuries later when many of his proposals reappeared in the writings of Feijóo, Torres Villarroel, Olavide, and Jovellanos. Buttressed by a conservative inquisition and by religious orders equally intent upon keeping new ideas out of Spain, the universities themselves did nothing to modernize from within.

Instead, pointing to the past and to a long list of famous leaders with an even longer list of achievements and offices attached to their names, the universities and their overseers on the Royal Council could see little reason why they should break from a tradition that had done so much in order to institute changes which promised neither certain nor immediate advantages. Although they were able to recognize the need for administrative tinkerings in order to shore up what was an already decaying situation, in doing so, they refused to take their inspiration from the present, but continually harked back to aged constitutions and statutes, the proper observation of which was supposed to bring prosperity anew. Rather than create a new university with new goals, they attempted to revive the university of the "Golden Age." The restoration of mythical glories out of the past and the continuance of practices sanctioned by time were integral to the politics and thinking of early modern Spain.[7] And the university, mentor for so many of Spain's leaders, was no doubt partly responsible for such ideals. These were reinforced by the fact that membership in the governing class was more of a test of blood than of knowledge or technical expertise; therefore, there was little or no concerted pressure, either from the elite, or from those seeking entrance to it, to force either the universities to change or the monarchy to reevaluate its aspirations and

[5]Cited in Julio Mathiás, *Torres Villaroel, Su Vida, Su Obra, Su Tiempo* (Madrid, 1971), p. 35. This scholar's autobiography, *Vida, ascendencia, nacimiento, crianza, y aventuras del Dr. D. Diego de Torres Villarroel . . . Escrita por él mismo . . .* (Madrid, 1743), deals extensively with life at Salamanca in the eighteenth century.

[6]Pedro Simón Abril, "Apuntamientos de cómo se deben reformar las doctrinas y la manera del enseñallas . . .," *Biblioteca de Autores Españoles* (Madrid, 1875): 293–96.

[7]On this point, see J. H. Elliott, "Revolution and Continuity in Early Modern Europe," *Past & Present* 42 (February 1969): 35–56.

goals. Spain's letrados looked back, not ahead; they pointed to precedents out of the past, not aspirations on the horizon; and the universities, dominated by viewpoints similar to these, merely stood still. As a result, they were allowed the luxury of remaining as they were and of leaving the hard work of educational innovation to other institutions: the Seminario de Nobles, preceded by the Colegio Imperial, and the royal academies for history, law, medicine, and the arts, all products of the eighteenth century. Intellectual leadership in Spain subsequently deserted the university for the academy, leaving the former to toy with the interests of vocationally-minded students and the social aspirations of the rich.

Yet even with this express purpose, the universities fell short of expectations. University-educated clerics were supposed to have healed the breaches in Christendom, and even though the threat of internal religious dissent had diminished by the seventeenth century, Protestant heretics were still at large and dangerous. University-educated lawyers, wielding their manuals of Roman law, were supposed to have helped the monarchy to unify its realms, yet the problems raised by local traditions and customary law in the Basque country and Catalonia in the seventeenth century were more troublesome than ever before. And once economic decline became apparent, for many contemporaries the universities, like the grammar schools, only added to the nation's woes by encouraging young men to enter the economically unproductive cadres of officials, lawyers, and priests. One who felt this way was the Bishop of Badajoz, Fray Angel Manrique. He wrote in 1624 about the excess of *bachilleres* in Castile, while complaining that "the abundance of licentiates who ignore necessary jobs is not good for the Republic."[8] In his opinion, four universities, in addition to twenty-four grammar schools, would be sufficient to meet Spain's requirements for educated men. Even the Cortes, a body usually in favor of university education, expressed alarm in 1627 at the overabundance of estudios generales in Castile.[9]

There were other complaints as well. Throughout the sixteenth century the Cortes of Castile repeatedly criticized the universities for their failure to prepare adequately students for the magistracy, maintaining in 1528 that "when the letrados leave the universities, they cannot handle judicial business properly nor even understand the law well enough to make proper judgments."[10] One reason for this was the universities' reluctance to teach Spanish law. Such instruction began only in the middle

[8]"Socorro del clero al estado, escrito por un religioso en 1624," cited in Zarco Cuevas, "El Lic. Miguel Caja de Leruela, y las Causas de la Decadencia de España," in *Estudios sobre la ciencia española en el siglo XVII* (Madrid, 1935), p. 527.

[9]Cortes de Madrid, 1627, vol. 45, p. 332.

[10]Cortes de Madrid, 1528, pet. 30. For later criticism of the quality of university graduates, see the Cortes de Valladolid, 1542, pet. 20; de Valladolid, 1548, pet. 39; de Madrid, 1551, pet. 2; de Toledo, 1559, pet. 10; de Madrid, 1570, pet. 49; de Madrid, 1576, pet. 8; de Madrid, 1583-85, pet. 16; de Madrid, 1600, pet. of Juan de Lugo.

of the eighteenth century, and then only after thirty years of prodding by Philip V. In spite of this advance, an English visitor to Spain in 1774 commented that law students learned only "corruption and royal edicts."[11]

In the other faculties, teaching was even worse. Fray Benito Feijóo, writing in the early eighteenth century, claimed that medical study was nothing more than a joke, and his opinion was corroborated by a friar named Norberto Caino who visited Spain in the 1750s. He reported that the topic of discussion in one public thesis in the medical faculty at the University of Sigüenza was "Of what utility or of prejudice would it be for a man to have one finger more or less?" And this was followed by another imponderable: "If, in order to enjoy good health, it is necessary when cutting one's fingernails to begin with the right hand or the left?"[12] He reserved the following comment for a theology thesis at Salamanca:

The Latin is of the oddest, most barbarous, most detestable, most stupid style that I have ever heard. It is a mixture of ridiculous and insipid phrases recklessly taken from the texts of the Bible and the Holy Fathers, put together without order or method: a strange mixture of Latinized Spanish and Arabic words arranged topsy-turvy. And thus they speak Latin at Salamanca; what would it be like where there is no university?[13]

However exaggerated such reports may be, the professorate's apathy and neglect threatened all classroom instruction and the quality of university degrees, while the violence and ostentation of student life side-tracked many of those students who were capable of learning on their own. One astute seventeenth-century "visitor" to the chancillería in Valladolid noted that reform in government depended upon previous reforms at the universities, ". . . because the well-being of the *Audiencia* and of the nation's government in judicial matters depends on the universities, principally that of Salamanca, if those who study there are schooled in vices and become accustomed to them, they can never be made into good judges."[14]

The continuing dominance of the colegios mayores exacerbated an already decaying situation. Using university chairs primarily for reasons of appointment and prestige, they brought the law faculties to their lowest ebb. And thanks to their influence and example, the university as a whole emulated the careers and interests of the colegial.

Thus the universities of Castile turned away from society at large to focus on the colegios mayores, the study of law, and the acquisition of letrado jobs. Their teaching helped to impart out-dated ideas to genera-

---

[11]Cited in García Mercadal, *Viajes de Extranjeros por España y Portugal* (Madrid, 1962), 3: 677.
[12]Ibid., 3: 401.
[13]Ibid.
[14]BNP: Ms. Espagnol 261, folio 6.

tions of officials, and, in turn, these helped to perpetuate the social and political ideals of the Middle Ages in a rapidly changing world. Government leaders, schooled in the legal traditions of the past, drew their inspiration from it as well, attempting to recapture a Golden Age of Spanish glory instead of striving to create the foundations of a new age. It is not that the universities of other European nations were more up-to-date, but Spain, almost by reason of its archaic string of universities, was fated to fall behind much of the rest of Europe in the march toward the scientific and industrial world.

The letrado elite, insulated from the wider world through censorship, class exclusiveness, and the Latinized culture which they represented, moved away from the higher, humanist ideals of service in which they had first been trained. In the sixteenth century they had given to the monarchy the legal expertise needed to create a strong, centralized government and a society that was eventually to be dominated by a rule of law. By the eighteenth century, however, the letrados lacked the expertise that Spain's ailing empire required. Turning their back on higher education in the national interest, this elite used the university to promote its own narrow ends. Strangled by this control, the leading universities of Castile would not revive until more enlightened leaders forged a new set of educational goals and granted them a measure of autonomous, independent life, free of strict ministerial censorship and control.

But ultimately, the history of the Castilian university lay in the way members of the university community, both students and teachers, viewed themselves and their place in Castilian life. Having chosen to emphasize the production of letrados or, at the very least, of gentlemen lightly schooled in the law for reasons of practicality and prestige, the fate of the university rested with the market it served, the classes for whom it catered. Lacking the protective family ties of the colegios mayores and the spiritual allies of the religious colleges, the university of the seventeenth and eighteenth centuries fell apart as its market contracted and the bulk of its following turned to alternate forms of education and careers. Its revival had to be achieved on the basis of a new and less restricted clientele, the product of improved primary and secondary schooling. It depended too on the emergence of larger and more diffuse labor markets and on the diffusion of bourgeois values which placed a new emphasis on the education and advancement of the young. But the beginnings of these special conditions, all products of the nineteenth century, were slow to develop in Spain, marking this country's belated and often turbulent entrance into the modern world.

appendix a
ADDITIONAL TABLES

Table I.   Growth of the Colegios Mayores: Number of Students (decennial averages)

	College					
Decades	Arzobispo	Cuenca	Oviedo	San Bartolomé	San Ildefonso	Santa Cruz
1550–59	14.4	9.9	12.9	13.2	21.2	—
1560–69	10.7	8.6	9.4	12.2	20.0	—
1570–79	10.1	9.4	8.3	10.6	16.9	—
1580–89	12.9	8.8	10.1	10.4	12.4	—
1590–99	12.6	9.6	10.0	11.5	16.5	—
1600–09	18.8	12.0	14.5	12.4	12.8	—
1610–19	17.3	13.0	14.3	12.7	18.9	14.0
1620–29	18.7	17.3	15.8	11.8	16.0	13.1
1630–39	18.6	13.5	16.5	14.6	25.3	17.0
1640–49	22.6	16.0	17.3	13.9	29.4	22.0
1650–59	25.0	16.8	18.5	11.7	32.9	21.4

Table I (continued)

			College			
Decades	Arzobispo	Cuenca	Oviedo	San Bartolomé	San Ildefonso	Santa Cruz
1660–69	27.0	24.3	22.2	15.8	40.9	25.3
1670–79	30.5	26.9	21.9	18.9	44.8	26.8
1680–89	27.9	22.2	21.4	18.1	41.9	28.7
1690–99	27.5	27.5	24.6	21.3	36.1	21.6

Number of Colegiales Mayores in the Eighteenth Century

Year	Arzobispo	Cuenca	Oviedo	San Bartolomé*	San Ildefonso	Santa Cruz
1705	25	27	22	19	—	29
1710	29	26	24	26	32	—
1715	37	24	19	28	—	29
1720	30	31	19	19	34	27
1725	29	25	22	25	—	31
1730	30	24	23	24	38	27
1735	32	28	28	28	—	25
1740	30	28	n.d.	31	42	31
1745	29	23	32	29	—	—
1750	27	20	27	29	34	26
1755	32	20	27	29	—	28
1760	36	23	25	32	31	—
1765	36	30	28	26	—	—
1770	n.d.	n.d.	n d.	n.d.	—	—
1775	5	3	—	1	—	—
1780	9	12	9	18	—	—
1785	12	11	7	17		
1790	4	3	5	2	—	—
1795	1	—	2	—	—	—

*Excludes chaplains.
Source: Libros de Matrículas of Alcalá, Salamanca, and Valladolid.

Table II. College Students at the University of Salamanca

Year	Enrollment	Religious colleges		Secular colleges		Total colleges	
		no.	%	no.	%	no.	%
1551–52	5,150	209	4.05	—	—	—	—
1555–56	5,146	217	4.21	110	2.13	327	6.34
1560–61	4,905	238	4.85	—	—	—	—
1565–66	5,262	261	4.96	124	2.35	385	7.31
1570–71	6,089	319	5.23	—	—	—	—
1571–72	5,888	—	—	—	—	443	7.52
1575–76	5,145	327	6.35	—	—	—	—
1581–82	5,543	321	5.79	154	2.77	475	8.56

Table II (continued)

Year	Enrollment	Religious colleges		Secular colleges		Total colleges	
		no.	%	no.	%	no	%
1585–86	6,705	315	4.69	130	1.93	445	6.63
1588–89	6,555	371	5.65	—	—	—	—
1595–96	5,460	377	6.90	159	2.91	536	9.81
1599–00	4,156	229	5.51	—	—	—	—
1605–06	4,983	521	10.45	235	4.71	756	15.17
1610–11	4,721	393	8.32	256	5.42	649	13.74
1615–16	4,974	499	10.03	—	—	—	—
1620–21	6,212	457	7.35	178	2.86	635	10.22
1625–26	5,791	369	6.37	254	4.38	623	10.76
1630–31	4,170	382	9.16	—	—	—	—
1635–36	4,797	419	8.73	249	5.19	668	13.92
1640–41	4,194	457	10.89	245	5.84	702	16.73
1645–46	3,401	441	12.96	194	5.70	635	18.67
1650–51	2,836	482	16.99	213	7.51	695	24.50
1655–56	3,096	479	15.47	—	—	—	—
1660–61	2,795	634	22.68	201	7.19	835	29.87
1665–66	2,533	562	22.18	192	7.57	754	29.76
1670–71	2,313	500	21.61	—	—	—	—
1675–76	3,115	725	23.27	188	6.03	913	29.30
1680–81	2,220	642	28.91	—	—	—	—
1685–86	1,821	606	33.27	275	15.10	881	48.38
1690–91	2,132	642	30.11	—	—	—	—
1695–96	2,199	749	34.06	224	10.18	973	44.24
1700–01	1,923	784	40.76	123	6.39	907	47.16
1705–06	1,575	674	42.79	241	15.30	915	58.09
1710–11	1,236	597	48.30	220	17.79	817	66.10
1715–16	1,443	670	46.43	209	14.48	879	60.91
1720–21	1,620	733	45.24	189	11.66	922	56.91
1725–26	1,627	724	44.49	213	13.09	937	57.59
1730–31	1,843	875	47.47	216	11.72	1,091	59.19
1735–36	1,737	894	51.46	230	13.24	1,124	64.70
1740–41	1,904	913	47.95	184	9.66	1,097	57.61
1745–46	2,349	899	38.27	250	10.64	1,149	48.91
1750–51	2,036	923	45.33	242	11.88	1,165	57.22
1755–56	1,950	943	48.35	245	12.56	1,188	60.92
1760–61	2,073	931	44.91	253	12.20	1,184	57.11
1765–66	1,832	808	44.10	283	15.44	1,091	59.55
1770–71	1,950	—	—	—	—	634	32.51
1775–76	1,398	279	19.95	77	5.50	356	25.46
1780–81	1,329	311	23.40	113	8.50	424	31.90
1785–86	1,428	353	24.71	102	7.14	455	31.86
1790–91	1,374	400	29.11	72	5.24	472	34.35
1795–96	1,389	323	23.25	86	6.19	409	29.44
1800–01	1,192	258	21.64	64	5.36	322	27.01
1805–06	1,017	407	40.01	54	5.30	461	45.32
1810–11	—	—	—	—	—	—	—
1815–16	185	46	24.86	—	—	46	24.86
1820–21	633	5	0.08	26	4.10	31	4.89
1825–26	427	61	14.28	29	6.79	90	21.07
1830–31	544	—	—	—	—	—	—
1835–36	776	—	—	—	—	31	3.99

Table III.   University of Alcalá de Henares: Students by Diocese

	1550	(%)	1610	(%)	1650	(%)	1690	(%)	1750	(%)
CROWN OF CASTILE										
Andalucia:										
Córdoba	33		7		5		9		2	
Granada	3		5		4		3		1	
Guadix	—		2		—		—		—	
Jaen	13		20		16		3		—	
Malaga	3		4		2		6		—	
Seville	35		10		10		4		1	
Total	87	(3.6)	48	(2.1)	37	(1.9)	25	(1.6)	4	(0.7)
Asturias:										
Oviedo	5		4		6		9		5	
Total	5	(0.2)	4	(0.2)	6	(0.3)	9	(0.6)	5	(0.8)
Castile (New):										
Cuenca	342		329		283		147		60	
Sigüenza	207		260		128		66		29	
Toledo	949		975		836		863		350	
Total	1,498	(62.5)	1,564	(68.1)	1,247	(62.5)	1,076	(68.2)	439	(74)
Castile (Old):										
Avila	38		20		6		3		5	
Burgos	61		71		80		73		20	
Calahorra	115		6		215		109		32	
Logroño	—		1		—		—		—	
Osma, Burgo de	99		81		53		23		13	
Palencia	93		15		10		7		—	
Santo Domingo de la Calzada	—		—		1		—		—	
Segovia	69		54		35		15		1	
Valladolid	—		13		4		2		1	
Total	475	(19.8)	261	(11.4)	404	(20.3)	232	(14.7)	72	(12.1)
Extremadura:										
Badajoz	17		3		—		1		4	
Coria	3		—		4		2		—	
Plasencia	13		8		8		1		—	
Total	33	(1.4)	11	(0.5)	12	(0.6)	4	(0.3)	4	(0.7)
León:										
Astorga	4		1		3		2		—	
Ciudad Rodrigo	2		3		—		1		—	
León	13		9		19		8		1	
Salamanca	8		4		2		—		1	
Zamora	—		—		—		—		—	
Total	27	(1.1)	17	(0.7)	24	(1.2)	11	(0.7)	2	(0.3)
Galicia:										
Lugo	—		1		3		3		2	
Mondoñedo	—		—		1		8		—	
Orense	—		1		—		2		—	
Santiago	2		3		1		2		3	
Tuy	—		—		1		—		1	
Total	2	(0.1)	5	(0.2)	6	(0.3)	15	(1)	6	(1)

Table III (continued)

	1550	(%)	1610	(%)	1650	(%)	1690	(%)	1750	(%)
Murcia:										
Albacete	—		—		—		—		—	
Almeria	—		—		—		—		—	
Cartagena	6		15		—		1		2	
Murcia	3		2		14		12		1	
Total	9	(0.4)	17	(0.7)	14	(0.7)	13	(0.8)	3	(0.5)
Total Crown of Castile	2,136	(89.1)	1,927	(83.9)	1,750	(87.8)	1,385	(87.8)	535	(90.2)
Kingdom of Navarre:										
Pamplona	64		77		52		40		10	
Total	64	(2.7)	77	(3.4)	52	(2.6)	40	(2.5)	10	(1.7)
Basque Provinces:										
Alava	—		—		—		—		—	
Victoria	20		—		2		—		—	
Total	20	(0.8)	—		2	(0.1)	—		—	

CROWNS OF ARAGON

	1550	(%)	1610	(%)	1650	(%)	1690	(%)	1750	(%)
Aragón:										
Albarracin	—		13		1		1		—	
Barbastro	—		—		—		—		—	
Calatayud	—		1		—		—		—	
Huesca	1		3		1		—		—	
Jaca	—		1		1		—		—	
Tarazona	53		101		22		10		4	
Teruel	—		4		5		1		—	
Zaragoza	—		—		—		—		—	
Total	54	(2.3)	123	(5.4)	30	(1.5)	12	(0.8)	4	(0.7)
Catalonia:										
Barcelona	3		1		2		2		—	
Gerona	—		3		1		1		—	
Lérida	4		7		—		—		—	
Mallorca	—		—		2		—		1	
Tarragona	—		1		—		1		—	
Tortosa	1		—		1		2		1	
Urgel	—		12		1		3		—	
Vich	—		3		—		—		—	
Total	8	(0.3)	27	(1.2)	7	(0.4)	9	(0.6)	2	(0.3)
Valencia:										
Orihuela	1		5		—		—		1	
Segorbe	—		1		—		1		1	
Solsona	—		—		—		—		—	
Valencia	6		12		3		2		1	
Total	7	(0.3)	18	(0.8)	3	(0.2)	3	(0.2)	3	(0.5)
Total Crowns of Aragón	69	(2.9)	168	(7.3)	40	(2)	24	(1.5)	9	(1.5)

Table III (continued)

	1550	(%)	1610	(%)	1650	(%)	1690	(%)	1750	(%)
Miscellaneous:										
Canary Islands	1		—		—		1		—	
Ceuta	—		—		1		—		—	
New World	1		—		—		3		—	
Nulius diocese	38		94		81		34		16	
Foreign:										
France	—		1		—		—		—	
Italy	1		3		—		—		—	
Portugal	3		18		1		1		—	
Bayonne	2		—		—		—		1	
Perpignon	—		—		1		—		—	
Total miscellaneous	46	(1.9)	116	(5.1)	85	(4.3)	39	(2.5)	17	(2.9)
Unknown	63	(2.6)	9	(0.4)	65	(3.3)	89	(5.6)	22	(3.7)
GRAND TOTAL	2.398		2,297		1,994		1.577		593	

Source: AHN: Univs., Libros 431 ff.

Table IV.   University of Salamanca: Faculty of Canon Law, Students by Diocese

	1570	(%)	1620	(%)	1650	(%)	1690	(%)
CROWN OF CASTILE								
Andalucia:								
Córdoba	51		29		30		7	
Granada	9		15		9		5	
Guadix	1		—		1		—	
Jaen	34		25		23		2	
Malaga	26		26		8		1	
Seville	103		71		35		19	
Total	224	(11.8)	156	(5.3)	106	(7.1)	34	(4.7)
Asturias								
Oviedo	35		5		41		26	
Total	35	(1.8)	5	(0.2)	41	(2.7)	26	(3.6)
Castile (New)								
Cuenca	74		80		57		7	
Sigüenza	18		29		9		1	
Toledo	192		225		182		72	
Total	284	(5)	334	(11.3)	248	(16.5)	80	(11.3)
Castile (Old)								
Avila	76		100		34		8	
Burgos	127		227		158		68	
Calahorra	83		225		86		39	
Logroño	1		2		—		—	
Osma, Burgo de	32		63		17		1	
Palencia	126		80		86		24	
Santo Domingo de la Calzada	—		—		2		—	

Table IV (continued)

	1570	(%)	1620	(%)	1650	(%)	1690	(%)
Segovia	31		60		19		5	
Valladolid	—		75		21		4	
Total	476	(25.2)	832	(28.2)	423	(28.1)	149	(20.7)
Extremadura:								
Badajoz	36		99		23		24	
Coria	45		78		40		51	
Plasencia	66		101		40		40	
Total	147	(7.7)	278	(9.4)	103	(6.9)	115	(16)
León:								
Astorga	34		54		52		19	
Ciudad Rodrigo	21		63		32		8	
León	55		65		26		13	
Salamanca	143		184		113		98	
Zamora	46		69		15		24	
Total	299	(15.8)	435	(14.7)	238	(15.3)	162	(22.5)
Galicia:								
Lugo	3		27		6		4	
Mondoñedo	1		9		7		2	
Orense	21		69		45		9	
Santiago	16		22		16		5	
Tuy	11		43		21		5	
Total	52	(2.7)	170	(5.6)	95	(6.3)	25	(3.5)
Murcia:								
Albacete	—		—		—		—	
Almeria	5		—		—		—	
Cartagena	26		34		14		2	
Murcia	—		—		2		2	
Total	31	(1.6)	34	(1.2)	16	(1.1)	7	(1)
Total Crown of Castile	1,548	(81.8)	2,244	(76)	1,270	(84.5)	598	(83.2)
Kingdom of Navarre:								
Pamplona	53		77		44		23	
Total	53	(2.8)	77	(2.6)	44	(2.9)	23	(3.2)
Basque Provinces:								
Alava	—		—		—		—	
Victoria	—		—		—		—	
Total	—		—		—		—	
CROWNS OF ARAGON								
Aragón:								
Albarracín	—		2		2		—	
Barbastro	—		—		1		—	
Calatayud	—		—		—		—	
Huesca	—		—		—		—	
Jaca	—		—		—		—	
Tarazona	25		34		8		4	
Teruel	—		2		4		2	

Table IV (continued)

	1570	(%)	1620	(%)	1650	(%)	1690	(%)
Zaragoza	13		11		7		—	
Total	38	(2)	49	(1.7)	22	(1.5)	6	(0.9)
Catalonia:								
Barcelona	3		1		3		—	
Gerona	1		—		—		—	
Lérida	1		1		1		—	
Mallorca	—		—		—		—	
Tarragona	—		1		—		—	
Tortosa	1		5		3		—	
Urgel	—		1		—		2	
Vich	—		—		—		—	
Total	6	(0.3)	9	(0.3)	7	(0.5)	2	(0.3)
Valencia:								
Alicante	—		—		1		—	
Orihuela	1		7		1		1	
Segorbe	1		1		—		—	
Solsona	—		—		—		—	
Valencia	2		12		7		1	
Total	4	(0 .1)	20	(0.1)	9	(0.6)	2	(0.3)
Total Crowns of Aragón	48	(2.5)	78	(2.6)	38	(2.5)	10	(1.4)
Miscellaneous:								
Canary Islands	3		15		12		3	
Ceuta	4		—		—		—	
New World	—		17		3		—	
Nullius diocese	64		150		100		56	
Foreign:								
France	—		—		—		—	
Ireland	—		—		2		—	
Italy	—		3		1		1	
Sardinia	—		1		2		—	
Germany	—		—		1		—	
Madeira	—		2		—		—	
Perpignon	—		—		1		—	
Portugal	172		317		7		28	
Total miscellaneous	243	(12.8)	505	(17.1)	129	(8.6)	88	(12.2)
GRAND TOTAL	1,892		2,953		1,503		719	

Source: AUS: Libros de Matrículas.

Table V.   University of Valladolid: Students by Diocese

	1570	(%)	1620	(%)	1671	(%)	1700	(%)
CROWN OF CASTILE								
Andalucia:								
Córdoba	1		1		—		—	

Table V (continued)

	1570	(%)	1620	(%)	1671	(%)	1700	(%)
Granada	1		1		—		—	
Guadix	—		—		—		—	
Jaen	1		1		—		—	
Malaga	—		—		—		—	
Seville	4		2		1		2	
Total	7	(1)	5	(0.3)	1	(0.08)	2	(0.4)
Asturias								
Oviedo	6		25		18		18	
Total	6	(0.9)	25	(1.5)	18	(1.5)	18	(3.3)
Castile (New)								
Cuenca	4		6		—		4	
Sigüenza	4		24		3		10	
Toledo	12		23		11		9	
Total	20	(3)	53	(3.1)	14	(1.2)	23	(4.2)
Castile (Old)								
Avila	3		6		6		8	
Burgos	106		560		608		169	
Calahorra	23		151		87		44	
Logroño	—		1		1		—	
Osma, Burgo de	20		58		27		23	
Palencia	348		282		128		96	
Santo Domingo								
de la Calzada	—		—		—		1	
Segovia	5		49		23		7	
Valladolid	—		248		135		80	
Total	505	(74.6)	1,355	(78.7)	1,015	(85.2)	428	(78.4)
Extremadura:								
Badajoz	2		2		—		—	
Coria	3		2		1		—	
Plasencia	3		6		—		—	
Total	8	(1.2)	10	(0.6)	1	(0.08)	—	
León:								
Astorga	10		47		32		7	
Ciudad Rodrigo	2		—		—		—	
León	39		119		39		31	
Salamanca	14		1		1		1	
Zamora	14		14		14		7	
Total	79	(11.7)	181	(10.5)	86	(7.2)	46	(8.4)
Galicia:								
Lugo	1		4		7		1	
Mondoñedo	—		3		—		—	
Orense	1		2		1		1	
Santiago	5		3		3		3	
Tuy	—		4		2		3	
Total	7	(1)	16	(0.9)	13	(1.1)	8	(1.5)
Murcia:								
Albacete	—		—		—		—	
Almeria	—		—		—		—	

Table V (continued)

	1570	(%)	1620	(%)	1671	(%)	1700	(%)
Cartagena	1		3		—		—	
Murcia	1		—		—		1	
Total	2	(0.3)	3	(0.2)	—		1	(0.2)
Total Crown of Castile	634	(93.6)	1,648	(95.6)	1,148	(96.4)	526	(96.3)
Kingdom of Navarre:								
Pamplona	14		19		16		4	
Total	14	(2.1)	19	(1.1)	16	(1.3)	4	(0.7)
Basque Provinces:								
Alava	—		—		—		—	
Victoria	—		—		—		—	
Total	—		—		—		—	
CROWNS OF ARAGON								
Aragón:								
Albarracín	—		—		—		—	
Barbastro	—		—		—		—	
Calatayud	—		—		--		—	
Huesca	—		—		—		—	
Jaca	1		1		—		—	
Tarazona	—		8		6		—	
Teruel	—		—		—			
Zaragoza	1		—		1		—	
Total	2	(0.3)	9	(0.5)	7	(0.6)	—	
Catalonia:								
Barcelona	—		—		—		—	
Gerona	—		1		—		—	
Lérida	—		—		—		—	
Mallorca	—		—		—		—	
Tarragona	—		—		—		—	
Tortosa	—		—		—		—	
Urgel	—		—		—		—	
Vich	—		—		—		—	
Total	—		1	(0.05)	—		—	
Valencia								
Orihuela	—		1		—		—	
Segorbe	—		—		—		—	
Solsona	—		—		—		—	
Valencia	—		3		—		—	
Total	—		4	(0.2)	—		—	
Total Crowns of Aragón	2	(0.3)	14	(0.8)	7	(0.6)	—	
Miscellaneous:								
Canary Islands	—		—		—		—	
Ceuta	—		—		—		—	
New World	3		—		—		—	
Nullius diocese	5		16		19		13	

Table V (continued)

	1570	(%)	1620	(%)	1671	(%)	1700	(%)
Foreign:								
France	—		—		—		—	
Portugal	5		6		—		1	
Malta	1		—		—		—	
Total	14	(2.1)	22	(1.3)	19	(1.6)	14	(2.6)
Unknown	13	(1.9)	18	(1)	1	(0.08)	2	(0.4)
GRAND TOTAL	677		1,721		1,191		546	

Source: AUV: Libros 32 ff.

Table VI. University of Salamanca: Matriculations (Quinquennial Averages)

Academic years	Students	Academic years	Students
1550–55	5,982.0	1700–05	1,894.8
1555–60	4,511.6	1705–10	1,429.4
1560–65	4,998.8	1710–15	1,420.6
1565–70	5,958.3	1715–20	1,692.8
1570–75	5,917.6	1720–25	1,698.4
1575–80	5,607.0	1725–30	1,809.0
1580–85	5,976.5	1730–35	2,041.6
1585–90	6,633.3	1735–40	2,038.0
1590–95	6,359.0	1740–45	2,336.0
1595–00	4,740.8	1745–50	2,350.0
1600–05	5,131.0	1750–55	2,054.8
1605–10	4,711.0	1755–60	2,139.0
1610–15	5,006.0	1760–65	2,035.4
1615–20	5,314.6	1765–70	2,112.0
1620–25	5,918.6	1770–75	1,609.2
1625–30	5,534.4	1775–80	1,499.4
1630–35	4,428.0	1780–85	1,385.2
1635–40	4,484.2	1785–90	1,599.4
1640–45	3,748.4	1790–95	1,533.0
1645–50	3,009.6	1795–00	1,452.6
1650–55	2,949.4	1800–05	1,149.4
1655–60	3,133.4	1805–10	717.6
1660–65	2,709.6	1810–15	82.4
1665–70	2,383.4	1815–20	420.8
1670–75	2,747.4	1820–25	517.0
1675–80	2,659.8	1825–30	611.2
1680–85	2,029.0	1830–35	602.2
1685–90	2,001.2	1835–40	654.2
1690–95	2,201.0	1840–45	567.2
1695–00	2,150.4		

Source: AUS., libros 268–359 and A. Vidal y Diaz, Memoria Histórica de la Universidad de Salamanca (Salamanca, 1869), appendix II.

Table VII. University of Granada: Matriculations (Quinquennial Averages)

Academic years	Students	Academic years	Students
1635–40	222.6	1745–50	35.6
1640–45	240.6	1750–55	1.0
1645–50	238.8	1755–60	6.4
1650–55	175.8	1760–65	34.8
1655–60	182.2	1765–70	37.4
1660–65	168.4	1770–75	204.6
1665–70	160.4	1775–80	373.8
1670–75	160.8	1780–85	468.2
1675–80	126.2	1785–90	555.6
1680–85	110.2	1790–95	613.6
1685–90	97.8	1795–00	684.4
1690–95	156.0	1800–05	703.6
1695–00	128.4	1805–10	605.0
1700–05	84.0	1810–15	220.6
1705–10	65.4	1815–20	716.4
1710–15	42.6	1820–25	947.8
1715–20	66.6	1825–30	1,157.0
1720–25	159.2	1830–35	1,408.0
1725–30	119.2	1835–40	1,478.0
1730–35	89.0	1840–45	1,032.0
1735–40	64.0	1845–50	777.0
1740–45	118.0	1850–55	982.0

Source: Francisco Montells y Nadal, *Historia del Origen y Fundación de la Universidad de Granada* (Granada, 1870), pp. 799–806.

Table VIII.   University of Alcalá de Henares: Matriculations by Faculty

Year	1550	1560	1570	1580	1590	1600	1610	1620	1630	1640	1650	1660	1670	1680	1690	1700
Grammar	1,493	1,250	1,085	634	323	351	199	200	175	217	94	65	58	54	53	77
Arts	594	931	1,202	1,417	1,346	1,145	1,206	1,390	776	1,032	862	828	874	662	714	571
Canon Law	221	325	457	497	599	587	650	1,223	636	1,140	799	760	505	452	565	465
Medicine	67	126	86	121	148	97	117	165	133	88	88	119	118	72	81	61
Theology	157	364	354	506	627	537	450	637	367	348	202	316	299	147	143	139
Colegio Mayor	35	34	33	33	23	19	18	17	18	30	28	43	45	45	41	38
Total	2,567	3,030	3,217	3,208	3,066	2,736	2,640	3,632	2,125	2,855	2,083	2,131	1,899	1,432	1,597	1,351

Year	1710	1720	1730	1740	1750	1760	1770	1780	1790	1800	1810	1820	1830
Grammar	7	12	33	44	48	50	88	—	—	—	—	20	—
Arts	353	641	425	392	358	364	470	197	195	169	—	183	105
Canon Law	228	359	170	106	132	148	198	51	61	77	—	12	19
Civil Law	—	—	—	—	—	—	—	125	110	149	—	198	251
Medicine	52	54	28	23	12	23	9	12	4	—	—	3	—
Theology	78	95	115	50	71	67	106	107	140	147	—	26	38
History	—	—	—	—	—	—	—	27	—	—	—	—	—
Colegio Mayor	32	34	38	42	34	31	—	—	—	—	—	—	—
Other colleges	121	61	156	196	236	214	—	—	—	—	—	—	—
Total	864	1,244	932	809	843	847	783	519	492	542	46	451*	413

*Includes 34 students labeled "protestors."
Source: AHN: Univs. Libros 431 ff.

Table IX.   University of Salamanca: Matriculations by Faculty

Year	1551	1555	1560	1565	1571	1575	1581	1585	1592	1595	1599	1605	1610	1615	1620	1625
Grammar	—	1,668	—	1,755	1,320	—	816	893	547	448	—	331	401	227	265	279
Arts	596	706	533	583	701	570	728	924	977	693	448	627	495	496	522	408
Canon Law	1,436	1,063	1,026	1,324	2,118	2,147	2,277	3,137	2,939	2,776	2,178	2,386	2,437	2,682	3,043	3,128
Civil Law	621	636	518	637	623	556	537	643	686	768	289	314	282	258	1,244	1,282
Medicine	129	157	148	138	115	110	144	194	234	208	161	164	155	178	163	177
Theology	318	420	391	440	565	519	470	571	626	—	294	343	278	293	210	211
Greek & Rhetoric	—	—	—	—	—	—	—	—	—	—	—	—	—	—	—	—
Hebrew	—	48	18	8	—	—	—	—	—	—	—	—	—	—	—	—
Surgery	—	—	—	—	—	—	—	—	—	—	—	—	—	9	10	—
Mathematics	—	1	—	—	—	—	—	—	—	—	8	7	—	22	3	20

Year	1630	1635	1640	1645	1650	1655	1660	1665	1670	1675	1680	1685	1690	1695	1700
Grammar	—	359	391	288	142	173	166	208	110	247	158	70	102	115	53
Arts	233	329	257	190	192	214	162	207	257	264	173	126	166	231	188
Canon Law	2,209	2,407	2,099	1,595	1,459	1,652	1,259	952	940	1,246	745	596	724	581	444
Civil Law	734	733	618	455	138	143	139	265	121	174	141	83	107	121	103
Medicine	143	108	75	38	42	49	61	70	60	88	59	39	57	52	50
Theology	156	107	137	95	89	84	89	70	66	80	34	32	45	32	27
Surgery	—	20	12	3	5	2	1	—	2	1	1	—	—	—	—

Year	1705	1710	1715	1720	1725	1730	1735	1740	1745	1750	1755	1760	1765	1770	1775	1780
Grammar	69	70	83	105	78	168	151	199	228	100	43	69	30	316	32	24
Arts	105	88	90	207	225	239	142	262	451	358	322	331	241	532	398	328
Canon Law	245	130	167	194	184	151	93	131	224	147	126	159	142	114	81	96
Civil Law	111	72	104	111	120	132	137	150	187	155	163	225	223	199	177	193
Medicine	52	12	33	42	49	33	24	23	46	57	46	54	46	31	15	24
Theology	36	8	16	17	11	7	18	15	19	9	14	12	22	27	255	196
Greek & Rhetoric	—	—	—	—	—	—	—	—	—	—	—	—	—	—	16	41
Surgery	1	2	1	—	1	1	1	—	3	—	3	14	4	2	13	8
Mathematics	—	—	—	—	—	—	—	—	—	—	—	—	2	1	16	16

Year	1785	1790	1795	1800	1805	1810	1815	1820	1825	1830	1835	1840	1850	1855	1860
Grammar	23	7	8	30	58	—	18	23	59	180	275	111	—	193	—
Arts	351	230	125	163	115	9	55	34	35	33	9	12	—	72	—
Canon Law	110	116	169	149	95	1	13	—	—	—	—	—	—	—	—
Civil Law	175	188	238	196	126	5	16	146	138	158	247	197	136?	149	126
Medicine	13	19	12	—	46	29	14	17	36	24	32	157	—	32	—
Theology	246	307	237	172	128	3	8	22	44	34	105	53	—	—	33
Greek & Rhetoric	22	13	5	2	6	—	—	—	—	—	—	—	—	—	—
Hebrew	—	—	—	1	—	—	—	—	—	—	2	—	—	—	—
Surgery	10	8	—	—	—	—	—	—	—	—	—	—	—	11	—
Mathematics	—	—	71	4	1	1	—	300	—	—	21	8	—	—	—
Music	—	2	2	2	4	4	4	4	8	21	15	10	7	14	4
Algebra	6	—	9	14	6	—	—	—	—	—	—	—	—	—	2
Experimental Physics	12	—	95	66	15	—	—	—	—	—	—	—	—	—	1
Moral Philosophy	—	—	—	—	—	—	—	—	3	—	—	—	—	—	—
Political Economy	—	—	—	—	2	2	—	11	—	—	—	—	—	—	—
Humanities	—	—	—	—	—	—	—	—	—	—	—	—	—	—	—
Greek	—	—	—	—	—	—	—	—	—	—	41	25	—	—	—
Astonomy	—	—	—	—	—	—	—	—	—	—	2	11	—	—	—
Botany	—	—	—	—	—	—	—	—	—	—	—	68	—	—	—

Year	1865	1870	1880	1885	1890	1900
Arts	—	134	186	149	156	68
Civil Law	133	672	216	164	617	129
Medicine	—	603	129	132	206	—
Theology	34	—	118	138	82	—
Sciences	—	82	—	3	3	—
Notary	—	30	—	—	—	—

Source: AUS Libros 268–539.

Table X. University of Valladolid: Matriculations by Faculty

Year	1567	1570	1575	1576	1588	1616	1620	1625	1640	1645	1650	1655	1660	1665	1670	1675	1680
Grammar	231	138	—	220	130	61	55	34	7	18	8	11	—	73	—	—	—
Arts	91	98	129	111	158	264	215	181	167	160	236	184	269	302	237	225	122
Canon Law	273	373	403	558	755	1,005	1,335	1,236	1,157	930	847	981	725	801	796	758	474
Civil Law	—	—	161	245	113	140	164	126	204	137	101	135	100	129	118	95	105
Medicine	11	22	14	—	35	28	43	38	19	30	22	42	34	43	64	32	26
Theology	90	112	119	123	114	112	57	38	31	19	36	31	43	53	38	56	24
Colleges	—	—	—	—	—	—	—	—	172	232	242	225	—	241	—	—	—

Year	1685	1690	1695	1700	1705	1710	1715	1720	1725	1730	1735	1740	1745	1750	1755	1760	1765
Arts	141	210	366	152	481	202	64	105	71	262	60	392	56	87	99	55	55
Canon Law	405	540	462	307	328	142	110	123	140	171	91	106	109	140	145	131	38
Civil Law	71	133	87	76	78	70	120	136	93	95	55	—	35	56	98	76	60
Medicine	33	28	22	29	32	26	32	33	32	28	10	23	—	12	—	23	—
Theology	37	26	43	38	49	12	26	25	26	17	19	50	56	71	67	67	—
Colleges	254	—	264	—	—	153	—	95	—	194	162	238	—	251	289	245	—

Year	1770	1775	1780	1785	1790	1795	1800	1805	1810	1815	1820	1825	1835	1840	1845	1850	1855	1860
Arts	285	529	456	410	397	526	358	319	75	148	336	453	593	336	—	67	115	55
Canon Law	22	217	219	230	276	313	343	207	14	19	44	59	59	20	—	404	394	—
Civil Law	121	318	357	286	310	344	395	292	54	87	277	446	802	566	—	*	*	365
Medicine	—	20	28	19	23	29	33	26	22	10	8	42	96	165	—	—	—	155
Theology	—	86	312	312	326	378	301	206	19	24	30	43	223	56	—	88	—	—
Sciences	—	—	—	—	—	—	—	—	—	—	—	—	—	—	—	—	19	—
Notary	—	—	—	—	—	—	—	—	—	—	—	—	—	—	134	—	132	—
Medical Clinic	—	—	—	—	—	—	—	—	—	—	—	—	—	70	—	—	—	17

*1850 and 1855 Canon and Civil Law enrollments are combined.
Source: AUV Libros 32–86.

Table XI. University of Baeza: Matriculations by Faculty

Year	1560	1565	1570	1575	1580	1585	1590	1595	1600	1605	1610	1615	1620	1625	1630	1635
Grammar	214	239	250	304	297	331	326	342	205	99	165	193	195	132	126	153
Arts	84	118	99	149	112	97	130	154	144	101	90	104	105	55	60	67
Theology	33	51	47	73	93	82	52	75	55	51	39	52	32	28	33	26
Total	331	408	396	526	502	510	508	571	404	251	294	349	332	215	219	246

Year	1640	1645	1650	1655	1660	1665	1670	1675	1680	1685	1690	1695	1700	1705	1710	1715
Grammar	166	81	116	100	128	108	209	76	85	46	59	21	19	27	99	57
Arts	102	90	68	59	67	98	144	110	85	45	67	58	66	93	58	54
Theology	26	33	33	24	25	39	52	41	28	29	25	39	37	39	36	29
Canon Law	—	—	—	—	—	—	—	—	—	6	20	21	7	10	4	—
Total	294	204	217	183	220	245	405	227	198	126	171	139	129	169	197	140

Year	1720	1725	1730	1735	1740	1745	1750	1755	1760	1765	1770	1775	1780	1785	1790	1795
Grammar	73	37	73	55	71	64	85	86	87	63	40	71	75	91	113	128
Arts	73	82	75	92	64	78	59	106	95	72	86	49	80	87	87	—
Theology	13	35	43	39	34	23	40	39	36	33	47	31	49	42	73	84
History	—	—	—	—	—	—	—	—	—	—	—	—	—	—	5	—
Total	159	154	191	186	169	165	184	231	218	168	173	151	204	220	228	212

Year	1800	1805	1810	1816	1820
Grammar	90	72	—	112	102
Total	90	72	—	112	102

Source: Archivo del Instituto de Enseñanza Secondaria, Baeza: Libros de Matrículas.

Table XII.   University of Osuna: Matriculations by Faculty

Year	1598	1599	1600	1605	1611	1615	1625	1630	1690	1695	1700	1705	1710	1715	1720	1725
Grammar	126	126	61	60	77	—	54	61	—	—	—	—	—	—	—	—
Arts	29	26	30	13	28	10	11	13	21	11	14	7	3	11	22	9
Canon Law	128	127	109	73	128	120	103	82	29	48	16	17	15	13	43	21
Civil Law	8	9	7	2	3	—	1	—	—	—	—	—	—	1	—	—
Theology	23	25	16	19	5	6	23	4	—	1	—	1	—	—	—	—
Medicine	12	19	10	16	21	14	21	17	17	18	14	12	13	17	10	18
Miscellaneous	—	—	—	—	—	—	27	—	—	—	—	—	—	—	—	—
Total	326	332	233	183	262	150	240	177	67	78	44	37	31	42	75	48

Year	1730	1735	1740	1745	1770	1775	1780	1785	1790	1795	1800	1805	1810
Arts	16	18	19	33	19	41	30	25	43	71	51	58	22
Canon Law	28	29	19	19	1	3	4	9	12	11	10	13	8
Civil Law	—	—	—	1	8	21	18	32	33	40	36	13	1
Theology	1	—	—	—	2	3	1	7	10	27	15	20	5
Medicine	29	33	23	19	7	17	18	28	38	31	—	36	22
Latin	—	—	—	—	3	8	26	23	64	84	104	136	26
Moral Philosophy	—	—	—	—	—	—	—	4	12	—	—	—	—
Latin, Rhetoric, Humane Letters	—	—	—	—	—	—	—	1	—	—	—	—	—
National Law	—	—	—	—	—	—	—	—	—	—	—	10	1
Total	74	80	61	72	40	93	197	129	212	264	216	286	85

Source: Archivo del Instituto de Enseñanza Secondaria, Osuna: Libros de Matrículas.

Table XIII. University of Santa Maria de Jesús (Seville): Matriculations by Faculty

Year	1546	1550	1566	1570	1575	1580	1590	1605	1610	1620	1630	1640	1650	1660	1670	1680
Arts	64	43	51	42	—	—	—	5	—	—	—	—	—	—	—	—
Canon Law	57	59	—	188	—	—	—	185	236	250	235	178	121	108	80	73
Civil Law	8	1	—	24	—	—	—	—	—	5	—	—	*	*	*	*
Theology	1	7	—	32	—	—	—	1	3	1	23	—	—	—	—	—
Medicine	2	5	—	16	—	—	—	24	33	24	34	26	17	19	34	35
Total	132	115	321†	302	407	303	244	215	272	280	292	204	138	127	114	108

Year	1690	1700	1710	1720	1730	1740	1750	1760	1770	1780	1790	1800	1810	1820	1830	1840
Arts	—	1	5	—	—	—	—	—	—	—	265	—	29	323	154*	254
Canon Law	163	88	73	201	133	—	122	122	140	47†	64	46	†	72	†	†
Civil Law	*	*	*	*	*	*	*	*	*	*	—	—	—	64	†	†
Theology	—	—	4	—	3	—	—	—	16	50	44	32	—	—	—	—
Medicine	19	26	38	22	58	35	47	64	74	41	67	†	22	57	92	279
Total	182	115	120	223	194	†	169	186	230	138†	440	†	†	516	†	†

*Canon and Civil Law enrollments are combined.
†Total incomplete.

Source: AUSA: 478–515.

Table XIV. University of Oñate: Matriculations by Faculty

Year	1640	1645	1650	1655	1660	1665	1670	1675	1680	1685	1690	1695	1700	1705
Total	102	113	73	86	57	37	22	36	13	15	8	3	2	*

Year	1710	1715	1720	1725	1730	1735	1740	1745	1750	1755	1760	1765	1770	1775
Canon & Civil Law	18	6	—	—	—	—	6	5	34	50	37	48	39	52
Theology	—	—	—	—	—	—	—	—	2	—	—	—	42	—
Arts	—	—	—	—	—	—	2	2	3	2	—	—	—	30
Total	*	*	*	*	*	*	8	7	39	52	37	48	81	82

Year	1780	1785	1790	1795	1800	1805	1810	1815	1820	1825	1830	1835	1840	1845
Canon & Civil Law	81	—	—	114	160	162	—	—	160	153	69	—	145?	—
Civil Law	—	—	—	—	—	—	—	21	—	—	—	—	—	—
Canon Law	—	—	—	—	—	—	—	2	—	—	—	—	—	—
Arts	38	49	52	38	52	57	—	51	148	127	?	—	—	84
Total	119	49	52	152	212	219	—	74	308	280	69	—	146?	84

*Total incomplete.

Source: AUV: Libros 313–25.

Table XV. University of Oviedo: Matriculations by Faculty

Year	1608	1633	1634	1635	1636	1638	1639	1640	1641	1642	1643	1644	1645	1646	1647	1648	1649	1650
Arts	57	66	98	53	—	15	146	76	103	75	64	89	—	110	46	82	169	—
Law	—	—	6	8	—	5	26	13	—	28	11	6	3	16	7	—	5	6
Canon Law	—	—	93	49	69	66	118	86	64	57	42	41	21	62	—	50	52	68
Theology	8	—	18	37	—	4	—	13	7	6	6	6	9	—	—	—	21	—
Total	65	66	215	138	69	90	290	188	177	166	123	142	33	188	53	132	247	74

Year	1651	1652	1553	1654	1743	1744	1745	1746	1747	1748	1749	1750	1751	1752	1753	1754	1755	1756
Arts	106	15	—	93	60	72	20	75	11	12	28	28	29	16	65	42	48	34
Law	16	15	—	6	2	10	8	9	4	6	5	6	12	9	10	14	11	3
Canon Law	74	64	52	59	—	—	—	—	—	—	—	—	—	—	—	—	—	—
Theology	32	—	16	15	—	—	—	—	—	—	—	—	—	—	—	—	—	—
Total	228	79	68	173	62	82	28	84	15	18	33	34	41	25	75	56	59	37

Year	1757	1758	1759	1760	1761	1762	1763	1764	1765	1766	1767	1768	1769	1770	1771	1772	1773	1774
Arts	92	27	36	89	105	37	51	11	20	71	77	135	197	106	171	174	167	172
Law	3	5	13	2	4	4	—	7	11	6	14	25	34	35	49	49	61	36
Canon Law	—	—	—	—	—	—	—	—	—	—	—	1	5	14	11	17	13	35
Theology	—	—	—	—	—	—	—	13	—	23	12	28	31	45	49	58	32	52
Total	95	32	49	91	109	41	51	31	31	100	103	189	267	200	280	298	273	295

Year	1775	1776	1777	1778	1779	1780	1781	1782	1783	1784	1785	1786	1787	1788	1789	1790	1791	1792
Arts	169	213	202	231	229	243	298	249	264	196	212	229	212	248	171	230	239	212
Law	38	56	68	77	98	105	77	84	89	99	100	93	87	107	98	99	91	86

Table XV (continued)

Year	1775	1776	1777	1778	1779	1780	1781	1782	1783	1784	1785	1786	1787	1788	1789	1790	1791	1792
Canon Law	36	32	47	51	61	68	83	90	73	72	75	74	83	84	90	93	97	107
Theology	49	62	118	79	94	99	102	120	111	102	121	128	155	129	121	132	130	157
Medicine	a	a	a	a	a	a	a	a	a	a	a	a	—	—	—	—	—	—
Total	292	363	435	438	482	515	560	543	537	469	508	524	537	568	480	554	557	562

Year	1793	1794	1795	1796	1797	1798	1799	1800	1801	1802	1803	1804	1805	1806	1807	1808	1812	1813
Arts	209	266	251	241	272	215	211	162	177	176	172	169	161	172	209	—	22	64
Law	109	149	111	121	135	110	128	133	125	122	159	140	148	155	111	—	3	8
Canon Law	96	111	101	108	102	122	108	116	145	130	131	140	139	147	105	—	1	4
Theology	163	182	165	183	201	180	165	184	174	155	107	88	71	82	87	—	2	4
Medicine	—	4	4	1	3	3	—	—	—	2	4	5	4	5	—	—	—	—
Total	577	712	632	634	713	630	612	595	621	585	573	542	523	451	512	0	28	80

Year	1814	1815	1816	1817	1818	1819	1820	1821	1822	1823	1824	1825	1826	1827	1828	1829	1830	1831
Arts	92	126	204	256	316	198	285	224	157	153	154	173	217	259	231	221	281	312
Law	6	24	46	89	116	165	136	132	52	263	176	171	187	187	147	183	80	137
Canon Law	5	4	11	42	61	69	59	59	9	79	20	29	38	46	40	28	31	15
Theology	7	12	15	18	38	46	26	20	10	13	56	62	88	119	118	124	65	79
Medicine	—	—	—	8	5	3	8	6	4	3	4	3	—	—	—	—	—	—
Total	110	166	276	413	536	481	514	441	232	511	410	438	530	611	536	556	457	543

Year	1832	1833	1834	1835	1836	1837	1838	1839	1840	1841	1842	1843	1844
Arts	334	392	366	290	182	154	124	158	141	144	—	—	—
Law	195	81	122	93	48	39	98	106	167	167	144	143	113
Canon Law	7	16	6	19	8	8	7	11	9	18	—	—	—
Theology	120	138	97	71	60	58	55	45	34	28	17	13	19
Philosophy & Letters	b	b	b	b	b	b	b	b	b	b	95	96	96
Total	656	627	531	473	298	259	284	320	351	357	256	252	228

Year	1845	1846	1847	1848	1849	1850	1851	1852	1853	1854	1855	1856	1857
Law	100	95	99	105	91	82	85	97	88	106	105	105	75
Theology	18	15	19	18	13	20	18	—	—	14	19	—	6
Philosophy & Letters	82	80	33	27	30	31	39	14	14	24	—	22	19
Notary	c	c	c	c	c	c	8	6	5	8	7	—	6
Total	200	190	151	150	134	133	150	117	107	138	131	127	106

[a] Medicine course began in 1787.
[b] Philosophy & Letters course began in 1842.
[c] Notary course began in 1851.

Source: Canella y Secades, Universidad de Oviedo, app. XIV.

appendix b
UNIVERSITY
MATRICULATION
BOOKS IN SPAIN

Much of this volume is based upon the statistical analysis of the information contained in the matriculation registers of Castile's universities. Available primarily in manuscript (see below), these registers list the name, town, and diocese of university students and, in a few instances, their ages as well. In addition, they indicate in which faculty each student was enrolled, sometimes by year of study. Furthermore, by the simple addition of the number of students in each faculty, it is possible to determine the total student population of each university at any one time.

The information contained in these registers, however, has many flaws. For example, it is impossible to determine whether the town listed alongside each student's name was his birthplace or merely the community in which he was currently residing. Advanced students in many cases appear to have listed the university town itself as their place of origin, and others may have done so as well, but it would be difficult, if not impossible, to know how many students did this. Consequently, one is forced to accept the geographical information provided in the matriculation registers at face value, while recognizing its possible distortions.

There are similar difficulties in dealing with the ages listed for students in the matriculation registers. The students may have lied about their age, but there is no way of checking this except by tracing each student in the baptismal registers of his home town: an exhausting effort, even on the basis of a small sample, and one which would be very difficult to complete. Another problem connected with the age of students is that of determining the average age at which they first matriculated. This calculation is complicated by the fact that every student's age was rounded off to whole numbers. This practice is understandable, but it does tend to distort slightly the mean age of each beginning class.

Still another problem in dealing with the matriculation registers involves that of determining the total student population of each university. There were students who failed to matriculate, matriculants who were never students, and other students who matriculated twice (see pp. 166–67).

Moreover, in one year university authorities may have made certain that every student matriculated, while in others they may have been more lax. This would cause figures for university matriculations to fluctuate, even though the actual student population may have remained steady. There is no way of knowing, however, whether such inconsistencies ever took place or the extent to which the matriculation books are distorted or incorrect. One is obliged, therefore, to accept these registers as they are, albeit, of course, with caution.

Despite these problems, historians of Spain are fortunate in that so many matriculation registers have survived. Those employed in this study are listed below.

University	Archive	Years
Alcalá de Henares	AHN: Univs., libs. 431 ff.	c. 1550–1834[a]
Avila	Convento de Santo Tomás (Avila)	17th & 18th centuries
Beaza	Instituto de Enseñanza Secondaria (Baeza)	c. 1560—c. 1820
Granada	AUG	only fragments, 17th & 18th centuries
Irache	AGN: Instrucción Publica	17th & 18th centuries
Oñate	AUV: libs. 313–25	1640–1845
Osuna	Instituto de Enseñanza Secondaria (Osuna)	1598–1810
Salamanca	AUS: libs. 268–539	1546–1835[b]
Santiago de Compostela	AUSC: leg. 65; libs. A 227 ff.	c. 1650—19th century
Seville	AUSA: libs. 478–515	1546–1840
Sigüenza	AHN: Univs. libs. 1283–87 f.	fragments: 17th & 18th centuries
Toledo	AHP. Toledo	fragments; 18th & early 19th century
Valladolid	AUV: libs. 32–86	1567–1865

[a]In that year, Alcalá became the Universidad Central de Madrid. Subsequent matriculation registers are stored in the archive of that university located in the Calle de San Bernardo, Madrid.

[b]Subsequent matriculation registers for Salamanca are in the archive of the university rectory.

Note: The matriculation registers of the University of Oviedo were destroyed by aerial bombing during the Spanish Civil War, but they were previously summarized in F. Canella y Secades, *Historia de la Universidad de Oviedo* (Oviedo, 1903), app. XIV. Montells y Nadal, *Universidad de Granada*, vol. II, has done the same for this university's registers, many of which were destroyed in an archival fire.

BIBLIOGRAPHICAL ESSAY

I. MANUSCRIPTS

1. Municipal and Provincial Archives

I explored these collections with an eye toward materials concerning primary and secondary schools. These documents, where they exist, are generally found in the section *Instrucción Pública* in those archives which are catalogued, and even then these listings are frequently incomplete. The only general guide to these local collections is L. Sanchéz Belda, *Bibliografía de archivos españoles y de archivística* (Madrid, 1963). The local archives which I found to be particularly helpful for this study were those in Madrid, Córdoba, Cuenca, Granada, Toledo, and Seville.

My intentions were the same when I visited a number of provincial archives. These collections are located in the capital of every Spanish province. In some cases they are housed along with the municipal archives but contain materials from towns and villages over which the provincial capital had jurisdiction. In recent years modernization of the storage facilities for these archives have begun—the archives in Toledo, for example, are superbly housed—and card catalogues are being brought up to date, but much work remains to be done. Like Spain's municipal archives, these provincial collections remain largely uncharted and unknown, but in addition to local administrative, economic, and legal documents, they frequently contain long series of local *padrones* or tax lists, superb source material for the social and demographic history of Spain.

2. Archives of Churches and Cathedrals

I looked into a number of parish archives in the hope of finding registers of baptisms and marriages which had been signed or rubricked by the interested parties. Unfortunately, in most of Spain, registers of this nature are signed only by the prist; therefore, the search was essentially fruitless. One should remember, however, that unlike France, where registers of vital statistics have been moved into the *Archives Départmentales*, parish churches in Spain hold onto their own, a situation which makes access to these documents difficult, since many priests are not accustomed to outside researchers.

As for the archives of Spain's cathedrals, I explored a number of these in order to obtain information regarding the educational backgrounds of the upper clergy. Such material is not always available, but most cathedrals keep biographical records (sometimes limited to proofs of Christian lineage or patents of appointment) of their chapter members. Access to these papers, however, is sometimes difficult, hours are sporadic and investigators are advised to arrange appointments with the cathedral archivist in advance, particularly in summer when they are often away. With a few notable exceptions, Granada and Salamanca for instance, published catalogues of these collections are few.

3. University Archives

These collections are much more diverse than their name implies, since they contain not only university records but also manuscripts and rare books on a wide range of subjects from the collections of individual professors, colleges, etc. The *archivo* and *biblioteca* of the University of Salamanca and the Biblioteca Santa Cruz (Valladolid) are especially rich in this regard. Both are well-catalogued.

As for documentation concerning the universities themselves, the best collection is that for the old University of Alcalá de Henares, now housed in the Archivo Histórico Nacional: Sección de Universidades, which also contains records of the University of Sigüenza, suppressed in 1807. This material has been catalogued in C. Gutiérrrez, *La Sección de Universidades del Archivo Histórico Nacional* (Madrid, 1952). There are additional materials for Alcalá de Henares, including some important registers dating from the early sixteenth century, in the Archivo de la Universidad Central de Madrid. This archive, poorly catalogued and maintained, also contains matriculation and graduation registers for the University of Madrid in the nineteenth century as well as papers concerning Madrid's Seminario de Nobles and numerous dossiers dealing with secondary education in nineteenth-century Spain.

The University of Salamanca's archives, housed in that university's library, are virtually complete after the mid-sixteenth century. Graduation and matriculation registers are plentiful, and the ancient *Libros de Claustros* which record the correspondence and deliberations of the university council exist in an almost unbroken series, extracts from which have been published in volume I of Esperabé Artega, *Universidad de Salamanca*. Papers for this university's colleges are also in this collection, although a number of the old religious colleges still in existence, San Esteban, for example, maintain archives of their own. Records for the University of Salamanca in the nineteenth century can be found in the archives of the university rectory, but this little collection suffers from neglect and researchers may be turned away. Anyone interested in working in the university archives of Salamanca is advised to contact P. don Florencio Marcos Rodríguez, *bibliotecario* of the university and archivist of Salamanca's cathedral.

The archives of the other universities which survived the suppression of 1807 are generally housed in the university library and are readily accessible. Those in Santiago de Compostela and Seville are in good order and fairly complete. On the other hand, the University of Granada's archives were largely destroyed by fire and Oviedo's by Civil War bombs, but many manuscripts survive in both. In better shape are the University of Valladolid's archives, currently stored along with the Archivo Provincial in the Facultad de Filosofía y Letras of the university. Its graduation and matriculation registers and its *Libros de Claustros* are complete after the later sixteenth century, though materials regarding its instructors are few. The archives also contain documents proceeding from the old University of Oñate. The Biblioteca Santa Cruz contains records of the colegio mayor which gave it both its building and its name.

Records for the universities suppressed in 1807 are harder to find and to use. Toledo's papers have all but disappeared, except for a few *Libros de Claustros* and *de Matrículas* housed in that city's Archivo Provincial. What is left of Ávila's archives belong to the Convento de Santo Tomás (Ávila) which was once the core of this university. There are no catalogues, and the monastery is not accustomed to researchers. Equally difficult to work with are the archives of the universities of Baeza and Osuna, now housed in the *Institutos de Enseñanza Secundaria* into which the universities' buildings were transformed. Neither has a catalogue and both collections—stuffed into bookshelves and thrown about on the floor—require both muscle and patience on the researcher's part. Oñate's old Colegio de Sancti-Spiritus (at present a secondary school) keeps the small part of that university's archives which was not sent to Valladolid. Don Ignacio Zumalde, author of the *Historia de Oñate*, is the local resident to contact for information concerning this collection. The archives of the University of Burgo de Osma are currently housed in the seminary of that city. It has many old manuscripts, but few which relate to the university. Finally, what remains of the University of Irache's archives are part of the Archivo del Reino de Navarra, while papers for the University of Santo Tomás (Seville) have apparently been lost.

Outside the Crown of Castile, records for the universities of Gandía, Orihuela, and Valencia can be found in the library of the University of Valencia, the Archivo Municipal de Valencia, and the Archivo del Reino de Valencia. The latter also contains an important collection of papers concerning the Jesuit colleges of that kingdom. Barcelona's university archives (part of the university library), closed the two summers I visited there on account of *obras* (building repairs), supposedly have records of its own past as well as others for the University of Cervera and the Catalan universities which were suppressed in 1714 by order of Philip V. The

University of Huesca's surviving registers belong to that city's municipal archives.

Ajo, *Historia de las Universidades*, vol. VII, contains a listing of manuscript materials, both in Spain and abroad, which refer to these institutions. This listing, however, is frequently inaccurate and misleading, since the author commonly notes documents which no longer exist.

4. Archives of the Audiencias, National Archives, and Other Collections

I initially explored these archives to gather information about letrado officials appointed by the crown. This search led to the *consultas de oficio*, which provide capsule biographies of candidates for royal offices, or, when these did not exist, salary records and patents of appointment which could at least provide the names of officials and their dates in office.

Among the *audiencias* of the crown, the Archivo de la Chancillería de Valladolid is the most important, although it lacks modern catalogues and other guides to research. Fundamentally, it is a large collection of lawsuits and other legal transactions proceeding from Castile in areas north of the River Tagus, but its contents, invaluable for the social history of northern Spain, are little known. Its *Libros de Acuerdos*, registers of the *chancillería's* official correspondence with the crown, make note of the judges and *abogados* who served in this tribunal.

The Archivo de la Chancillería de Granada, housed along with the Archivo Provincial, covers the same material as that in Valladolid but for regions south of the Tagus. The collection is well-catalogued and carefully preserved, but unfortunately its *Libros de Acuerdos* were lost during the Spanish Civil War.

The archives of the audiencias at Seville and La Coruña have also suffered serious losses. A fire early in the twentieth century cost Seville most of its materials dating from the Habsburg epoch, while La Coruña's archives, housed in that city's Casa de Cultura, lost a large part of its sixteenth-century papers when Sir Francis Drake raided the city in 1589.

The archives of the audiencia or *consejo* of Navarre forms part of Pamplona's Archivo General del Reino de Navarro. For information about its holdings, see J. J. Salcedo Izu, *El Consejo Real de Navarra en el Siglo XVI* (Pamplona, 1964). There is also an archive for the audiencia that was located in the Canary Islands; see L. de Rosa Olivera, "La Real Audiencia de Canarias: Notas Para Su Historia," *Anuario de Estudios Atlánticos* 3 (1957): 91–161.

For information concerning other letrado officials of the crown, one must turn to Spain's three great national archives. The Archivo General de Indias, for example, contains *consultas* of the Council of Indies which deal with the appointment of audiencia officials in the New World. *Legajos* 741,940, and 942 in the vast section *Indiferente General* are helpful in this respect for the reign of Philip II, and similar materials for other reigns must surely exist. The appointment records of Castile's other councils belong to the Archivo General de Simancas and the Archivo Histórico Nacional in Madrid.

In the former, the section Estado-España, leg. 11–17 contain *consultas de oficio* dating from the reign of Charles V, while the *Registro General de Sello* includes patents of appointment for royal offices. This vast section, however, is catalogued only for the early years of the reign of the Catholic kings and is, therefore, difficult to use unless one is searching for specific patents and happens to know names and approximate dates. The section *Cámara de Castilla* records *mercedes* and appointments to *capa y espada* offices, but not important letrado posts. On the other hand, the small series *Nóminas de Cortes* provides annual lists of letrado councillors and other court officials from the late fifteenth century until the 1570s, and the series *Quitaciones de Corte* contains individual salary records for councillors and court officials throughout the Habsburg period. Salary records can also be found in the *Contaduría Mayor de Cuentas, épocas* 1 and 2, while the series *Dirección General de Tesoro* is invaluable for the sale of offices in Castile.

With regard to materials concerning the history of schools, colleges, and universities, the archives at Simancas are relatively weak, although the section *Gracia y Justicia* does include some sources for the history of higher education, particularly for the eighteenth century. The series *Diversos de Castilla* has a few items relative to university history, while the *padrones* compiled at the order of Philip II provide an insight into the distribution of letrados, schoolmasters, etc. in late sixteenth-century Castile (see section *Expedientes de Hacienda*).

The essential guide to this archive as a whole is Angel de la Plaza Bores, *Archivo General de Simancas: Guía de Investigadores* (Valladolid, 1962). In addition, there are catalogues, some published, for the individual sections.

The Archivo Histórico Nacional, weighted toward the seventeenth and eighteenth centuries, takes up where Simancas leaves off. Within the vast section of *Consejos Suprimidos*, the series *Audiencias y Chancillerías* contains the consultas of the Cámara de Castilla for all tribunal appointments after 1588. Consultas for mercedes, church offices, and other positions can be found in the series *Consultas de Gracia* and *Consultas de Viernes*, while additional materials regarding clerical appointments in Castile are in the series *Libros de Iglesia*. There are no *consultas de oficio* for any of the major letrado councils during this period, although these might turn up once the *Consejos Suprimidos* section is properly arranged. Fortunately, the names of these councillors can be found in the series *Libros de Plazas*. This contains, in chronological order, patents of appointment for all *plazas de asiento* in Castile, except for places on the Council of the Military Orders and those of the inquisition. There exist, however, consultas de oficio for the former (cf. AHN: Cons., leg. 51708), while *Libros* 246–49, 356–61, 366–408, 426–30, 489–95, 572, and 1232 of the section *Inquisición* list those letrados who served with the Holy Office. Also of interest for the appointment of letrado officials is the series *Relaciones de Méritos* of the *Consejos Suprimidos* section. This contains the capsule biographies which candidates for office sent to the Cámara. A catalogue of the series, arranged in alphabetical order by name, is available.

As for sources relating to the history of education in Castile, the AHN is well-stocked. The series *Archivo Antiguo de Consejo* of the *Consejos Suprimidos* section, leg. 7138, contains important source material on university administration and reform, while the series *Enseñanza* and *Universidades de Castilla* are devoted to the educational history of Castile during the eighteenth and early nineteenth centuries. In addition, the section *Ordenes Militares* offers papers concerning the history of the Colleges of the Military Orders at Alcalá de Henares and Salamanca. And for Jesuit institutions, the section *Jesuitas* houses most of what is left of the archives of the individual colleges and seminaries (see A. Navarro Guglieri, *Documentos de la Compañía de Jesús en el Archivo Histórico Nacional* [Madrid, 1962], although there are other large holdings of Jesuit papers in the Real Academia de Historia (Madrid) and in semi-private Jesuit archives in Alcalá de Henares. The latter, a little known collection which is especially rich in materials concerning the history of the Society in nineteenth-century Spain, has a typed catalogue that is stored in the Biblioteca Razón y Fe (calle Pablo Aranda 3, Madrid).

Elsewhere in Madrid, the manuscript collection of the Biblioteca Nacional is very diffuse and largely uncatalogued. Only a few modern guides have been issued and the old registers and card indices are incomplete, misleading, and frequently incorrect. Important letters and memorials are often bound indiscriminately into manuscript volumes of little general interest, but those helpful in the preparation of this work are listed in the footnotes to the text. The Real Academia de la Historia also contains a large collection of manuscripts, but here as well, adequate catalogues are few. Aisde from various memorials listed in the footnotes, Ms. 9-22-3-4147, "Colegios de España y sus personas" was especially important, since it provided the names of a number of early sixteenth-century colegiales mayores which were not listed elsewhere. Another important archive in Madrid is the Instituto de Valencia de Don Juan. Largely unknown, its manuscripts, particularly abundant for the reign of Philip II, form one part of the famous Altamira Collection, of which the remainder lies in the British Museum and the Favre Collection of Geneva. This archive is difficult to work, since the hours are short (two hours daily), but its excellent catalogue, long inaccessible, is now being made available. I found *Envio* 90, which includes a report made by the Cardinal Espinosa on Castile's universities and their graduates, particularly helpful.

Two other important manuscript collections in Castile are located in the *bibliotecas* of El Escorial and the Palacio Real (Madrid). The former, an incredibly rich collection of rare books, has a diverse collection of manuscripts, the contents of which are available through Julian Zarco Cuevas, *Catálogo de los manuscritos castellanos de la Real Biblioteca de El Escorial* (Madrid, 1924). The latter is a major source for the history of the Royal Court.

Outside Spain, the manuscript collection of the British Museum is rich in papers regarding higher education and the appointment of royal officials in Castile. Consultas for openings on the important councils in the 1580s and 1590s can be found in Add. 28, 347; 28, 349; 28, 353; 28, 358; and 28, 363. Add. 28, 351–53 contain lists of candidates for *corregimientos* and other offices during the 1560s and 1570s, while Eg. 439 includes a comprehensive review of higher education in Spain that was carried out in the reign of Charles III. There are also numerous isolated memorials and consultas, a few of which are referred to in the footnotes of this book. V. Beltrán de Heredia, *Cartulario de la Universidad de Salamanca* (Salamanca, 1971), 3: 575–622, publishes a number of these British museum manuscripts, particularly those concerning the University of Salamanca in the sixteenth century; however, Pedro Gayangos, *Catalogue of the Spanish Manuscripts in the British Museum* (4 vols., London, 1875–93) remains indispensable for work in this collection.

The Bibliothèque National (Paris) and the Archives des Affaires Étrangères (Paris) have important holdings relating to Spain, but little material directly concerned with the subject matter of the present volume. The Collection Eduard Favre in Geneva is essential for an understanding of the part which the royal secretary Mateo Vázquez played in the appointment of crown officials during Philip II's reign. In this regard, manuscript volumes 31 and 38 were particularly helpful. L. Micheli, *Catalogue de la Collection Manuscrit de Eduard Favre* (Geneva, 1914) provides an introduction to this archive's contents. And, finally, in Rome, the Archivium Historicum Romanum Iesu houses the letters and catalogues which were forwarded by Spain's Jesuit colleges to the Society's central headquarters. The collection is well-catalogued and is readily accessible to outside researchers.

II. PRINTED SOURCES

The following bibliography is intended only to serve as a guide to further reading in the major topics treated in this volume. Listed are works of a general nature, many of which contain bibliographical entries which are fairly complete and need not be duplicated here. However, full references to those works which have been cited directly in this study are presented in the footnotes of the text.

1. *Education and Society in Early Modern Europe.*

There is no introductory work available on this subject, although specialized studies are many. Philip Ariès, *Centuries of Childhood, A Social History of Family Life*, trans. Robert Baldick (New York, 1962) is fundamental for any study in family life and childhood education, while a recent listing of other works on these topics is available in C. John Sommerville, "Towards a History of Childhood and Youth," *Journal of Interdisciplinary History* 3 (Autumn, 1972): 439–47.

The subject of literacy in history can be approached through Carlo Cipolla, *Literacy and Development in the West* (Baltimore, 1969). Lawrence Stone, "Literacy and Society in England, 1640–1900," *Past & Present* 42 (February 1969): 69–139, is much broader than its title suggests and offers what is perhaps the best conceptual framework available for studies in the history of education. See also J. R. Goody, ed., *Literacy in Traditional Societies* (Cambridge, 1968).

Latin or Renaissance education has been examined in many specialized articles and books, but there are few general studies of importance on this topic. Still useful is W. H. Woodward, *Studies in Education during the Age of the Renaissance, 1400–1600* (Cambridge, 1906) (this has been reprinted by Columbia University Teachers' College Press, New York, 1967, with an excellent introduction by Lawrence Stone). However, E. Garin, *L'Educazione in Europa, 1400–1600* (Bari, 1957) (also available in French) remains the best available work on the subject. Latin pedagogy is another subject about which much has been written, but Georges Snyders, *La Pedagogie en France aux XVIIe et XVIIIe Siècles* (Paris, 1965) stands out both for its quality and breadth. Its equivalent for England, though in a somewhat earlier period, is Joan Simon, *Education and Society in Tudor England* (Cambridge, 1959), and this can be supplemented by Kenneth Charlton, *Education in Renaissance England* (London, 1965). The best general study of the education of the aristocracy in Europe remains J. H. Hexter, "The Education of the Aristocracy in the Renaissance," in *Reappraisals in History* (London, 1961), although this has been updated for England by Lawrence Stone, *Crisis of the Aristocracy, 1558–1641* (Oxford, 1965).

The universities of early modern Europe are unfortunate in that they have never merited a study comparable to H. Rashdall, *The Universities of Europe in the Middle Ages*, ed. by F. M. Powicke and A. B. Emden (3 vols., Oxford, 1936). The only general survey, and one that is less than satisfactory, is S. D'Irsay, *Histoire des Universités Francaises et Étrangères* (2 vols., Paris, 1933). More specialized but dealing with universities in much of Europe are the articles published in two recent collective volumes: *Les Universités Européenes du XIVe au XVIIIe Siècles, Aspects et Problems* (Institut D'Histoire de la Faculté des Lettres de Genéve, vol. 4, Genéve, 1967) and *The University in Society*, ed. Lawrence Stone

(2 vols. Princeton, 1974). English higher education in the sixteenth and seventeenth centuries has been the subject of a number of good recent studies, among them Lawrence Stone, "The Educational Revolution in England 1560 to 1640," *Past & Present* 28 (July 1964); Hugh Kearney, *Scholars and Gentlemen; Universities and Society in Pre-Industrial Britain 1500-1700* (London, 1970); and Wilfrid R. Prest, *The Inns of Court under Elizabeth I and the Early Stuarts, 1590-1640* (London, 1972). The only works of a general nature available in English for German universities are F. Paulsen, *German Universities and University Study* (Leipzig, 1902) and J. Conrad, *The German Universities for the Last Fifty Years* (Glasgow, 1885). Nothing on this scale exists either for Italy or France, although studies of individual colleges and universities are numerous.

2. Early Modern Spain: General

J. H. Elliott, *Imperial Spain* (London, 1963) and John Lynch, *Spain Under the Habsburgs* (2 vols., Oxford, 1964–69) remain the best introductory works in English for early modern Spain, although they can be supplemented by Antonio Domínguez Ortiz, *Spain in the Golden Age 1502-1659* (New York, 1971). Spanish economic and social history in this period may be approached through the *Historia Económica y Social de España y América*, ed. J. Vicens Vives, (5 vols., Barcelona, 1957) and Antonio Domínguez Ortiz, *La Sociedad Española en el Siglo XVII* (2 vols., Madrid, 1963-70). The eighteenth century is covered in Antonio Domínguez Ortiz, *La Sociedad Española en el Siglo XVIII* (Madrid, 1955) and Richard Herr, *The Eighteenth Century Revolution in Spain* (Princeton, 1958). For additional bibliography, see B. Sánchez Alonso, *Fuentes de la Historia Española e Hispanoamericana*, 3rd ed. (3 vols., Madrid, 1952). Recent books and articles are listed in the periodical *Indice Histórico Español* (University of Barcelona).

3. Early Modern Spain: Education and Society

a) Family Life and Childhood
Except for studies based wholly upon literary sources and those dealing with individual families, this area remains totally unresearched. Even demographic studies are few; Bartolomé Bennassar, *Valladolid au Siécle d'Or* (Paris, 1967) is the only study, to date, which makes an attempt at "family reconstitution" in Castile. Juan Luis Morales, *El Niño en la Cultura Española* (4 vols., Madrid, 1960) is perhaps the best starting point for a history of children in Spain, particularly for its detailed bibliography of pediatrics.

b) Literacy and Latin
This area, too, has been poorly researched. Though a number of local studies exist, works of a general nature are very few. Lorenzo Luzuriaga,

Documentos Para la Historia Escolar de España (2 vols., Madrid, 1916) is a useful collection of documents on Spanish education from the Middle Ages to the nineteenth century, but offers little in the way of a narrative, while J. Raymond Perz, *Secondary Education in Spain* (Washington, 1934), gives only a brief historical introduction to his subject. The history of Spanish pedagogy is treated in two older but still useful works: Antonio Gil y Zarate, *De la Instrucción Pública en España* (Madrid, 1855) and E. García y Barbarín, *Historia de la Pedagogía Española* (Madrid, 1909). And an introduction to "Renaissance" education in Spain is provided in Aubrey F. G. Bell, *Luís de León: A Study in the Spanish Renaissance* (Oxford, 1925), a work which can be supplemented by Caro Lynn, *A College Professor of the Renaissance* (Chicago, 1937).

c) Universities and Colleges

There are a number of general works available on the history of higher education in early modern Spain. Alberto Jiménez, *Historia de la Universidad Española* (Madrid, 1971) offers an impressionistic (and undocumented) account which is not nearly so good as the classic in this field: Vicente de la Fuente, *Historia de las Universidades* (4 vols., Madrid, 1884–89). This has recently been updated by G. Ajo y Sainz de Zúñiga, *Historia de las Universidades Hispánicas* (8 vols., Madrid, 1957–72), a massive work which continues to appear. Ajo is especially useful for the detailed bibliographices of manuscript and printed sources provided in vols. I, VII, and VIII. Bibliographies for Spain's colleges and seminaries have been published by F. Martín Hernández, "Fuentes y Bibliografía para el Estudio de los Seminarios Españoles," *Salmanticensis* (vol. X, 1963) and "Noticia de los Antiguos Colegios Universitarios Españoles," *Salmanticensis* (vol. VI, 1959). Volume I of the *Bibliographie International de l'Histoire des Universités* (Geneva, 1973) contains an excellent section (pp. 3–100) on Spain and Portugal prepared by Rafael Gilbert, while still another useful bibliography appears in María Soledad Rubio Sánchez, *Historia del Real Colegio de Estudios Mayores de la Purísima Concepción de Cabra (Córdoba), 1679–1847* (Sevilla, 1970), App. II. Specialized studies of Spain's universities and colleges are numerous; many of these have been referred to in the footnotes of this volume.

INDEX

Abogados, 84

Academies: at court, 35; of Juan de Herrera, 38; literary, 38; for nobles, 39–40; royal, 234

Agustín, Antonio (1517–86), jurist, 33, 162

Albornoz, Cardinal Gil de (1310–67), 33

Alcalá de Henares, University of: colleges in, 65; faculty of grammar in, 51; foundation of, 41, 69; *pupilajes* in, 191–92; religious orders in, 189. *See also* Colegio Mayor de San Ildefonso; Universities
—instructors: absenteeism among, 173
—students: ages of, 176–77, Figs. 1, 3, Table 14; attrition among, 178, Fig. 4; geographical origins of, 179–80, 203, 228–29, Table 15, Map 5; graduate careers of, 97–98, 104; matriculations of, 197, 213, 225, 228, Figs. 7, 9

Alfonso V, of Aragon (1416–58), 33

Alfonso X, of Castile (1252–84), 62

Almagro, University of, 198, 211

Andalucia: Jesuit colleges in, 53; universities in, 64

Arabic, study of, 216–17

Aragon, kingdom of: universities in, 64

Aranda, count of (1719–98), minister of Charles III, 59

Arbitristas, 43–44

Aristocracy: in the colegios mayores, 127–28, 130–31, 133; education of, 9–10, 34–40; as letrado officials, 87; at university, 183–86, Table 16. *See also* Nobility

Audiencias, 83, 85. *See also* Chancillerías; Letrado hierarchy

Augustinians, 56, 189, Table 2

Avila, University of, 197–98, 202, Fig. 7

Azpilcueta, Martín de (1491–1586), professor at Salamanca, 162, 231

Baeza, University of, 197–98, 202, 225, Fig. 7

Barbosa, Aires, professor at Salamanca, 162

Barcelona, University of, 229

Beltrán, Felipe (d.1783), bishop of Salamanca, 149

Benedictines, 57, 189, Table 2

Bologna, University of, 63; Spanish college of, *see* Colegio de San Clemente

Bureaucracy: development of 70–71, 104; expansion of, 82–83, Table 3; professionalization of, 91; recruitment into, 94–95. *See also* Letrado hierarchy

Burgo de Osma, University of, 198

Cadiz, medical faculty at, 229

Cámara de Castilla, 39, 93–95; bias toward colegiales mayores, 100–02; clashes with

king, 97; recruitment of professors by, 173–75; role in royal appointments, 96–97

Campomanes, Pedro Rodríguez de (1723–1803), *fiscal* of the Council of Castile, 23, 47, 59, 148, 227

Cano, Melchor (1509–60), Dominican theologian, 162, 232

Canon law, study of: in the colegios mayores, 135–36, Table 9; in the universities, 161, 212–13, Figs. 9–11

Capa y espada, 80–81, 219, 223

Carmelites, 57, Table 2

Cartagena, Alfonso de (1385?–1454), bishop of Burgos, 34

Casas, Bartolomé de las (1474–1566), Dominican, 217

Castile, kingdom of: grammar school students in, 47; litigation in, 218; universities in, 64–65, Map 2; university graduates in, 201; university students in, 199–200

Catalonia, principality of: revolt of, 224; universities in, 64, Map 2

Catholic kings: promotion of learning by, 34–35; university policy of, 71, 183; use of letrados by, 70–71, 88–89

Cespedes, Baltasar de (d. 1615), grammarian, 41

Chaldean, study of, 216, 266

Chancillerías, 58, 92–93, 98, Table 4. *See also Audiencias*; Letrado hierarchy

Charles II (1665–1700), 100

Charles III (1759–88), 17, 22, 227

Charles IV (1788–1808), 17, 58, 227, 229

Children, early education of, 6–9

Chumacero y Carillo, Juan, president of the Council of Castile (1643–49), 147

Church: educational policy of, 11, 36; letrados in, 80, 84; nomination of bishops in, 102–04, Table 5

Cisneros, Cardinal Jiménez de (1436–1517), archbishop of Toledo, 69, 89, 110

Civil law, study of: in the colegios mayores, 135–36, Table 9; in the universities, 161–62, 212–13, Figs. 9–11

Clergy: colegiales mayores among, 102–04, Table 5; foundation of universities by, 66–68; number of places for, 82, 84; university education of, 186–88
—regular: as schoolteachers, 23, 56–57; as university instructors, 189–90, Table 12. *See also* Religious orders; Society of Jesus

Cobos, Francisco de la (1477?–1547), royal secretary, 89

Colegio de la Concepción de Teologos (Salamanca), 66, 194

of, 85; sons of in the colegios mayores, 127–28, 133; values of, 233–34

Liberal arts: rise of in Spain, 33–36; study of in the colegios mayores, 134–36, Table 9; in the universities, 163, 212, 215–16, 226, Figs. 9–11

Limpieza de sangre, 90–91, 130, 146

Literacy: cost of learning, 11–12; demand for, 25; measurement of, 14n, 26; rate of, 23; teaching of, 9–10, uses of, 18–19. *See also* Schools; primary

Litigation, 218

Loaysa, Garcia de, Archbishop of Toledo (1598–99), 146

López de Mendoza, Iñigo, archbishop of Burgos (1527–31), 67

López de Montoya, Pedro, 16th century teacher, 37

Lucena, Juan de (d. 1506), 34

Macanaz, Melchor de (1670–1760), *fiscal* of the Council of Castile, 102

Madrid, 123, 173; Central University of, 224, 229; grammar schools in, 41, 53; Jesuit colleges in, 53–55; Normal school in, 17; primary schools in, 13–18, 29; university students from, 181

Manrique, Fray Angel de, bishop of Badajoz (1645–49), 234

Manteistas, 102, 150, 221

Marineo Siculo, Lucio (1444?–1533), Italian humanist, 35, 216

Martin de Canto, Alonso, 16th century schoolteacher, 13

Martínez Siliceo, Juan (1485–1557), archbishop of Toledo, 131

Martin V, Pope (1417–31), 63, 71

Martyr d'Anghiera, Peter (1457?–1526), Italian humanist, 35–36, 216

Masters of primary letters, 11–12, 21

Mayorazgo, 6, 86, 218

Medicine: as a career, 132, 218; study of in the colegios mayores, 134–36, Table 9; in the universities, 162, 215, 235; Figs. 9–11

Medina-Sidonia, 7th duke of, 183

Mendo de Benavides, don, bishop of Segovia (1633–41), 147

Mercado, Tomás de, 16th century theologian, 162

Mercedes, 86

Military Orders, 218; colleges of, 67, 154–55, 158, 194; council of, 80, Tables 3, 4

Minimos of St. Francis de Paul, 57, Table 2

Mondéjar, marquis of, 92, 128

Monterrey, Jesuit college in, 55

Morales, Ambrosio de (1513–91), chronicler of Philip II, 10

Moriscos, education of, 29–30

Münzer, Jerónimo, 196 ⸗

National law, teaching of, 162

Navarre, kingdom of: colegiales mayores from, 113; schools in, 25n; university students from, 181

Nebrija, Antonio de (1444–1522), humanist and grammarian, 27, 33, 162, 232

New Castile: colegiales mayores from, 113; schoolboys in, 48; university students from, 181

Nobility: of the robe, 60–61, 86, 101; types of, 182–83; at the University of Salamanca, 184–85, Table 16. *See also* Aristocracy

Núñez de Guzmán, Hernan (1475–1533), El Pinciano, Greek scholar, 162, 232

Olavide, Pablo de (1725–1823), reformer, 46, 49, 227, 233

Old Castile: colegiales mayores from, 113; schoolboys in, 48; universities in, 64; university students from, 181

Olivares, Count-Duke of, Gaspar de Guzmán (1587–1645), favorite of Philip IV, 98, 101, 173; educational schemes of, 38–39; on "lack of leaders," 224; at the University of Salamanca, 185

Oñate, College-university of, 79, 198, 211

Oposiciones. See Universities: instructors, appointment of

Osuna, University of, 66, 198, 211, 228

Oviedo, University of, 69, 228–29

Palacios-Rubios, Juan López de (1450–1525), jurist, 88

Palafox y Mendoza, Juan de (1600–59), bishop of Puebla and Burgo de Osma, 31

Pamplona, Jesuit college in, 55–56

Papacy, 160; role in Spanish universities, 63, 71

Peasantry, education among, 25–26

Pérez Bayer, Francisco (1711–94), tutor to the royal *infantes*, 102, 111, 127, 148–49

Philip II (1556–98), 23; ban on university study abroad, 72

Philip III (1598–1621), 97

Philip IV (1621–65), 44–45, 152, 173

Philip V (1700–46), 46, 226

Philosophy. *See* Liberal Arts

Plazas de asiento, 80, 83, 92, 94, 157, Table 3. *See also* Letrado hierarchy

Polyglot Bible, 231

Portugal, revolt of, 224

Portuguese, at the University of Salamanca, 203, Map 5

Printing, 11, 35

Puberty, 16th century ideas on, 8

Pupilajes. See Universities: student life

Quevedo y Villegas, Francisco Gómez de (1580–1645), 85

The Johns Hopkins University Press

This book was composed in Times Roman text and Helvetica Compressed display type by the Jones Composition Company, Inc., from a design by Beverly Baum. It was printed on 60-lb. Warren 1854 paper and bound in Holliston Roxite linen by Universal Lithographers, Inc.